The Oral History of Admiral Paul David Miller U.S. Navy (Retired)

Interviewed By
Stanley D. M. Carpenter, PhD
Professor Emeritus
U.S. Naval War College

U.S. Naval Institute • Annapolis, Maryland

Copyright © 2022

Preface

This set of oral history interviews with Admiral Paul David Miller, US Navy (Ret.) spans his career in the United States Navy, from his youth through his endeavors as a board member and executive officer of multiple private sector companies. Admiral Miller served in the surface warfare community in his initial division officer tour, and through multiple warship command tours. As a flag officer, he commanded a cruiser-destroyer group (CruDesGru 3) and fleet (7th Fleet). Due to his exceptional administrative ability and the trust placed in his leadership and judgment by senior officers and Department of the Navy civilian officials, Admiral Miller served in many Pentagon staff and OPNAV positions, including as executive assistant (EA) to the Secretary of the Navy. The amalgamation of his superior command leadership, administrative acumen, professional expertise, adept diplomacy, and ability to work in a high stress environment all contributed to his rapid promotion to and within flag ranks. Emblematic of his skill and effectiveness as a senior flag officer, he had the rare distinction of having served as the commander in chief, U.S. Atlantic Fleet (CINCLANTFLT), North Atlantic Treaty Organization (NATO) supreme allied commander Atlantic (SACLANT), and commander in chief, U.S. Atlantic Command (USCINCACOM). Based on his administrative ability, leadership expertise, and forward-looking innovative concepts, his post-naval service career led him to membership on multiple boards of directors of private sector companies and executive leadership at the president and chief executive officer (CEO) level at firms such as Litton Marine Systems, Sperry Marine, Inc., and Alliant Techsystems, Inc. (ATK).

The oral interviews were conducted in 2017 and 2018 at his homes in Williamsburg, Virginia, and Naples, Florida. Admiral Miller is still active in many ventures; therefore, the sessions were conducted as his and the interviewer's professional and personal schedules allowed.

The primary organizing principle and themes of the interviews revolved around five distinct topics that wove throughout all levels of his career, ranks, and positions: effective leadership; strategic communications; leadership moral authority and obligations; innovation; and, the application of military executive experience to the private sector economy. The interviews were organized chronologically starting with his youth and progressing to his current endeavors. A secondary aspect of the progression was the chronicling of the main characteristics of each era in terms of how the Navy and Department of Defense operated, planned and fought conflicts, developed and executed doctrine and tactics, innovated, and conducted force structuring in the pre–Vietnam War era up through the post–Cold War/post–First Gulf War years, which saw the transition to a smaller force. The nature of the various positions, from division officer to department head, executive officer, commanding officer, group commander, to fleet command as well as the ashore administrative billets, was examined in depth so as to create a perspective on the roles, duties, and responsibilities inherent in each position.

Additionally, many of the questions were framed based on the admiral's perspective as a highly successful retired flag officer and revolved around what advice he would give a newly appointed or promoted officer on how to conduct his or herself and how to manage the responsibilities as an effective leader. The intent here is to provide some perspective to future generations of naval officers on how to approach their leadership and responsibilities based on Admiral Miller's highly successful career. Many of the questions addressed his perspective on the traits and characteristics of an effective and efficient leader. Recommendations as to what activities, skills, experiences, and credentials that an officer at all levels of their career should acquire or participate in also shaped many of the questions and responses.

The greatest value of these oral interviews is in providing to future officers and leaders a perspective on how to conduct themselves and how to carry out their roles effectively based on the experience of a highly successful retired flag officer. Ideally, these interviews will be used in the future as part of the curriculum at the officer accession schools—U.S. Naval Academy (USNA), Officer Candidate School (OCS), and Reserve Officer Training Corps (ROTC).

Admiral Miller is an accomplished commentator on issues relating to U.S.-Allied technological transformation and innovation, as well as future naval and maritime strategy and tactics. Throughout the interviews, he weaved in that perspective, which is especially helpful in light of the need for the modern Navy and othermilitary services to be integral players in the international realm. Finally, an essential mission of the oral histories is to provide future generations with a perspective on how the Navy operated and what operations it undertook while the interviewee served. Therefore, many questions and responses addressed the environment and nature of the Navy, the political nation, and the military in general during Admiral Miller's tenure from the mid-1960s to the mid-1990s. His perspectives on the various civil and military senior officials in the Cold War and post–First Gulf War periods are especially insightful in understanding how the nation dealt with issues of regional conflict and alliance relations in an era of superpower peer competition.

Thanks go to Eric Mills of the Naval Institute, who coordinated and managed this oral history project, providing timely and helpful support and guidance. Additionally, the Naval Institute expresses its gratitude to the Tawani Foundation and the Pritzker Military Library of Chicago for their generous financial support of the oral history program.

Stanley D. M. Carpenter, PhD
Captain, USN (Ret.)
Professor Emeritus
U.S. Naval War College
Newport, Rhode Island
December 2020

The U.S. Naval Institute Oral History Program

Researchers and authors have been drawing on the Naval Institute's Oral History Program since 1969, the year it was established by Dr. John T. Mason Jr. He and his successor, author and historian Paul Stillwell, sought to capture, preserve, and disseminate a permanent record of the stories of significant figures in naval history. In recent years, the program has expanded, with increasing numbers of historians conducting more interviews.

These oral histories are carefully fact-checked and reviewed by both historians and interview subjects before being made available. The Naval Institute is known for this high level of editorial intervention and polishing. The reader is reminded, as with all oral history interviews, that this is a record of the spoken word.

The Naval Institute wishes to acknowledge the many donors who make this program possible, in particular the generous support of the Pritzker Military Foundation of Chicago and the late Jack C. Taylor of St. Louis.

ADMIRAL PAUL DAVID MILLER
UNITED STATES NAVY (RETIRED)

Paul David Miller was born in Roanoke, Virginia, on December 1, 1941, and spent his childhood years in Newport, Rhode Island and Norfolk, Virginia. He served in the United States Navy from 1964 to 1994, retiring on October 31, 1994 with the rank of admiral. Promoted to admiral (four-star) on February 1, 1991, his final active duty billets included commander in chief, U.S. Atlantic Fleet (CINCLANTFLT), North Atlantic Treaty Organization (NATO) supreme allied commander Atlantic (SACLANT), and commander in chief, U.S. Atlantic Command (USCINCACOM).

Following graduation from high school in Jacksonville, Florida, in 1958, he attended the College of William & Mary in Williamsburg, Virginia, and later transferred to and graduated from the Florida State University in Tallahassee, Florida, with a BS in economics in 1963. Admiral Miller then earned a Master's in Business Administration (MBA) from the University of Georgia in 1964. In mid-career, he graduated from the Harvard Business School Executive Management Program in 1978 and the U.S. Naval War College in 1974. Following graduation from the University of Georgia, he applied for and was accepted for officer training and was commissioned from Officer Candidate School in Newport, Rhode Island in 1964.

Admiral Miller began his Navy career as a surface warfare officer (SWO), serving as a division officer on the fleet tug USS *Papago* (ATF-160). Due to the small wardroom of *Papago*, he took on many divergent duties, including communications, navigation, and operations as well as underway bridge watch standing, a dynamic that gave him a vast array of shipboard experiences and skills not normally inherent in the initial division officer tour. Due to his multifaceted skills and proven leadership, the commanding officer (CO) of USS *Seneca* (AT-91), also a fleet tug, specifically requested Miller to serve as the ship's executive officer (XO) despite his junior status. That tour further enhanced his capabilities, leadership acumen, and promotability, a factor in his rapid promotion to flag rank well ahead of his peer group. He then served as the operations officer (OPSO) of USS *Parsons* (DDG-33), with fleet operations service in the Vietnam War; a Navy junior officer detailer at the Bureau of Personnel in Washington, D.C.; commanding officer of USS *McCloy* (FF-

1038) from 1972 to 1973; flag lieutenant and executive assistant (EA) to the vice chief of naval operations from 1974 to 1978; commanding officer of USS *Luce* (DDG-38) from 1978 to 1979; and as EA to commander in chief, Pacific (CINCPAC) from 1979 to 1981.

As a senior officer (captain O-6 and flag), his billets included tours as EA to then–Secretary of the Navy John Lehman from 1981 to 1985. Miller was promoted to flag rank (one-star) in 1985 after only twenty-one years of naval service and was one of the youngest flag officers in U.S. Navy history. Other senior officer tours included Commander, Cruiser-Destroyer Group 3 in 1985 to 1986 (ComDesGru 3) and commander, U.S. Seventh Fleet (Com7thFlt) from 1986 to 1988. When promoted to vice admiral in 1986, he was the youngest vice admiral in the Navy. In an extraordinary move, he was promoted from rear admiral lower half (one-star) directly to vice admiral (three-star), skipping over rear admiral upper half (two-star). He served as deputy chief of naval operations, naval warfare (OP-07) from 1988 to 1991 prior to promotion to full admiral in early 1991.

Admiral Miller has had a robust business career in technology, marine industries, and finance since Navy retirement and has served on the board of directors of multiple business entities, including Teledyne Technologies; SunTrust Bank; Huntington Ingalls Industries, Inc. (shipbuilding company); Crestar Financial Corporation; Crestar Bank; Donaldson Company, Inc., (filtration systems company); UGS Corporation; Atlantic Marine, Inc.; Anteon International Corporation; and Siemens Product Lifecycle Management Software, Inc. He also served as a member of the operating executive board at J. F. Lehman & Company. On Navy retirement in October 1994, he joined Litton Industries, Inc., where he was head of the Litton Marine Systems and President of Sperry Marine, Inc. In other executive positions, Admiral Miller served as the chairman of the board and chief executive officer (CEO) of Alliant Techsystems, Inc. (ATK), an advanced weapon and space systems company.

Admiral Miller not only practices management, executive leadership, and technological innovation but writes about leadership and strategic issues as well. For example, he is the author of "Both Swords and Plowshares: Literary Roles in the 1990s" and "Harmonising the Alliance with the Dynamics of Change" in the Royal United Services Institute (RUSI) *Journal* (1993).

Admiral Miller's military personal awards include the Navy Distinguished Service Medal; Defense Superior Service Medal; Legion of Merit; Meritorious Service Medal; Navy Commendation Medal; Navy and Marine Corps Achievement Medal; and numerous campaign and service medals.

Admiral Miller and his wife Becky reside in Williamsburg, Virginia, and Naples, Florida. The Millers have two children, Chris and Colby, both of whom have served as naval officers, and several grandchildren.

Key Terms

Leadership

Innovation

Strategic Communications

Newport, Rhode Island

Norfolk, Virginia

Mayport, Florida

Officer Candidate School

Becky Miller

USS *Papago*

USS *Seneca*

USS *Parsons*

USS *McCloy*

USS *Luce*

USS *Enterprise*

Vietnam

U.S. Naval War College

Carrier Strike Group (CSG)

ComCruDesGru 3

7th Fleet

CincPacFlt

CincLantFlt

Pentagon

OPERATION DESERT SHIELD/DESERT STORM

Antisubmarine Warfare (ASW)

Chief Engineer (CHENG)

Admiral Elmo Zumwalt

Secretary of the Navy John Lehman

Executive Officer (XO)

Commanding Officer (CO)

Officer of the Deck (OOD)

Engineering Officer of the Watch (EOOW)

OPNAV

Chief of Naval Operations (CNO)

Navy Promotions

Secretary of Defense (SecDef)

Secretary of the Navy (SecNav)

Chief of Naval Operations (CNO)

Joint Chiefs of Staff (JCS)

Chairman of the Joint Chiefs of Staff (CJCS)

Deputy Chief of Naval Operations for Naval Warfare

Commander in Chief, U.S. Atlantic Fleet

Supreme Allied Commander, Atlantic

Commander in Chief, U.S. Atlantic Command

Deed of Gift

The U.S. Naval Institute is hereby authorized to make available in any format it chooses, from bound-book hard copy to electronic/digital Internet access and as part of videorecordings, the audio recordings, transcripts, and videorecordings of the oral-history interview series conducted concerning the life and career of the undersigned. Disposition, repositories, and access shall be at the discretion of the Naval Institute. The undersigned shall be offered the opportunity to review the transcribed oral history prior to its finalization, and to make any corrections thereto that the undersigned deems necessary.

The undersigned does hereby release and assign to the U.S. Naval Institute the rights and title to these interviews, with the exception that the undersigned and heirs retain the right to use the material for personal, noncommercial purposes. The copyright in the oral, transcribed, and videorecorded versions shall be held by the U.S. Naval Institute. All recordings, transcriptions, and videorecordings of the interviews shall remain the property of the U.S. Naval Institute.

Signed and sealed this 21 day of January 2017.

Signed name _____

Printed name Paul David Miller

Interview with Admiral Paul David Miller, USN (Ret.)
Date: January 21, 2017

Stan Carpenter (SC): Admiral, you were born in Roanoke, Virginia, then very shortly afterwards moved to Newport, Rhode Island, and spent your first few years there. You initially resided on Fenner Avenue. For those not familiar with the City of Newport, that area is just off Broadway and very close to the Bellevue Avenue section. Newport changed dramatically when the Navy pulled the operational forces out in the early 1970s, leaving essentially the training and education commands such as the U.S. Naval War College, Officer Candidate School, Destroyer School, and so on. The city made a dramatic transformation to a high-end tourism destination in the 1970s that featured the rich maritime history combined with the "Gilded Age" mansions that are interestingly called "summer cottages." But, when you lived there in the post–World War II period, Newport was more of an operational "Navy town" rather than a tourist mecca. Your mother remarried a Navy chief petty officer and that factor brought you to Norfolk, Virginia, and the real start of your lifelong U.S. Navy association. Let's start with your move down to Norfolk in the mid-1950s. How did you react to that move, and what about the adjustment to a new school and a new set of friends?

Paul David Miller (PDM): Stan, it was not only an adjustment to a new school; it was an adjustment to a new family environment. We had moved from Fenner Avenue to the next street over—Caswell Avenue; however, I was still close to my cousins. But when we left Newport, Rhode Island, and moved to Norfolk, that was like moving far away. Memory-wise, I left behind a whole set of people that I had seen every day and I knew I was on my own. I was now this person called Paul David Miller, moving to Norfolk, Virginia with my natural mother and this man who came into my life that I did not know. He exercised the responsibilities of being a father, so I appreciated that. We moved into a small house on Sunset Drive. I don't know why I remember the numbers of the house. I lived at 1205 Sunset Drive. It was in the Bayview section of Norfolk, Virginia.

He was on the USS *Prevail* (AM-107). What is that? That's a naval ship that was painted white that was sent only to the Persian [or Arabian] Gulf. There were three ships in rotation—the *Duxbury Bay* (AVP-38), the *Greenwich Bay* (AVP-41), and the *Prevail*. They were on one-in-three rotation in the Persian Gulf. Back then, that was how the Navy's presence was kept in the Gulf. He was gone on those long cruises, so my mother and I were left to continue on in our small house.

I finished seventh and the eighth grade at a Catholic school in Oceanview—St. Mary's. It was fine, but I took away not a single memory of that period. Then came Norfolk Catholic High School as my mother wanted to continue my Catholic education. My time in high school, Stan, was unremarkable. What do I mean by that? I was not a star student. I was a very good three-sport player but not an outstanding athlete. I made the mistake that I think too many youngsters do that were given some athletic ability, that you decided that you needed to do everything instead of become really good at one sport. I would advance from the football season to basketball season to baseball season; you didn't hone any skills, you just became damn good at everything, but not exceedingly well-gifted in any sport. But anyhow, I had a good high school run athletically.

Then academic-wise, it was fine, but I didn't set any records. The four years, one went into the other. I don't have lots of recollections of milestones that I had met, goals that I had achieved, or marks that I had set. I was a Mk 1, Mod 0 [Mark and Model] high school student who successfully completed the course of instruction, and that was it. [*laughs*]

SC: Did you participate in any school political leadership activity?

PDM: Absolutely not.

SC: You've mentioned sports. Were there any other curricular activities or nonschool extracurricular activities that you participated in?

PDM: No, because it was all sports. I was myopic on whatever sport was in front of me at the time.

SC: In sports, was there any aspect of it that you think influenced your concepts of skills as a leader?

PDM: At that time, I was more of a team player as opposed to a team leader. The leadership construct hadn't developed at that point in time, and I can see that some are gifted in being able to turn that leadership switch on earlier than others. I was one that it didn't get turned on until a little later, but that was okay. I look back at that period and have some memories. Unlike the first eleven years that I just tried to muddle though, this period was fine.

I had good experiences with the chief boatswain. He was promoted to chief warrant officer during this period. He was a hard-nosed sailor. He was at Pearl Harbor when Pearl Harbor was bombed. He joined the Navy at seventeen years old and he made the Navy a career. He would introduce me to the Navy. He would take me to the ship when he was a chief and then as a warrant, because he wanted to do one thing: he wanted to teach me that if I went into the military, that I should do it as an officer, not as an enlisted man. Not that he had anything against enlisted service, but he knew that being an officer in the military was something very special. He had always looked up to people that were in authority. And so once I was adopted by him, he did not have any natural children, so he wanted to use whatever time he was given with me, which was essentially five years, to influence me that if I was going to have to serve, to do it as an officer. At that time, the draft was still on going, so it was in our thought processes that we would probably have to serve at some point in time.

I remember being in the Brooklyn Navy Shipyard when the ship was in for an extended availability. We lived in some rental quarters, but I went to the ship with him almost every day. Back then, you could do this in the Navy. Today you couldn't get away with it. And he would turn me over to his petty officer and say, "He's one of your hands. I'll collect him at the end of the day." And I did what sailors do in a shipyard. Do I know how to chip paint, use a needle gun? Yes, sir. Do I know what red lead [primer paint for ship hulls] is? Yes, sir. Could I rig a boatswain's chair when I was fourteen years old?

Yes, sir. So it gave me a real grounding in what the enlisted life is like on board, at least in the deck force of a Navy ship.

A nasty event took place—at least I thought it was nasty—and I can still recall being yelled at. We had just completed redoing the paint locker. The paint locker is often the foulest place on the ship, where they would put paint away before going to sea. It would often spill. Anyhow, we had this compartment pristine, and then for some reason, there was this five-gallon can of primer— red lead— and someone said something to me, and I backed up. I knocked over the five-gallon can of red lead, and it went all the way down three decks and sprayed the whole paint locker that we had just spent days chipping and cleaning and repainting. The whole world came crushing down on me at that time. What did that tell me? It told me to be careful when someone does something, because the way that one reacts to that is remembered. I remember exactly what that first class petty officer called me, exactly, and I'm seventy-five years old now, but I can still remember it. Throughout my career, I remembered events like that. When someone does something, you've got to choose your words and choose the way you want to influence the outcome carefully, because it leaves a mark. But spilling that red lead was vivid, and you know who had to clean it up, Stan? I had to clean that up. I must have used three bales of rags, trying to sop that spilled red paint up before it dried.

But those are the things I remember about the "old boatswain." He was a boatswain, warrant, then he got the full stripe, he was W-2, W-3, and retired as a W-4 warrant boatswain. They don't hold the position today, but a warrant boatswain was a seagoing proven sailor, and in the '40s and '50s and early '60s, they were the backbone of how ships were sailed and how they were sailed proudly. Every chance that he had, he tried to instill in me to reach further, to not be satisfied with what he had accomplished, and for someone that entered the Navy at seventeen, he had accomplished a great deal, leaving the Navy after thirty years of service as a W-4 warrant boatswain, with a solid war record, spent all that time in the Pacific. He was a real sailor.

SC: Sometimes when people are young, specific books or literature influence their thinking. Do you recall any specific authors or books that were influential in your development?

PDM: Stan, you ask that question to lots of people, but for P. D. M, it's not a good question and I'm embarrassed to say I don't have an answer.

SC: Fair enough. Well, let's do this question. Many of us of our generation who grew up in the '40s through the 1970s have some really fond memories of specific TV shows. In my case, a reason why I went into the "U.S. by God Navy" was *McHale's Navy*, believe it or not. [*Miller laughs.*] And the movie *PT-109*. And what's interesting is a lot of these old TV shows are very popular, MeTV, Nick at Nite, they're coming back because our generation treasures those. Do you have any particular TV show or movie that you remember from those days that was particularly influential?

PDM: Stan, we didn't have a TV.

SC: Didn't have a TV. [*laughs*] Well, let's move on then. As we progress through your life and career—

PDM: We didn't have a TV probably till I was in high school. I didn't spend a lot of time watching TV. When I came in at dark time because I'd been out playing sports, there wasn't much time left other than schoolwork. Did I watch a couple of the programs that you just mentioned? The answer's yes. But did I key on them? Were they an influence? No.

SC: You've mentioned the red lead incident as shaping and formative. Can you think of any other moments or events that gave you a profound revelation or life experience that influenced your future career or worldview?

PDM: When I graduated from high school in Norfolk, Virginia, 1959, the boatswain was given a "twilight tour." He was given a two-year assignment to a locale that he wanted to retire in. He wanted to retire in Florida, so he was sent to a place called Green Cove Springs. Have you ever heard of that?

SC: It's near Jacksonville.

PDM: Yes. It's thirty miles south of Jacksonville on the St. Johns River, where they had retired ships, not quite as big as the bone yard that they had in the Chesapeake Bay [Naval Defense Reserve Fleet, or James River Reserve Fleet]. As a warrant boatswain, he was put in charge of those ships.

So to answer your question directly, we closed shop in Norfolk, Virginia, but I had graduated from high school with little preparation for college. Why? It hadn't been emphasized. So I had to default into what I was going to do. I was seventeen. I graduated from high school quite early, and so I moved to Jacksonville with them and started at a junior college. It's Jacksonville University now, but it was Jacksonville Community College then. The takeaway from that is, which I've remedied with my sons, was that parents have a responsibility to mentor, guide—you choose the phrase—help make options available. The old boatswain offered little guidance. If I had become a sailor, even though he wanted me to become an officer, it would have been fine. He would have said, "do it right." The takeaway from that was that I wasn't helped along the way. I didn't take enough initiative myself either on deciding how I was going to approach university. With the boatswain, academics was not high on the list. It just wasn't. Work, but not academics.

So when we went to Jacksonville, I lived at home to go to this community college, and I worked. He got out of the Navy at that time and he bought a gas station, where I worked some afternoons and on the weekends to try to save money, because then I realized I wanted to try to go to school, and they didn't have any money. The work was useful. I learned a hell of a lot by working in that environment for a small entrepreneur that tried to take a little gas station and build it into something more than a gas station, a repair capability, then trying to bring more people on, you know, to try to be a small businessman. I look back, and that was very useful to learn and to play a very small role in it. It just showed that the old boatswain took the values that he had in the Navy, which were hard work and stick-to-it-iveness, transition them to business, and made a good little business out of that. So that stuck somewhere, because I think I repeated that, but at a different plateau [*laughs*] later on.

SC: If you were tasked to address a group of high schoolers on how to approach their future lives and careers, based on your experiences growing up, what would you advise them to do?

PDM: I've done that with high schools, and I've talked at a few high school graduations. I've learned that is a very tough assignment to be an advisor to a seventeen- or an eighteen-year-old. I think that giving them illustrations was the best way I was able to connect—hold their attention for a little bit—using personal experiences as to what in military parlance is prepping the battlefield. They had to prep their future. You just didn't go into battle without doing some preparation, and trying to get young people to understand that they have the responsibility to get themselves prepared and they're the only ones that can do that, the parents could be helpful, their teachers could be helpful, but they were the ones that had to write their own mental "operations order" [OpOrder] as to how they wanted to pursue their future.

And I try to use a military analogy in any environment with youngsters, usually by using a military analogy; it gets their attention. When you use a phrase like "prep the battlefield" or use phrases like "an operation order," these were new phrases to them. I could tell I had their attention in being able to advise and maybe help them work through this very difficult thought process of thinking about their future.

SC: Building on that, if you were to recommend a curriculum for high schoolers to undertake in terms of their future lives and careers, what courses or what curricula would you recommend they strive for?

PDM: I would have to recommend exactly what I didn't do. I would recommend getting a technical education or at least an appreciation for engineering, math, and computer sciences. I think that is so important. Today it's essential. When I was growing up and when you were growing up, Stan, it was important, but now it's essential to have an appreciation for the sciences, for mathematics, for technology. We see so many mistakes in young people wanting to avoid that. I think it needs to be embraced, and anytime someone of experience can influence a young person, to steer them in that direction it's important. Without it, without that foundation, you're playing catch-up ball the whole time. I played catch-up ball for a long time in the Navy.

SC: In addition to the specific academic endeavors you just mentioned, are there any other activities you recommend for high schoolers to strive towards a career in the military or the business world?

PDM: Again, it's probably what I missed. I would advise anyone to be a voracious reader of military history if they wanted to participate in the military. I would advise them to have an appreciation of some of the military leaders. That information is available and ubiquitous. There's lots of information about great generals, great admirals along the way, and to know about how they thought would be helpful. I had to play catch-up ball here also. Youngsters need a recipe card given to them when they are in their last couple of years of high school, gates they really need to pass through to get into college and then to pursue whatever career they wanted to pursue. The recipe card wouldn't be myopic; it would have lots of activities in a broad range of subjects. I missed that, and I tried to give that opportunity to my youngsters, somewhat successful. You have to expose them. You have to give them an opportunity to say, "Don't pass this up. Read about this. Study about that. Take a field trip on this." That's a parent's job. If you're able to do that, I think you've contributed a lot, whether it's your own family or whether you're mentoring someone outside your family. High schools do a so much better job today in preparing students for higher education.

SC: In the early twenty-first century, many heroes of youth are celebrities or sports figures. In your early years, who did you see as the heroes and why? What appealed to you about the certain public figures?

PDM: [*laughs*] I had a lot of baseball heroes, some football heroes, a couple of basketball heroes, but outside of sports, I had few heroes. Why? Because I was never given that recipe card. I developed my own, and I defaulted to doing whatever schoolwork I needed to do. I liked athletic activity, so I followed pro sports. Some remember Warren Spahn, a baseball pitcher. Many remember Yogi Berra and the famous Yankee Phil Rizzuto. Those are your baseball cards. Now youngsters don't follow things like that. Instead, they often become engaged in electronic games. They know manual dexterity, but they don't read batting averages on the back of a card and say, "I'd like to hit 243 instead of 218." So that's all I did.

SC: I was in day camp listening to the radio, to the Yankees game when Roger Maris hit his sixty-first home run.

PDM: That's it.

SC: So if you could wave your hand and bring back to American and Western society some cultural values from years back that have changed with the decades, what might they be and why?

PDM: [*laughs*] That's a tough one. Cultural values, my recipe card there is family unity, hard work, result-oriented teaching, a foundation of faith, and then being able to share with your friends, your family, that you're working together, you're trying to succeed together, the proven cultural values that brought us to where we are today.

    We watched yesterday the inauguration of our forty-fifth president. I spent some time watching it on both sides of our political spectrum; the values are different on each side. I was shocked, listening from one channel and then to another, of how they perceive things. But for myself, what I just mentioned, being able to pull it together as a unit, to have unit integrity, whether it be your team, your club, your family, your nation, that's a home run. And right now in 2017, I don't think we're hitting a single, let alone a home run.

SC: As we progress through your life and career in this oral history, we'll cover your concepts of leadership, some of which you just outlined and described, and your personal philosophy of—and I'm using your words here—steering in the right direction. So to sum up your youth experiences, are there any other events, activities, or experiences in your youth that you see as exerting the most influence on your future actions and attitudes? Did we cover everything?

PDM: You know, looking back, it wasn't the affirmative period. It wasn't what actions positively influenced my youth, it was the absence of positive actions that I knew I had to make up for. Sadly, there was very little remarkable positive activity for Paul David Miller's first eighteen years, very little.

SC: Were there any particularly memorable teachers that influenced you? You've talked a lot about your stepdad. How about while you were in high school? Any memorable teachers that you remember that had a particularly positive influence on your future attitudes?

PDM: Yes, I had one teacher in high school; she influenced me more than she'll ever know, but it wasn't positively. This teacher told me I would never make anything of myself. I didn't know exactly at the time why she said that. I probably did something in her class that day that she didn't like, and probably my performance in whatever class she was teaching wasn't great, and she probably had some reason to react to whatever I did, but when she said, "You will never make anything of yourself," that stuck. I still think about that. Why does one say that? It goes back to what I said earlier; you have to be very careful about what you tell people when you want not necessarily discipline, but when you want to get their attention and correct something, because you never know how long that lasts. I was probably sixteen when she told me that, and that has lasted for sixty years.

SC: Were there any other youth leaders, ministers, or adults that influenced your thinking and your attitudes?

PDM: No. I did not pay a whole heck of a lot of attention to them. I was the type of high school student, and even late grammar school student, that simply wanted to be a participant, to go through that period of time unobserved, to pass through it, to complete it, and to go on to the next step.

SC: Let's turn now to that next step. You mentioned earlier that you started out your college career there in Jacksonville at the community college, which is now Jacksonville University (JU). What were your perceptions at that time as you started college as to your future career, and did that include the U.S. Navy?

PDM: No, it did not. It was still a canvas with nothing on it. I embarked on a general course of studies. I was just beginning to focus on what it is that I had to pull together to be able to complete college and then go on. I knew that I wanted to complete college. That had been drilled into me by the boatswain. There was no turning back from wanting to do that, but it was how I was going to do that, and I knew that this place called Jacksonville University wasn't the right place. I knew that it was okay to start there, but I knew that I had to find a better outcome, but I still wasn't sure of the path. But now I'm a little older, I'm eighteen, I'm working in my father's gas station, not a glamorous thing to do, but important work, and I'm trying to decide what's next.

SC: You attended Florida State University (FSU) in Tallahassee for finishing your undergraduate studies. What dynamics influenced your decision to attend FSU as opposed to, University of Florida (UF) or some other four-year university?

PDM: Well, this is embarrassing. While at JU, I said I've got to try to go to some place that had more cachet to it—I didn't use that word at the time—but was better known, was a place that I would have been more proud of. This is me now at nineteen, about. And so I start looking around. I wanted to improve my college outcome.

So of all the places—recall, I grew up in Norfolk and I remember the College of William & Mary, which had a good reputation. I had a decent junior college record, so I applied to the College of William & Mary, and lo and behold, I got in as a transfer student. I didn't exactly know how we were going to do this because I hadn't quite saved enough money to pay for William & Mary, but through the good auspices of my stepfather and my mom, they were able to pull it off, so I went to William & Mary.

This was the turning point. This is where the next four months I knew that I had to pull it together, that meandering was no longer allowed. That's what I had been doing. I had meandered from living under Aunt Mary's tough tutelage, to my mother being equally as tough as Aunt Mary, particularly when my father was deployed. I was not coming to grips with being properly prepared for the future.

So that's when I went up to William & Mary. But it did not work. I knew that if I stayed at William & Mary I might not have been able to complete it. I knew my shortcomings. So that's when I said, "I've got to get into a different environment," because trying to play catch-up ball in an elite academic place was really tough. I realized that I can pull the ripcord now. I had a bunch of bad paper [grades] at William & Mary. So that's when I transferred to FSU.

SC: Tell us about your studies at FSU. What was your major? Why did you choose that?

PDM: I went to FSU and again it seems like I had to play catch-up. You can't transfer a D. I had to make up some academic ground. The business school was a path. I went to summer school to catch up, and it all worked. I even decided that I needed to have a decent academic record with well over a 3.0 average even though I was distracted by this young girl named Becky Norcross. [*laughs*]

SC: And we're going to talk about that shortly. Just as an aside, talking about transfer hours, in the history department, for example, at Florida State, they will only accept six hours of graduate credit if you're transferring in from any other university.

PDM: I was in the same situation. That's why I had to play catch-up.

SC: Did you have any professors that were particularly memorable, positive or negative?

PDM: Stan, I can't remember any professor I had, so it wasn't positive.

SC: But they weren't negative.

PDM: They weren't negative either.

SC: You joined Alpha Tau Omega fraternity. What else can you say about the social life at FSU in the early 1960s?

PDM: Other than in the fraternity and then trying to rebuild some semblance of an academic record, I had given up any thoughts of more college athletics. I had made the basketball team and tennis team in Jacksonville, but I knew I wasn't going to play any big-time "ball," but still I participated in every intramural athletic activity.

SC: So your major focus then was on academics?

PDM: If you call it focus, yes. I knew that I had to repair a record in academics. That took more time than I thought it would, but I knew it was essential and I knew I had to do my role within the fraternity, which took some time. I worked a little bit to supplement, as the boatswain couldn't afford but so much. Florida State at that time was a full-fledged state school, so it wasn't a real burden like William & Mary had been.

SC: If you had to go back to those years and relive your undergraduate days, is there anything that you would do differently, better, or not at all?

PDM: If I could start over, I probably would do a hell of a lot of things differently, but when I look at the outcome, I'm wondering if I did things differently, would I have the same outcome. The proof is always the outcome. So to answer a question like that is tough.

SC: Granted that the world has changed a lot since we were in college in the '60s and '70s, are there any enduring lessons that you would like to impart to any high schooler embarking on a college education today, based on your experiences at Florida State and from your perspective as an extraordinarily successful military and business professional?

PDM: The singular thing that I would be compelled to recommend is be totally involved in whatever you are doing. In academics, be involved more than just doing the required course of study. Student government, be involved. Be involved in being the best athlete you can be. Don't sit on the sidelines once you've decided you want to do something. I found myself sitting on a lot of sidelines, maybe not because I didn't have the ability to be involved but for some reason I often never pulled the trigger to be involved. So it's so important to gain that experience early. But depending on an individual's makeup, it's a lot easier for some than it is for others, but if you have the opportunity to influence an individual, regardless of age, based upon your experiences, you should be able to share that total involvement is essential, absolutely essential. Don't sit on the sidelines anytime.

SC: Excellent advice. You graduated from Florida State in 1963, just as the Vietnam War was kicking into higher gear. The Gulf of Tonkin incident occurred just after your graduation, for example. There was a lot of social and societal flux starting to build in American society in that year, and that exploded in the late 1960s. Did you perceive or detect any of that ferment during your undergraduate years?

PDM: Not in my undergraduate years. I actually graduated from Florida State in April of '63, and then I matriculated at graduate school at the University of Georgia in August of 1963. Because I had tended to business in more ways than one in my last three semesters at Florida State, I was able to get a fellowship to the University of Georgia Business School. Now, this was in '64. There I had good professors, I was a serious person, I was even teaching Paul A. Samuelson Economics 101 to sophomores as they were taking their first economics course. The UGA Business School had the convention of having a professor give a big lecture and then the class would break into smaller groups to be led by mostly graduate students—to answer questions, to talk about the topic of the lecture, etc.

I enjoyed that phase of college work very, very much, but that's when the murmurings of the Vietnam War first were shared among students. The program called the draft was still part of the code. So most men—I was probably twenty-one at the time—had to think that if they continued ratcheting up the troop commitment that the draft is something that one might have to worry about. That hit the target when I personally received a draft letter in 1964. They hadn't started the lottery system yet. I had a student deferment for graduate school. Becky and I weren't married. So I had to make a choice. I wasn't going to go any higher academically, so I said the boatswain taught me to be a naval officer, so I visited the Navy recruiter in Macon, Georgia, and showed him my draft letter and said, "What do you have that I can complete this obligation in the Navy?"

And that's when I took the tests and the physical. There was this program called Officer Candidate School (OCS), and that's where the story begins.[1] If there hadn't been a draft, I don't know if I'd have ever gone down the path of military service.

SC: Everyone occasionally wishes they had done something differently in their youth or made different choices or taken different paths, and to sort of put a reflection or a retrospect on this period, can you think of any actions, activities, decisions not taken that, in retrospect, you wish you had taken? I know you mentioned earlier that the outcome is the thing, but just thinking back and reflecting back, would there have been any that you think would have value or added value to your career had you done so?

PDM: Probably, but not feeling sorry for myself, my early years from birth till twelve, thirteen, fourteen were unusual. They impacted the future much more so than I realized at the time. If I could go back and change where I was born, who I was born to, yeah, hell, yeah, but you can't change that. Along the way, given the set of circumstances that I grew up in, the answer's no, I wouldn't.

SC: One of the most critical aspects of effectiveness in the civil and the military realm is strategic communications or what is known by other terms such as information operations, public relations, etc. Do you recall any events or experiences in your youth

---

[1] Officer Candidate School (OCS), located at Naval Station, Newport, RI is a multi-month curriculum that prepares officer candidates for commissioning. Many students are former enlisted sailors who have attained a bachelor's degree, but most are college graduates without prior military or naval experience. The curriculum includes leadership and management, navigation, basic ship operations, basic engineering, and Navy administration.

that shaped your attitudes on the value of effective strategic communications in the public arena?

PDM: Boy, that's a tough question to ask. I would say that most of my colleagues didn't pay attention to lots of strategic activity. The strategic message during the mid-60s was not meant for people of our age. It might have been for people that were older and in a different stage of their life, but I'm not so sure that it was targeted for the college student, the high school student.

I'm not so sure the messages delivered today are targeted for college students. I think some of them should be, because that's where you start to begin to think about all these things that will influence the path that one takes. Some people come from families that are adroit enough to provide that strategic communications overlay, but there are so many, like in the environment I had, that had no person or group to provide an overlay. If it wasn't sourced where I could reach it, there was no such thing that you would call overarching strategic communications for people like myself.

SC: Let's get back to your decision to go and talk to the Navy. Other than the draft, which you've already mentioned, were there any other influences on your decision to apply to OCS?

PDM: Yes, the boatswain.

SC: So you never considered any other service?

PDM: Not even a whisper of a thought. He started as an E-1 and finished as a W-4. If I was going to do anything, I was going to pick up at O1 and see what happened. Not a thought of serving in another branch of the Armed Services.

SC: Did you ever consider applying to the Naval Academy?

PDM: I considered it, but I knew I wouldn't make it. I didn't have the record. I sort of regretted that later on, but I'm a realist, and so I knew I wouldn't be able to follow that path.

SC: We've already covered a lot of what would be an answer to this question, but I just want to see if you want to amplify anything or add to it. What aspects of the military most appealed to you such that you said, "I'm going down to apply to Officer Candidate School," once you graduated from University of Georgia?

PDM: I think that [*laughs*] the single criteria of going to the Navy recruiter was it was a viable option to being drafted, full stop. But, I knew a little about the Navy because of the boatswain. So it had appeals, going on a ship, being able to be a participant in a crew. So it was easy to decide—would I rather become a naval officer or a platoon commander. It was easy to choose, as it was familiar and comfortable territory.

SC: Tell us about how you met your lovely bride, Becky, and how that transpired.

PDM: [*laughs*] That's going to take a long time. [*Carpenter laughs*] Becky is from a small town in western Illinois. She wound up at Florida State after two years at Stephens College in Columbia, Missouri, so we were both transplants to FSU. She was in a sorority, the first time I saw her was at this gathering called a "Greek Sing." It was a contest between fraternities or sororities about vocal prowess. Neither one of us were participants, but we were there. Just like in a book or movie, you see somebody across the way, and for some reason you're attracted. Becky was a beautiful coed. I thought she was stunning and had to figure out a way to meet her. The meeting was about a week later. If she were answering this question, it might be a little different. Becky will come up throughout my answering questions. I want to say straight away, I was most fortunate that Mary Rebecca Norcross payed attention to me. Our backgrounds are so very different. I was hooked the first time we went on a date. When she said yes to marrying me, I was blessed then and have been for fifty-four years. I knew little about a career in our Navy. She knew less. We learned and together we raised a wonderful family, went to the heights of military leadership as a four-star, and finished with a successful run as a corporate CEO [Chief Executive Officer]. Becky Miller played a vital role in each of these phases of life and deserves so many accolades as a young Navy wife, as a mother, as a partner to a ship's captain, as a representative of our Navy and when I reached senior positions such as Seventh Fleet commander, CinC of the Atlantic Command/NATO supreme allied commander Atlantic. I admire her, thank her, and love her. She made my journey possible.

SC: In our next few sessions, Admiral, we're going to take you to Officer Candidate School (OCS) back in Newport, your initial officer training, and commissioning as an ensign in the U.S. Navy, and your first years of sea duty. Since we will be referring back to and discussing the experiences and lessons from the Officer Candidate School experience many times throughout the first several sessions, we will go directly to session number two, question set number three and pick up the story with your first duty station following OCS.

PDM: Great.

SC: This is session number one, question set number one, USNI oral history interview with Admiral Paul David Miller, U.S. Navy (Retired). The date is Saturday, January 21, 2017, and the interviewer is Professor Stan Carpenter from the U.S. Naval War College. Thank you, Admiral.

[End of January 21, 2017, interview]

Interview with Admiral Paul David Miller, USN (Ret.)
Date: January 22, 2017

Stan Carpenter (SC): This is USNI oral history interview with Admiral Paul David Miller. This is session number two, question set number three. The date is Sunday,

January 22, 2017. The interviewer is Professor Stan Carpenter of the U.S. Naval War College. These questions cover the first sea duty tour as a junior officer.

Admiral, let's pick up with your first duty station following your time in Newport at Officer Candidate School. Looking back from the perspective of a long and successful naval career, are there any courses or curricular areas that you would recommend adding or deleting from the officer commissioning program, especially at Officer Candidate School today and in the future?

Paul David Miller (PDM): Not really. The career begins with the first duty station. The academic work that goes on before that is sufficient, whether it be the Naval Academy, OCS, NROTC [Naval Reserve Officers Training Corps]. The meter begins when you go to that first duty station and take up your first set of responsibilities.

SC: Did you leave immediately from OCS following graduation and commissioning?

PDM: I did leave immediately from Newport, Rhode Island, but I think we need to go through the story of me getting my first set of orders. Before I left Newport, there was that "dance" the one that goes on while everyone waits around to be told what his first duty station might be. It came to my turn, and I went to the initial assignments detailer, and he told me I was going to the USS *Papago*.[2] I said, "What's a *Papago*?" And he really didn't know what a *Papago* was.

There was a line so I thanked him and moved aside. Rather than act like I didn't know naval ships, I went to *Jane's Fighting Ships*. There was a volume nearby and I looked up this thing called *Papago*. Much to my amazement, it was a fleet tug. I said mentally, "Oh, my gosh." I thought I was joining the Navy and I was supposed to go to a warship, and I was going to a fleet tug. I didn't understand its mission, I didn't understand its position in the fleet, but I did recall serendipitously that "the old boatswain" was on a fleet tug in Newport, Rhode Island, when he met my mother. I

---

[2] USS *Papago* (ATF-160) was an *Abnaki*-class fleet oceangoing tug commissioned in 1945 and decommissioned in 1992. She displaced 1,200 tons and was crewed by eight officers and sixty-eight enlisted men. She was homeported in Norfolk, VA, and at Naval Station, Guantanamo Bay, Cuba.

remember going on that ship as an eleven- or twelve-year-old, and to me then, that ship was a relatively decent size, but it truly isn't.

That was it; I had received my first set of Navy orders. Not happy but having accepted this outcome, I packed my stuff, and rather than going straight to the ship, I went to Bushnell, Illinois. Becky had agreed that we would be married between commissioning and having to report to my first ship. She did a great work with planning and we were married in a perfect church ceremony—a very beautiful bride married in her home town at her home church. Knowing there was limited time (we knew that right after the wedding) we had to drive to Norfolk, Virginia, to find a place for her to live, I had to get on the ship after about five days in Norfolk. I had to leave for Guantanamo Bay, Cuba, on ship's duty. We carried it off. Becky was amazing about accepting it. She was now a Navy wife—no longer a Midwest small-town farm girl. And we were off on a journey. We had no idea where it was going to take us. Sadly, there was to be no honeymoon—to this day when a couple is telling us about their honeymoon, I get this special "look."

So we start off to Norfolk in her Nash Rambler—two young adults with little to our names heading off on a life together. I remember clearly an ensign in 1964 earned $242 a month, and there was a small stipend for housing. So we had to find a place to live within the limits of that budget, and we found a small one-bedroom furnished apartment on Granby Street.

I reported to the ship, and I found something that even made me feel worse about my first set of orders: I was the sixth officer on a five-officer ship. Mentally, I think I was amazed at how could this be happening. How could I have been assigned a billet on a ship that had no billet and I was on this thing called the *Papago*? I just swallowed hard. I met the captain. He was a mustang, which meant he had previous enlisted experience and worked his way up to get his own command. To him, this was a cruiser; this was an amazing position for him to be in having started as E-1 some time ago. He was an outstanding commanding officer, and he treated myself and his wife treated Becky like a wardroom captain and wife should do. We were embraced and they tried to make us feel at "home."

Becky was absolutely terrific and made our little apartment the best it could be. I did feel awful about leaving her alone in Norfolk, a bride of two weeks, and I'm sure she wondered often what did I get myself into. I knew I had a lot to prove that she made the right decision in marring this young naval officer.

The *Papago* got under way for Gitmo [slang term for Guantanamo Bay]. It was all independent steaming. Of course, we were a fleet tug. We didn't steam with anybody. So then I started to learn the rudiments of all the things that made that ship work. I didn't like the smell of the ship when I first went down the amidship passageway. It smelled of diesel, and if you take the ladder as you walk into the amidship passageway, it leads down to the engine room with four great big diesel engines. I knew zero about diesel engines.

I was an officer, so the captain had to give me a job. All the larger ships had an electronic warfare officer (EWO). This ship had only some communications equipment, so it was the communications/electronics officer. The other billets were an engineering officer, a diving officer, which was, in fact, the ship's main battery. It had full hard-hat and scuba capability. It had a decompression chamber. That was its main battery, salvage, and if something had to be taken up from the bottom of the ocean, they had that capability. It had an XO and it had a CO. So I was in charge of everything else that wasn't in the main line of what the ship did.

I learned quickly that the XO was the navigator, by assignment, but he had zero interest in it, and since he had this new fresh ensign, he just said that's part of my additional duty, but he kept the responsibility. So that kept me busy because there was no SATNAV [satellite navigation system]. We had a LORAN [Long Range Navigation], but it worked half the time. You had to pay attention to DR [dead reckoning]—you had to pay attention, period. When you were in open ocean, to taking the sun lines so you at least knew your latitude.[3]

But this is a long-winded way of saying I went to a ship that I was terribly disappointed in, and I didn't know what to do other than to do what I was told and to do it

---

[3] LORAN is a radio-based long-range navigation system developed by the United States during World War II. Ships receive radio signals and, by measuring the intervals between signal pulses from widely dispersed transmitting stations, can determine their position at sea.

the best that I could. That's the simple lesson. No matter where you go, you just have to show that you have the talent to do more and see where it takes you.

SC: I think you said earlier that you would have preferred something like a cruiser, destroyer, frigate type first, amphibious ship [amphib] second, service force third. Let's look at that process for assigning billets. At the time, was it completely at random or was it based on some rational system such as needs of the Navy?

PDM: Probably in between, but that was where I learned my first lesson about things don't always work the way that they're advertised. I wound up on this thing called the *Papago* because the captain, before he took command of that ship, had been in the Bureau of Naval Personnel, and he was in enlisted detailing. He was an officer in charge of some section. Before he left to go to the schools that he had to complete prior to taking command, he shared with me that he stopped by the initial assignments officer desk and asked whoever was there, since he was going to this ship, which was to be totally operational during his time, "Can you send me a bright, ready-to-go ensign, and we'll give him a lot of things to do." And so they found this person called P. D. M. and sent him to that ship.

So then I realized that, you know, things don't always work, even in a large organization like the Navy, the way that they're advertised. There are things that happen which "help" the system work differently—a good lesson and I was always mindful of that.

SC: We're going to get back to your time on the *Papago* and bore in on that, but first I want to explore some of the preparations in general that a young officer has before assuming that first sea duty tour. What would you recommend to future newly commissioned ensigns on leave in between whatever commissioning source and their first billet, as to what they should do in that time before reporting aboard to their first duty assignment?

PDM: I would recommend doing nothing except mentally preparing yourself that your life was going to change. Whatever you knew before going to that first assignment—and

I believe this applicable to the Navy, to becoming a platoon leader in the Army, or the Marine Corps—that you were going to enter an environment that would be totally different than anything you had done up until that time, and so you'd better go in with your eyes wide open with a positive attitude and that you're not only going do your damnedest but also we're going to learn every single day.

SC: The Surface Warfare Officer Basic Course evolved in the 1970s, well after you'd been commissioned, so in the mid-1960s, was there any officer training, surface warfare-type officer training pipeline prior to your first sea tour?

PDM: Not to my first sea tour. It was from OCS straight to whatever assignment you were going to get, but then I started to hear about this thing called Destroyer School.[4] It wasn't a Department Head School; it was Destroyer School. It was started a few years before that in Newport. One reason I wanted to do a destroyer tour was because the lieutenants that were in that school seemed to be of the main line. If you were going to be a surface warfare officer, that's the path you should follow—aim for serving in destroyers.

SC: So you went straight from OCS, with a few days' leave, to the ship.

PDM: A few days' leave to get married. I probably had two weeks in between graduation and going to the ship.

SC: At that time, there were no other basically billet-related officer training schools?

PDM: Maybe for some. For me, nothing.

---

[4] Destroyer School, later renamed Department Head School, at the Surface Warfare Officers School (SWOS) at Naval Station, Newport, RI, is a multi-month school that an officer attends prior to their first department head tour.

SC: Once you got to your first ship as a division officer, what parts of the OCS curriculum did you find most useful in having taken and what about least helpful?

PDM: The way things worked out, the most helpful was the smattering of navigation instruction as I wound up needing to get the *Papago* from Point A to Point B. If you had a crew like you had on *Papago*, you needed all the training you could get. *Papago* was manned with all the people that other ships didn't want. We were at the bottom of the list for manning. It's sad to say. I had very unkind names for the outfit where I started my professional career—the Navy's "junk force."

SC: You might recall the early 1980s there was a thing called Project Upgrade, but in the fleet known as Operation Bottom Blow.

PDM: That's it.

SC: People who took up entirely too much administrative time for what they were worth.

PDM: It wasn't a real close wardroom. I was the only serving naval officer commissioned without prior service. I was a reserve officer, 1105 [surface warfare officer, Navy Reserve designator], at that time. The others were the mustang I mentioned; the engineering officer was LDO [Limited Duty Officer]; the diving officer, he was sort of a regular person, but he had gone through almost a year's worth of special schooling, so he wasn't much interested in things on board. He was interested in doing his diving work.[5]

SC: You were commissioned in the early Vietnam War era. What was your impression now of civilian attitudes towards the military as the 1960s and the Vietnam War wore on?

---

[5] LDO is a limited duty officer. LDOs are former enlisted sailors who are technical specialists based on their previous enlisted rate or specialty. They are commissioned officers and can advance to captain and serve as division officers, department heads, XOs, and COs. However, all their assignments will be within their technical specialty.

PDM: At that point in time, in '65, we were in Norfolk, Virginia. We were in a bubble. And since I had been assigned a noncombatant, we weren't involved, but they were starting to send destroyers around to participate in Vietnam deployments. I was not involved other than watching news and infrequent conversations with other officers. There was not much hype about Vietnam in 1965.

SC: With the growing negative public attitudes that evolved through the 1960s towards the military, and particularly in the later 1960s, the services often took in both officer candidates and enlistees to fill quotas that in ordinary times would not have been qualified. That dynamic really didn't manifest itself until the 1970s. Did you have any negative experiences with that dynamic either at a training command or as a division officer?

PDM: [*laughs*] Not at a training command, but I wondered where they got some of the sailors that we had on the ship. I just marveled at their inability to even carry out some of the basic tasks, and it was a tough ship. There was a lot of hard work being done. When you get into salvage work and you lay this stuff called "beach gear" when you try to hook up to tow a large ship, there's a lot of dangerous work that goes on, and you have to have a trained element of your crew to do it all. Keeping those diesels running required training and ingenuity. You didn't get a lot of help from your squadron or your group staff. You were expected to keep the ship running.

    I went into it with a degree of "What the hell am I doing here?" But once I got there, I knew that I could keep myself very, very busy trying to keep all the elements of that ship together and not having anything pass through to the XO or CO without my imprint on it.

SC: As part of the officer development curriculum today and really for the past few decades, tactical simulation is an important part of the teaching pedagogy. You've already mentioned that that was fairly minimal, but what little tactical training you did have at OCS, was that applicable to anything you did aboard *Papago*?

PDM: No and no. The thing that was applicable was limited time with ship-driving and ship-docking simulations.

SC: You've already mentioned that navigation was critical. Anytime the whistle blows under way, you're navigating.

PDM: That's it. Even with the ship's draft of 15.6 feet. It doesn't seem like much, but in keeping 6 feet beneath the keel you had to be mindful of where you were all the time.

SC: When did you first go to Navy Firefighting School? Tell us about that experience and what impressions it left on you.

PDM: I went to Firefighting School two days at OCS—very realistic training—taught you about all the class—Bravo, Alpha, Charlie—fires, all the things that you needed to be aware of. The other training that I was really taken with was damage control training, getting into a simulator ship that they flooded gained a real appreciation and understanding of shoring and other techniques of how to stop flooding.

SC: The *Buttercup*.

PDM: The *Buttercup*. That was the name of it. That simulator was helpful, because it made you understand and appreciate the force of water in a confined space, and that you'd better be mindful that if you had to use those skills, you'd better know what the hell you're doing, because it meant something.

SC: At Firefighting School, after the *Forrestal* (CVA/CV-59) fire incident off Vietnam in 1967, a standard feature, and I assume still today, is they show *Trial by Fire*, which is essentially a TV camera that recorded all landings and takeoffs and it caught that particular incident. Do you remember at Firefighting School prior to that, did they do any of what I would call the shock movies to show you exactly what could happen?[6]

PDM: Yes, I'm sure they did. But the basic damage control trainings was good. I'm sure they're infinitely better now, but I would be a fan of spending as much time as available in that kind of training.

SC: Typically, in a career, sailors attend Firefighting School regularly. How many times do you think you went to refresher-type firefighting training over the years?

PDM: Zero. But I did go when I became a fleet commander. I used to visit the Firefighting School in Norfolk, Virginia, every once in a while just to show that there was top interest in this training.

SC: Let's turn now to your time on USS *Papago*. Tell us about your first day aboard.

PDM: [*laughs*] I alluded to it earlier. You just walk aboard, you try to get acquainted with it, and I didn't have much time. I had two days before we got under way. I was an observer the first time we got under way, but my learning curve was steep. As soon as we got past 1 Charlie [navigation buoy] in the Chesapeake Bay, turned south, we were going against the Gulf Stream, not hours later, I became sick. It was terrible. As I went through the ensign sickness pattern, it lasted a long time. It was serious. Every time it got rough, because the tug was shaped like a turned-over turtle—it wasn't a cutting-through-the-water ship—every wave, every time you came up and bounced back down, I felt awful. I was happy our first assignment was in Gitmo. I was happy to get down to the Caribbean and calm water.

SC: Did you have a sea daddy or mentor who showed you the ropes in your first few weeks aboard *Papago*?

---

[6] The *Forrestal* fire occurred on July 29, 1967 while the ship was conducting flight operations off the coast of Vietnam on Yankee Station. It was started by an errant electrical signal that ignited a Zuni rocket, which fired off striking a parked aircraft. The resultant fire killed 134 sailors and airmen, injured a further 161, and damaged or destroyed 61 aircraft.

PDM: No, the ship is so damn small, everybody's your mentor and you get to know everybody quickly. To get familiar with the main propulsion, you'd go down to the engine room and you have a second-class engineering officer of the watch [EOOW]. You could ask him anything. You become friends with the enlisted people as well as the officers because you're fifty-five to sixty people, you're all in this together, to get the thing where it's supposed to go and do the assigned mission.

SC: In general, why is having a sea daddy or a mentor critical to the development of every new junior officer?

PDM: If one did have someone that took you under his wing to guide him through the initial time in one's job that would be important because no one wants to make a silly mistake. If someone can help you prevent that, it helps prevent embarrassment, it reinsures confidence, and that's what a mentor does. I did it for hundreds of people in later assignments.

SC: I would say you really need two mentors, a senior and a junior, meaning if you're a division officer, your department head should mentor you and your leading enlisted, typically chief petty officer, first class petty officer as well. Would you say that's a valid concept?

PDM: Yes. For a newbie in his first tour, that's valid. But then I found that the mentor that would be on the enlisted side or lower in your leadership structure, the chief or first class, he's not looking for a trainee; he's looking for someone to support him. So, therefore, with him, after you've gotten to learn the way around, your association with him can still be one of learning from him, but, more importantly as you're doing that, you've got to show him that you are ready to support him and his troops in completing their task.

SC: Let's turn now to what you did aboard the *Papago*. What watches did you typically stand in your first few months aboard, both in port and under way?

PDM: I never stood an in-port watch in my whole naval career, and that is a fact. I say it again: I never stood an in-port watch in my whole naval career. I stood CDO [command duty officer] watches.[7] There were people on the quarterdeck, but I never stood a quarterdeck watch. I was automatically a CDO of the tug. We'd go down, we have a six-week period in Guantanamo where we did [*laughs*] the cherished assignment towing targets for the destroyers that I wanted to be on. We would tow the sled and we would mark the fall of shot as they tried to qualify in gunnery. Then we'd bring the sled back, we'd bring it up tight and go back into port every day.

There were people interested in learning to drive the ship. I was very interested. I started with the CO under his tutelage. I got it under way just about every day. Because the engineer was the LDO [limited duty officer], he would do it if he had to, and so was another LDO. They were happy to have this youngster that would take every ship handling opportunity and they didn't have to worry about it. But I learned a lot about ship driving during that little period, the first six weeks I was on board.

SC: Did *Papago* ever have any senior enlisted officer of the deck?

PDM: Yes, it had a chief petty officer. In fact, there were four qualified OODs. I was one, the engineering officer, and then the other two were enlisted. The captain was a traditionalist and never let us be in more than four sections. That was fine.

SC: Tell us about your typical in port day for a new division officer in the 1960s. Basically, what was the usual ship's routine like aboard the *Papago*?

---

[7] The CDO is the captain's representative in port when the CO and XO are ashore or not aboard. The CDO may be, but does not have to be, the most senior officer aboard. In an emergency, the CDO may take action that is usually reserved for the CO, such as an emergency sortie.

PDM: In port, we had one-in-three duty sections. If you're on an old ship and you don't have a lot of talent to keep things going, your day is busy working and trying to make things ready to go to the next evolution.

Becky, as a new Navy wife, would come down and we would eat in the wardroom on my duty nights, and she did that often during the sixteen months I was on the *Papago*. We tied up in Little Creek [Naval Amphibious Base].

I would spend my day running around getting things done, and there was a myriad of tasks. If I didn't have anything in communications, I would help the engineer because he had so much to do, he was overloaded. The diving officer sometimes needed help. I just assisted everybody. It was a close-knit group. It wasn't a line of command on a small ship like that. It was truly that we were all there to just get our jobs done and move on. It was a different world.

SC: I have to ask this question.

PDM: Shoot.

SC: You remember the—it was a stage play and later a movie with, I think, Henry Fonda—*Mr. Roberts*. One of the dynamics there was he wanted to be on board a destroyer in the Pacific war, and he was assigned to essentially an auxiliary supply ship. Did you ever have times when you felt like Mr. Roberts?

PDM: I probably felt worse than Mr. Roberts, especially when towing targets for the FRAM [Fleet Rehabilitation and Modernization Program] destroyers shooting 5"/38 guns they would return as sleek destroyers, and tie up. Of course I often thought, "What the hell am I doing here?"[8]

---

[8] The Fleet Rehabilitation and Modernization or FRAM program modernized World War II era destroyers, particularly the weapons systems, electronics, sensors, and engineering/propulsion plants. The intention was to modernize the ships with the latest technology systems to get at least another decade of service. The FRAM program dated from the early 1960s. The 5"/38 Dual Purpose gun was the standard main battery weapon on destroyers and other surface ships and the standard secondary battery on battleships in World War II. It was used for anti-aircraft defense, surface gunnery, and shore bombardment. The bore size was 5" firing a round 5" in diameter and with a barrel length of 38 calibers, thus the designation of the weapon system.

SC: Let's talk about your typical day at sea on the *Papago*. You've already mentioned some of the activities that would happen, but let's say you're not actually in a gunnery exercise or doing a tow. Let's say when you're steaming, what would your typical day be like?

PDM: Sometimes if you had everything working and, of course, there was no formation steaming, part of the day would get a little boring, especially if it was rough. If it was rough and we were independent steaming, it was tough just to get through the day. I don't know how many days I ate peanut butter and jelly sandwiches, sitting on the floor in the little wardroom. You couldn't sit in a damn chair the ship rolled and pitched so much.

Early on, I'd say three months into my assignment, we did get a unique task. There was a B-52 [U.S. Air Force strategic bomber] that had crashed off of Thule, Greenland. Our task was to get up there as fast as we could with the diving capability. We rendezvoused with a Coast Guard icebreaker. I have a couple of pictures. That was unique. After a couple of weeks on the ice, most of the support facilities came from the beach, and we were just a platform to do what needed to be done. It was just unique. I went over to the icebreaker and rode it for a couple of days, just to understand and appreciate how that task is done, and then trying to navigate back through the ice floes was challenging. I never went back to the ice again, but it was a great experience.

We had another task. We were task-oriented. Other than going to Gitmo, if you were the ready salvage ship, you never knew what you were going to get involved in. Somebody goes aground, you go out there to help pull them off. So the days were filled not with OPORDERS [Operations Orders], fleet assignments, everybody trying to put a warfare task together. The days were filled with getting a specific task done oriented to the capabilities of your small ship. Different world. It was Navy because it was a Navy ship, but other than that, there aren't many interconnections with what most people understand and appreciate as the operational Navy.

SC: You've mentioned several of the functions of the *Papago*, such as diving and salvage and towing and what have you, and you've also mentioned some of the other officers and their responsibilities. On a typical much larger Navy warship at the time, you would have had an operations department, weapons, engineering, navigation, and supply. These have changed somewhat over the years, but how did the fleet tug organization compare to that pattern of departments?

PDM: There's no comparison. I'll talk about this later when I went to a destroyer. You had clear lines and you had a separation of responsibilities. There were no separations of responsibilities on that tug. When you had a chief storekeeper, he's the one that did what a supply officer does, but if you needed certain parts or whatever, you weren't able to go and get the federal stock numbers and all from some supply person; you had to figure it out yourself and write your own chits [paper forms] and turn them in and be a supply officer for eight hours. You just did everything.

SC: Let's turn now to something that is extremely important to every naval ship, and that's general quarters. For those not completely familiar with the implications or meaning of the term "general quarters" or GQ, tell us exactly what that means on a Navy ship.[9]

PDM:[*laughs*] Believe me, what that means on the fleet tug versus what that means on a ship of the line is totally different. The damage control's the same. Damage control is damage control. If you have a flooding issue, you have to take care of water coming onto your ship. I did not face that in the tug. The tug was sturdily built. But we did have probably more small fires than most because we were a diesel. If you took a heavy roll, sometimes in the catch basins under each of the main engines, if its fuel splashed or it spilled over, you could have a fire in a heartbeat. We had one that got my attention for having a fire at sea. Nobody wants to do that. So later in my ship assignments, I paid more attention to damage control. I had experienced what it meant to have a space fill

---

[9] General Quarters or GQ, is the highest state of combat readiness. The ship goes to GQ or battle stations whenever a threat of combat is imminent or when other threat conditions are encountered such as fire, flooding, or collision.

with smoke and to actually put on an OBA [Oxygen Breathing Apparatus] to fight a fire at sea in rough weather.

SC: If I throw out the term "maximum condition of readiness," how would that relate to General Quarters?

PDM: [*laughs*] We have to talk about that when I get to my department head and being in command two times. We've talked enough about fleet tugs. They do their job. Now they're not even in the Navy. They're part of the MSC [Military Sealift Command].[10] They're all civilian-manned. They're probably manned with thirty people now or twenty people or ten. I don't know how many. Different, different world.

SC: And probably a lot more automation.

PDM: Yes, and probably some good navigation equipment that you can get from Point A to Point B. It was a full-time task when we were at sea to know where the hell we were and to get where you are going. I was probably one of the few that navigated to Iceland and England in an ATF. Celestial [celestial navigation] only.

SC: A lot of celestial navigation.

PDM: A lot.

SC: What was your GQ station?

PDM: I was the officer of the deck, of course. [*laughs*] Let's go from there to me being XO of one of these beasts.

---

[10] Military Sealift Command (MSC) provides all the transportation and service force assets for the Navy. The fleet, largely manned by civilian mariners, includes hospital, expeditionary fast transport, special mission, fleet oilers, fleet ordnance, tanker, sealift, maritime prepositioning, and dry cargo ships.

SC: We're going to do that in the next question set. Let's wrap up your time on *Papago*.

PDM: I learned on *Papago*, I look back, and while I did not appreciate being assigned to this thing—I used to say "this thing called the *Papago*," [*laughs*] I never even said "USS *Papago*." The environment that I was thrust in, the crew that I had to work with, it taught me a lot of life's lessons which later stood me in good stead, so while I was disappointed at the time, the fitness reports were great. I had them written by admirals later on, but they weren't any better than those written by my LDO captain. I was proud of those reports.

SC: It strikes me that being on a small ship like that, where you have many, many duties, when you come out of that tour, you are far more experienced than someone who is a smaller cog on a larger ship.

PDM: Amen.

SC: Let me ask about your collateral duties. You've already mentioned some. You did a lot of navigation, you did pretty much anything. Did you have any formal collateral duties like wardroom mess treasurer or some type of collateral duty of that nature?

PDM: No, we didn't. Again, duties weren't administered that way. A wardroom mess treasurer, we had stewards then, right? We had one, even on that fleet tug, and that second-class was our mess treasurer. Everybody did what needed to be done. It's hard to characterize, if one is only a fleet sailor, what goes on in the junk force. It's hard to characterize.

SC: When I came aboard my first ship as a new communications officer, the senior chief radioman asked me politely to avoid playing with or handling the communications equipment. Actually, his words were a lot saltier, but you get the point. In retrospect, there was a lot of powerful truth in those few words, "Mr. Carpenter, don't touch my 'expletive deleted' gear." What did the senior chief mean by that, and why was that excellent advice to a brand new ensign?

PDM: You're in a different world, Stan. On board that cruiser, there were sophisticated receivers, transmitters, and he probably wanted only someone that had been to school, trained, touching his equipment because if for some reason it got out of tune, out of calibration, there was a lot of effort to make it right. On board a small ship, where you have just two receivers, that's all you have, two, and I remember the designations, R-1051. We had a second-class radioman, and he and I had a little alley-like radio room. So you had to be a participant. You could not be just an observer as there was no one else to "touch the gear."

SC: How important is a cadre of talented senior enlisted subordinates? Let's take us out of the *Papago* realm and put you on a larger ship.

PDM: When we talk about that later, it's an essential to have that degree of support needed to make any mainline ship achieve its maximum capability. Without talent, one never gets maximum capability.

SC: As we wrap up your time on the *Papago*, let's talk about a few little lighter things. What was your worst day and your best day on board *Papago*?

PDM: [*laughs*] That's a good question. I have to really search back into the files for my worst day. I think my worst day was probably being deathly ill, seasick, and as officer of the deck losing navigational reference to where we were in the Windward Passage [strait between Cuba and Hispaniola]. We were in waters that even a ship with a fourteen-foot draft could get into trouble then. I was really sick. The wind was coming against the flow of the Gulf Stream. We were into really good seas in the Windward Passage. The captain came to the bridge and asked me where we were exactly, and I couldn't answer him. That LDO taught me a few things about situational awareness and never, never, ever lose it again.

SC: I think the term is "lose the bubble."

PDM: That young ensign had lost the bubble.

SC: I'm going to assume that your answer to this next question is the day you saluted the quarterdeck and "I report my departure," but what was your best day aboard *Papago*?

PDM: That was true, I was happy to leave, but my best day was probably our second time back down to Gitmo, and I was the OOD, and the captain let me bring it in. There was a ship on the other side of the pier, and I brought it in hot. I told the engineers that when I rang up a bell [speed orders from the bridge to engineering main control], make sure that we get it. And the people on the other side of the pier started looking at "That ship's coming in too fast," and we slid into that space and the ship parked. It was a single-screw ship, so it would back to port. So I came in at a rather steeper angle than normal, and when I put on all back two-thirds, the engineers hit that and we just parked. The captain said, "Wow, that was a little fast, but that was a great landing." That was the day I knew I could drive a ship.

SC: Were there any particular recognition or reward techniques that you found useful or would recommend to junior officers in helping to draw out the best efforts from their division?

PDM: Yes. Know your division, know not only their shipboard duties but know if they had a family, know about their family, know about what they were interested in. Be concerned about their success and make sure that they were comfortable in coming to you before they got into trouble. If you can do that with a fourteen-man division, you can do that with a hundred-man department and you can go right up the ladder to a five thousand-man ship. If you are CO of an aircraft carrier or air wing detachment, if you tree-down that philosophy all the way to the newly reported seaman, it really works.

SC: *Papago* was home ported in Little Creek, Virginia, which is part of that whole Norfolk area naval community. What was life like there for a Navy family in those days?

PDM: It was routine. Norfolk was a naval town. We did not have children during my time on that ship or my whole seagoing time as a junior officer. So Becky worked. She was in the school system of Virginia Beach. We were a Navy couple. We went to the commissary. We used exchanges. On Friday evenings, if we had the ability with some friends, we'd go to the Little Creek Officers' Club. We were in a cocoon of Navy activity It wasn't grand, but we were happy with what we had, and if you approach it that way, it all works.

SC: You went next to another fleet tug, the USS *Seneca* (ATF-91), as executive officer or XO.[11] This is called a split tour, and it's a little unusual for a junior officer in his or her first sea tour. Why and how did that occur, and what were your perceptions of the new orders at the time?

PDM: Again, disappointment. I thought I had done okay. I thought I was going to get a split tour to at least maybe an amphib [amphibious ship]. I thought I had been tarred or in some fashion negatively marked as a junk force officer. The XO of the *Seneca* got ill. They were getting under way and they needed an XO. My skipper knew the skipper of that ship, and it happened fortuitously because H. J. Robinson, the skipper that I had in *Papago*, was being relieved. It was just time to slip and proceed, and he recommended to the skipper of *Seneca* that I was pretty well trained in things ATF, and so he called the Bureau and said, "Don't send anybody. Why don't you just give us this lieutenant (j.g.) across the pier?" So it had been eighteen months, because I had made LTJG [lieutenant junior grade], or maybe fifteen months, right in that area. The Bureau [Bureau of

---

[11] USS *Seneca* (ATF-91) was a *Navajo*-class fleet tug. She was commissioned in 1943 and decommissioned in 1971. Originally designated as a fleet tug (AT-91), she was redesignated as an ocean fleet tug or ATF in 1944. She was laid up in the James River Group, National Defense Reserve Fleet, Lee Hall, VA, until being sunk as a target in 2003. At 1,235 tons displacement, her compliment was five officers and eighty enlisted. Homeported in Norfolk, VA, her primary duties were target towing, rescue and salvage work, and ship towing.

Personnel] moved this JG to be XO. At that time, I still had sort of planned that I was going to leave the Navy at the end of three years and I went to *Seneca*.

SC: We will discuss your XO tour in our next session, but for now, looking back from a distance of having achieved four-star flag rank, what are your perceptions of having been a ship XO so early in your career?

PDM: It was a continuance of being assigned to a small ship as my initial assignment. I had responsibilities that were the same as XO of a larger ship, but it was just in a miniature way, but everything was the same. There's no difference, just the numbers were smaller, the departments were smaller, the reach was a little narrower, but the responsibilities were the same, and I learned a hell of a lot.

SC: Based on your experiences in those days as a young junior officer with a family and just starting in a career, what recommendations would you make to someone today in similar circumstances?

PDM: I would recommend seeking out a tour on as small a vessel as you can early. The Navy has those opportunities; they had them and they still have them—because you're exposed to so many different things that you have to rely on your own ingenuity, your own facility to accomplish whatever job you have. There's little help. You have to get the job done. You learn to do it, and that experience puts you in a good position when you go to a larger ship.

SC: This wraps up our discussion of your first sea tour aboard USS *Papago*. Are there any other thoughts or reflections that you would like to add at this point?

PDM: Looking back, service on this small, poorly manned ship left some lasting impressions that every person in the crew was vital. As a leader, you had to be very agile in drawing out of each sailor their maximum contribution to make your ship sail proudly, to meet every commitment, and return to port safely with the satisfaction of a job well done.

SC: Thank you, Admiral. In our next session, we will continue our discussion of your first years of sea duty aboard USS *Seneca* and, in particular, your duty as the ship's executive officer. This is USNI oral history interview with Admiral Paul David Miller, U.S. Navy (Ret.). The date is Sunday, January 22, 2017. The interviewer is Professor Stan Carpenter. This is session number two, question set number three.

SC: This is USNI oral history interview with Admiral Paul David Miller. This is session number two, question set number four. The date is Sunday, January 22, 2017. The interviewer is Professor Stan Carpenter from the U.S. Naval War College. These questions cover the tour as executive officer of USS *Seneca* (ATF-91).

Admiral, let's now turn to your years as an XO of USS *Seneca*, a fleet tug. You had an unusual start to your Navy career in that you were the executive officer, or XO, while still in your initial sea duty years. Tell us about the training and preparation pipeline, if any, for new XOs of smaller warships such as the *Seneca*. What about that experience?

PDM: There was no training. All I had to do was walk across the pier, take the XO's cabin, and begin doing what I was essentially doing on *Papago*, except doing it as the number two officer on board.

The thing that changed, I learned, is that captains can be so different. I had a relationship with the captain on *Papago*. I met the CO of *Seneca*, I knew immediately I could never have a close relationship with this man. You just knew it. And so I said, "Oh, mercy. Here I am, I've been transferred to this new ship, but now I have to understand, I have to be able to serve this captain, but he is by far a different individual than the captain that I had in the *Papago*." This was a straight naval officer. He had been through the destroyer pipelines and he wanted to go to command. He was a very ambitious guy, only to be surpassed in ambition by the guy who relieved him. I had to serve both of them. It was a big change and I had to adapt, and that's what people have to do. When they get a new boss, they have to adapt. The boss isn't going to adapt, nor should the boss adapt, but you have to adapt. And that was strikingly clear after my first meeting with Charles Alves. I'll not forget it.

SC: In retrospect, in looking back, do you think that there was any training or preparation that the Navy could have or should have done for someone in your position going aboard as an XO in such a junior time in your career?

PDM: Not in the junk force. That kind of ship belongs where it is today. It belongs in the Military Sealift Command manned by civilians. It's a different world and it should be handled as such. So, no, additional training wouldn't have helped.

The only thing that might have been helpful was ship's administration. Everyone on board, which was between fifty-five and sixty-five people, had a Navy personnel record. There were responsibilities to maintain properly each record and probably if I had even two days of understanding what goes into keeping personnel records it might have been helpful, but other than that, no.

SC: One of the dynamics that we'll address as we advance in these interviews through your career is the issue of strategic communications. We've already talked a little bit about that. I think as you get much more senior, this is going to become far more important because you become more and more the generator, if you will, of strategic communications. As XO, how did you try to project yourself to the sailors, to your shipmates, to the seniors, which would have been, of course, the CO and maybe even the commodore, and the world at large in your tour as an XO?

PDM: The dynamics need to be appreciated. I came from a ship that was manned by professionals in the world that they operated in. By that I mean they weren't destroyer sailors; they were fleet tug, they were minesweeper, they were small-ship sailors. They knew their job; they knew what needed to be done. When I go to *Seneca*, I come in front of a skipper that thought that this was a mini-destroyer because he tried to make people dress like it was, tried to have the daily routine like we were a combatant. I saw straight away that my job was going to be to protect the crew from this guy. That was a hell of a thing for somebody twenty-four years old to decide. This guy was probably thirty-six; I don't know. But I knew that was going to be my job. I knew because if he led that ship the way he had in his departments on board a destroyer, it was going to be a tough tour. So I took that on as my job.

The lesson there is you have to, when you go to any new assignment, you have to judge and make pretty quick judgments about how you're to operate, what your range of motion is going to be, what your freedoms are going to be in being able to carry out assigned tasks. I can say it now because, sadly, he's deceased. This captain was afraid of his shadow. I don't know how he got to be a captain of a U.S. Navy ship. It was tough.

SC: XOs have a huge administrative responsibility, and we've already addressed personnel issues being one of them. So in addition to all the other duties that you had on the small ship, what did you regard as your primary administrative duty as the XO?

PDM: Like any XO does, the job is to make that ship work as efficiently, as effectively as it can, both in port and at sea, and to relieve the captain of any anxiety about the preparedness, the readiness, and the ability to carry out whatever mission that had been assigned, and that's what I spent my next eighteen months, two years, eighteen months at least doing. And it was challenging.

SC: What was your typical day like as the XO in port?

PDM: Problem solver. If I had engineering problems, I helped the engineer. If we had communications issues, I would help to fix it. I was just a number one problem solver and making sure that things got done with regard to the deck force. It was a fleet tug, but we tried to make it the best-looking fleet tug on the piers, and it all worked, but it was tough because the captain, instead of letting us do the work, he felt that he had to be the one to micromanage the work, and that really got people confused.

SC: We're going to discuss later on in these sessions leadership styles and, in particular, the problems inherent with the senior being a micromanager, which is what it sounds like you were faced with. So what about a typical day under way for you as the XO?

PDM: Under way, I was the formal navigator, so that was my main task. For some reason, they sent ATFs on six-month deployments to the Mediterranean. So it wasn't too long after I was on the ship that we were assigned as ready salvage ship Mediterranean. Preparing a small ship for a cruise of that length, with no infrastructure to support it, you have to think through a lot of things, because the replenishment apparatus in the Mediterranean didn't even have an adjunct capability to support a thing called ATF. Federal stock numbers and all that stuff. If you're a destroyer, they keep a certain percentage of spares positioned forward. Not so when you're at the bottom of the food chain. So it was a great deal of preparation, preparing for ship's deployment to the Med.

SC: On that note, *Seneca* made the Mediterranean deployment attached to Sixth Fleet in 1966. What duties did *Seneca* perform while you were deployed to the Med?

PDM: We positioned ourselves first in the Western Med and then the Eastern Med [Mediterranean Sea] and we were simply assigned to "wait and see until something happens, then we can give you a task." So, fortunately, in the first few months nothing of note happened that they needed our services, so we worked with the Spanish navy, we worked with the Italian navy, particularly in the salvage area and providing sort of school call for other navies that didn't have the expertise we had, particularly in diving and salvage.

SC: Did you do any target towing?

PDM: We didn't tow targets. Combatants deployed to the Med are fully ready, including gunnery. Getting to the Med deserves comment. Gibraltar, if you draw a rhumb line, is on about the same latitude as Norfolk. To go the shortest distance, of course, is a great circle route. But I was the XO and I had to get to Gibraltar with, again, no support electronically. Even the radar on those ships was substandard, and they had the LORAN-C again, but it worked just like the one we had on *Papago*. The only thing that I had was celestial navigation. And when you have a CO like Charlie Alves, who wanted to know where he was every second of the day, you can imagine what a fifteen-day transit was like. I was up most of the time. I took star fixes, I took all manner of navigational fixes. I was fortunate to have on board that ship a second-class quartermaster that knew a little bit about celestial navigation. So we both were in this little bitty chart room, pretending like we knew everything so that the captain didn't drive us absolutely bonkers. Sometimes we'd get celestial fix triangles that worked. If I had a triangle that had a half inch on each side, I was happy. I knew about where we were. [*laughs*] The ship's actual track was between a "great circle" and a rhumb line. I was quite happy to see Gibraltar on time and on a course that had us in the middle of the Strait of Gibraltar.

SC: Since a lot of people that will be listening to this, particularly in future years where celestial navigation as a skill has pretty well deteriorated—

PDM: They won't even know what the hell I'm talking about.

SC: Exactly. So I'm going to throw a phrase out to you. Could you define it and give us an idea of some of the techniques and dynamics of celestial navigation? So let me throw this term out: "the declination of Aries."

PDM: [*laughs*] I don't know if I ever used Aries as a star fix, but you hit on the right point. The hardest thing to do is to identify the celestial bodies. Now they have an app on your iPhone and can easily identify what celestial bodies there are. But in 1966, you had no app. So I relied on star fixes on the few nights we had them. I relied on sun lines so at least you knew what latitude you were on.

If I was on the latitude that was close to the rhumb line between Norfolk and Gibraltar—and we didn't go full great circle, because that ship was diesel and we had sufficient fuel—I felt comfortable in knowing where we were. There were no two sailors happier than when we picked up land on this little surface radar. We knew we were going to be OK and hit Gibraltar on the mark. It was on the mark. The CO, I think, he was surprised. He pretended like he knew we were there all along, but he was surprised. And then we just did our duties in the Med. I don't need to make a long case of what we did on *Seneca*. It was more of learning the people and developing leadership skills for a different set of shipmates than I had on the *Papago*, and that is huge, because when one moves from one environment to another, particularly in the military, you will face a different set of circumstances, and your ability to adjust to those circumstances quickly and to become a "producer" as opposed to being someone that is calling upon others to help was important. If you're able to shorten that period of time and then start adding value, you have a much better chance to succeed. That cross-deck taught me a lot. I had sixty different individuals on board one ship, then another ship, and as XO, I took more time to understand the entire crew. We had problems. We had some brig [Navy jail] people. We had racial problems. It was a tough time in the Navy in that regard, and we had the bottom of the bottom as part of our crew. It was tough.

SC: Did you still have the system where African Americans were basically relegated to things like mess steward, or was it more fully integrated by this time?

PDM: No. We had a Filipino steward. But most of the cooks were minorities. We had the "racial thing" in the ship. We had cells, and even on a small ship, that troubled me greatly. You knew you had tensions. So I spent a lot of time on tension easing, and even I had to face down a sailor in front of other sailors. It was a touchy time.

SC: Let's get back to your navigation. Was *Seneca* equipped with a DRT or dead-reckoning tracer?[12]

PDM: No.

---

[12] The Dead Reckoning Tracer, or DRT, uses course and speed inputs to make a horizontal plot of the ship's movement. A lighted compass rose moves across an enclosed cabinet based on the inputs and projects onto white paper laid out above. Watch standers can then make pencil marks of the position of the ship as the compass rose projection moves across the paper. In this fashion, the ship can estimate the course, speed over ground, and distance traveled over a discreet time period. The position of contacts and their bearing can also be recorded relative to one's own ship.

SC: No DRT?

PDM: I had a dead reckoning tracer with my pencil and slide rule. [*Laughter*]

SC: *Seneca* carried some defensive armament. [*Miller laughs.*] Her initial World War II configuration was a 3" gun, two twin 40mm gun mounts, and two single 20mm gun mounts. By the late 1960s, was any of that still aboard?

PDM: The 3" gun mount was, and we had an armory of small arms. We didn't have any 40mm guns onboard. We would fire the 3" every once in a while just to make sure it worked.

SC: Did you have any gunner's mates assigned?

PDM: Yes, we had a gunner's mate. We had a second-class gunner's mate, and that was his total world, but it did not have a fire control system. We couldn't slew that gun around electrically. We had to move it around with hand wheels. It was an old vessel.

SC: *Seneca*'s propulsion plant was diesel driven.

PDM: Same thing. Old.

SC: Same thing as *Papago*. Were there any particular advantages or disadvantages to diesel engines compared to the dominant steam turbine plants of the day?

PDM: The advantage was that you didn't have to fuel every three days, but the disadvantages, to me, was the smell, the annoyance of diesel burning. It was adequate for that brand of ship. To have any other kind of propulsion would have been too difficult, and the motor generator set, of course, was diesel, so the people that played the greatest role on a ship like that were your machinist's mates that kept that damn diesel going. An engine could break down, if it cracked a liner, it could be put back together while under way, because without your mobility, your ability to contribute was zero, so that was your main battery. Carrying the salvage equipment and being able to have the power for it was what you tried to make sure that you kept going on a 24-hour/360 basis.

SC: You said that you were the general quarters officer of the deck, or OOD, on *Papago*. Same position on *Seneca*?

PDM: I was the same position on *Seneca* because we did not have the extra ensign to give it to. We only had five officers on *Seneca*.

SC: Which was the normal manning level.

PDM: It was the normal complement.

SC: Were there any what I'll call real-world operational events that the *Seneca* participated in?

PDM: There was nothing remarkable, but I remember this probably happened on *Papago*, the one real-world contribution that we made was being assigned to help the USS *Thor* (ARC-4), which was a cable layer, put down our first SOSUS system from the far reaches of the North Atlantic and tie it into Iceland.[13] It was an absolutely amazing deployment because we were shadowed by the Russians. I have a picture in Williamsburg of me on the bridge wing of the ATF with a Russian destroyer close aboard. And I went and rode that cable layer for a couple of days to learn how things work, and I always took time, like I did with the icebreaker, this time with a cable layer. They put up their own Decca

---

[13] SOSUS or Sound Surveillance System was a series of underwater hydrophone arrays laid on the ocean bottom to detect the sounds of Soviet submarines during the Cold War. The hydrophones were connected by underwater cables to receiving stations ashore called Naval Facilities or NAVFACS where the contacts were analyzed and plotted. The intelligence gathered was then passed to the antisubmarine forces. With the end of the Cold War and the increasing quietness of submarines, the system has been drawn down considerably.

Navigator System. You may have heard of Decca, which was a precise navigation equipment system needed to be able to lay the overall cable network very accurately on the bottom of the ocean.[14] That one made everybody feel good because we were making a contribution, but most of the other time that you were on an ATF, you waited for something to happen.

SC: When you were operating out of the Western Atlantic, I assume out of Little Creek as well?

PDM: Yes.

SC: What typical missions or tasks did you perform when something would happen?

PDM: Besides the Mediterranean deployment, I had more time in Gitmo. I knew Gitmo too well. And then we had one oceangoing tow. That was impressive. We towed a big ship. I can't remember the name of it, but we towed it from Norfolk to Port Arthur, Texas. That is a long way when you're going three and four knots. Making that towing machinery, keep the tension proper, there's a lot of dangerous work that goes on on those small ships that they get no credit for. It's seamanship. You have to be mindful of safety, every moment of the day on those small ships. And later on, that stood me in good stead for future jobs in both the military and in civilian life, the importance of safety.

SC: We'll dive into that as we get into higher levels of your career. Did *Seneca* ever take part in any major fleet exercises?

PDM: On a standby basis only. We did every exercise that they had in the Mediterranean. We were sort of there because you never knew what was going to happen. They always

---

[14] The Decca Navigator System grew out of the British Gee navigation system developed in World War II. It uses a phase comparison of two low frequency signals to determine precise locations, especially in inland and littoral water.

had us with the fleet, not on the other side of the Mediterranean, because they wanted a response capability, but that was all.

SC: When you were in the Med, did you operate out of Naples? Was that your primary home port?

PDM: We operated out of Naples, Italy, and we went as far east as Israel, but a milestone was we spent Christmas, if you can believe this—I didn't believe it—in the harbor of Monaco. Becky flew over, and we had a little place on the harbor in Monaco. Here you had a fleet tug and a diesel submarine. I know the little town must have said, "Oh, no. A submarine and a diesel boat." And to our amazement, the captain received invitations to have dinner with Princess Grace. For some reason, the captain did not go, so he let Becky have the invitation. It was an amazing experience to be able to meet Princess Grace and Prince Rainier. They were very generous, very wonderful to all of us. They had invited a couple of enlisted folks also. They treated the Navy fleet very, very well during her lifetime.

But we soon steamed back from the Mediterranean. I was an old salty navigator by then. I didn't have any problems finding Norfolk.

SC: Later in your career, you served as the operations officer on USS *Parsons* (DDG-33).[15] The normal progression is from division officer to department head to XO. But in your case, the department head and XO tours were inverted. That's not a problem in that since we're already on the subject, I'd like to talk a bit about the XO billet in general terms throughout the Navy. Then as we advance down in your career path, we'll circle

---

[15] USS *Parsons* (DDG-33) was a *Forrest Sherman*-class destroyer originally commissioned in 1959. In the 1960s, she was reconfigured as a guided missile destroyer and renumbered as DDG-33. The ship was named for Rear Admiral William S. "Deak" Parsons. She was decommissioned in 1982 and sunk as a target ship in 1989. Parsons (1901–53), a 1922 U.S. Naval Academy graduate, was an ordnance and gunnery expert in the U.S. Navy prior to World War II and was instrumental in developing the radio proximity fuse early in the war. He was assigned in 1943 to the Manhattan Project for the development of an atomic weapon as the head of the Ordnance Division. Parsons was instrumental in researching and developing the firing mechanism for the first atomic bomb. On the attack against Hiroshima, Japan, on August 6, 1945, then-Captain Parsons armed the weapon in flight aboard the B-29 Superfortress *Enola Gay* that dropped the weapon. *Enola Gay* is now on display at the Smithsonian Institution National Air and Space Museum Udvar-Hazy Center.

back and talk about the dynamics of the department head tour on a major combatant. If you were to define the ideal working relationship between an XO and the department heads, what would that look like?

PDM: The ideal relationship isn't with the department heads. The ideal relationship is with the commanding officer. If the CO and XO are able to operate on the same frequency and understand and appreciate what's important for that ship at any moment in time, and the commanding officer attends to things that the commanding officer should attend to and the executive officer should, in coordination and conjunction with the department heads, attend to things they should attend to, you achieve harmony. You get off kilter a bit if you don't have harmony. So as an XO, whether it was on a large ship or a small ship, what I just suggested is terribly important. When you have a relationship that I had with my CO in *Seneca*, it made the XO's job infinitely more difficult because the commanding officer was an interference as opposed to someone who was able to help and pull in the same direction that all the operators in the ship need to go. And it's tough. Some people have the facility to pull this off; others don't.

Later on, after all the sea tours that I had, when I would go on a ship as a battle group or as a fleet commander, I knew instantly who was in charge of that ship after meeting both the CO and XO. I knew instantly who had the personality that that ship took on.

SC: What about the relationship between the XO and the senior enlisted leadership, specifically the chief petty officers, first class petty officers, division leading petty [LPO] officers, etc.? As XO, how does that differ from that of your department head or division officers?

PDM: The relationship is delicate. The tightness of a relationship should be, in my view, between the E-7, -8, or -9, with his division officer first and then department head.[16] The XO has to take a passive, not active, role, but in taking that passive role, he has to have the adroitness, the ability to understand, the ability to appreciate what the "temperature"

---

[16] E-7 is chief petty officer; E-8 is senior chief petty officer; E-9 is master chief petty officer.

is between those positions that I've mentioned. And an XO can do that really informally by getting out of the XO cabin, having lunch in the chief's quarters. "Chief, didn't you invite me for lunch today?" They always say yes. And you really want to test that. That's what you've got to do. You can't interfere, but you have to know where you need to adjust the meter, and with some people, you have to adjust the meter a little more than others.

SC: That really leads on to our next question. When a brand new department head or division officer reports aboard, what is the XO's role as a mentor as, as you've just alluded to, adjusting the meter?

PDM: I never experienced being the XO of a destroyer or a large ship. However, the top job of any CO or XO, in addition to formal duties, is to mentor, to be an example, to set standards, to coach, to be a sounding board, to discipline, to correct, to praise, to connect all in the spirit of mentoring, not commanding.

SC: Right. Or division officer.

PDM: Or division officer. Every ship has the welcome board and you have to go through the check-off sheet to see all the proper people and become a crewmember. What's instrumental there is the first session that the reporting person has with the XO and CO. The dynamics are so very important. There's that old adage: "You never have a second chance to make a first impression." In the military, that is so very important, because if you don't cement that budding relationship the first time you meet somebody aboard a ship, particularly a combatant ship, then you always are working at it a little bit harder than you need to.

I felt confident, both as a department head and then as a CO, that if I was able to have an individual leave and mentally say to himself, "I can trust the captain as my boss," I had done my job. If you won that person's trust the first time you met him and you looked him in the eye, and you conversed with him and you told him what you expected of him and that you were there to make sure that he achieved success, then he walked out of that cabin and mentally he said, "This is a good place," you've won the game.

SC: So it really is a two-way street.

PDM: It's a two-way street.

SC: As an XO, if you were to construct a list of the top things you would advise a newly reported-aboard junior officer to do or not to do, what might that list look like?

PDM: This is a list for the junior officer?

SC: For someone junior to the XO, so that would be a department head or, more specifically, I think a division officer.

PDM: Number one—it's a caution. I've seen this happen too many times. Apply the adage that I live by of "never overestimate your importance." When you come aboard as a division officer or department head reporting to the XO, there are people that overestimate their importance. You don't have to underestimate it, but you have to chat and express that you are there to support, to learn, to be a leader in your respective sphere of influence, and to be a team leader and to work for the department head or for the XO—that you want to listen, appreciate, and understand what's expected. You do little talking and a lot of listening. I've seen too many cases where someone thinks they're the savior to the ship in their first conversation. I'd look at them and think, "Where'd they get this yahoo?" And it wouldn't work. Initially, I wouldn't pay any attention to them. The element of being able to strike up a trusting relationship—it means so much—begins at the first meeting. Some people never get it. Others, they have it instinctively.

SC: We're going to talk a lot, as you progress and become more senior in your career, about various leadership styles that you've seen that are effective or not effective, and I think you've established the stage here in terms of some leadership traits. Let's turn a little bit to wardroom life back in those years. Did you begin to see the wardroom culture changing at all during your first years at sea?

PDM: We had no wardroom culture on the ATF. Period. There were five or six guys trying to do their job, but it wasn't a closely-knit organization because there were such different people coming from different walks of life.

SC: Well, let's expand that a little bit. Let's say that you are the XO on a much larger ship with, say, twenty, twenty-five, even thirty officers, a typical destroyer or cruiser type. Typically, the XO would serve as the president or the head of the mess. What would you advise an XO undertaking that duty to do or not to do? How would you approach that if you were the XO on a larger ship?

PDM: I personally would approach it as if I'm the captain of the ship. I would look at it from that vantage point, and I would want to be able to have everybody in that wardroom thinking higher than their particular position on board that ship, that if they were a division officer, they would think like a department head. Should something happen, should something go wrong, there would be absolutely no loss of contribution if he had to instantly move up. The same way for a department head to an XO, and that's why if I were an XO, everything that I did I would be doing it from the vantage point as if I was CO. That way if you instill that mindset throughout the wardroom, you have a leadership dynamic that's much wider than you see in most ordinary ships.

SC: And I think this is particularly critical in a military environment, where that senior may be out of action, killed, wounded—

PDM: Yes, the military can be a very tough environment.

SC: One of the most difficult issues most XOs face is how to rate their juniors on periodic fitness reports. This dynamic is particularly difficult when there are several top performers who must be ranked. What advice would you give to newly reported-aboard XOs on how to address the fitness report?

PDM: Call the shots the way you see 'em. Enlisted people, in my time, they'd get efficiency evaluations. The biggest shortfall that I saw and immediately remedied is that too many division officers, too many department heads, left that task to the last minute and they did not do a good job in taking the time that they needed to evaluate properly the people that worked for them. They wanted someone to take time and to write their evaluation with the proper thoughtfulness. So I used to emphasize from chiefs on up through the XO, that that aspect of their responsibility to write thoughtful and honest evaluations ranks very high on their "to do" list, really high. That's the number one thing that he's working and busting his ass for, is to come out with an evaluation that he/she can be proud of and can support advancement. Terribly important.

SC: And it has a lot to do with promotion and job assignment and—

PDM: Self-esteem.

SC: Self-esteem, all those elements that you really have to deal with, and you're dealing with somebody's career. It's incumbent on the senior rater to take as much time and interest in it as the person being evaluated.

PDM: Exactly.

SC: The reality is that not every commissioned officer has the capability or the traits or the behaviors for effective leadership, so as an XO, if you're faced with such an officer, how would you counsel and advise that person on how to improve their performance?

PDM: That's totally dependent on the personality of the individual. Some you needed to use a direct, unbridled, harsh dynamic that said straight away, "I've got your attention now, and this is it." Others, subtle, a small word was crushing and then you had to be careful that you did not set him too far back. Being able to appreciate, to understand, and to feel the human spirit that you're dealing with is a huge characteristic of a good leader, huge.

SC: Many sailors have personal or familial problems that impact their professionalism. Alcohol abuse is a big one, so are marriages that are going badly. You've already referenced at the time that the racial component was a problem. What techniques or actions might an XO take to mitigate the impact of these dynamics?

PDM: You must challenge a division officer or department head to not only know a subordinate's professional capabilities but also to know what's going on in that individual's life, not that he wants to interfere in any way, but he has to be able to have that individual know that he is there to help any situation. So he has to build the confidence of everybody in his division. Some people were able to do that magnificently; others, it's very, very difficult. But good leaders are able to do that instinctively; they worry about the people that work with and for them. I'll give you illustrations of that later on.

SC: We'll refer that to part of a leader's moral authority. That's one of the key traits there. Many XOs are faced with a severe personality or professional conflict between officers and often between the officer and the senior enlisted leaders. It's a dynamic that can crush the effectiveness and efficiency of a division or its morale. So did you ever encounter such a situation as XO of the *Seneca*? And how did you address it? And if not, what advice might you give to an XO facing such a situation?

PDM: I faced it every single hour of the day with my *Seneca* CO. [*laughs*]

SC: And how did you handle it?

PDM: Gingerly. Maybe sometimes with a little bit of firmness. I actually took the conn from the captain when I was an XO on *Seneca* because I wouldn't let him crunch the ship. The people around us on the bridge must have thought, "What the hell is he doing?" And I said from the beginning that this gent was afraid of his own shadow. This was after the Med deployment. I thought he had learned stuff by then. But it was Gitmo, and I had so much experience with the prior landings in Gitmo. I could see we were literally going to wipe out a pier. And I just said, "Captain, I think I'd better do this," and he didn't know what to do. I said, "I've got the conn." I pulled the chestnuts out of the fire. That guy never mentioned it again, never brought it up, and I certainly didn't mention anything.

But the lesson there was regardless, if you're in a situation that you absolutely know is going south and if you're in a position to arrest the situation and get it back where it should be, you'd better do it. You'd better muster the courage to do it. Otherwise, you're complicit. There were experiences later on that it was reversed as CO; I had to pull chestnuts out of the fire for other reasons. So the question is, about relationships, people are made differently, and you have to have the ability to know who you're dealing with. Without that ability, you sort of fumble along. You get things done, but you don't get them done harmoniously and with everybody pulling in the same direction.

SC: And let's bore in on that particular subject, because that's critical, talking about safety of human life and the safety of your ship. In general, what would you advise an XO in terms of where and when to take the individual action and where to be more cautious and attain the CO's approval first? And not necessarily in an in extremis situation [critical danger].

PDM: If you're not in an in extremis situation, it's a judgment call. You have to judge on how much time do I have. Usually things are so dynamic [that] time is closing fast. Unless you're dealing with a real odd personality, if you're able to act and save an extremis situation, you'll get recognized. You won't receive any reprimand unless you're with some guy that doesn't appreciate common sense, and you've met one or two of those along the way, I bet. [*laughs*]

SC: I have indeed. More than a couple. We're going to get back to the general questions on being an executive officer a little bit later, so for now what I want to do is turn to some lighter subjects as we wrap up your years as an XO on the *Seneca*. What were your favorite liberty ports, if any?

PDM: It was a blessing that Becky and I had the experience in Monaco. It'll be something we'll always remember. Naples. That's where we spent most of our in-port Mediterranean time. We were small enough to get into a small port called Valletta, Malta. From the historical perspective, that was a very interesting place to visit. We stopped in Bermuda. That was a hell of a sea detail as it's not an easy place to get in and out of. All my time in the junk fleet, as I call it, passed quickly even out in the middle of the ocean, independent steaming on four Atlantic crossings. We were busy. I was sometimes busier on the ATF than I was on the destroyer as a department head because I had no help. There's a difference when you have help and when you don't have help, and it taught me to be self-sufficient in problem solving.

SC: Tell us about your most humorous or memorable event during your time on *Seneca*.

PDM: I don't have any humorous events on *Seneca* because Captain Charlie Alves was relieved in my last few months by a Naval Academy graduate named Alan Bissell. I can remember well those two COs. Lieutenant Bissell was worse. He was absolutely worse in being a more intense micromanager than Charles Alves. He had come from a destroyer. He was a hard-charging guy that wanted command. We weren't a destroyer. We were an ATF. We were a fleet tug. So there weren't that many happy days.

SC: That leads to my next question. What was your best day as an XO?

PDM: I'll tell you what, the best day was departing the ship. There's absolutely no doubt. I departed the ship in Port Arthur, Texas, after we finished that tow that I talked about earlier. That closed that chapter. All the while in my last six months there was the dynamic of what I was going to do at the three-year point—the date was coming closer and closer.

SC: I'm going to ask that question once we get wrapped up, so we'll come back to that. Was there any particular worst day that you remember on board *Seneca*?

PDM: Happily, no, because I never had any navigation problems. On this ship we didn't have any fires. We did everything that we were supposed to do, so I really didn't have a worst day. It worked.

SC: Sounds pretty much like *every* day was a worst day. [*Laughter*] So let's play a counterfactual here. If you were to go back to your XO days knowing what you now know, is there anything that you might do differently? I know we've talked about this previously in terms of that's all irrelevant, it's in the past, really what's important is the outcome, but I like to play the counterfactual, thinking back.

PDM: It actually was better to be fresh, young, not having a set pattern of doing things, being able to call audibles because that was the way to get things done. So would I have done anything differently? Probably yes. I wouldn't tell the CO that he was going to crunch the ship. I was very fortunate that it happened in the sequence that it did to get an XO tour quickly, even if it was only a small ship. I would tell people that I started my Navy service on an ATF, they would look at me and wonder what is that. They didn't understand. But the work and experience turned out to be very helpful.

SC: Would it be fair to say that your career really benefited from having been steeled in the fires of adversity?

PDM: That's an almost poetic way of saying it. [*laughs*] But the answer is yes, it helped markedly.

SC: Let's do something a little bit lighter here. How about family life? Assigned to a ship in the late 1960s in the Norfolk area, what was your family life like at that time?

PDM: Becky and I had not had our first child. We had little money. As a LTJG, I think I was making $292. The pay scales then were very different. We would try to make an annual trip back to her home, the town of Bushnell, Illinois. We had some very good friends in the same milieu of the ATF world. The diving officer that I had in *Seneca*, he left the Navy. They still visit every year, so we've been friends for fifty years. The social life was limited. We'd go to a movie, go to the Little Creek Officers' Club sing-along on Friday night if we were in port. But nothing remarkable.

    An aside, we went to the NOB [Navy Operating Base] Officers' Club, I think one time, and I was a bit apprehensive as a LTJG to walk down the street where all those big houses were.

SC: Admiralty Row.

PDM: Yes. It was very curious that a scant twenty-three years later we would come back and occupy Virginia House.

SC: You were onboard *Seneca* during the midst of the Vietnam War. Did you see any changes in attitudes towards the military in those years by either Navy personnel or the civilian community?

PDM: Not change in attitudes, but change in awareness. You asked that about when I was on *Papago*, and even a scant eighteen months later, activity associated with Vietnam and Navy involvement had ratcheted up and you heard about it more on the news in Norfolk. Ships from Norfolk became involved. So the answer is yes, but attitudinally, I did not see any big change.

SC: At the end of your first XO tour, what was your perspective on the Navy and your professional future? I did promise this question coming back to you.

PDM: Blurry. I knew that I was reaching a decision point. Becky wasn't totally enamored, because she hadn't experienced the Navy. You don't experience the Navy driving two ATFs for three years. It's not the Navy. So I was going to get out, and since I had my MBA already, I was going to come back down to Florida to go to law school. By that time I was twenty-five, twenty-six. But I was haunted—and I think that is the proper word. I had mentioned in the first chapter of my personal background, I did not want to leave my three years of naval service by being assigned to two fleet tugs. I would have felt bad, even though I did fine, I did what I was assigned to do, I did my job, but I would have still felt bad. In fact, if I had children and they asked what the record was, it would be hard to explain to them what I did in the Navy. [*laughs*] Hard to explain.

So Becky and I spent time thinking about it, and I came to the conclusion that I'd give it one more tour if the Navy would send me to Destroyer School. Wow. This was tough, but I will say for that Naval Academy guy, Alan Bissell, he had been to Destroyer School and Department Head. When I told him and when I wrote an application, he was kind enough to endorse it, to say that I deserved a chance in Destroyer School, even without destroyer experience. I thought that was very nice of him to do that. He didn't have to. My request was addressed to the commander SERVRON EIGHT (Service Squadron EIGHT) for endorsement. I guess they needed people at Destroyer School [*laughs*] because they were scraping the bottom of the experience barrel—I did get accepted.

I told Becky, and we decided that it was going to be a two-and-a-half-year investment because half a year would be in Newport, Rhode Island, going through Destroyer School, and then two years of active duty in a destroyer this time, because that was the obligation. One of the stipulations was augmenting to the regular Navy (dropping my USNR designation). I did not do that and stayed a Reserve officer because I wanted to be able to have that fire break without it being contested. The only thing I needed to do was at least ride a DD [destroyer] for a few weeks—a set of orders of TAD [Temporary Additional Duty] to a destroyer in Newport. I spent a short period of time on (two or three weeks) the *Radford* (DD-446) and the experience only served to acquaint me with the activity on a destroyer.

We moved from Norfolk to Newport, Rhode Island, into the quarters that were set aside for Destroyer School students. Becky and I had decided to go down this path and we did it.

SC: And we're going to talk in our next session about that Destroyer School, Department Head School experience. So, wrapping up your years as the XO of *Seneca*, are there any last thoughts on those years or areas that you'd like to delve deeper into or that we missed before we move on?

PDM: No. I'm just glad I walked away from them with my head high and that I was able to get the paper (fitness reports) that I did get from four different skippers in those ships. I still have them. The reports were different, even unique, but all said that this young guy had potential.

SC: Admiral, we're going to continue on here with talking about executive officer in general. We can relate it back to your time as XO of the *Seneca*, if you like. This is more geared towards executive officer positions in general.

The next few questions address the issue of effective leadership, which is an extremely important topic to you. We'll deal with leadership effectiveness questions from the commanding, senior, and flag officer perspective in greater depth in future interviews. From the first moment a new XO reports aboard, the senior officer and enlisted leadership and the various divisions and departments look to the XO for guidance and direction. How important is it to give the crew a vision statement of how the new XO expects the ship to run?

PDM: A vision statement has importance only in that his subordinates would have a full appreciation that this officer knows the landscape. One has to have the confidence of those he leads that there is a full understanding of the landscape in which operations are going to take place. If you're able to transmit to the crew or to your subordinates on a shore facility that you appreciate, you understand, you have more than just a surface knowledge of what the unit is to contribute to the overall force, you're ahead of the game.

As to a separate vision statement, I don't think that's essential in the military, even though it's become fashionable to do so. I never wrote a vision statement in either the Navy or in business, but there was never any doubt that those that worked with me appreciated the goal setting and the other attributes that went along with making sure an organization looked forward and was successful.

SC: Everyone at some point in their career, whether a civilian or military, is faced working with a difficult senior or boss or supervisor or manager, etc., and in particular for the Navy it could be a ship, squadron, a station CO. We're going to address this critical issue at all levels of your career, and as you've indicated earlier, you actually already encountered this particular dynamic, but in general, what advice would you give to any XO on how to approach working under a difficult superior?

PDM: Carefully. If you discern that the relationship that you're going to have with a senior is going to have speed bumps, it's incumbent on you to assess and find out how you can best even out those "speed bumps." But if you're unable to grasp quickly what that action would be, it's absolutely mandatory that you make sure those speed bumps don't become barriers. At least if you do that, roll out the speed bumps and make them less of an event every time you have to cross one of them.

It's difficult. Personalities are unique. Strong-willed people don't convince easily. But it's something that has to be worked out. You might not be able to do it along a timeline that you think is best, but if you're able to do it over time, that's what's important—it's not a need; it's an absolute must. And you cannot let the reporting cycle of the military get in your way, whether you're three months away from your receiving a fitness report or a full twelve months away from your reporting date, you must work on closing any distance between you and the CO.

SC: There's clearly a legal authority in leadership, but there's also a moral authority that derives from one's actions and behaviors. We're going to delve into this critical leadership issue at all levels, from division officer to department head to XO to CO to flag officer as we advance through these oral history interviews. What moral authority attributes, actions, and behaviors do you see as essential in a shipboard XO?

PDM: I'd use two words, whether it be at the XO level or at the four-star level. Those two words are "do right." If you exercised those two words in every single situation you faced, you could never go wrong, and the best way of doing right is just set the example. If you're able to set the example on board ship or going ashore, whatever the situation, you knew the right thing, you knew the wrong thing. No one needed to tell someone that had been in the military for five years or ten years what was right and what was wrong, if you set the requisite example, you would have 95 percent follow you, and then you'd only have to pay close attention to the 5 percent of people that didn't.

SC: Here's a related question on moral authority. By the time one's a shipboard XO, they're typically a very senior lieutenant commander or commander, depending on the ship type. Again, you had an unusual career in that regard. But as the second-most senior officer, an XO is expected to have a demeanor and decorum that fits with the level of responsibility and authority. How might you advise an incoming XO on this critical aspect of effective leadership and specifically what to do and not to do in terms of their moral authority?

PDM: Straight away, I say one would have to guard against being aloof. An office such as XO brings with it a certain status but one should earn that position every day. Show those that work for you that you recognize the position is more than a title. You set the example. Again, the vast majority of people will take your example and try to copy it and at least be able to mimic what you want to happen.

That's what leadership is all about. It's being able to have the large number of people understand, appreciate, and go in the direction you want to go in and then give them the space to lead. Let them do it by themselves, and you concentrate on that smaller slice that don't understand, don't appreciate, and need a little more directional assistance in making sure they get the job done. If you narrow that number of those that need additional direction with every step you take, all of a sudden you have a 99 percent following you without any assistance. That's when you are on the right track.

SC: We've already talked about an example or two from your first sea tours of some leadership problems, but can you tell us about any other particularly poor leadership examples that you experienced or witnessed from either juniors or seniors while as an XO?

PDM: On the ATF, leadership was thin. There was, however, a willingness to learn and if I saw something that wasn't right, I tried to turn the improper action into a training or mentoring event.

Thankfully, the more complex a ship, [the] more resources are available. The hardest things to manage are those things that are at the end of the talent and resource food chain. An ATF was at the end of the manning and resource line. The larger, more important ships got their allocations of resources first. That happened in business too, so you had to pay attention to the "least of the brethren" as opposed to the ones fully manned, fully resourced, and [that] had the best leadership. The people that are on the other side, even from 50 percent down, don't have those attributes, so they need the attention and the help to make the entire squadron, group, or fleet work. That's what it's all about. If you leave one unit behind, then you didn't do your job.

SC: There's a certain term in the Navy and I would like you comment on what it is and what's the danger or hazard in doing this; it's called "gun decking."[17] Tell us about that.

PDM: "Gun decking" is not acceptable. There are no good outcomes from someone not doing the maintenance or training properly.

---

[17] "Gun decking" is the Navy slang for reporting or recording that a task is completed when it has not been and is usually found in falsifying official records.

SC: Another aspect of gun decking is falsifying records, claiming something was done or something was not done that had to be. What is the danger or hazard with that particular aspect of gun decking?

PDM: It's obvious, especially in the PMS records.[18] That's where a lot of it takes place. For example, you had the number two lube oil strainer or something on the gun mount to perform maintenance on. You had to open and inspect. It required you to go get a box of tools you didn't have time or desire to do the check. You rationalized: "This has been operating really well." So you sign it off that you did PMS check 206 or whatever. And then, "kaboom," the thing goes out in the middle of an operation. You check why did it go out. Then the outcome is obvious. Someone signed off on completing the check. They "gun decked," which translates to they lied and you have to hold them accountable.

SC: The Planned Maintenance System, or PMS, checks are especially critical on damage control-type equipment.

PDM: Sure.

SC: Can you think of any particularly effective leadership examples?

PDM: Leadership happens in important settings and more often in routine environments. You don't need to set the stage for leadership. I've seen leadership by whispers, nothing that other people saw. It was great leadership because it helped someone do his task, and be able to take credit for doing his task, but that person knew he was helped by somebody else. If you can lead quietly, subtly, that's much more important than doing it in some overt "I am the leader, you are the follower" manner.

SC: There are many leadership styles in the Navy, as there are in business and in the world at large. Some XOs are very proactive and exercise individual initiative in

---

[18] PMS or the Planned Maintenance System is a system that identifies when periodic maintenance checks, servicing, or inspections are to be done on all equipment and systems.

decision-making, and some are more reticent to make a decision or execute an action unless it's been approved by higher authority. What was your leadership and decision-making style as an XO, and did this style ever create a problem for you?

PDM: As an ATF XO, I led firmly. There were lots of leadership voids to fill. I didn't have any resistance. But later on, I guess I believed in the axiom of "Act bravely and beg forgiveness," because I felt that it was a shortcoming on my part if I really had to go ask my superior about something. I can't think of a case where I didn't have the solution presented before I even began to ask permission to move forward. I sometimes had that position changed a little bit, but I never let any superior or boss start a blank sheet of paper. I had thought through the problem the best that I possibly could, I had recommended the best solution that I possibly could, and then if someone wanted to say maybe we should add this or subtract that, it was OK. I can accept that. I understood that and I appreciated that, because the next time I would never commit that same mistake again. And as you move forward and up the ladder, you tucked it away. You've got to be careful because people look at things differently, so you've got to add something that you might not have added before. But never did I go into a situation where a "sheet of paper" was blank. It was always: "What do you think about this?" I always tried to set the conditions I thought appropriate—subtle leadership.

SC: Let's turn now to the role of the XO in terms of getting the ship ready for operations and exercises. Of course, fleet exercises are critical to the training, effectiveness, and efficiency of the force, and as we move into higher levels of command responsibility for you, we're going to home in on this, but just in general, tell us what impact an XO really has on the training and readiness of the command.

PDM: Every operation in the military, in the Navy, is done under some brand of operations order. That's just the way things are done. I always made sure that people were familiar with the annexes of a training or operations order [OPORDER]. That's where the treasures lie. The basics of the training directions, etc., were easily understood. What was expected of you, what was required, were not in the basic tenets of the task order, but in the annex. It held all the jewels. So if you were more familiar with those annexes than anybody else, you came out ahead of the game in any operation, any inspection or training evolution because you didn't have to pause and look up anything. You knew precisely all aspects of the mission, training requirement, and were able to properly complete the order.

SC: Taking this training and preparation a bit further, what's the role of an XO in terms of just general crew training and preparation to carry out their regular routines, duties, functions, roles, etc.?

PDM: His role is no different than the CO's role. He makes sure that it's all ready to go when the CO says, "Carry on." Anybody who looks at it any differently isn't ready for the next step—to be the CO.

SC: As an XO, if you think of this like the CEO of a ship, if we regard the CO as more like the chairman of the board, is that a fair way to describe an XO?

PDM: No, the commodore is chairman of the board. A CEO is the commanding officer. [*laughs*]

SC: The CO would be the CEO?

PDM: The CEO is a better comparison. He is the chief executive officer that's responsible for everything that happens within his command.

SC: The XO would be more like, in the business world, an executive vice president?

PDM: Chief operating officer.

SC: The COO?

PDM: The COO.

SC: Delegation of authority is a key aspect of leader effectiveness. We've all worked for the boss who came into work at zero-dark-thirty and left in the middle of the night, yet never seemed to get anything accomplished because they micromanaged or wouldn't delegate authority. What's your perspective on delegation of authority?

PDM: I'm for it. I guess the best compliment you can receive as either a CO or the flag officer is that when people leave, they say a simple thing—"Admiral," or "Captain, thanks for letting me do my job. I appreciated the help along the way, but letting me do what I was supposed to do without a lot of help, without a lot of checking, without a lot of interference, it made this a great two years. Thank you very much." The more times people told me that, the more times that I knew I followed the proper leadership path.

SC: Admiral, this wraps up our look at your time as XO of the *Seneca* and also some general comments and observations on executive officer, or XO, in general. In our next session, we're going to discuss your return to Newport for Destroyer School and then we'll delve into your follow-on tours on board destroyers. Thank you very much, Admiral Miller.

PDM: Thank you. My pleasure.

SC: This is USNI oral history interview with Admiral Paul David Miller, U.S. Navy (Ret.). This is session number two, question set number four. The date is Sunday, January 22, 2017. The interviewer is Professor Stan Carpenter of the U.S. Naval War College.

[End of January 22, 2017, interview]

Interview with Admiral Paul David Miller, USN (Ret.)
Date: September 30, 2017

Stan Carpenter (SC): This is USNI oral history interview with Admiral Paul David Miller, U.S. Navy (Ret.). This is session number three, question set number five. The date is Saturday, September 30, 2017. The interviewer is Professor Stan Carpenter from the Naval War College. These questions cover your time at Department Head School and as operations officer of USS *Parsons* (DDG-33).

Good morning, Admiral.

Paul David Miller (PDM): Good morning.

SC: Your first department head tour was as the operations officer on the *Forrest Sherman*-class destroyer USS *Parsons* (DDG-33), named for Rear Admiral William S. Parsons, also known as "Deke" Parsons, who worked on the atomic bomb Manhattan Project and actually armed the Hiroshima bomb aboard the *Enola Gay* in August 1945. Before we turn to that tour, let's discuss the preparation that all prospective department heads in the surface fleet undergo. When you were finishing your XO tour on *Seneca*, what was the Navy's process for detailing prospective department heads?

PDM: Once leaving the *Seneca*, I had applied for and been accepted to this thing called Destroyer School. It was a school in Newport, Rhode Island, which had about one hundred students, and their task was to introduce the individuals, the lieutenants there, to what they were going to face as fleet department heads in destroyers. My issue was I had not served on a destroyer, and even though my performance had warranted an opportunity to go to Destroyer School, they believed that I needed to get familiar with things destroyer, and I was sent to the USS *Hawkins* (DD-873), which was a DD in Newport, Rhode Island. I went there for a period of weeks to go through a familiarization period of each department and then go to the Destroyer School and begin my six-month course of studies there.

Destroyer School was a bit of a phenomena [*sic*] for me, because when I talked with all of the classmates that I was going to have, I suddenly realized that I was the only one that had not had destroyer duty. That sort of fazed me a bit, because I knew that I would have to run a little faster, study a little harder, pay more attention, because I was obviously a bit behind, because without that experience, I had a lot of catching up to do.

The course was divided into three sections, and it was operations, weapons, and engineering. The course was relatively easy in that you were given not only the requisite texts but also you were taught by outstanding fleet sailors. Some were chiefs, some were lieutenants that had had their department head tour and had gone back to instruct at the Destroyer School.

I remember that the CO of the school was Captain Redgrave, and he upped the ante for the students. He told all the students that your assignment upon completion of Destroyer School was going to be dependent upon where you stood, where you ranked on a 4.0 system with your classmates. What this did, this took an already competitive group of one hundred officers and made them a little more competitive because everybody wanted to go to become an ops officer or a weapons officer on a guided missile destroyer out of San Diego. [*laughs*] So I knew that things were going to become a little bit more difficult because that's exactly what I had placed on my dream sheet when I graduated from Destroyer School.[19]

The course was relatively benign. You take the material, you study the material, you take the test, you don't have to memorize it for a final, you then go do another section, you take the test, and you go through that for six months. I came out of Destroyer School in relatively good shape, because I was assigned as operations officer on a destroyer out of San Diego. I knew that my competitive ranking had to be okay. I don't remember many remarkable things about Destroyer School, other than that I had to pay attention, had to study. The school taught me a lot. I gave Destroyer School high marks for making a student appreciate the rudiments of each of the disciplines I

---

[19] A "dream sheet" is where an officer requests the preferred command he or she would like to be assigned. It typically includes warfare specialty such as surface ship, aviation, submarine, special forces, etc., and includes type of billet (combat systems, engineering, etc.) and preferred homeport. Navy detailers can use the "dream sheet" to assign officers to specific billets; however, it is a desired assignment and carries no real weight in the assignment process. The "needs of the Navy" are always the highest priority in billet assignment.

mentioned. Highlights were tracing the fuel system of the destroyer, actually on a destroyer getting down into the main spaces and tracing it, tracing the lube oil system. You're learning the condensate system. It prepared you, even without an engineering background, to go to a ship and be an engineering officer on a destroyer. The same way with the weapons systems. You learned about gunnery, ASW [antisubmarine warfare] weapons, missile systems, and you just didn't learn about them academically. We went down to ships. You went into 5"/38 mounts. You learned exactly what went on.

In operations, it was report writing, making you familiar with all aspects of op orders, CASREPs [Casualty Reports], those things an operations officer must be mindful of. And being reminded that don't miss any scheduling conferences for your ship, because you could make it a happy ship by getting in some liberty ports that they might not have gotten into had you not attended a scheduling conference. So that was Destroyer School.

Becky and I lived in a small apartment provided by the Destroyer School leadership. They had a set of quarters set aside for you and you could take residence for six months. We enjoyed Newport very much. That summarizes that six-month period of being schooled in and being accepted in this thing, what I will term later as the destroyer community. With that ticket, I was able to proceed to my destroyer and start my real Navy career after spending three years in what I will again term "the junk force of the Navy."

SC: What attributes did the Navy look for in an officer's initial sea tour or tours at the division officer level or, in your case, also as the XO in terms of selection for Department Head School, and has that selection criteria changed over the years?

PDM: I hope not, but apparently, with what we're seeing in our fleet today, something has changed. What they were looking for then and, I would hope, are looking for now were young division officers that were eager to participate in every aspect of shipboard operations, were able to demonstrate clearly that they were able to lead at the division officer level, but more than that, they demonstrated potential, and I have always placed high regard for potential. I think the only reason that I was able to be selected to

Destroyer School was that thing called potential, because I did not have the requisite experience, knowledge, and other attributes that they looked for in a division officer on a destroyer to move forward. These were folks that had seen hundreds of officers go through this course of instruction. They could tell what attributes made that officer successful, and they skewed their selection process to those attributes.

SC: One of the dynamics that we want to bore in on in these oral history interviews is your perspective on and recommendations to contemporary and future naval officers as to what career credentials and accomplishments are most fundamentally important for career advancement. With that dynamic in mind, for those officers aspiring to department head selection, what should they achieve in their initial sea tours?

PDM: I'm probably not the one to comment on that from an experience perspective, because I did it differently. That theme will be seen throughout this whole taping. But what they look for, and what I looked for when I became a CO, was the ability of an officer to complete all tasks assigned, but, more importantly, to be able to look at what needed to be done next and begin completing the next evolution, to put into his mind that he was looking to complete his work as if he was the department head, to think like the department head. And I'll say later for the department head to think like he was the XO and for the XO to think like he were the captain, to always view things not from your perspective but from the perspective of the leader over you, to be able to know that you needed to not only complete the given task but to set the framework for what comes next. So that's what they look for. They look for potential.

SC: Between your time on *Seneca* and Department Head School, as you mentioned, you were sent to a destroyer for temporary additional duty, or TAD, for a couple of months to familiarize you with destroyers and their operations. That ship was USS *Hawkins*. What duties did you perform while you were aboard *Hawkins*?

PDM: Sadly, when one comes aboard a ship for, quote, "familiarization," it can be a good experience, it can be an adequate experience, or it can be a poor experience. My experience bordered between poor and adequate. I say that simply because when you don't belong to the ship, it's the interest that they take in you to be able to do what I was there for, to familiarize myself with things destroyer. They did an adequate job, but I clearly knew that I was there as sort of an extra person that had to be there for the assigned period of time, and I think I received a four-line additional duty fitness report that, in my words, said, "This officer was here for two months and departed."

SC: *Hawkins* was a World War II *Gearing*-class destroyer that underwent FRAM modernization in the 1960s. What was the FRAM modernization program all about, and what was its purpose?

PDM: That was a program to modernize World War II destroyers to make them more technologically current, particularly its weapon systems and, in some, engineering systems to be able to get another decade out of the ship and to sail it in a more modern fashion. The biggest enhancement on those ships were the gun mounts. They went from single-barrel gun mounts, 5 inches, to twin 5"/38s. They had a complete overhaul of their engineering system to be able to burn lighter fuel, and I learned that much on *Hawkins* because they were a FRAM destroyer.

SC: Well, the reason why I asked the question was because to use that term, a lot of people are not familiar with what was going on to try to get that additional few years out of those World War II–class destroyers, and most of them did last another ten or fifteen years.

In 1969, *Hawkins* had some notable events, was testing out the new Polaris ballistic missile system with the Royal Navy submarine HMS *Renown*, a near catastrophe with USS *Chopper*, a U.S. Navy sub, and participation in the Apollo 12 Atlantic recovery force, which was quite a remarkable year. Were you aboard *Hawkins* during any of those evolutions?

PDM: I missed them all.

SC: At Department Head School, was the class integrated with all students in a common curriculum, or were you separated into cohorts based on your prospective future tours?

PDM: We were all taking the same course of study where they placed equal emphasis on the three areas mentioned: operation, engineering, and weapons. You did not know which discipline you were going to serve in till the orders were given.

SC: So tell us about your typical day at Department Head School. Start with when you reported aboard all the way through to the time you were completed.

PDM: We went to school five days a week. We went to school from 8:00 to 4:00 or 4:30. It was run in academic style. When we were off the ship, we were able to do the things that I mentioned. We would go to a ship for a practical lesson in engineering, and the one that's most vivid was tracing of systems, because I would have never traced a lube oil system or a freshwater system or a fuel oil system in a destroyer had I not gone to Destroyer School. So it was classroom 92 percent of the time, and maybe 8 percent of the time outside the classroom.

I gave Captain Redgrave, who was the skipper at the time, high marks for running an outstanding school, and when I left it, I felt comfortable. Even though I never served a day in a destroyer before I went to the *Hawkins*, I felt comfortable that no matter where I was going, I knew a sufficient amount about operations, engineering, and weaponry that I could go on any destroyer and start performing as if I had been on a destroyer and having division officer experience. It was that good.

SC: Was there any time allotted for PT, physical training, recreation? Was that part of the curriculum then?

PDM: I don't recall, but there was always time that you got off for some reason, and we did have a competitive class, and they encouraged it, for basketball in that good gym in Newport. But there was no emphasis, extra emphasis placed on that outside of the academics and learning the workings of the destroyer Navy.

SC: That gym, Building 109—

PDM: Building 109, I spent a lot of time there.

SC: I did as well. It's gone now. They tore it down and built a parking lot about three or four years ago, but they replaced it with a very, very nice modern gym with a pool in it. It's a very nice facility, but those of us that have spent a lot of years in Newport remember Gym 109 fondly.

PDM: That's it.

SC: You mentioned earlier the nature of the faculty was a mixture of chief petty officers and former successful department heads, and so I want to bore in a little bit on that. What do you think was the value of having very experienced chief petty officers as faculty?

PDM: I go back to the boatswain I mentioned in earlier pages. A chief in the Navy who's learned his discipline and also has gained the ability to talk to the officer community with clear appreciation that he knew what he was talking about allowed students such as myself to pay close attention. Because when a gunnery chief was going over all aspects of the respective gun mounts, you knew that man was not only a practitioner, but he also knew the science behind what made it all work. They were absolutely experts in their discipline, and students like myself paid careful attention to them. I would say that the chiefs were a better cadre of instructors than the officers.

SC: Let's talk about the officers. You mentioned earlier that they were post–department head tour officers. What was the value of having those type of persons on the faculty?

PDM: The officers were found mostly in the Operations Department. They had the experience and the background knowledge about what a ship does as opposed to what allows the ship to do it. The engineers knew how to get the ship from Point A to Point B, and the weapons people knew the equipment that fought the ship. So they had classified the school appropriately and, in my view, put the appropriate instructors in the right slots.

SC: Were there any curricular areas that you found not useful once you assumed your new tour?

PDM: Probably, but it wasn't remarkable, and I would not say that there was anything that detracted from the overall course of instruction.

SC: And, conversely, what curricular areas did you find to be most helpful in preparing you for your operations officer tour?

PDM: Elements of all of them. I won't detail the particulars, but there were elements in each of those phases that I can remember to this day that were very helpful, particularly because I never served as an engineer on a naval combatant. I never served as a weapons officer on a naval combatant. But I can recall when I was a CO that I was much more comfortable with my interactions with weapons and engineering officers because of the foundations laid at that Destroyer School.

SC: What subject did you have the most difficulty with and why, and how about the least difficulty?

PDM: Tough question. Probably engineering, but I say that because I had no real interest in the engineering plant, so having to remember, having to draw all the cycles caused me to spend a lot of time studying them, appreciating the science behind them took a little bit of effort. The easiest, of course, was operations. You started off with piloting and navigation. After my ATF experience and my navigating across the ocean four times by sextant, I had no problems with navigation or the things that were in the operations world, so I was much more comfortable there than I was in engineering. Weapons was just a good middle spot and, happily, the chief that was the head of the weapons course of instruction made it interesting with lots of stories about what happens when you don't handle with care, not only the gun mounts but the ammunition. [*laughs*]

SC: Understood. As we've already discussed, at the accession schools and at the SWOS Basic, there were a lot of tactical training evolutions in terms of bridge watch standing, CIC simulators, underway time in the YP training craft, tabletop exercises, and so forth. How much did the Department Head School curriculum focus on tactical training of this nature?[20]

PDM: I recall some. Did it add value? Marginally. Simulation, the art of simulation, let me say, had not progressed sufficiently to give the realism, to give the dynamics of a situation, what you can see today on a simulator. So this is a long time ago, this is in 1969, so the simulators were very basic, and while you could see how they would help, they added little value because of their limited capability.

SC: I want to bore in on something that a lot of people have difficulty with and, as we have likely seen in the last year or so in the Western Pacific, they may still be having difficulty with, and that is understanding relative motion. With that in mind, would you explain to those who might not be familiar, what is the maneuvering board or the MO board? What's that all about? What is relative motion and how should an officer pay particular attention to learning the dynamics of relative motion and maneuvering board?

PDM: I'm disappointed in what I read today has happened on a few of our ships. Relative motion is a basic concept. You don't really need this thing called the maneuvering board to understand its relevance. We did not have a maneuvering board onboard our ATF. We did not have a radar of any value onboard the ATF. Yet as an officer of the deck, I knew what relative motion was. I knew that if I took a bearing to a ship, a light, or any other

---

[20] SWOS Basic Division Officer Course (BDOC) is the basic school for newly commissioned surface warfare officers. Junior officers generally attend prior to taking up their first division officer tour; however, they may spend some time on board their ultimate assignment between the commissioning source and starting SWOS. The commissioning date and the school schedule drive this dynamic. SWOS Basic schools are located in Newport, RI, and San Diego, CA.

target that I wanted to look through the alidade and get a bearing on, I knew that if I came back to that same alidade and I took another bearing, it did one of three things: the bearing drift was left, the bearing drift was right, or the bearing drift was steady. So then you learned that the pace of that bearing drift moving left or right would sort of give you the distance that you were going to miss that object by, at least in your mental maneuvering board, and you knew that if it was steady, you were going to face a problem. Because of that old adage, "constant bearing decreasing range," you knew that there was an issue.

So I don't understand how these things that has [sic] happened in the last few months, I don't understand how they happened. I look forward to seeing the investigations. I'm sure they'll reveal to us what the problems were. But that basic concept is taught by skippers, by courses of instruction, and you learn by common sense and experience what relative motion is. But relative motion comes in really handy, Stan, when you're driving a ship. When you appreciate different speeds, coming alongside another ship, you're able to judge how your ship is moving alongside another, or in flying formation in an airplane where your wings are almost very, very close but they're moving against each other, the relative movement. So it's a basic concept that all mariners, all aviators know about, and so I have to automatically default that when we have a problem like that it's simply because somebody wasn't paying attention.

SC: And for those unfamiliar with it, a maneuvering board is basically just a compass rose where you're in the center and all you're doing is plotting the movement of an object that you're observing, and then in that way you can judge or determine course and speed and bearing and all those important relative motion elements.

PDM: You're able to plot, in addition, Stan, what they call the CPA, the closest point of approach to your ship. I subscribe that once you are able to think relative motion, you can just about do what the maneuvering board does in your head to the numbers of contacts that you have out there.

SC: Exactly. It's a critical concept. It might even be *the* most critical concept of someone who has the conn on the deck. What were the assumptions made by the Navy in terms of an officer's foundational knowledge of basic tactics, watch standing, navigations, weapons, engineering, Navy admin [administration], and so on when they arrived at Department Head School? And you've already mentioned your preparation was not quite up to the same standard that other officers had, but what were the assumptions, in general, made of a student who would walk into Department Head School on the first day?

PDM: I think the assumptions were that everybody that matriculated had a basic appreciation for the operations of fleet destroyer operations. As a division officer, they may have served in one division, in engineering, say, as opposed to weapons and operations. But they knew that you had some appreciation for what the other divisions did. What Destroyer School did was approach it from that vantage point. They knew if you had been the main propulsion assistant in a destroyer, that you'd probably have a pretty easy time with the engineering course of instruction, but the gunnery and the operations portion would be important, because you might not be assigned as an engineer. So the whole cross-training was very applicable to every student that began the course of instruction. For the peculiar background that I had, I had to pay close attention to every one of them because there was no preconceived notion that I could ease up on one of them because I already knew it. I did not know any of them.

SC: One of the functions of department heads on the cruiser, destroyer, and frigate community is standing tactical action officer watch, or TAO. In those years, was there any preparation at Department Head School towards being a TAO?[21]

---

[21] The tactical action officer or TAO, is the commanding officer's representative in the Combat Information Center (CIC) and has cognizance and control over all ship's systems related to "fighting the ship," including the weapons, sensors, and propulsion when the captain is not in CIC or on the bridge. The TAO is typically a department head or a very senior division officer depending on the ship type.

PDM: The TAO concept had not come into full blossom by the time that even I'd left *Luce* (DDG-38) as a commanding officer. It was still combat and bridge, and the TAO system was just coming into being.

SC: Would you say that was because by the late seventies, early eighties a lot of those type combatants would have the NTDS system and those sorts of electronic aids?[22]

PDM: Technology, absolutely.

SC: Once you completed Department Head School and in preparation to assume your duties as the operations officer, were there any other schools that you attended?

PDM: No.

SC: So you went straight to the ship?

PDM: Straight to the ship.

SC: So let's turn a page here and do something completely different. Tell us a little bit about your personal life in those years. As a more senior officer in the wardroom, did you experience any great life changes during those years now?

PDM: Are we speaking of when I was a department head?

SC: Well, in that general timeframe.

PDM: The answer is no. The first five years that Becky and I were associated with the Navy, which included the ATF and my tour in *Parsons*, I spent an inordinate amount of

---

[22] NTDS is the Naval Tactical Data System, which was first fielded in the 1960s. It collects and displays data from multiple sensors in an integrated display. It assigns symbology to types of contacts and can be used to calculate dynamics such as a contact's course, speed, etc.

time at sea. I caught all the ships on their deployment cycles, not their overhaul cycles. When we left Newport, we went to San Diego. We had to find a place to live in a relatively short time, because, once again, I had to leave Becky by herself and fly away. This time I flew to meet the USS *Parsons* in a place called Kaohsiung. It is a port in southern Taiwan. They had been with the carrier in the Gulf and got a port visit in Kaohsiung. So that's where I boarded the ship after a long flight to Taipei and a ride in a unique train setting down to this town called Kaohsiung, and Becky was left to set up a household in San Diego.

SC: Once you completed Department Head School and [were] about to report to the *Parsons*, what was your attitude towards continuing your naval career?

PDM: Undecided. I did not augment to the regular Navy. That was one of the stipulations was unspoken, that if you were going to go to this thing called Destroyer School, that was for regular Navy officers. That was getting a degree of training and then a pathway for you to be a full sailor in the destroyer force. I was undecided and I wanted to keep the option of leaving the Navy after this department head tour open, and so my fitness reports contained the designator 1105, which meant that I was still a reserve.

SC: Let's turn now to your tour as a department head on the USS *Parsons* from 1969 to 1971. If you were to define the ideal relationship, working relationship, between a department head and the division officers, what would that look like?

PDM: The ideal relationship between department head and division officers is simple. The division officers' tasks are to support the department, to support through the XO and the commanding officer in completing all aspects of operation on board the destroyer. The communications officer is vital, equipment knowledge, association with his radiomen, care for crypto top-secret custodial activity. Electronics maintenance officer knowing the respective equipment, and navigation on board the bridge, your CIC officer, all of them having the knowledge of what makes those parts of the ship work, them knowing that they have the channel to you as a department head, that if anything is needed to support them, it's there. And, most importantly, that they have an appreciation that you trust them to do their job without interference.

I always entered a leadership position with trust in a subordinate until they did something that said, "Uh-oh, I'm giving that officer too much leeway." So it was the relationship they started off at 100 percent, and if they demonstrated at 100 percent, they were left alone because I knew that that part of the milieu would be covered. At times I was lucky in *Parsons*. I had three division officers that were great, so I could spend more time worrying about what the XO and CO worry about. And that's the pattern I used. That's the pattern I used as a department head, as a CO.

SC: What about the relationship between the department head and the senior enlisted leadership, specifically the chief petty officers, the first-class petty officers, and division-leading petty officers? Does that differ from that of a division officer?

PDM: It really doesn't, but it has to be done in a different way. It's delicate. Because of my upbringing and because of my time in the ATF world, I had great relationships with the chief petty officers and senior petty officers. I relied on them. I appreciated their counsel. So I would often visit the chief officers' quarters and get to know better the chiefs that were in my department and later chiefs that were on board the ship, to try to get a feel for which one of them that I wanted to encourage to break out of becoming a chief and go for one of the officer programs, to become an LDO, to become an augment, to become a NESEP in the training programs.[23] So it was delicate. I couldn't go and let the division officer think that I was checking up on him, that I didn't think he was doing a good job, but to knowing what the contributions of the chiefs and senior petty officers were to wring out more potential for themselves and for the Navy. I just thought that was part of my task.

---

[23] NESEP is the Navy Enlisted Scientific Education Program that allows enlisted sailors to attend various universities and major in technical and engineering fields. They can then attend OCS and receive a commission.

SC: As a department head, when a brand-new junior officer reported aboard in your department, what was your role as a mentor?

PDM: Simple. To welcome him, to spend time with him, to know about him as a person, that he had a family, his family, what his interests were, what he wanted to get out of his time in the Navy, and tell him that he's starting off at 100 percent confidence, and the only person that can let that fall from 100 percent is himself. And if he ever had any issue that he wanted to talk about, that he could always share it with me, and we would work out the problem together, and then that was the end of the conversation. "Happy to have you here. Get to work."

SC: If you were to construct a list of the top five things you would advise a newly reported-aboard department head to do or not to do, what might that list look like?

PDM: Number one was work as hard as you can for every moment that you're aboard this ship. Number two is to get your qualifications as early as you can. Three, be a shipmate to all of the fellow servicemen on this ship. Four, spend time with your enlisted people; know them as well as I know you. That's speaking from department head to division officer. And number five is engage in extracurricular activities, such as sports, other things that are going on, to show that you're well-rounded and that you want your people that work for you to be the same. And the overarching thing for all of these is to do right, do right on board ship and off ship, and if you wrap all those things together, you'll be a good division officer.

SC: Are there any things that you would advise a new department head to never do or not do?

PDM: Embarrass the ship.

SC: And that leads on to the next question, interestingly enough. What was wardroom life like back in the late 1960s and early seventies, and how and why had the wardroom culture changed since you were commissioned in the early 1960s?

PDM: We didn't have a wardroom life in the ATF world. But the wardroom life in a destroyer wasn't exactly what I thought it might be. During that period—and I think probably we see it now—the operational schedules were so intense. My whole time on *Parsons* was spent at sea, so the wardroom was that place on board ship where you had time to talk with, to associate with the other officers on board. But the pace of operations that I particularly found in the Gulf, everybody was working so damn hard that there wasn't much time to be able to get not only together as a wardroom but to feel that you had a group of fraternity brothers there. These were professional guys. Every one of them was working hard. There were always problems. The best thing that you could feel about your fellow officers was that they were there to help when there were problems. That was good. But as far as off ship, I don't recall much association at all as a wardroom.

SC: One of the most difficult issues that many department heads face is how to rate their junior officers or division officers on periodic fitness reports. This dynamic is particularly difficult when there are several top performers who must be ranked, as you've just indicated with at least three of your division officers. This is a dynamic that I want to explore with you at all levels of leadership in your career and an area that I think is especially helpful to potential future leaders. So what advice would you give to a newly reported department head on how to address fitness reports for junior officers in their department?

PDM: This is probably one of the most important things that they'll do outside of their professional work. It's a very sensitive area. The fitness report program that we had when I was a participant forced you to break out officers between outstanding, excellent, and on down. It was a fine line between where you would put the x on one as opposed to the other. But you have to recall you drafted the report. The commanding officer was responsible for the report, so you were writing a recommendation via the XO to the CO.

So the CO was then seeing how you saw the respective junior officer through your eyes, and he might have seen him through different eyes.

So I never stepped away from marking an officer for accelerated—then the term was "accelerated promotion"—that deserved such marks. Never. I never tried to balance the grading of the officer with another. I called the marks as I saw them, and I knew that when I did that, I would have to talk to that officer as to what I did. That is a hard thing when you have a twenty-four-year-old division officer and you're probably telling him for the first time that he wasn't quite as good as another one, especially youngsters from the United States Naval Academy that thought they should all be in the top ranking. But then I had to take that to the XO, tell him why, and then to the CO. Very few times did I have the CO change anything, very few times, so I felt confident that my review was one that was substantiated by higher authority reviews within that ship.

SC: The reality is that not every commissioned officer has the capability or the traits or the behaviors for effective leadership. As a department head, when faced with such an officer, how would you counsel and advise that person?

PDM: Very few were in the category of "I think you should find something else to do right away." [*laughs*] Most were youngsters that hadn't had the opportunity to show the ability that he had. Anybody that gained a commission in the military has a modicum of ability in lots of areas; otherwise, he wouldn't be there. Then it becomes personality-driven. You don't know what motivates them. You don't know what he's thinking about, whether it's his girlfriend all the time. There's so many things that come into play. And there were very few that were in that category. I'd spend some time with them trying to understand, to appreciate the problems. You just reminded me of probably four or five officers in my whole career that were in that category that were not redeemable, and you sadly had to, when it came time for their tour to be over, you had to recommend that even if they wanted to stay in the Navy, you had to recommend that they slip and proceed.

SC: The next question is a particularly sensitive and perhaps difficult one. We all know that sailors have personal or familial problems that impact their professionalism. Alcohol abuse is a big one. So are marriages that are going badly. I had a first-class signalman, the LPO [leading petty officer], in fact, whose mother was murdered in a drive-by shooting.[24] What techniques or actions might a department head take to mitigate the impact of these dynamics, and what about something like basket leave, for example?

PDM: Basket leave, that's leave for someone you just give and don't charge him for it, [is] a very helpful technique. To answer the question briefly, you have to give them space, you have to show support, and you have to demonstrate that it's okay for him to deal with that problem because you and his subordinates will deal with his problems aboard ship. You have to make him feel that while he's taking care of an issue like you illustrated, he's not letting down the ship. And that way when the situation is resolved and he returns, then he fills the spot that he filled before the problem, and everything is as it was. And you can show no greater support for an individual that faces an issue that when he returns from that issue, it's like nothing ever happened in his professional life.

SC: Here's another hard question, but one that every officer has to come to grips with at some point. When you have a sailor or even a junior officer who is facing some sort of discipline from a nonjudicial punishment or even up to a court-martial, but you regard that person as an excellent performer otherwise, how do you approach that dynamic as a department head? And this is a question that I'll delve within to at all levels of leadership, particularly at the CO level, but let's start looking at it from the department head level.

PDM: Tough, tough response. At the department head level in the space that you're given to lead, you have to be quite hard on subordinates for doing stupid things. If you set the parameters carefully and if you are able to articulate clearly what should not be violated in those parameters, when they are, then the chips fall as they may. I can recall some examples where folks did some not-so-smart things, and they thought that they deserved a second or third chance or whatever. It's a close call, but I gave fewer second chances than most, because your life on board that ship and off ship is pretty simple. The choices

---

[24] The LPO or leading petty officer is the most senior petty officer within a division below any chief petty officers. The LPO is typically the work center supervisor.

that you take are pretty easy to do what you're supposed to do on board ship and to act like you're supposed to act ashore. So when one of those things were violated, I felt no compelling reason to go out of the way to provide additional support. Later on, I did, but at that level, you have to know what you're dealing with, and if they happen to fall down at that level, the chances of them falling down later are greater, in my view.

SC: Thank you, Admiral Miller. In our next session, we'll continue to look at your tour as operations officer aboard USS *Parsons*. This is session number three, question set number five, USNI oral history interview with Admiral Paul David Miller, USN (Ret.). The date is Saturday, September 30, 2017. The interviewer is Professor Stan Carpenter.

Thank you, Admiral.

SC: This is USNI oral history interview with Admiral Paul David Miller, USN (Ret.). This is session number three, question set number six. The date is Saturday, September 30, 2017. The interviewer is Professor Stan Carpenter from U.S. Naval War College.

These questions cover your time as operations officer of USS *Parsons* (DDG-33). Admiral, let's continue with your years aboard the *Parsons* and your tour as operations officer. Many department heads are faced with a severe personality or professional conflict between a division officer and his or her senior enlisted leadership, especially the chief and the first class petty officers. Did you ever encounter such a situation, and how did you address it? If not, what advice might you give a department head facing such a situation?

PDM: Never faced a situation with a senior petty officer that's worthy of talking about. I respected highly the chiefs' mess, where the chiefs sort of did their relaxing and did their talking about the respective officers, the commanding officers, and individuals that worked for them. Having that respect, I went to them often if I had an issue with a sailor, giving them the opportunity to remedy it first. And, secondly, talking to them about themselves and what I could do to enhance their advancement if they were a 7 to an 8 or an 8 to a 9, and every once in a while, find the kind of chief petty officer, the E-7 that went through the ranks quickly and demonstrated qualities that would make him a good naval officer. Simply put, I respected the chiefs' quarters and everybody that had made that rank in the United States Navy.

SC: The next few questions address the issue of effective leadership, which is an extremely important topic. We will deal with leadership effectiveness questions from the commanding, senior, and flag officer perspective in greater depth in future interviews, but from the first moment a department head reports aboard, the senior officer and enlisted leadership in the various divisions within the department look to you for guidance and direction. How important is it for you to give your crew a vision statement of how you expect the department to run?

PDM: Running a department on a combatant or an amphibious ship, an aircraft carrier, I do not believe is a terribly difficult task because of the parameters. They're fixed. You know what is expected. There have been many that have accomplished this before you, many that will do better after you, and it's incumbent upon you, when you have that opportunity, to be able to exercise the leadership and the execution of required taskings and get them precisely correct and to relieve from higher authority, in your particular ship, your XO and CO, relieve the burden from them to having think twice about what your department contributes to the ship. It's not hard.

SC: Everyone at some point in their career, whether civilian or military, will face working with a difficult senior or boss of supervisor or manager, what have you. We will address this critical issue at all levels of your career. So what advice would you give a department head on how to approach working under a difficult superior?

PDM: Make your contributions to that difficult superior so clear, so correct, that even a difficult superior has a hard time being difficult. That's it.

SC: Good advice. In the military, there is clearly a legal authority in leadership, but there's also a moral authority that derives from one's actions and behaviors. We're going to delve into this critical leadership issue at all levels, from division officer to department head to CO to XO to flag officer, as we advance through these oral history interviews. So what moral authority attributes, actions, and behaviors do you see as essential in a shipboard department head? And what I really mean by "moral authority" is essentially the way you conduct yourself.

PDM: I hear this term "moral authority" often. I think that's, I guess, a more scholarly way of saying "set the proper example." And if one is in a position, if he sets the example of leading others, of caring for others, of respecting others, he's fulfilled that moral aspect of his duties. The "respecting others" plays the largest role. Setting [a] personal example is a close second. Marry those two together, and he's completed the moral example requirement.

SC: A good way to look at this is the authority that one derives not from any legal authority, but just because of your actions, your behaviors, or, as you say, how you set the example.

PDM: Yes, that's it.

SC: Without naming any names, can you tell us about any particularly poor leadership that you experienced from either juniors or seniors as a department head, and how about any particularly effective leadership?

PDM: As a department head, I was blessed with outstanding leadership. You're assigned. You really don't have a choice to go to one business or the other. You're assigned to go to this unit. The unit has a commanding and an executive officer, and it is what it is. But in *Parsons* I had one XO and two COs, and all of them, all three of them, were *absolutely* outstanding. I was lucky to be assigned there, fortunate. So given that top cover by leadership, I was able to do my prescribed duties, to earn qualifications, because, recall, I had no destroyer duty, so I had to learn to become what they call fleet officer of the deck. I had to be able to work in a destroyer environment with regard to evolutions from gunfire support to refueling, rearming, doing those things that I had not been experienced in. And the leadership in *Parsons* not only was helpful, they gave me every opportunity to learn, to establish my credentials, and to advance in every way possible my shipboard strengths as a destroyer officer.

SC: That is good examples of particularly effective leadership from seniors. How about particularly effective leadership from juniors, say, your division officers or your leading petty officers and chiefs?

PDM: On board *Parsons*, too much water has passed beneath the keel for me to give you an illustration of anyone in particular, but it was clear that because I was able to come away from *Parsons* with the fitness reports I did, that I had great support from the division officers and senior petty officer leadership on that ship.

SC: Would say that there wasn't any particular episode of poor leadership at the junior level?

PDM: No. If I can't recall it, there wasn't an example.

SC: I'll be asking this question as we go down the road, because I'm sure at some point you encounter some and I think it would be instructive to cite that as to—

PDM: [*laughs*] We'll get to some of those.

SC: I'm sure we will. There are many leadership styles in the Navy. Some department heads are very proactive and exercise individual initiative and decision-making, and some are more reticent to make a decision or execute an action unless it's been approved by higher authority. What was your leadership and decision-making style as a department head, and did this style ever create a problem for you?

PDM: As to my leadership style, I evaluated pretty quickly anybody that worked for me and in my domain of responsibility. If I found that that individual, regardless if he was a division officer or a leading petty officer in the comm shack [radio central or the main shipboard communications space], if I saw that they had the ability to carry out all their duties, I'd leave good leaders alone. I concentrated on those leaders that aren't at 100 percent, to try to bring them up to 100 percent. That was my leadership, I'd say, recipe card all the way through.

SC: What, in general, would you advise a newly appointed department head in terms of where and when to take initiative, individual initiative, or action, and where to be more cautious and obtain higher authority approval first?

PDM: Anything that one thought the outcome would reach higher authority, pay attention to it in a way that it was going to reach authority. If it wasn't going to reach higher authority, be confident that your decision would stay below the higher authority level.

SC: What was your best day as a department head?

PDM: Wow. I had a lot of good days as a department head. Qualifying for fleet officer of the deck in a remarkably short time and then having the CO rely on me as being the officer of the deck during all underway evolutions that required close-in maneuvering. And it was a good day or a best day when the ship participated in operations that supported our activity in Vietnam. In coming away with the feeling that one played a small role in the overall contributions because it fulfilled exactly why Becky and I decided to go to a department head tour, because I would have never experienced that if I had left the Navy after the ATF tours. But I went to *Parsons* when she was in the last three months of a deployment to the Gulf, the Tonkin Gulf—this wasn't the Persian Gulf—or to Southwest Asia. We participated in true fleet operations with the carrier, air ops, gunfire support, all the things that one wants to have on his record as a naval officer. So it wasn't a single day, but it was three months of good days because we did it all and I gained all the requisite qualifications. And I was going to be blessed to have another opportunity because ships were rotating quickly, and I would take the ship back under a different CO for three or four months of deployment there before I was relieved.

So it wasn't good, it was outstanding, because, Stan, I had the opportunity to fulfill what Becky and I wanted to accomplish to give the Navy a look as to whether I was going to stay in it. So I guess it worked, because I stayed in it.

SC: What about your worst day?

PDM: I did not have a worst day on a destroyer. I did not.

SC: You were very fortunate.

PDM: Everything, everything that I touched, that I did, came out just right. Never. Honest.

SC: Are there any lessons that you learned from these experiences? I would say good and bad, but since no bad, all good.

PDM: No, there were so many lessons that I learned. Rather than detail them, I would summarize it by saying in this period of time, under the two skippers and an operational schedule second to none, for someone that was in my position that wanted to gain as much experience as possible in the shortest possible time, that every brand of fleet operations that one can think about for a destroyer, I participated in. And whether it be some degree of luck, which there was, or whether it be hard work and a relationship with two outstanding commanding officers and an XO, that permitted me to do more than a department head usually gets the opportunity to do, and to come away with fitness reports at the end to be marked as the number one department head on that destroyer, for a non-destroyer person, it was a good feeling. And to this day, I've always attributed my staying in the Navy to those commanding officers and to the experience that I was given as a department head aboard that ship.

SC: One of the dynamics that we will address as we advance through these interviews through your career is the issue of effective strategic communications. People often equate that term with large entities such as military services, government agencies, State Department, etc., but there's a good argument that at the individual level everyone engages in strategic communications all the time. Call it the projection of yourself to the world. How did you try to project yourself to your sailors, your shipmates, seniors, and the world at large in your years as a department head?

PDM: Quietly and effectively.

SC: Let's play the counterfactual here. If you were to go back to your department head days knowing what you know now, is there anything that you would do differently and, if so, why?

PDM: No. When I look back at what was achieved during that period of time, for me as a reserve officer trying to go through the filters of whether I wanted to do this, with having three years of not-so-wonderful experiences, then transitioning to a great experience, I was not going to sort of roll the dice and decide that I should do this as a career.

SC: Let's turn now to some of the dynamics of your time as the operations officer. *Parsons* was one of the four all-gun *Forrest Sherman*-class (DD-931) destroyers converted to the new *Decatur*-class (DD-936/DDG-31) guided missile destroyers, or DDGs, in 1967, and designated as DDG-33. You joined the ship while she was on a WestPac [Western Pacific] deployment. What were your expectations as you first walked aboard?

PDM: I walked aboard that ship, as mentioned earlier, in the harbor in Kaohsiung, Taiwan. The difference from my previous fleet experiences were so different with regard to equipment, with regard to spaces, with regard to size, that I knew that when we got this ship under way that I was starting from a zero-experience point and that I had to then gain as quickly as I can not only familiarization, but a working knowledge of all this new equipment that I'm seeing, that I heard about in Destroyer School but I'd never worked with. That engineering was different. What could I expect from this now 1,200-pound (psi) steam plant instead of what we were schooled on, a 600-pound (psi) steam plant? And this was my first introduction to a missile capability on board ship. So it was a totally new canvas for me to work with, and we were thrust into operations with the carrier two days after we left Kaohsiung, and so it was the flurry of activity that was the proving ground of whether I was going to be able to ratchet up every aspect of my response capability to be able to meet all the varying demands of a ship in that very high tempo of operations. I was delighted to have that opportunity, I thrived on that opportunity, and, as I've mentioned, it worked, and I look back on it as one of the best nearly two years I had in the Navy.

SC: What were the general duties of the operations officer on a DDG in those days?

PDM: The primary duty was to take all of that incoming what we called message traffic, which was always changing what one was doing in the overall tactical situation, to be able to make sure the ship was where it should be at the time it should be, ready to do what it was prescribed to do. And not only the CO receives that, but take the time to make your colleague department heads know what is going on, so that they could tree it down to the whole ship. That's what I took as one of my real responsibilities. No one told me to do that, but if I knew that the captain knew and I knew that the ship knew, then when we were in some tight situations, we would be able to better perform as a ship. And operations at that time were consistent with the importance of what was being done. Things were being changed all the time in an environment of a carrier—the destroyers, protection of the carrier, lifeguarding for flight ops, supporting things ashore. It was a very dynamic situation that you had to be on top of every second of the day.

SC: For those not familiar with the operations of a destroyer in those days, how was the Operations Department organized and what divisions were you responsible for?

PDM: The Operations Department was responsible for the non-gunnery main battery of the ship; that is, you're responsible for the eyes and ears of the ship, the Combat Information Center, all the equipment that goes with that. You're responsible for the communications of the ship, which was absolutely essential. And at that time and in that environment much of the communications would come in classified, and so you had to make sure that you handled that information correctly. You're responsible through the electronics material officer, the EMO, that that equipment worked on a 24/7 basis, and that was a huge task when you had been deployed for some time. And support for all equipment, whether it be in weapons, engineering, or operations, was not instant. They didn't have "FedEx'ing" of repair parts. The system got them to you when they could. So it was just a flow of activity, and operations was the centerpiece for letting everybody know what they were doing and why they were doing it, and that's what I was responsible for.

SC: *Parsons* was reconfigured with the early anti–air warfare, or AAW, Tartar missile system, and the antisubmarine rocket, or ASROC system.[25] Without discussing anything still classified, tell us about your experiences with both those weapon systems.

PDM: Because we were deployed with a carrier in support operations in the Gulf over there, or South China Sea, I should say, we had very little real experience with both those systems. The air threat to the carriers were minimal. We had to be mindful, but we never went to GQ with the air threat in which you were going to engage in anti-air missile capability. And there was zero submarine threat, so we did not have to engage in the anti-submarine world either. The tempo of ops was with the carrier and the carrier support for the ongoing effort in Vietnam.

SC: What was your general quarters station, and how did you prepare yourself for that role?

PDM: I was the general quarters officer of the deck shortly after I came on board, and the only place that I felt that I was minimally not up to speed in was in damage control. So I remember getting together with the DCA [damage control assistant] and, as the officer of

---

[25] ASROC is an antisubmarine rocket, which is essentially a rocket-propelled torpedo. The range provided by the rocket allows for a greater standoff distance from the target. The RIM-24 Tarter missile weapons system was first fielded in the late 1950s and was a surface-to-air medium-range missile deployed on smaller combatants, such as destroyers with a range of 8.7 nautical miles at up to 40K feet altitude.

the deck during GQ, having him go over with me the communications between the bridge and damage control central so that I had an appreciation for and an understanding of what they were going to do should we have to practice damage control.[26] And so knowing that, I was more comfortable to discharge and then to give information to the XO and captain about what was going on in different places during general quarters drills and if we went to general quarters for real.

SC: Granted that you're talking about *Parsons* was not in a, say, hot war situation with a peer competitor—at that time it would have been the Soviet Union—once *Parsons* was reconfigured as a Tartar ship with ASROC, had there been a hot war situation such as that, what would have been her role?

PDM: It would have been close-in missile defense for the carrier, because the Tartar missile had limited range. I had the Terrier missile.[27] We'll talk about [that] later on in *Luce*. The ASROC, honestly, I was happy we'd never had to use that system, because we carried this thing called nuclear ASROC weapons. I did not have an appreciation for what might happen if we ever had to use that capability. But I'll leave these thoughts to when I was the CO in *Luce*, in which we went to the North Atlantic and participated in very real exercises against the then-Soviet threat, and I think you'll find some of my answers enlightening then.

SC: When a destroyer operates with a carrier task force or carrier battle group or strike group, depending on the common term of the day, what has changed over the years, if at all, in terms of the role that a destroyer plays?

PDM: I think the destroyer during the time that I was in *Parsons*, the way that ships were in formation was a much tighter scheme than they were ten years later when I was CO of

---

[26] The DCA is responsible for all damage control training and operations aboard the ship.

[27] The RIM-2 Terrier was the next generation surface-to-air missile. Using an expanding rod warhead, the Terrier was mainly designed to intercept and destroy incoming air-to-surface missiles launched from Soviet high-level bombers. In the final variant, the Terrier had a range of 17 nautical miles and a ceiling of 80,000 feet.

Luce. Why? Weapon systems had been changed in being able to give more range. You bought more range with new radars, with NTDS, so you operated with the carrier, but you didn't operate as closely around the carrier as you did in the old destroyer force.

SC: What used to be called naval gunfire support, or NGFS, was an important destroyer mission, and since *Parsons* retained the forward 5-inch gun mount, what role did the ops officer play when you were undertaking an NGFS mission?

PDM: *Parsons* was the last ship to be assigned NGFS role because of the single mount, because if you had a casualty in that mount, then there was no backup if you were supporting direct fire. *Parsons* was never assigned a direct-fire mission. You had indirect fire, which was in an area, it could be assigned that mission, but the tension of direct fire support was not felt by that ship because it was limited with one gun.

SC: *Parsons* also retained the torpedo tubes for antisubmarine warfare, ASW, purposes. Understanding that you did not have to do that in the Vietnam War, had it been in a hot war situation where you did worry about submarines, what role did the ops officer have in that aspect of a ship's combat mission?

PDM: The ops officer had just a general role of knowing what the tactical picture was around that ship. Inside of combat, you had the ASW center and you had the transfer of information, but with regard to this interface of sonar, the weapons capability, torpedo tubes, and ASROC, you fused that information to be able to give the XO or, more importantly, the skipper, the tactical picture upon which he would evaluate whether you had reached a fire control solution or not. We did that in training only in the Tonkin Gulf. We did not have any real-world experience in that role.

SC: You mentioned earlier that the TAO concept was evolving. By the time you reported to *Parsons* off Vietnam, was there any TAO watch set or is that something that's going to come much later?

PDM: No, there was no TAO watch set. It was CIC watch officer and the bridge. The interface was through that. There was no central point like the TAO that would go right to the captain, and sort of the bridge watch was secondary once you have the TAO. So we were the old-fashioned watch standing variety.

SC: In 1971, *Parsons* deployed again to WestPac [Western Pacific] for a tour of duty in Vietnam. You made the first half of that deployment before detaching. Tell us about your Vietnam experience.

PDM: Well, it wasn't extensive. The biggest thing that we did in the second phase of my time in *Parsons*, I think—hold on. The paper shuffling was me going through a fitness report that came from the commodore that we had embarked in *Parsons*, and he wrote an endorsement of my report from my commanding officer, Jim Kelly, and he described what went on quite well: "As operations officer of my flagship during two months of combat and combat-type operations, that knowledge and imaginations permitted us to successfully carry out several intensive operations in support of our operations in Cambodia. As an intense time, it was real, and we were able to successfully do our supporting role." That phase of the deployment, since I had been over there before just for three months, gave me six months of operations in the theater and it sealed, for me, that I would make this a career.

The support I had from the CO, the commodore, the support of this entire ship meant that I left *Parsons* with a feeling that I had earned a place in the future of our Navy, and I left *Parsons* to go back to Washington and become what they call a Navy detailer of junior officers. I had to augment into the regular Navy to be given this follow-on assignment. And it all worked, and so I left *Parsons* with some regret, because I really enjoyed my time and my responsibilities. And to show that it was a good ship with good operations, the person that relieved me in *Parsons*, Bud Flanagan, became a four-star naval officer also.[28] [*laughs*]

---

[28] Admiral William J. "Bud" Flanagan, Jr. (1943–) graduated from the Massachusetts Maritime Academy in 1964. He served in the U.S. Navy from 1967 to 1996 following three years as a merchant marine officer. His final assignment was as commander in chief, U.S. Atlantic Fleet and NATO commander in chief, Western Atlantic from 1994–96.

SC: A high endorsement. If you had to define the ideal department head, how would you describe that person?

PDM: It's tough in describing an ideal person. I would simply respond by saying, number one, it's a person that is laced with humility, that approaches his job as being a center for support of his commanding officer and the center of knowledge about the department that he is leading, and the leader of his department and divisions that always embodies confidence so that the XO and CO never has to think a moment about what they are being told because they know it is the absolute truth, that they know that is the absolute best that could have been done at that point in time. That's a hard task.

SC: It is. Looking back, were there any particular schools or training that you would now add to the preparation and schooling for a prospective shipboard department head?

PDM: I was thrust into an operational environment that gave me more than any school would have been able to give me. Conversely, if you get thrust into a shipyard environment, where you do nothing but worry about the rehabilitation or reworking of the engineering aspects of the ship, your only way to enhance your knowledge of some brand of fleet operations might be through those schools. Then they would be very helpful.

SC: Since you were the ops officer, the weapons officer and the ops officer have been merged into combat systems officer. What's your perspective on that evolutionary step?

PDM: Even through my CO tour, I operated under the old management style of three department heads, engineering, weapons, and operations and did not have experience with a combat systems officer. I can see why they made that decision, I can see it's perfectly evolutionary to do that with the technology and the weapons systems interfaces, but I personally didn't experience it.

SC: In late 1971, the ship was sent to Yokosuka, Japan, as part of the forward-deployed DESRON 15 or Destroyer Squadron 15. Were you still aboard when the change in home port occurred?

PDM: No, I was not.

SC: Let's turn now to some more personal subjects as we wrap up your years as department head. What were your favorite liberty ports and why, and what were your less favorite and why?

PDM: We had very few liberty ports in my six months, three and [a] half months and six months of deployment. The only liberty port that we visited was the famous Subic Bay, visited there more than once, and we had a brief three days in Hong Kong before we came back, I think. I do not have any recollections about those ports, other than Subic lived up to its reputation that it earned during the Vietnam era, and I'll have comment on that when I came back there at Seventh Fleet. But I don't have any.

SC: Subic Bay, obviously, is very notorious in Navy lore, if you will. Did you, while you pulled in there, have any discipline troubles or troubles with your crew in dealing with Subic Bay?

PDM: No, because the cautions were laid out clearly. I never went into the liberty bastion of Olongapo City. I cannot report any tales of Olongapo. I did not visit it. I played golf, and I remember they had the best caddies in the world because they used their toe to tee up the ball. I remember that clearly. But I did not go into Olongapo. I listened to a lot of stories about Olongapo. But I always tried and always did what I have espoused more times than once during this interview: set the example. My example there was there could be no trouble if you did not even go into Olongapo.

SC: The Officers' Club at Subic Bay is a pretty famous place, particularly among the aviation community. Did you ever have an opportunity to go to the Officers' Club there? And tell us about it.

PDM: Absolutely. I went over there. During that period of time, it was a thriving Officers' Club with all the camaraderie you would expect, all the competitiveness between squadrons that had been conducting combat operations and back there for a few weeks or a few days ashore. They had this catapult thing set up there, I forget what they call it, that you could take a ride on. And it was just a spirited place. Even when I went back as Seventh Fleet, it was not in wartime, but it still kept some of its mysticism and its allure as being one of those famous clubs revered in naval aviation. There were very few like it.

SC: Do you have any particularly memorable or humorous liberty call or significant stories during your years on board *Parsons*?

PDM: No. I think what probably the wardroom had me pegged as was someone who worried about work more than he worried about liberty. I don't say that in any self-aggrandizement way, but that's just simply the way I faced it. I spent most of my time when I was in an in-port status being concerned with what we were going to do next, because I knew that it would hit us fast, hit us hard, and I couldn't make a mistake.

SC: One of the problems that senior officers and especially at the department head and XO level face with junior officers who are typically very young, early twenties, [is that they] sometimes can get in trouble on the beach, particularly with alcohol. Did you ever have any of these type of difficulties on *Parsons*, and, if so, how did you deal with it. If not, how do you think you might have dealt with it?

PDM: To my recollection, I did not have any officers in the department, and I cannot recall any enlisted get[ting] into any trouble. I spent a lot of time counseling, advising before we made our first stop in Subic, because the lore about Subic is famous. The fleet chatter is legendary. So you had ample opportunity to caution everybody so that you didn't face issues because of those cautions. But things happened, but I cannot recall any that were in my lane while we were in Subic.

SC: Is there any advice that you might give to current and future department heads as to how to deal with this situation, other than, as you mentioned, the counseling beforehand?

PDM: Counseling beforehand and then setting the example if you're ashore with them. Between those two things, you've sort of bracketed what can happen. And I did that when we would visit in WestPac. I did that when we would visit Stavanger, Norway, and on the *Luce*. Those two things, making the crew appreciate the environment that they're going to get into and then setting the example, and the outcome, the vast majority of the time, would be good. It's not difficult.

SC: One of the more onerous duties that junior officers are often faced with, certainly not at the department head level typically, but at the division officer level is having to be the shore patrol officer, essentially either manning a liberty launch or being ashore as the sailors come back from liberty, and especially from a place with the reputation as Subic Bay. Looking back, if you had to give any advice to a junior officer faced with going to be the shore patrol officer, and [who] is probably going to have to deal with sailors coming back who might be in trouble from alcohol or something else, what would be your advice to that officer before they headed out for that duty?

PDM: As a junior officer, I never stood an in-port quarterdeck watch or I was never a shore patrol officer, so no real advice on that duty.

SC: You were very fortunate. [*laughs*]

PDM: Never. But being involved in each of these evolutions, even though I wasn't the shore patrol officer, the thing that one has to do is to identify a potential problem early. If someone came back to get on to the liberty boat and wasn't quite right, identify that early and make sure he's buddied up with one or two people that can get him back to his berthing space without a problem. So it's incumbent upon either an officer of the deck if they were coming directly aboard the ship, or at the landing area if they were ashore and had to get on a liberty boat, to make sure that everybody was identified at that point and the problem was resolved then before it could continue on and get worse in a different environment aboard ship.

SC: One of the things as officer of the decks in port may have to face, and some of us have, in foreign ports are incidents where someone tries to come aboard the ship, and it may be completely innocent, they're just curious, and they would like a tour of the ship, or in these days of terrorism, it could be a lot worse. Granted that you never had to stand OOD in port, what would you advise a junior officer who's about to strap on the sidearm and assume the watch as officer of the deck in port in a foreign port, in terms of handling that type of potential situation?

PDM: First, as CO I would make sure that every officer that I signed off as qualified to stand those watches were, in fact, qualified, including with sidearms. They had to be qualified. Given the qualification, then the set of instructions that were approved by the commanding officer—and I took time to approve them in each situation—that if you followed those instructions, that there were very few off-ramps to get himself into trouble. So if he followed them, if he knew what they were and he followed them, if he needed additional help, there was a way to call for additional help, and he knew what his authorities were, he was able to implement the measures that needed to be implemented, to cause without embarrassment someone trying to get on a ship, and, as you suggest, just to take a look around.

And in the other situation, if you had innocent people on the other side of the ship in a small boat that wanted to get too close, even though terrorism was not in full blossom then, you had the instructions to cover that. There's one thing good about the Navy and most military organizations, they've got pretty set proven instructions because of [*sic*] every incident that we've had has a lessons-learned with it. And so you're able to rework to amplify those instructions, and it's not hard to follow instructions. It's just not hard. And that's what you have to expect of those people to do.

SC: You mentioned being qualified with the sidearm. There's a term in the Navy called "fam fire off the fantail." Tell us what means.

PDM: It's more than "fam fire." What it means is familiarization and then actually firing of the weapon. You don't have an extensive armory on board a destroyer-type ship. You have a sufficient amount for the watches that need to be stood, and then you have a few other long rifles that are there, and shotguns for either rioting defense or a milieu of things. But the thing was, is that you had to take seriously that if you were going to put a young petty officer or officer in a watch station with authority, that they had to know how to use that weapon should it be required. Lots of times you couldn't qualify someone at a range to a shore, but you wanted to qualify them so you could have your gunner's mate take the person or the group of people for training, and the obvious place was the fantail, to be able to shoot. And what I would do often was to bring the ship to under way but no way on [movement through the water], put something in the water for them to shoot at, so that you could legitimately sign off their sidearm qualifications. And the term was "fam fire," but that's what it all meant.

SC: One of the defensive mechanisms to prevent someone from boarding is a charged fire hose. Tell us how that operated.

PDM: You always kept a charged fire hose. I was never in an environment to use one. Came close in Australia one time, but didn't have to. It's just simply charging a fire hose, and then it takes the opening of one valve, and you get, I don't know—I forget the pressure, psi, but it's high. It would knock you on your butt if you were hit by it. And it was just one of the nonlethal defense mechanisms that the ship had for adverse situations about boarding the ship.

SC: You mentioned earlier that there were mechanisms in place for the officer of the deck to call for help should there be a situation that required it, particularly on a warship that carried nuclear weapons in those days, as almost all DDGs did, or guided missile cruisers. Tell us about that security team and how that operated.

PDM: There's a team that you could call away, and it was also trained in each watch section. Taken to its endpoint, the security team would then go to the armory, and they were qualified in the shotguns and the other weapons that they had on board, and they would deploy to different points of the ship. Basic security was not a departmental, but a shipboard responsibility because you had people from all departments standing those respective watches, all integrated in the security. So it's something that you need to train on, and you did rely on, and you knew you had to—I go back to it all the time—you needed the confidence in that before you signed off any individual as the qualified officer of the deck with the requisite authorities and responsibilities that he was, in fact, qualified. And you could be anywhere off the ship and you knew that he was going to act in the way that he was trained.

SC: One of the things that always happens anytime a ship is in port and tied up and the full crew is not there, is the watch section, and one of the responsibilities for junior officers is to be a duty department head. What did that mean?

PDM: It totally depended on the material condition at the time. It is different if you were in a restricted availability alongside, where your machinery and engineering capability was cold iron, and then your ops was just about nonexistent because you didn't even have communications. You were in repair availability. Same with weapons. But in any other time but that, the thing that I was concerned with most was fire and flooding, inadvertent flooding. So the officer of the deck, in making sure that the sounding and security patrol reported as he was prescribed to do, and then every once in a while that he would send his messenger of the watch to go out and do the running, I would have them ask the messenger of the watch to go to every place that he should go, because sometimes they would take shortcuts. They're sailors, right? And so you had to have a backup to every situation that might come up, and so you had the informal as well as the formal way to make sure your ship was secure.

SC: What is meant by the term "cold iron"?

PDM: "Cold iron" is a euphemism that there's nothing hot going on on the ship. There's no steam. You're getting your electric power from ashore. Probably you've left cooking arrangements, unless you were really cold iron where the crew went ashore. Cold iron can mean either you have nothing on board that ship that is related to power, or you have modified cold iron, the engineering plant's cold but you still have the capability to run your mess decks.

SC: When the petty officer of the watch in port announces, "Now lay before the mast all 8:00 o'clock reports," what does that mean?

PDM: It means that whether you're ashore or whether you're afloat, that the reporting chain is sequenced to start at the elementary level and go all the way up through each of the departments, that they're reporting that their lane of activity is secure. And then it gets reported to the CDO or, at sea, to the commanding officer that everything is secure.

SC: You were married to your lovely bride, Becky, during those late 1960s years. How did married life change your perspective on your naval services?

PDM: Becky was totally unfamiliar with the United States Navy. The three years that we spent together in ATFs didn't advance very much her knowledge of the United States Navy. When we went to the destroyer, because we had tremendous COs and an exceptional XO that knew how to run a ship with a twenty-five-officer wardroom and do the best they could of making it a unit, a close unit, that involved the wives and families, they did it in an absolutely stellar manner. So that period in that destroyer gave us both a different feeling than we had, of course, in the first three years. And when we talked about my augmenting, it was based on the experience in *Parsons*, not the previous experience. That said, we were going to go forward and see where it took us.

But the first five years, the time I spent at sea was intense. Becky had to support herself the majority of the time, and we did not have any children, and so she was called upon to make her own life, because we were married but it was married with a hell of a lot of absence in those five years. But the experience was such that we thought that we could make it all work if I stayed in the Navy.

SC: *Parsons* was homeported in San Diego when you served aboard. In general, what was family life like for a midgrade naval officer in the early 1970s in San Diego?

PDM: It was fine for the amount of time that we had in San Diego. We lived in a unique place. We had a wonderful apartment in a unique place. We both enjoyed that. But I simply wasn't there that much.

SC: Thank you, Admiral Miller. In our next session, we'll continue to discuss your tour as the operations officer onboard USS *Parsons*. This is UNSI oral history interview with Admiral Paul David Miller, USN (Ret.). This is session number three, question set number six. The date is Saturday, September 30, 2017. The interviewer is Professor Stan Carpenter.
    Thank you, Admiral Miller.

PDM: Thank you.

[End of September 30, 2017, interview]

Interview with Admiral Paul David Miller, USN (Ret.)
Date: October 1, 2017

Stan Carpenter (SC): This is USNI oral history interview with Admiral Paul David Miller, U.S. Navy (Ret.). This is session number four, question set number seven. The date is Sunday, October 1, 2017. The interviewer is Professor Stan Carpenter from the Naval War College. These questions cover your time as the USS *Parsons* operations officer and, more specifically, [focus] on the nature of the Navy in the early 1970s.

Admiral, the early 1970s experienced some changes in the training, qualification, and certification of surface warfare officers, specifically the creation of a SWO, or surface warfare officer, designation, with a distinctive badge as the aviators and submariners had long had. When and why did the surface community finally start receiving their SWO pins?

Admiral Paul David Miller (PDM): I remember clearly when the surface warfare officer pin was instituted. There had long been a desire of surface warfare officers to earn, not to be given, but to earn a similar recognition that aviators and submariners had, so the senior offices of surface warfare put together a program and got it approved through CNO/SecNav [Chief of Naval Operations/Secretary of the Navy] for a surface warfare officer designation.

The first group of people to receive this pin were those that had already served in destroyers and did not have to go through a regimen that they had established in D.C. I recall that I was—I think I was in *Parsons* then. I'd left there with a surface warfare officer pin, but with the experience that I had gained there, when you looked at the criteria that had to be met to be designated a SWO, as they called it, S-W-O, most department heads that had sailed on deployments to the South China Sea had certainly met all the requirements. So the designation was given. But over the years, I think the qualifications became clearer, their requirements were set, and officers had to meet each of the requirements and be designated by their commanding officer and higher authority as a surface warfare officer. I believe it sort of boosted SWO officer morale, and it clearly put them on par with their brethren in aviation and in the submarine community. It didn't have the history of those designations, but they were proud to start a designation in the community, and I think it has served the community very well.

SC: The Navy uses a qualification program called PQS, or Personnel Qualification Standards, system.[29] What did the PQS system look like in the early 1970s?

---

[29] The Navy's Personnel Qualification Standards or PQS program is a system of basic training performance objectives (TPO) designed to establish the minimum competency level required for a member to perform successfully in their grade, rank, billet, or position. It involves actions or examinations to demonstrate that the member has mastered the requirements or can perform the function.

PDM: Ragged. PQS, it was, as you suggest, a set of standards for qualifications in different arenas. As a division officer or as a department head, you pursued that as part of your responsibility to get as many people signed off in the PQS realm as possible. Over time, it gained more discipline, it gained more rigor, and it gained a greater degree of institutionalization—a good program, and I think the surface Navy profited from it.

SC: In the Navy, routine maintenance of equipment, gear, and systems relies on the planned maintenance system, or PMS. What, in general, is the PMS system, and how did it operate in the early 1970s?

PDM: Another program that was needed, but as with most programs, when it is initially put into process, it overreaches. By that I mean each unit of equipment that you wanted to conduct PMS on, a planned maintenance system, the cards, the requirements were written by a shore establishment and probably a contractor. I don't know. But they were rigorous, the periodicity was often questioned by fleet sailors, but, on balance, it was an outstanding program because the fleet sailor probably would not work on a piece of equipment until it had to be worked on, but the system had data that showed that if you change the bearings of this pump with this periodicity, the life of the pump would be extended by x.

So it was a thoughtful program, it was a good program, but it took careful leadership on behalf of senior or leading petty officers, chief petty officers, and division officers to make sure that the checks were done and the checks were done properly. It even required department heads and XO and CO to show interest in the program, to show that it was important for the ship's material well-being, and I believe the program served the Navy very well.

SC: We've already discussed in general your service in Vietnam aboard the *Parsons*, but let's now bore in a bit on the specifics of how an early 1970s destroyer operated. Naval gunfire support, or NGFS, now known simply as naval fire missions, was a major task of the destroyers. What was the purpose of these NGFS missions?

PDM: The naval gunfire support was generally divided into two areas I believe I mentioned earlier: direct fire, indirect fire. There was a liaison that was required with the unit you were supporting, and that gave birth to an acronym called NGLO, and that was a naval gunfire liaison officer. He would go to a school, and sometimes he would even join a unit ashore to be able to communicate with the ship, not always, but they had a direct link between the units you were supporting and the naval gunfire liaison officer and the ship, particularly for direct fire. Indirect fire was where you were given an area in which you could free fire, and I think the label put on it was harassment and interdiction [H&I] fire. So, those are two elements of gunfire support.

The ships that received the majority of that tasking were those ships that had two 5"/38 mounts, and they were able to put a lot of shells ashore. The largest ship that we had in the arsenal was *New Jersey* (BB-62), and it was called on to fire some ultra-long-range NGFS.

SC: Tell us about the procedures that a ship would follow during such a mission. In other words, once the ship received a call for fire from the beach or some other entity, what was the flow of events?

PDM: The flow would go—you would set the naval gunfire support team, you had fire control, you had folks in combat, you had folks in the mount that were all linked together, and the captain had to give batteries release, unless you were on an interdiction H&I mission, and sometimes the captain, because of time of day, because of lots of other reasons, would permit the officer of the deck to do that. But you trained at it. It was a careful flow where target was designated, where the naval gunfire support solution was made in combat, and fire control officer, they were linked. The battery was slewed to the right degree angle, and the equation was solved for the amount of powder, what the humidity was, and all those factors that went in to get the range that you needed. And each ship, before it went to the South China Sea, had to qualify in a rigorous naval gunfire support regimen and receive qualifications before they were able to go on line, the gun line, they called it.

SC: Let's talk a little bit more about the NGLO in naval fires, or NGFS. Who were these people and how did they basically operate?

PDM: Sometimes they were shipboard and other times they were good naval officers operating with the Marines or the Army units. They were instrumental because they understood what was happening aboard ship. Unlike an artillery battery that the Marines and Army were used to, this was something coming from often over the horizon for the people ashore, and there needed to be a careful liaison between who was shooting and where the fall of shot would go. So the naval gunfire liaison officer, in coordination with the battalion, whether it was the battalion or whether it was a company that were being supported, the liaison there was terribly important. They would actually spot the fall of shot and relay back to the ship that they needed to go right fifty or up fifty or down fifty, and particularly in defilade fire, which was the most difficult aspect of gunfire support. The NGLO played a key role in accuracy of fire.

SC: In Vietnam, the Army used a lot of airborne spotting for artillery. Were there procedures to use an airborne other-service spotter in NGFS or was it all strictly the NGLOs?

PDM: There may have been, but I personally was not involved in that, so I can't lay out the methods and the way that worked.

SC: When a destroyer would go on the gun line, I understand that *Parsons* didn't simply because she had the one turret, and if you suffered a casualty, you'd be basically nonfunctional in terms of NGFS, but for a typical destroyer that had multiple mounts, tell us about what the gun line duty was all about, how long it lasted, what type of fire missions one would get, and basically anything you can tell us about being on the gun line.

PDM: A battle group at that time would have three or four destroyers attached to it, and they would be available for various missions. The carrier would always keep one destroyer close by, usually for plane guard duty; that is, following the ship very closely, should they have a cold cat [catapult launch] or should they have a requirement for a pilot to eject on landing.[30] You'd have the capability there to pick them up right away. Then the other ships, since we had no submarine threat, the other ships were assigned to support other activities. Some were assigned to support the interdiction of supplies up and down the coast, and one might get gun line duty. The duty was periods of days or hours, and the requirement was to be in a zone or an operating box to be able to go up and down at the captain's wishes and to be ready to receive a call for fire, just as the definition designates.

The crews were buoyed by receiving that duty because they thought they were making a direct contribution to the combat that was going on, and they would shoot probably a little bit more than was needed in H&I missions, and they would only shoot as designated for direct fire. Then they would leave the gun line, be replaced by somebody or not be replaced, and then they would go rearm, because you needed to maintain a full magazine at all times. The destroyers in the group would rotate through those stations while the carrier was launching planes day and night. The tempo of ops was rigorous.

SC: You mentioned earlier that *New Jersey* (BB-62) spent some time off Vietnam providing NGFS. This was still the day when there were several big gun cruisers left over from [the] World War II period operating. Did they ever get tasked with going on the gun line, or was that strictly a destroyer function as well as the *New Jersey*?

PDM: I know the *New Jersey* by reputation and because I know well the CO of the *New Jersey* that was there. He's a retired two-star now. I did not know of any heavy cruisers that were involved. I'm sure there were. Vietnam went on a long time, thankfully not as long as this operation that's going on in Afghanistan, but it went on for, what, six or seven years. So there were many activities, many ships that participated, and I'm not familiar with every brand of ship that was tasked with Vietnam ops.

---

[30] A "cold cat" means that the catapult system has not been warmed and pressurized adequately for a successful launch based on the weight of the aircraft. It can result in insufficient speed and lift for a successful launch, resulting in the aircraft falling into the ocean.

SC: In the gun mounts on those destroyers, which was still largely World War II–era technology, you mentioned the 5"/38s, which were the standard. What kind of range were you looking at for those guns? In other words, how far inland could you provide actual gunfire support?

PDM: We had a 5"/54 in *Parsons*, and we were comfortable shooting at twelve miles. The 38s, eight, ten miles. The closer you could get, the more accurate you would be. The gunfire support equation that you had to solve, of course, would get a little bit more ragged with the more distance that you added to it, and so what the book said and what happened in reality is always a little bit different, and that's the way it was with those that were on the gun line. Also, one's an automatic system and one is a hand-loaded system.

SC: How fast could you lay out rounds?

PDM: Five-inch/54s were very rapid-fire because the loader would be down on the third deck, and then it would go mechanically up to the breech into the mount and boom! So it was as fast as the mechanical system could move those shells, they would go out. On a 5"/38, the shells had to be placed into the breech by the gunner's mates.

SC: Was there any difference in the number of crewmen required between a 54 and a 38?

PDM: Yes, there were more in the 38, but the 5"/54 system was a bit more temperamental as you can imagine, all the interlocks and movements that it had to go through to get that shell into the breech. An interlock failure had to be fixed before the gun could fire again.

SC: One of the technological advances in recent years has been a complete[ly] automated loading and fire system, where there are no gunner's mates in the actual turret. Had that technology come into the fleet in the early 1970s, or were we still operating with the manual?

PDM: You didn't have to have men in the turret for the 5"/54. It was an automatic weapon system. Five-inch/38s, you definitely had to have them, and, of course, the 16," you did too.

SC: Were there any specific duties that the operations officer would have during a naval gunfire support mission?

PDM: It depends if you were at GQ. I was a GQ OOD on the *Parsons*, and other ships probably had an operations officer, but those that were on the gun line for large periods of time, the operations officer would do what operations officers do.[31] They never worried about what the ship was doing then; they had to worry about what the ship was going to do next and being able to have a seamless set of activities. So everybody participated in an evolution like gunfire support because everybody in the ship knew exactly what was going on. Every time you fired one of those things on a destroyer, you knew that there was activity, that activity was part of a real operation, and so everybody was paying just that little bit more attention to what they did during those type of operations.

SC: What type of targets would be typical in Vietnam for an NGFS?

PDM: The gunfire support targets for direct fire was the enemy, because they would not call for a direct fire unless there were troops that needed some kind of support. If air cover wasn't there, if they didn't have a gunship or they didn't have an aircraft to support them, naval gunfire could put shot down to support troops directly.

The H&I fires, I do not know where that term came from, I do not know who decided that that would be a good thing to do, but there were areas that were designated so ostensibly you would not have collateral damage if you shot in that area, but any

---

[31] The officer of the deck, or OOD, is the captain's representative on the bridge, who is responsible for all ship movements, safety, navigation, routines, etc. when the captain does not take direct control. The OOD may or may not "have the conn" (orders and controls actual ship movements). OODs are typically very experienced in ship handling and tactical maneuvers and are generally senior division officer LTJGs or LT (lieutenant/O-3) department heads.

enemy troops that were on movement could definitely be harassed and might have been interdicted by that kind of fire.

SC: One of the missions of the fast-attack submarines in Vietnam was to support Special Operations ashore, to launch the SEAL teams and recover them.[32] Was this ever a role for the destroyers in Vietnam?

PDM: Not to my knowledge, but I'm sure there was, and a lot of them were inserted by the swift boat, which certainly had more maneuverability, was able to get into places that larger ships couldn't get into, so the Special Ops forces played a key role. Support came from different vessels, and it ranged from helicopters to small ships, larger ships. They had LSM(R)s, I remember, which was a ship that was loaded with close-in fire support capabilities.[33] So there was a whole range of support activities for Special Ops. I recall in *Parsons* that's what we were supporting when I mentioned Cambodia before.

SC: One of the missions of destroyers traditionally has been in the twentieth century rescuing downed airmen, and one of the things, if you were an airman over Vietnam and you took fire and you had a casualty, you tried to make it back out to "feet wet," or over the ocean, as opposed to bailing out over the land and possibly becoming a POW [Prisoner of War]. In general, how did the rescue of downed airmen work, and did *Parsons* ever pick up any downed airmen?

PDM: The scenario that you talked about was first worked from behind the aircraft carrier. There were more downed airmen or as many downed airmen off the carrier as there were shot down and parachuted at sea. You kept a lifeboat at the rail, they called it, which the ship could put it into the water easily. You kept the communication lines open, the Mayday communications [aircraft in distress] lines open, so that you could hear, just

---

[32] The SEALs are the Navy's Sea, Air, and Land Teams and are the U.S. Navy's primary special operations force. The SEAL Teams are a component of the Naval Special Warfare Command.

[33] Landing Ship Medium (Rocket) are a class of ships that originated in World War II that can add fire support capability to forces on the beach.

as the carrier could hear, what was happening and if someone needed help. So when you were operating with a carrier in those waters, you were always prepared to support any downed airmen.

SC: Did *Parsons* ever pick up any downed airmen while on plane guard duty?

PDM: We did not. There was one opportunity while we were on station, but the carrier, if they have the helicopters onboard, they usually put what they call an "angel" up, and the angel plucked that pilot out of the water within seconds.

SC: I remember an incident where we were in plane guard to the *John F. Kennedy* (CV-67), and a plane exploded on deck while trying to land, and all we ever recovered was the flight helmet of the pilot. So it's a dangerous duty.

PDM: Dangerous work.

SC: Let's talk a little bit about destroyers and aviation. At that point did destroyers start becoming configured to handle helicopters?

PDM: Oh, you're testing memory. It started with the system, I believe, called DASH, which was sort of—I would put it in the realm of a drone now.[34] It was a capability where you had a small platform on the destroyer and you could extend your weapons capability because you could drop a torpedo from DASH, and the search capability, visual search and others, it started with that. The first LAMPS helicopter on board a destroyer, I don't know, but I know that in *McCloy*, which was then just three years later, both helicopter operations from a ship and HIFR, helicopter in-flight refueling, was done routinely so that particularly in ASW operations, a helicopter could stay in flight for a

---

[34] The Gyrodyne QH-50 DASH or Drone Anti-Submarine Helicopter was the first rotary-wing unmanned aerial vehicle to enter Navy service and expanded the reach of an ASW ship for detection and weapons delivery. First fielded in the early 1960s, it was soon replaced by manned helicopters and deemed highly unreliable. Once the DASH launched, it was often never seen again.

longer duration before he had to return to the carrier or the mother ship.[35] So it was in that period there that helicopters became prolific off of small ships.

SC: Did *Parsons* have any sort of flight capability?

PDM: We did not.

SC: Today, if you're going to do a transfer of personnel from ship to ship, it's almost always by helicopter, but back in those days, there was a thing called highline. Tell us about highline and if you remember any interesting stories about this particular evolution.

PDM: No interesting stories, but I have highlined two or three times. That is just simply setting up rigging between two ships and putting a chair, dangling a chair down from one of the set of riggings. You jump in it and you get pulleyed across to the other ship. The key thing there was the delivering ship would have to come in as close as reasonable so that the individual, particularly in rough seas, would be able to get across in a very short period of time and, the good Lord forbid, never be dunked into the ocean.

I've been delivered by helicopter tens of times, and that's always an exciting maneuver with the helicopter hovering over the deck of a pitching ship, and you get lowered. You can generate some static electricity. They take care of that first and then try and get [you] out of your harness. Those are all evolutions that are taken for granted, but each one of them can go south very quickly.

SC: It was always fun to dunk the chaplain when he was coming across by highline.

PDM: [laughs] Never dunked anybody.

---

[35] The Light Airborne Multi-Purpose System (LAMPS) is a shipborne helicopter primarily designed for antisubmarine warfare. It can carry detection gear as well as an ASW torpedo, thus giving significant standoff detection and attack capability.

SC: You mentioned the static electricity, and this is getting a little bit beyond our period here, but as long as you brought it up, let me ask this. What is a "dead man's stick" and what's the purpose?

PDM: It's basically a metal hook that you hook around, if you're dropping somebody on deck, you lower the line and you hook this stick around it, and it's attached to the ship, so it allows any static electricity to run down and be grounded on the ship.

SC: It's a safety function, and I suspect that they found out in some of the early flight operations that they killed people with the static electricity. Basically you ground it and suck that electricity out, ground it into the ship. As a more senior officer and department head aboard *Parsons*, what watches did you stand, other than officer of the deck, if any?

PDM: I stood officer of the deck watches and that was all. I was probably the more senior watch officer the second portion, the second time we deployed to the South China Sea, and I took over the responsibilities of the senior watch officer, which was setting the watch, who was going to stand what, when, etc. The engineer was the senior watch officer in seniority, but we took him off the watch list because being the chief engineer of a 1,200-pound plant of one of those destroyers was more than a full-time job. We let him tend to keeping us going and keeping the electricity flowing throughout the ship.

So I took over senior watch officer, and we were in mostly in one-in-three sections while we were deployed, because the second skipper I had was not very generous with OOD qualifications. He was pretty tight. So we stood lots of watches, but it all worked well. We had outstanding young officers on that ship. We were very lucky.

SC: Let's talk a bit about the organization on the bridge of a destroyer, which has changed a quite a bit with automation and technology, but back in the seventies and eighties, what was the typical bridge watch and what were the functions of each of the watch standers?

PDM: There were too many people. I realized that the first time I walked onto a destroyer bridge. I had been used to standing watches on my ATF with two people, and on this destroyer there were helmsmen, lee helmsmen, quartermaster, quartermaster's helper, JOOD [junior officer of the deck in training to become a qualified OOD], signalmen. There were lots of people on board that bridge. I remarked then that if I ever got senior enough, that I was going to look at this issue, because I felt it was a misuse of valuable manpower, particularly when you were in transit operations, that you certainly didn't need that many people, and I will have a good illustration later on, on what I did about it.

SC: Some other watch functions while the ship is under way are the lookouts, the forward, aft, and others. Tell us about what their function was in the bridge watch.

PDM: To do just as the name implies: look out and report what they see. Lookouts were terribly important in inclement weather. Lookouts did little to support a ship steaming, particularly in transit in open ocean. When I became CO, I did not have lookouts when we did not need them, because I always looked out for individuals being utilized in something that the individual knew was a useless activity. Standing with a headset on the stern of a ship transiting in bright sunlight doesn't have a lot of utility. So in situations where you begin to get low visibility, they're terribly important. At nighttime, some people said that they were essential. I didn't think so. When we get to *McCloy*, I limited my numbers of people on the bridge. I tried to use manpower efficiently.

    The surface Navy had a hard time changing the way they did things, and the numbers of people on board a bridge, the numbers of lookout stations, the numbers in all watch stations were very, very rich, and that's what made crews of destroyers come out to be very high numbers, because the captains had the people, he used the people, and I don't think over time they were used efficiently. Now we've probably gone too far with the USS *Zumwalt* (DDG-1000) in having less than a hundred people.[36]

---

[36] The *Zumwalt* class, a new generation of destroyers named for Admiral Elmo Zumwalt, is designed for maximum multiroles and stealth. The USS *Zumwalt* (DDG-1000) was commissioned in 2016.

SC: On the bridge, you've already mentioned officer of the deck and junior officer of the deck. What is that, and what's the function of the junior officer of the deck?

PDM: To be trained, and he is usually given the conn [gives speed and rudder orders to the helmsman and controls all ship movement]. The OOD usually passes the conn to the junior officer of the deck so that he can learn his responsibilities about making sure the ship is headed in the proper direction, check the navigation, check the contacts that he might have to make sure there's no problems in having an untoward incident. Just learning the operations of the ship from the junior officer of the deck vantage point was very helpful and gave the opportunity for a captain spending time on the bridge to watch the junior officer, watch his initiative, see how much interest he took in other things than just what was designated in driving the ship. And observations by the CO and the officer of the deck either led to pretty quick designation as OOD or for some it took longer.

SC: Let's look at some of the enlisted bridge watchstanders. What about the quartermaster of the watch? What was his function?

PDM: His function was to keep the chart updated of where the ship is at all times. We didn't have satellite navigation then, so you had electronic, you had LORAN, and you still had celestial, but I think that was the beginning of rudimentary satellite navigation [SatNav]. Carriers had it, so when you were with a carrier, you always knew where you were exactly. I can't recall SatNav being on *Parsons* when I was on it. It may have, but I can't recall.

SC: What about the boatswain's mate of the watch? What was his function?

PDM: To uphold the heraldry of a boatswain mate at sea on a ship with his boatswain mate's whistle to signal to the crew what time reveille, what time chow was, knock off ship's work. All those evolutions were accompanied by a whistle blown into the 1MC [general announcing system] so the ship's crew would know what was going on.[37] Was it necessary? Absolutely not. Was it in keeping with the fine traditions of U.S. naval service? Yes, it was.

SC: At one point in the twentieth century, ships would use a bugler in addition to the boatswain's pipe. Did you ever have an experience with any buglers onboard?

SC: No bugles on any ship I ever served on.

SC: Let's turn now to the helmsman. What was the helmsman's duty?

PDM: The helmsman duty was very simple: to keep the ship on the course designated by the officer of the deck.

SC: And what about the lee helmsman?

PDM: Another person on the bridge that I question its utility, but he was stationed behind what they call an engine order telegraph [EOT used to send speed orders to the engineering main control below decks], and when the officer of the deck called for the engines to be moved to all ahead standard, ring up turns for fifteen knots, the lee helmsman said, "Aye, aye, sir." Then he would move the dials to all ahead standard and move the turns to 115 turns, or whatever to make fifteen knots.[38]

SC: There's a peculiar Navy term for a piece of gear called the "bitch box." Tell us what the "bitch box" was or still is.

---

[37] The 1MC or 1 main circuit is a one-way announcing system originating on the bridge that transmits general information and orders to all internal ship spaces and topside areas. It is used to put out general information to the ship's crew and for transmitting alarms ship wide—general, chemical, collision, and flight deck crash.
[38] Turns are the number of times the propeller shaft completely rotates in one minute or revolutions per minute (RPM). RPM determines the speed through the water.

PDM: It's internal communications and it has the functionality of having a bunch of buttons and you press them for whomever you wanted to talk to, the CIC, the captain, whatever, and then you press the button and you would dialogue. It became a "bitch box" affectionately because people used it to bitch about something all the time. "Fix this, fix that, do this, do that."

SC: There's an older technique for communications between the bridge and other parts of the ship, basically a brass voice tube. [*Miller laughs.*] Did you ever have any experience with those?

PDM: No, we just had to keep them polished.

SC: What about sound-powered phones? A lot of people are intrigued by how one can communicate without any electrical power. Tell us about sound-powered phones.

PDM: Sound-powered phones is just a mechanism to communicate from rather long ranges on board the ship, with this unit that you strung around your neck, particularly for damage control evolutions. They were the predecessor of what would be like the walkie-talkies, the portable communications gear which is what's in use today, separate channels, and much more efficient, more effective. But sound-powered phones were in our Navy for a long time.

SC: And the idea here is the vibrations from the voice actually create an electrical current that then travels to wherever. So if you were to lose complete power or, as we say, drop the load, then you can still communicate throughout the ship.

PDM: Well, you can still communicate with your portable gear, too, because the batteries were still there. I mean, that's the way they did it then. Now, the way we've done it for the last thirty years now has not been with sound-powered phones, it's been with portable communications.

SC: What about the signal bridge, the signal watch? What was that typically like on a destroyer in the seventies?

PDM: We still paid some degree of attention to signal flags because we operated close enough to other ships to be able to use that as a form of communications with the flag, and then you have your HO 102, your signal book, to break what they were saying.[39] All these were vestiges of probably World War II and before, when you would operate in radio silence. You still wanted to be able to communicate. A signalman had what he called a flag bag, a flag for each letter in the alphabet and a series of pennants and other flags that had different designations. You could go into a publication to read what that ship was telling you, or a commodore would use them to give orders to ships to change formation. They were good to practice, they were good for remembering what went before you, but they serve little utility in the modern Navy.

SC: And that leads me to a term EMCON [emissions control] in communications.[40] What did EMCON mean?

PDM: It means do not use communications that you did not want to emit something that could be picked up by someone listening. This was particularly important during the Cold War, because ships' positions could be given away very, very easily with electronic emissions. So there were times in later experience, particularly on *Luce*, where we would operate in the North Atlantic totally in EMCON, where the carrier group would try to stay undetected by the then-Soviets.

---

[39] HO 102 or Pub. 102 is the *International Code of Signals* that originated in the mid-nineteenth century as a way for ships to communicate despite language differences. Signal flags are the most common transmission medium, but flashing light and radio transmissions are also used.

[40] EMCON or emissions control is essentially "radio silence." There are various degrees of EMCON, from partial to total, depending on the tactical situation. Transmissions in the electronic spectrum are restricted or selectively prohibited depending on the EMCON condition to prevent detection by an adversary.

SC: There's a particular formation, a circular-type formation that evolved during World War II around a carrier, where a sector screen is assigned to ships. Tell us about some of the dynamics of maintaining station in a sector screen on an aircraft carrier.

PDM: I haven't heard that term in so long.

SC: This is why we do these oral history interviews, sir.

PDM: That was probably one of the more difficult maneuvering board [known as mo board] questions in destroyer school, in which you were given Sector 2 or whatever, and you were to switch stations with the destroyer in Sector 4, and you were all proceeding on a course, a designated course [base course] at a designated speed, and you had to figure out the course and speed that you needed to take to wind up in your new station without causing any consternation to the overall force, because all these ships were moving at one time. The maneuvering board would help figure out your relative-motion answer.

And it was used in practice, but never, even when I was in the North Atlantic, never for real, because during that period of time, we were moving away from the old-fashioned close-in direct support of carriers to sort of a distributed battle group because you had better sensors, you had helicopter support, you had fixed-wing support, you had underwater support in SOSUS, and then you tried to fuse all the information. But the times that sector screens became used prolifically was particularly during World War II, when the submarine detection capabilities were limited and you had to put a tight ring around your high-value units to protect them. But whenever we exercised with sector screens, it was always a hoot, especially at nighttime. The captain, all you had to do is tell him, "We've got to change station," and there was nothing that brought the captain to the bridge faster than that.

SC: Or the carrier, you're right in the middle of your sector, and the old man comes out, takes—

PDM: Flight ops.

SC: Flight ops, and says, "Well done, sir." And then heads off to his sea cabin, and next thing you know, the carrier's decided to change course and crank it up to thirty knots. Captain comes out and you're six thousand yards out of sector and in trouble. It happens to every OOD.

PDM: When you hear "Foxtrot Corpen" over the air net, you knew that you were in for some kind of maneuvering fun.

SC: Indeed. Tell us about FleetTac [Fleet Tactical] radio circuit. What was that all about?

PDM: The Navy, particularly in tactical operations, had many circuits that you had to monitor. Usually the tactical net that you had was only used by the ships that were under the operational command of the task unit you were sailing with, and most of the tactical signals came over that net.

Then a secure phone capability was put onboard ships. On *Parsons*, we had two. We had one in combat and one on the bridge. Because of security, the nets onboard a destroyer became confused. By that I mean while you had nets designated for separate tasks, people being people, when they wanted to really talk about something important and you wanted to make sure that the other unit understood it, you'd just get on the phone, the red phone, and talk in plain language, because you didn't have to worry about it. So primarily they never taught you this in Destroyer School, but that red phone was sort of a crutch for leadership, because while they could use all the tactical nets, so often that phone would ring and the confirmation of your signals of what you were supposed to do came over the secure phone. I always listened for that phone first, because I knew it was priority information coming over there, and what was coming over the fleet tactical net was routine.

SC: You mentioned SOSUS. That was a closely guarded but well-known secret back then. What were the SOSUS stations, or the SOSUS system? What was that all about?

PDM: I know too much about SOSUS. I don't know if I mentioned it in *Papago* or not—I should have—but *Papago* was assigned, along with the cable layer *Thor* (ARC-4) to lay our first SOSUS station far into the North Atlantic. We tied it into a SOSUS station north of Iceland, and then it went from land to a first SOSUS unit in Keflavik [Iceland]. These were towed arrays placed on the bottom of the ocean, microphones, that could hear sound, could absorb the sound, everything. *Thor* put a string of those on the ocean's bottom.

Much undersea charting had gone on before *Thor* was sent to do this mission. A special DECCA, which was a British high-def [high definition] navigation system, was set up on *Thor* so that it knew precisely where those phones were going to be laid. And what *Papago* did is we had a tow line hooked up to *Thor* so that she would be able to stay on a very precise track. We did that for days and days and days, because she would lay the cable at two to three knots. But that was the only time I ever received a top-secret message on a fleet tug. It was the whole OPORDER [operations order]. We did not sail with *Thor*. We sailed independently and rendezvoused with her north of Iceland.

SC: Let's turn now to—

PDM: You didn't think you were going to get a whole lesson on SOSUS, did you? [*laughs*]

SC: That's why I asked the question. Let's turn now to Combat Information Center, or CIC. This is a concept that also evolved out of World War II, primarily to track incoming aircraft raids and designate ships to provide anti-air warfare protection. But by the 1970s, this had evolved quite a bit. Tell us about CIC [Combat Information Center], what its roles were and essentially how it operated on a destroyer in the early 1970s.

PDM: Totally depend[s] on the brand of ops you were in. If you were with a task force, particularly in the South China Sea, the CIC area was a bustling place to be, because it was monitoring the air nets. It was always ready for the NGFS nets because to plot for gunfire support, you manned ASW stations, but you weren't concerned that that was going to be a threat. You had your air search radars and the consoles manned because on *Parsons* we had a capable air search radar, and you kept track of the aircraft in the vicinity as backup to whatever the carrier was doing.

So you were charged with knowing what was in your surface space, in your air space for the whole area that the task group operated in, and its job was to share necessary information with the officer of the deck. The officer of the deck, conversely, shared with combat his picture of what he was [seeing] while engaged in driving the ship. The pace of activity was quick, the requirements of every watch stander were thorough, and it was a satisfying professional time to operate under those circumstances for someone who was in a combatant in the early seventies.

SC: What was the DRT, or the dead reckoning tracer, and what was its function?

PDM: Its function was to do what the name implied: it traced the movement of the ship. It was attached to the pit sword, which was able to determine the speed at which the ship was going. It had gyro inputs, and so you could trace on this dead reckoning DRT a solid input that was your ship. Then radarmen [radarman rate] could mark on this chart other sets of activities so you had another picture of what was going on.[41]

SC: In CIC, there are always a number of what are called vertical plots. What was this and what was its function?

PDM: Vertical plots were exactly that. They were vertical screens. This was before we had flat screens, where we could display things electronically. We had radarmen and other CIC personnel behind the screens. They would take the information given to them by someone on a radar, about where an aircraft might be. You had a surface plot where the surface ships were, and so manually you kept a full tactical picture. As you walked into combat, you could see this straight away. All that has been changed by our flat panels and everything being fused automatically, replacing the individuals doing it. Now they just appear as different symbols on board a screen, much more efficiently, much

---

[41] The radarman (RD) rating was disestablished in 1971 and broken into and replaced by operations specialist (OS), electronic warfare technician (EW), and electronics technician (ET).

more effectively. But that was what we did, that's what we had, so you trained at it, you used it, and it was an important source of information for the CIC watch officer and for the XO or CO when they walked into combat.

SC: One of the technological developments about this time was the NTDS, or the Navy Tactical Data System. Had that come into play when you were on *Parsons*?

PDM: Yes, but we weren't an NTDS ship. We'll get to that in *Luce* because that was an NTDS ship. I would just simply say night-day. The old-fashioned CIC was night. If you had NTDS, it was day, because you had so much more capability, so much more reach, so much more fusion, that the picture that you saw was really enlightened compared to what you had in the older capability, but the older capability was sufficient because you did not know you could reach into the future of NTDS. So it all evolved.

SC: And we'll discuss that in a little more depth when we get to USS *Luce*. What about radars? What type of radars did you have on board *Parsons*?

PDM: We had the surface search radar, two air search radars. That's all we had in our radars. The air search radar was a Mk-29.[42] It was a long-range air search radar. The thing that I had to pay attention to and make sure that I had more than my allotment of spares going on my second deployment to South China Sea was CRTs [cathode ray tube], because they would constantly blow the cathode ray tube on those things, and you were allowed one spare or whatever, so you had to make sure that you used your ability to have more than one. But they were just fleet radars, the SPS surface radar. SPS-25 [surface search radar]?

SC: Yes.

PDM: Gosh, it's amazing I remember that designation. That's a long time ago. It was SPS-25?

---

[42] AN/SPS-29 air search radar.

SC: It was. What about Damage Control Central [DCC]? What was that and what's that all about?

PDM: I mentioned Damage Control Central before. It is that responsibility on the ship to make sure that they are ready should the ship have fires, flooding, or any other untoward activity that needed to be resolved quickly. They were the fire brigade on board ship. I had high regard for damage control folks. The damage control assistant [DCA] had a tough job. He had to train constantly, because unless you've been in a fire aboard ship, you don't know how bad that is. I was in a bad fire aboard ship on board *Papago*, and it was frightening in the North Atlantic. I had high regard for supporting the DCA when I was the operations officer in *Parsons*, and even higher regard when I was CO of *Luce* to make sure that that capability was second to none before we went to sea.

SC: What was the intent behind multiple damage control lockers?

PDM: The larger the ship, the more you needed to have your equipment. On different frames of the ship because—I'm getting too deep here—because the ship's damage control plates [diagrams of spaces] and the damage control illustrations were set into how many frames a ship had, and then after so many frames there's a whole set of damage control gear, where the fire stations were. In the engine rooms, you had a separate capability called Halon, in which you could suppress the fire all at one time.[43]

Damage control aboard ship is probably one of the most thought-through things that we have on board ship, because everybody recognizes that at sea, when you're away from everything, you can rely on only yourself and your resources of these trained folks that have been through not just two days of Firefighting School or not two days or one day of Underwater Damage Control School, but have been there for weeks and knew how to practice their art. Then they were responsible aboard ship to train the designated party for repair locker one, repair locker two, repair locker three. All of them had different functions. They were working together separately when they needed to and in unison

---

[43] Halon is a liquefied, compressed gas that stops the spread of fire by chemically disrupting combustion.

when required. Damage control is an art and a practice that receives great attention, and any skipper who didn't pay attention to that almost daily was remiss should something happen.

SC: One of the great advantages the U.S. Navy had over the Imperial Japanese Navy in World War II was our damage control procedures were far more robust and developed. What is an OBA, and did you have those on board *Parsons*, or was that a later innovation?[44]

PDM: We had them. I used one for real. Oxygen-breathing apparatus is a hood thing with a canister in front, and you're able to open it up and you have your oxygen inside your closed habitat. If a space fills up with smoke, you couldn't operate without them.

SC: Tell us about some of the basic firefighting gear that would have been used in the 1970s.

PDM: They made advances for engine-room fires with this thing called the Halon system. They probably call it something different now because they probably have a better chemical for it. But that was terribly important. The rest of the fire capability was, of course, in hoses. You had to be able to treat the movement of fire, should you have one in one compartment, to be able to know not to open up a hatch and be blown away by flames because the fire would be wanting new oxygen and get sucked right towards it. So it was just the regular fire equipment that you fight fires with every other place.
The hoses and the nozzles were particularly novel. They had lots of capability. They could spray hard, they could spray wide areas, so the valves were unique to large fire hoses. I don't know what else to add. It's just important stuff.

---

[44] The Oxygen Breathing Apparatus, or OBA, is a self-contained emergency breathing device that produces oxygen from a chemical reaction in a canister connected to an airtight facemask. It allows firefighters to enter an oxygen-deficient or smoke-filled space.

SC: There's a fire retardant or suppressant called AFFF.[45] Did you have that?

PDM: AFFF is foam that is emitted like a sprinkler system that puts a foam barrier and it smothers the fire that way. I never had to use it, but I heard fleet stories that if you ever used that stuff, it was so hard to clean up. People didn't use it till the last second, because if they could take care of the fire before it got to requiring AFFF, they would.

SC: It's also very corrosive, and a lot of people don't know, but the root ingredient is actually made from bird guano.

PDM: I never read the recipe card for AFFF.

SC: We've covered several areas aboard ship. Are there any that you think might be important to describe how operations worked on a 1970s destroyer?

PDM: No, other than refueling. When you're in a task force group operations and you're moving that ship around, you use more fuel than you think you would, and the requirement was always to stay at 70 percent fuel because you did not know when you would be sent off on a task that you didn't have support. So the fueling detail, the fueling-at-sea equipment you had to make sure worked 100 percent all the time. Your detail, whether it refueled in detail or at nighttime, was a dangerous evolution, and it required a good ship handler and it required him to talk with the people that were receiving the fuel and talking with the delivering ship to make it all work in unison. I paid a lot of attention to refueling at sea.

SC: We've already discussed a little bit about navigation, and it's certainly changed over the years. Today, mariners largely rely upon satellite-based navigation, which was just

---

[45] AFFF or Aqueous Film Forming Foam is a fire suppressant agent that attacks flammable liquid pool fires. At a 3 or 6 percent solution, it is mixed with seawater to form a foam that is sprayed on liquid-fueled fires (such as fuel oil, gasoline, petroleum lubricants, etc.) and thus smothers the fire.

coming into practice in the 1960s and seventies. Tell us a little bit more about navigation in those days?

PDM: Stan, we went over navigation earlier, particularly celestial, when I was on *Papago* and *Seneca*, because that's all we had. Later navigation, you didn't give it a second thought. Even in *Luce* in the late seventies, we had satellite navigation, and then later on it was integrated in industry. I integrated it, when I left the Navy, into a one-man watch capability that took the satellite, took the engine, took all these other capabilities, and you could drive the ship with it. So satellite navigation was one of those things that technology provided the mariner to make life easier.

SC: What's the watch quarter and station bill, and what's that intended to do?

PDM: Watch quarter and station bill. It was watches, what needed to be manned, when it needed to be manned, and to be manned by whom, and it was the—I'm looking for what I would call it in industry or on a manufacturing floor. I don't have a counterpart for it. Because it was just what people looked at to find out what was going on, when it was going on, and what the responsibilities were to execute their job.

SC: There's an old term in the Navy known as "rope yarn liberty." What exactly did that mean or does that mean?

PDM: Oftentimes the lore is remembered for a long time. There isn't enough time when you're in port or even at sea to get all your personal tasks done, and so lots of units would designate a Wednesday afternoon to do your personal stuff, to be able to get off the ship, or if you were onboard a ship, we would have rope yarn on an afternoon so that the sailor might be able to iron, press his outfit, press his clothing, press his dungarees, to be able to shine his shoes, to be able to do those things that you needed to do, to go to the ship's store to get your personal gear, just personal time. I have no idea why the old lore called it rope yarn, but that's what it was. It was personal time, and at sea it was looked at as, "I don't have to work for these four hours in the afternoon. I can lay in my bunk." It was good for the crew.

SC: Our last question in this question set, I want to ask about the geedunk stand. What was and is the geedunk stand, and why do you think that's important to the crew morale?

PDM: Geedunk is where you could get personal goodies. Everybody likes to store away Good & Plenty, M&Ms. You choose the confection. On a destroyer-type ship, we did not have a lot of automatic dispensers at that time, so you had a little ship store that was able to do that, and it was just a source of non-official goods that a sailor could go and buy and squirrel away in his respective bunk spaces, and have them when he wanted to have them, not when the ship wanted to give them to him in the chow line.

SC: This concludes session number four, question set number seven. The date is Sunday, October 1, 2017. The interviewer is Professor Stan Carpenter. In our next question session, we'll continue on with the USS *Parsons* as operations officer and also some of the dynamics of being in the destroyer Navy in the early 1970s. Thank you, Admiral.

PDM: Thank you.

SC: This is USNI oral history interview with Admiral Paul David Miller, U.S. Navy (Ret.). This is session number four, question set number eight. The date is Sunday, October 1, 2017. The interviewer is Professor Stan Carpenter from the Naval War College.
    In this session, we're going to continue talking about operations officer on USS *Parsons* and some of the dynamics of serving in the destroyer Navy in the late sixties and early 1970s.
    Good morning, Admiral.

PDM: Good morning.

SC: By the time one's a department head or senior, you typically don't stand bridge watches unless, as in your case, there was a minimum of qualified OOD. That dynamic is going to vary with the ship and the crew size, but I want to bore in a little bit on what are the specific duties of the officer of the deck on the bridge under way, and what are some of the particular things that an OOD under way must pay special attention to?

PDM: Officer of the deck [OOD], a heralded position in the Navy because you have the responsibilities of the commanding officer while that ship is in an underway situation. You have safe navigation. You're responsible to make sure you know where that ship is, with not only course, speed, etc., but making sure that you're in safe waters at all times, responsible for participating in any assigned exercise or, beyond exercises, any assigned group operations. You're the captain's representative onboard. You're one of two, three, four designated people that the captain trusts, and he has a set of orders that you're supposed to know very, very well and to carry out those responsibilities and to call him when you think or when he says that he's supposed to be informed, day or night, about the evolution the ships are going through. You're his guy, and it's a very serious duty.

SC: What was the qualification regime like for an OOD in a cruiser-destroyer-frigate-type warship in the early 1970s?

PDM: I would imagine like on any ship, whether it be small or large, you have to, first of all, gain the captain's trust, because when he's not there to oversee the ship's movement or the ship's operations, it's entrusted in you as the officer of the deck. So it takes different officers different periods of time to gain that. You have to demonstrate clearly you know all aspects of the ship's operations and that you can fulfill them as a second nature. You're able to look at a situation entering or leaving port and know what to do, when to do it. You're able to operate with other ships at sea, particularly in a task group environment, and know what circuits to listen to, know what [sic] coordination with the Combat Information Center, to discharge your ship's responsibilities correctly, and, I would even say, elegantly. Why do I use that word? Because there's a fierce competition among destroyers in how they operate and with pride, and so whenever you're operating with other ships, you want to be able to execute whatever mission it is better than the other ships that are in your task group. A good officer of the deck is able to demonstrate he's able to do that if he's paying attention to every aspect of operations, and when he gets a call to do something differently, to do it quicker, slicker, and better than the other ships. That's what I personally found as a real motivating factor when I was in task group operations, particularly in the South China Sea.

SC: That leads me to the next question. You've mentioned that the OODs are designated and selected by the commanding officer. Are there any characteristics or personality traits that a commanding officer typically looks for in terms of a prospective underway OOD?

PDM: I would say leadership, and he's looking for that officer that is willing to step up, to take charge, to lead in his absence, and that's number one. Closely behind or on equal level is how much can I trust this officer to be able to do that when I'm not present. That's something that has to come between two individuals. There's no recipe card for it. You're either able to demonstrate that your captain trusts you or you can tell that he doesn't. If he's not too far from the bridge when you're in tough situations, you know that he's trying to give you the opportunity to earn that trust, but he doesn't fully trust you. My officers of the deck, if I gave them that position and I trusted them, I did not go to the bridge until they said, "Captain, would you please come to the bridge?" Because I wanted them to execute whatever the situation involved, without oversight.

When I was an officer of the deck on *Parsons*, I felt like I had not done something properly if the captain came to the bridge without my asking him to, unless he was just coming to the bridge to sit in his chair. It was my ship and I had his role, and I valued that position, and I did not want to do anything to call into question my ability to carry out the mission and have the captain not feel confident that I would do that. That's something that is a bond between captains and officers of the deck. It's a serious, serious job that you have, and you have to be able to do it knowing that you have the lives of all those sailors in your hands for that period of time, that four hours, that whatever.

You can see what's happened in the last three months, in which two large destroyers had terrible, terrible incidents, where officers of the decks were not paying attention to what they were supposed to do, and the captains obviously weren't involved, because those were serious situations. I never had an operational incident when I was officer of the deck or when one of my officers that I had qualified was officer of the deck.[46]

SC: The command duty officer, or CDO, is a critical position in the safety and security of the ship in port. What is the CDO and what are the typical duties?

PDM: Again, he's the captain's representative when in port, and he has a smaller duty section. He only has one-quarter of the crew, one-fifth of the crew, one-sixth, depending on how many sections that they were in, and their duty was to keep that ship monitored and to keep it safe during the period of time that the full crew was not on board. You had a command duty officer and he was in charge. He had full responsibility, just like the officer of the deck has full responsibility at sea.

SC: Who typically served as the CDO during the early seventies, and how was such an officer selected for the position?

PDM: They were usually the officers of the deck at sea, but then in port they were the command duty officer. If you had more command duty officers than you had fleet-qualified officers of the deck, then those next in line that were near qualification for fleet officer of the deck would serve as the CDO as recommended by the XO to the captain. It had responsibility, but nowhere near the breadth and depth of the responsibilities required at sea.

---

[46] The USS *Fitzgerald* (DDG-62), an *Arleigh Burke*–class guided missile destroyer, collided off the coast of Japan with a container ship on June 17, 2017 killing seven sailors. Investigations revealed that poor and inadequate training, watch stander errors, and equipment problems all contributed to the incident. The USS *John S. McCain* (DDG-56) collided with an oil tanker on August 21, 2017 off the Singapore coast, killing ten sailors. The cause of the collision was due to poor watch standing procedures and a lack of familiarity with emergency steering procedures due to inadequate training.

SC: In terms of managing, training, and leading young division officers as they learned the skills needed to be successful in a leadership role such as officer of the deck, what was your personal philosophy as a department head in this role?

PDM: The philosophy was giving a division officer as much opportunity as possible to appreciate, to understand all aspects of the shipboard operations. He had a particular division officer task. I would encourage him to branch out, to learn other division responsibilities so that when he started off as a junior officer of the deck, he could demonstrate that he knew what was going on ship-wide, not just in his sleeve of interest as a communications officer or whatever job [billet] he had, so that he was able to be competent to manage or to lead all departments on the ship and, therefore, gain the CO's confidence more quickly.

SC: What's meant by the term "sea and anchor detail?"

PDM: Before you enter or exit a port, it is a special evolution in which you are required to exercise a different set of the rules of the road. These are inland rules of the road, in which you are maneuvering in tight situations. Now it is less important than it was when I had time in ships, because I did not use pilots; that is, the outside source of knowledge that comes aboard your ship and knows the harbor really well and is able to help drive your ship in or out of a port. They use them now, but as the CO, I probably used them only in those foreign ports that required them. The sea and anchor detail were your special people and special places to be able to assist in tight maneuvering and into tight navigation until you reached the buoy that designated open seas.

Like in Norfolk it's Bravo-1-Charlie at the end of the Chesapeake Bay. So you had special people on the bridge, you had special people manning the engine room, special people in the deck force, so that you could handle the evolution with the best support that you could muster on board the ship, and they were sea and anchor detail folks.

SC: Clearly, as the OOD, primary OOD, you would have stood that watch in sea and anchor detail, but as the operations officer, was there any particular role in sea and anchor detail?

PDM: I was usually the officer of the deck, but other than that, no.

SC: For those not familiar with a ship at sea, what was meant by conditions of readiness and why was this important?

PDM: There were alphabet designations for conditions of damage control readiness. The most severe degree of readiness you could have would be to guard against radiological or chemical attack, and that was the designation of Circle William. Then it went to a lesser degree of damage control readiness. For general quarters, it was generally X-ray, in which you had all the hatches and gun covers over, but wasn't wrapped up as tight as it could possibly be. Then you would have another designation for general steaming, and for in port. So that was just a shorthand way of designating damage control readiness for your ship.

SC: A ship at sea must be replenished with food and fuel especially, but depending on the mission and actions, ammunition and other stores might be required. Tell us, in general, about underway replenishment in the period.

PDM: Underway replenishment was a vital operation in task force steaming. Independent steaming, not so much, but if you were independent steaming, you had to plan carefully for fuel usage and then going into port to refuel or to get stores for food and the like. Under way, you refueled about every three days if you had an oiler present. You rearmed only when necessary. The South China Sea, you did that more frequently.

You replenished probably every ten days. Most of the time destroyers from '70 on would replenish by vertical replenishment, and that is when a helicopter would bring a couple of pallets of goods and drop them on the fantail, as opposed to you taking them by highline, which is crossing between the ships on a rig. You would fuel probably from two fueling stations with a probe from the oiler to your ship. Each of these evolutions would take probably an hour of time to get a full bag of gas and to get a sufficient number of stores aboard till you ran out another ten days.

But those were normal evolutions, and when you heard over the 1MC, "Now set the fueling detail, now set the replenishment detail," the trained crew would know the stations that they go to, they know what the task would be, and most of the time those evolutions came off without any issue, except when that inadvertent action would take place, like the helicopter would have a problem with his hookup and he would drop a whole sling of stuff on the stern of your ship, or the fuel probe would not mate properly with your receptacle, and then someone would start sending fuel over and you would have a big spill on your portside. But those were infrequent incidents.

Navy ships practice underway replenishment all the time, and they did a good job, and that's what made our operations capable of being conducted around the clock, because we never had to take a break from leaving the station to go to a port to refuel or replenish.

SC: When you're alongside an oiler, as the officer of the deck or the conning officer, what are your biggest concerns?

PDM: Totally dependent on sea state. If you're alongside at one hundred feet and the seas are calm and you have a decent helmsman on the replenisher, the ship that you're receiving fuel from, the destroyer can maintain station relatively easily. If you have rough seas, then it becomes a little more tenuous because your seakeeping capabilities are not that of a larger ship, and you're bounced back and forth. You will close twenty feet in a heartbeat, so you have to look at the seas forward, gauge the movement of the ship, and order to the helm that course and those number of turns you think would be necessary to try to maintain your position. It took some ship handling skill to be able to think in advance what was needed, not for your condition now, but those seas coming forward, what it was going to be and how this wave was going to hit your bow, and you needed to know when to add those few turns, subtract a few turns.

It's a delicate situation, and if you got in too close, which happens all too often, you're in danger of bringing those ships together. It depended on the confidence of the commanding officer as to whether he would let one, two, or three people drive the ship during those evolutions or that he would train youngsters to do it, because the youngster doing it would feel really good at having conned the ship alongside in a replenishing situation, but it took a captain with confidence to permit that.

SC: As the operations officer, did you have any specific role in underway replenishment?

PDM: On board *Parsons*, once I gained my qualifications, under one CO I probably didn't have the conn two or three times. Under the other CO, I had it, again, the vast majority of the time, because I had his confidence as being a good ship handler, and he wasn't interested in training a lot of people. When I was CO of *McCloy*, I never had the conn in an underway replenishment. I always trained.

SC: We have discussed previously the concept of holding quarters, and I want to go back to that. From your perspective as a retired four-star flag officer, having attended and held many, many quarters, what advice would you give to a brand-new department head as to how to conduct effective and useful quarters?

PDM: Quarters is having the opportunity to meet with the people that are in your department, to talk with them about what you want to complete that day. The advice that I would always give a division officer was to look at what he was going to be responsible for from my position as department head, and I would often permit a different division officer to be the department head and to take my position at quarters so that they would gain that experience in knowing how to lay out the program for the day, what the requirements were, what the timing was for the evolution, and just to learn how to articulate good management for the period of time that you were covering. I probably attended quarters one-fifth of the time. The XO questioned me at first why wasn't I there, and then when I said what I was doing, he accepted that and it became a practice of other department heads too.

SC: At sea is always busy for all hands, and especially department heads. Looking back, are there any recommendations that you would make to a newly appointed department head as to how he or she should approach time management?

PDM: Use every minute that you have available to the maximum extent possible, particularly when you're at sea. There is nothing else to do but work, and so if you use every minute that you're not sleeping to work, you get ahead of the game quickly.

SC: How often did you conduct personnel inspections of your department on the *Parsons*? Was this a regular routine, and if so, how were personnel appearance and uniform inspections addressed, especially in a war zone?

PDM: Whenever I'd go to quarters, I would look at the general appearance of the folks in my department. The pace of ship operations didn't require a lot of spit and polish, but the pace of operations also did not permit anyone to be a slob, so it was a fine line between what was acceptable and what wasn't. As long as it was acceptable, I let it go when I knew they were standing one-in-three watches that we had very few rope yarn periods, and everybody maintained a modicum of uniform, dress, and appearance. I was never a stickler for hats on the bridge, but every captain I had has been. When I was a CO, I wasn't. But I never emphasized personal decorum, particularly in the South China Sea.

SC: You went on to become part of Admiral Elmo Zumwalt's staff, following your time as CO of *McCloy* and at the Naval War College, but prior to that time, the famous Z-grams began impacting Navy policy on appearance, uniforms, and so on. While you were aboard *Parsons*, were there many changes based on the Z-grams, or was this a later phenomenon?

PDM: I was still on *Parsons* when he became CNO. I was personally directly in line with Admiral Zumwalt's determination about how people should conduct themselves with regard to appearance. He was a little bit more lax than others. "Lax" is not the right word. He was a little bit more open to what society was doing at the time. But it was early on, I think, I went back to Washington right on the cusp of him being the CNO. I'm trying to remember exactly when it was, when his first Z-gram came out that shocked the fleet. I can't remember whether I was in Washington or on *Parsons*. The first Z-gram shocked the fleet.

SC: Yes, and we'll talk a little bit more about that as we get down the road, as you were on Admiral Zumwalt's staff later.

Routine maintenance is critical in keeping a ship fully operational. What were the facilities for regular overhaul, repair availability, and routine maintenance like in the early 1970s?

PDM: Fortunately, I did not go to a ship that had to go to a regular overhaul. That was one of the things that I did not want to do out of Destroyer School.

We had availabilities twice. Once we had a week availability in Subic Bay [Philippines] because we had some engineering issues, and when we were back in the U.S. in between deployments, we had what they call a restricted availability alongside the pier, not in a shipyard, for, I think, a four-week period of time. Then each department head tries to put together a maintenance program with outside assistance, to get as much help as he could to make sure his equipment is ready to go to the next operation or the next exercise, and in our case, the next deployment without going to a large overhaul in a shipyard.

SC: As we wrap up your time as operations officer on *Parsons*, are there any other areas that we should address before moving on?

PDM: No. I'd just like for the record to say that your time on board particularly the fast-paced operations of a destroyer, depends a lot on your commanding officer. I was blessed to have two commanding officers, totally different in personality, but they were equally good as leaders. One brought more leadership to the ship than the other. By that I mean he was able to delegate. He didn't have to do everything himself. That officer went on to be selected for flag at an early point in time. The other officer, while an outstanding commanding officer, was less ready to delegate. He opened up responsibilities to the department heads very carefully. He kept a tight rein on everything. That officer made captain.

I took away from that later on what I learned from each of those officers, and I put into practice those attributes from the first commanding officer that embraced delegation, embraced sharing his responsibilities and the authorities with his subordinates, while he kept the ultimate responsibility. He was secure enough to train and to let others gain experience, where the second one didn't.

SC: As we wrap up your two years as a department head on USS *Parsons*, if you were to go back and redo that tour, are there any things that you would do differently, in retrospect?

PDM: I would wish I had the time to complete my second deployment myself, but I had no control over that. I enjoyed that tour very, very much, even though we were at sea, as you can tell, an awful long time, and that wrapped up my ATF days in *Parsons* with six months ashore at Destroyer School, so that was a very demanding period at sea in which this sailor gained a hell of a lot of at-sea experience.

SC: Some officers leave the Navy at the end of their first department head tour, some officers go off active duty and roll into the Navy Reserve to complete their service. What was your perspective as you finished your tour as the ops officer on *Parsons* in terms of your future in the Navy?

PDM: I mentioned before that I went to Destroyer School to get the opportunity, and, fortunately, for some reason I was given the opportunity to serve on a destroyer that was going to WestPac. Even though they were in month increments, I got two opportunities to go to the South China Sea to get all the destroyer experience that one could get in that period of time, and it all left the feeling that I could make a career of the United States Navy. Still a reserve officer, I was given orders back to Washington, D.C., but the decision had mentally been taken that based upon the destroyer experience, that there was potential of a full career in the Navy, particularly in the brand of operations that I had completed in *Parsons*.

SC: What in those days was the process for a Navy Reserve officer requesting augmentation?

PDM: Finishing the first three-year obligation, I had to sign up for Destroyer School and then two more years and put in a tour after Destroyer School as a reserve officer. I was enticed to take a tour in Washington, D.C., by the first skipper that I had, who was then in Washington, D.C., and he was helpful in bringing me back to the detailing shop at the Bureau of Naval Personnel for junior officers. That was the shop that brought together twenty of the brightest junior officers that the surface Navy had from all over the fleet to be detailers in Washington.

To come back to there, though, I had to submit or I had to say that I was going to augment to the regular Navy. So when Becky and I moved back to Washington, we knew that we were on the path. I had not augmented, but we were on the path to becoming a regular Navy officer family.

SC: Once you detached from USS *Parsons* and then augmented to USN, you came to Washington and served as a Navy detailer, so let's turn to that. What exactly does a detailer do?

PDM: First, you have to realize that for most officers that were assigned to the detailing shop, it was the first time that you were assigned with the best that the community had, because each of them had been successful department heads, just as you had been a successful department head. So that was a unique set of individuals.

The task was as the name would show. You were in charge of a certain number of junior officers and you detailed them to their next assignment. You reviewed their records, you reviewed what was available, and you tried to match up what they wanted to do, what they were qualified to do, with what was available. I started off at the "Mc" and "S" desk. I had every last name that began with "Mc" and every last name that began with "S," and they were about three thousand. Each desk had about three thousand officers which they detailed. You sat there, you received letters from them, you received telephone calls from them, and you looked at when they were coming up from when they finished their eighteen-month tour, if they were going to split tour to something else. You looked to see what [sic] you racked the desires up with the requirements and you sent them a set of orders.

SC: There's an old myth in the Navy that says that detailers use a dartboard to determine one's next assignment. What is your comment on that, and how do officers' dream sheets play into the detailing process?

PDM: Not true on the former. Dream sheets play more of a role than they're credited with. Detailers looked at what you called preference cards and took that into consideration when they matched it up with requirements.

SC: What exactly is meant by the phrase "needs of the Navy" and what implications does that have for the detailing process?

PDM: The needs of the Navy were the requirements that you had to choose from. That's the billets that the Navy needed to fill at a particular point in time.

SC: The needs of the Navy always take precedence in detailing, but you try to match up the officer's career path and desires with the needs. How difficult is that dynamic?

PDM: If an individual had a desire for a particular home port, a desire for a particular ship, then on that preference card is which was more important, the particular ship or the home port, and then you did the best that you could with the listing of billets that would be available and you tried very hard to match it up.

But you had all these detailers, I think there were twelve, of alphabetical detailers. The alphabet was divided up like that. Now, each one of these officers were looking at this list of requirements, and so you had to pay attention pretty quickly. I would review this every day, what the requirements were. That was called the placement officer. They had to place the people where they needed to go. And I would go over to his desk and check everything that was available. We didn't have computer screens where I could just mouse it up in front of me. You had to physically go check. And then when I would detail somebody, I would try to remember that, hey, there was this job in San Diego [California], Mayport [Florida], whatever, and did my very best to match them up.

SC: If you had a situation where an officer had expressed a desire for a certain billet or type ship or job or home port and you knew it was not particularly career enhancing for them, how much intervention would you do there, or did you just simply match them up based on their desires?

PDM: Depends what kind of record he had. If he had a record that deserved additional opportunity to keep demonstrating his potential, I would work very, very hard not to send him to some place like someone sent me to the USS *Papago*. That experience defined lots of things that I did later on in the Navy.

SC: Tell us about your typical day at the detailing ship.

PDM: It's important to say at this time, by the time I went back to Washington, this Vietnam phenomena [*sic*], the resistance to it, was beginning to get in full blossom. They made that determination in Washington that military people would not wear uniforms to work. I didn't wear a uniform to work; I wore a suit to the detailing shop. I thought this was awful peculiar, but it started and that sort of gave a civilian flair to it, because we were all, even your superiors were in civilian clothes.

But the day, it was a workday from 8:00 in the morning till 4:00 or 5:00 in the afternoon, and somehow I didn't think it would fill up, but somehow the day filled up with issues here, issues there, and you tried to work them the best you could. You'd spend a lot of time on the phone. I never called a detailer, but I learned a lot of people called detailers, and you tried to do the best you could to match. I tried to match potential with premium jobs, not so much potential with the needs of the Navy.

SC: Were there any other surprises or dynamics other than you've already mentioned the uniform issue that you did not expect when you reported to D.C.?

PDM: It unfolded sort of as advertised, as you thought it would, but it's important to interject now that I had been an alphabetically designated detailer for about twelve months. We had two premium desks. This was the sea detailer and the shore detailer. Those were the people that you had to talk to about the billets. The shore detailer was getting relieved. He was also the Vietnam detailer. He had first refusal of anybody. So I said, "I've had enough experience at this desk." I wanted to do that. I had just been selected two years early for lieutenant commander. Captain Sackett was our boss.[47] He made admiral. He came down to my desk, the "Mc" desk, and said, "Congratulations." I had no idea what he was congratulating me for, but I was the last person on the lieutenant commander list that year, and I was still a reserve officer. Augmentation hadn't come through.

So then I said, "Maybe I have a chance for this desk," because I was the only one picked up early out of this group of hot-running people. They made a determination that while I had been in the South China Sea, I had some experience over there that I had not been in country, so it would be difficult for someone who had not been in country to detail people in the last couple of years of the conflict.

So I thought about it for about a week. I went to Captain Sackett one day, and I said, "Captain, you're right. I don't have in-country experience, but what if I go to Vietnam and visit every outpost that we have, every place we have a riverboat unit, every place we have a support detachment, and talk to every lieutenant and LTJG that we have in country, and then come back and I'll have the knowledge, I'll have better knowledge of anybody that's ever served over there, what our requirements were."

And he said, "Well, we'll think about it." He said, "We'll talk about it."

---

[47] Rear Admiral Albert M. Sackett (1920–2016) graduated from George Washington University. He enlisted in the U.S. Navy in 1937, was commissioned in 1944, and retired in 1977. His last billet was as commandant, Ninth Naval District and commander Naval Base, Great Lakes.

He came back and said, "Okay." Then he says, "If it's good for you, the lieutenant commander desk should do it too." The lieutenant commander detailer, because we had a lot of lieutenant commanders.

So we received TAD orders to go to ComNavForV [commander Naval Forces Vietnam], and with the task of visiting as many units as we could. That two weeks over there, I could do what you do, I could write a book about it, because it was so unusual to have someone looking out for the people's future come into the combat zone to take whatever vehicle they could find. We flew in helicopters, we rode in jeeps. No one gave us a dedicated transportation. We were free to do whatever we wanted to do. It was an amazing two weeks. I visited folks in every little place that you could name.

One of them that I remember was Fiksyen. It was an outpost for the riverine force, and we got in there because a helicopter was going about a couple kilometers away, and then we just hiked over to them. They had a station that was on stilts in the river because the river would pull it down. These four guys were in the most desolate part of South Vietnam, and I said, "Guys." After seeing this—they had decent records—I said, "You think about where you want to go and you will go there. I'll find a way to send you there." So I visited every place like that.

And we made it back. I took the Vietnam desk, and my second year as a detailer went smoothly, and it was punctuated by my going to command of *McCloy* from the detailing shop.

SC: What was your family life like in those first years in D.C.?

PDM: Family life changed remarkably. Becky and I had our first son while I was at the Bureau, 1971. She went through the pregnancy, and the youngster was born at Bethesda Naval Hospital, as most of the youngsters that were born of Navy families at the time. It was a total lifestyle change, of course, from her and I, who had spent a lot of time apart, and then life changed with an infant in the house. I was always a workaholic, so I had to change that a bit, not a lot, but a bit. We had bought our first house. We had become instead of two people married with doing sort of separate things, with me going to sea so much, it was the first time we became sort of a family. So that sort of changed my outlooks on things from then forward.

SC: We'll come back to that in just a moment, but first I want to address the concept of early promotion. You were selected two years early for promotion to lieutenant commander. To what do you credit that early promotion?

PDM: To this day, I don't know. I go back and I look at how does someone that served on ATFs for three years, go to Destroyer School, do one tour onboard a destroyer as a department head, still be a reserve officer, and be selected as the most junior selectee by that Selection Board. I can't tell you what did it. I can tell you that Admiral Zumwalt's program designated that he wanted 10 percent, some percentage of the selectees that year. It was his first year of emphasis of changing, bringing young people forward. His decision to do that, it permitted it. So the Selection Board had to look through the early records thoroughly, because historically they might have picked up one or something like that a year early, but they had been charged with picking up a percentage, like 10 percent, and the window be [sic] opened two years early.

Why I was chosen as opposed to the guy who sat right next to me that had five years of destroyer experience, I'll never know. I do know that I was fortunate to have the experiences in the South China Sea twice. I do know that my fitness reports were better than I ever thought that I could receive. I received endorsements that were unusual, by the commodore. I was teamed as the number-one onboard that ship. I was fortunate to have fitness report writers and particularly one that didn't emphasize what I did, but emphasized potential. In reading the reports on the Selection Board, I can only opine—I have no idea, but they were looking to select x number early, and this record happened to surface, in which even in the early days, there were more comments about potential than there were about completion of the current duties. So I think it was that, but there was nobody more surprised than me.

SC: You also mentioned that you got a commodore's endorsement on a fitness report as department head, which is strikingly unusual, and I'm sure that had a lot to do with it as well.

PDM: Yes, and he handwrote the things, and it was all potential.

SC: Once you completed your tour as a detailer, what was your perspective on the work that you had done there?

PDM: I was satisfied, particularly with the Vietnam approach. I was able to talk with anybody that I sent to Vietnam. I knew exactly where he was going, what he was going to do. I could tell him I'd been there two months ago. It was the winding down two years of the war. I only had the desk a year. This was in '72, and we were out of there in '73, so you're still sending people there when the mission, the enthusiasm were always on the downward trend, but I could tell them what to expect, I could tell them what we were going to do when it was completed, because I took each of those assignment and I wrote clearly in my own hand, I stapled it to his card, what I had promised—not promised, but what I said that we would take a thorough look at for when he came out of there, and I would make a commitment to them that I left with the person that relieved me, that as soon as there was an opportunity to relieve him, if the mission went away, we would do that with alacrity.

So I came away with the overall detailing experience of understanding and appreciating how the process worked, which was important. I understood clearly the importance that that function [has] to every individual, and it is an individual, not an organizational importance, and I was able to carry that all the way through my whole naval career.

SC: You'd now reached a point in your Navy career where many officers have to make that hard decision as to, as I said earlier, resign the commission, roll into the Navy Reserve, or, as the phrase says, go CivLant. What was your perspective on a full Navy career at this point?

PDM: Once I had submitted for augmentation when I came to the Bureau and once that [sic] I was selected for lieutenant commander two years early, much to Becky's surprise [laughs], to her complete surprise, then we had affirmatively made that decision and we knew that the launch pad was set as good as it could be set as I was going off to become CO of a frigate that not very many people had had the chance to do before they were thirty years old.

SC: Did you feel at this point in your career that it was fairly well on track, and did you, in fact, have any doubts?

PDM: One always has doubts, because one doesn't recognize that his performance deserves the recognition that it was given.

SC: This concludes session number four, question set number eight. The date is Sunday, October 1, 2017. This is USNI oral history interview with Admiral Paul David Miller, USN (Ret.). The interviewer is Professor Stan Carpenter.

Admiral, in our next session, we'll be discussing your CO tour on USS *McCloy*. Thank you very much.

PDM: Thank you.

[End of October 1, 2017, interview]

Interview with Admiral Paul David Miller, USN (Ret.)
Date: December 3, 2017

Stan Carpenter (SC): This is USNI oral history interview with Admiral Paul David Miller, U.S. Navy (Ret.). This is session number five, question set number nine. The date is Sunday, December 3, 2017. The interviewer is Professor Stan Carpenter. These questions cover the years leading up to and covering commanding officer of USS *McCloy*.

Admiral, before we move to your command tour on the *McCloy*, let's wrap up your time in D.C. at the Bureau of Personnel. Were there any other comments you'd like to make?

Paul David Miller (PDM): Thanks, Stan. I don't remember exactly how much we covered from the Bureau, but that was a terribly important tour for me. I left the *Parsons* with a sense of did I want to stay in the Navy, did I belong in the Navy. I asked all those questions of myself, and the commanding officers that I had in *Parsons* were encouraging. The first one, Robert Morris, was so encouraging; he helped bring me back to Washington, D.C., in a premier billet. I was still a reserve officer, and they didn't usually give those billets to reserve officers.

I went back to the Bureau and found myself in the midst of about fifteen other young lieutenants, all [of whom] had done equally as well as I had done in my department head tour on a destroyer. All of them were from the destroyer force, which sort of showed back then the segmentation between the destroyer force, the amphibious force, and the service force. There was a bit of being just a little bit more knowledgeable if you had gone through the combatants' trail as opposed to the others.

So Becky and I moved back to Washington. This was a huge move for us, going from San Diego to Washington, getting involved in trying to buy our first home in a real estate market like you'd find in Arlington and Fairfax even back then. We elected to live close in, in Arlington, not very far from the Pentagon, and so we had to mortgage our souls to be able to move into that small house on Dinwiddie Street.

The Bureau was a very enjoyable place to work. The camaraderie amongst that group was equally as strong as it was on a ship, and friendships I made then, a couple of them have lasted for fifty years, forty-five years, because we just had one of the detailers visiting here in Naples, Florida, two weeks ago. He was fortunate enough to become a rear admiral. So the professional opportunity there was very, very strong for me. I wanted to compete with the best that the Navy had. It wasn't a competition per se, but all of us knew that there were very important fitness reports that we got out of there, because it was the first time we were being looked at and graded with people that had proven their operational competency.

The first year there was unremarkable; it was just doing your duties. But then I saw at the end of the first year there was an opportunity to move up just a bit, and that was to become a coordinator for all the shore assignments and for Vietnam, and the other desk that was just above the detailer's was for all the sea assignments. But I showed that I wanted to move up; my performance was good.

The head of the section of the Bureau was Captain Al Sackett. He was a crusty seagoing captain, and he told me that he couldn't assign me there because I had not been to Vietnam on the beach on the riverine or swift boats. After that conversation, I thought about it, and about a day or two later, I went back and I said, "Captain, if you send me TAD [Temporary Additional Duty], I'll go to Vietnam. I'll go there for two, three weeks, and I'll visit every LTJG and lieutenant in country, no matter where they were."

He looked at me like I had two heads, but then he thought about it for a while and he sent myself and a lieutenant commander detailer; gave us open orders. We went to Saigon, and then the ComNavForV [commander, Naval Forces Vietnam] didn't know what to do with us because it was unusual to have somebody from the Bureau to ask to go visit their operational units. He couldn't assign dedicated support to us, dedicated transportation, dedicated this, but he set it up to give us our first leg, to go down and visit the boat drivers in Cam Ranh Bay. We went down there and then we saw a lot of lieutenants and LTJGs, the ones that were prosecuting the shallow-water war.

From there, myself and the lieutenant commander detailer found a boat or found a helicopter that was going to another site, and we went to it. When I visited them, they thought, "Who is this guy?" And I would tell them I had all their records, and I asked them where they wanted to go, and they could not believe I was sitting out there in the middle of nowhere, asking where they wanted to go.

The one that sticks in my mind clearly was we took a helicopter that dropped us off in the middle of the Mekong [River], in the middle of the river. They had some riverine boats, and the tide would go in and out. At that point in time, they were on a hooch with stilts [living quarters], we made it over to that and I found a couple of guys there. We had some great conversations. They could not believe this, in this place called

Phú Quốc. I asked this guy, "Okay, this is for real. You're getting out of here in three months. Where do you want to go, young man?" And he looked at me. He said, "I want to go to Europe. I'm tired of this. I want to go to some place in Europe."

I said, "Okay, guaranteed. I will go back and work on that, and you'll get a personal note from Captain Al Sackett, who is my boss, and you'll go there because I'll tell him that you were one of the toughest dudes out here and you had one of the toughest assignments, and you deserve it."

And we went away. We spent two weeks there. We hit all the major spots and even all the smaller spots. When I came back from that, I took the desk. When I had to call somebody up and tell them where they were going, I was able to give them a first-hand report of what they were going to experience, who they were going to be with, and it felt a lot better for me sending a youngster my age or just a couple of years younger over to do a year tour there. This was '71, so the activity was still going on. And it all worked. Captain Sackett, when I went back, he says, "That was a unique idea."

Then the next thing that happened not too far after that was my two-year early selection to lieutenant commander, and I was still a reserve officer. That shocked everybody. I honestly had no idea that I was even up for lieutenant commander. Captain Sackett came down the hall and said, "You're the last person on the lieutenant commander list."

I said, "Thank you." I really don't know what I said. But anyhow, that set me up. That clearly made my decision that the Navy was willing to make me part of the young folks that were going to be those modeled after the [Admiral Elmo] Zumwalt model of being able to get promoted as quickly as your ability permitted, your performance permitted, and that was it.[48] And I said certainly. It wasn't a quid pro quo thing, but the

---

[48] Admiral Elmo R. "Bud" Zumwalt Jr. (1920–2000) graduated from the U.S. Naval Academy in 1942 and served aboard destroyers in World War II, winning a Bronze Star for actions in the Battle of Leyte Gulf in October 1944. He commanded Naval Forces, Vietnam as a vice admiral in the late 1960s. He became the youngest ever Chief of Naval Operations in 1970 (nineteenth CNO) and was noted for his reforms in the personnel, tactical, and fleet right-sizing aspects of the naval service. He issued CNO directives and instructions called "Z-grams" that reformed personnel practices, rules, and regulations, introduced new ship and aircraft designs/concepts, and increased the capability and size of the nuclear ballistic submarine force by the end of the 1970s.

thing that came out of it for me, I was assigned to be the commanding officer of the USS *McCloy*.[49]

This was another step that was questioned. It was questioned by the Navy. I remember—I will not forget the man's name, but Rear Admiral Weschler, who was ComCruDesLant [commander, Cruiser-Destroyer Forces, U.S. Atlantic Fleet].[50] They had a ComCruDesLant. He was sort of the type commander for only the destroyers and cruisers, as they had one for PhibLant [amphibious forces] and ServLant [service forces such as oilers, ammunition ships, etc.]. He told Captain Sackett that he didn't want me; I didn't have the experience.

Captain Sackett didn't know exactly what to do, so he had to take it up to the chief of naval personnel. I don't know what transpired in those conversations, of course, but what I learned later, after going up there, was that, "He's going. If he doesn't do the job, you can fire him, Admiral." But I did not learn that until later on. All I knew is it came back that I was going to go to the *McCloy*.

That brings us up to getting orders to the USS *McCloy*. Becky and I then move up to Newport, Rhode Island. We moved into Navy housing and I had just put on lieutenant commander, moved into this place, and I had total flashbacks of being there with the chief that had adopted me after he married my mother. It was not the same housing, but it was close by. So we moved into that, and Becky and I made the best of that housing, but it was a set of housing that the Navy should have never approved for naval officers, never.

So *McCloy*'s deployed, and I have to fly over to Portugal, my home country, and take command. The only thing I had to do with that ship was to bring it home safely. I

---

[49] USS *McCloy* (DE-1078/FF-1078) was a *Bronstein*-class destroyer escort, later reclassified as a fast frigate in 1975. Commissioned in 1963 and decommissioned in 1990, the ship was named for Lieutenant Commander John McCloy, a two-time Medal of Honor winner. *McCloy* displaced over twenty-three hundred tons with a maximum speed of twenty-four-plus knots. Armed with 3"/50 guns, ASROC and torpedoes, her primary mission was antisubmarine warfare and her complement consisted of 16 officers and 183 crewmen.

[50] Vice Admiral Thomas R. Weschler (1917–2016) graduated from the U.S. Naval Academy in 1939 but was not commissioned until the start of the Second World War due to vision problems and served more than thirty-four years in the U.S. Navy. Following his retirement, he served on the faculty of the U.S. Naval War College in Newport, RI.

said, "This is going to be okay." I didn't have to worry about going into operations or anything. Get it home, relieve, bring the ship back to the U.S.

The next two weeks were the worst two weeks I had in the Navy [*laughs*], absolute worst. We got the ship under way. We were coming back as part of some task force that they had deployed with, and about three days out, we hit this hellacious storm. *McCloy* is not a good-righting ship under the best of circumstances, because it was two of a class that they hung the 26 sonar [AN/SQS-26 bow-mounted, low frequency SONAR] on the bow, which had a great big bulbous bow. So while it had the latest in sonar onboard, it disturbed the righting moment [based on a ship's metacentric height and center of gravity] that put it just within limits for it to go to sea. But we hit that storm and people were getting concerned. That night, we lost the mast. We lost the *mast*, carrying the SPS-29 radar [AN/SPS-29 air search radar]. Lost the *mast*. It was hanging down by the guy wires. I said, "This is a hell of a way to start my command tour." [*laughs*]

I was afraid that the sailors were going to get hurt, so I went with them up to the flying bridge. You take the rough seas and the rolls, then the pounding. If we didn't get the mast secured with wire and a turnbuckle, that thing would have beat the crap out of the mast and would have fallen overboard at some point in time. No telling what damage it would have done. Well, we got it secured, but that was just the beginning of my travails.

The *McCloy* only had one set of evaporators [for converting sea water to fresh water by evaporation/condensation], one set, and in that rough sea, it continuously lost suction, so we'd make a little water, then go offline. Feed water [purified water free of minerals and sediment for the boilers made by flashing sea water to steam, then condensing] kept going down. I can remember sitting on the ladder down in the boiler room looking at the Bureau of Ships Technical Manual on using saltwater in the boilers. I was that close, because I *knew* that we could not lose way in that sea. We kept 15 percent feed water. We kept going.

Night turned to day, and we got a little break. The other ship in the squadron, one of them was called *Voge* (FF-1047), and it had an outstanding captain. We got talking bridge and bridge. He said, "We're doing fine on feed water. I'll come alongside and we'll try to put over a feed water hose and pass some to you." As a captain, I admitted I only took this puppy four days ago, and I wasn't expecting this calamity, "But if you want to try it," I said, "I'm willing and I'll be grateful, because it'll save a lot of consternation."

So he came alongside, and I have pictures that he later gave to me after we got back to Newport, of the bow of *McCloy* coming out of the water, showing the SQS-26 sonar dome while *Voge* was alongside of us. That's how rough it was, and that was relatively quiet compared to what it was throughout the night. So I had to send SITREPs [Situation Reports]. I had to CASREP [Casualty Report] the radar. I was ready to CASREP the evaporators. We got enough. I think we got up to 40 percent of feed water. But it never turned really rough again, and we were able to begin to make feed water, mast was secured, boilers were boiling as they should have been. I had to have both of them online, because if we had lost one for some reason, I'd have gone dead in the water. So all those things that you're supposed to do, I think we did, and I was able to write decent messages, so we made it back.

I got off that ship. It looked absolutely terrible. [*laughs*] I looked at the XO and the crew, and I just said, "This is a hell of a start, guys." But it was a test. The ship passed it, the crew passed it, I passed it. There was nothing that ever happened, no one ever griped about the radar falling down, no one griped about the evaporators. They just helped us get everything fixed.

Then we became an integral ship of DesRon 28 [Destroyer Squadron 28], and the commodore I had was Captain Johnson. You always remember the tough guys, never remember the good guys. You remember the tough guys. C. J. Johnson, bachelor, probably forty-eight years old, captain. He came over and said, "What's the plan?"

We came back in the fall, so this was October. We were there in restricted availability, worked hard getting the ship looking decent again. We didn't have any underway time for about six weeks. Then we got under way for some small event outside of Newport.

Then Christmas came, our first Christmas there. I went down to the ship on Christmas Day. Something told me to go to the ship on Christmas Day. I said to Becky, "I've got to go down to the ship."

She looked at me and said, "Okay."

So I go down on the ship, and it's about eleven o'clock in the morning. Who comes on board? C. J. Johnson. He said, "Captain! I didn't think I'd see any CO on their ship on Christmas Day." And he said, "You brought the ship a long way." He wasn't much for talking a lot. He said, "Merry Christmas to you and the crew," then left. From that day forward—and I had him for about ten more months as my DesRon commander—he looked after *McCloy*. He knew that I was younger, and I recall in the fitness report that he wrote, he said, "Lieutenant Commander Miller is years younger than the other commanding officers in this squadron, but his performance is superior to any." And I tag that back to me being concerned on Christmas Day. As a starter, we performed well, but that was something that jumpstarted it. For him to show interest in the ship, to show interest in me was that right there.

We deployed with *Intrepid* (CV/CVA/CVS-11) [antisubmarine warfare carrier] to—I think they called them HUK [Hunter-Killer Group] group deployments. We were in the teeth of the Cold War. An ASW patrol in the North Atlantic was big sport back then, and the *Intrepid* had been changed because we had the *Forrestal*-class [CV-59] eclipsing it and it had been changed to an air wing of S-2s, ASW helicopters, and they had a DET [detachment] of four A-4 attack aircraft.[51] That was their air wing. So we deployed in that spring to the North Atlantic. It wasn't six months; it was only four or five months.

So we deploy, as four "small boys," a carrier, an oiler; it wasn't a large task group. It was just an ASW hunter-killer group. And on the ship, they would get "tippers" [submarine contact reports] from the SOSUS world, the VP [maritime air patrol] world, put the information together, and we would try to gain contact on submarines. That's how we spent all the time.

During that time, the only unique thing other than doing the ASW work, was our ship was the only one that had a working HIFR, helo in-flight refueling, capability. This is where the helo comes up behind the ship, you pass them a hose, a line and then a hose, they plug it in, and you provide fuel, and he's able to stay on station for a couple more hours. For helicopters in the ASW world, in the dipping sonar world, that was important because when they were in the hover, they used a lot of gas, and then they'd come back to us to refuel.

---

[51] S-2 Tracker ASW aircraft built by Grumman. A-4 Skyhawk built by Douglas.

We went into a couple of ports up in the North Atlantic, but it wound up that we did ninety-one helicopter in-flight refuelings [HIFR] in that deployment, and we became pretty proficient, no injuries. They did not lose a helicopter on that whole cruise, didn't lose any S-2 aircraft. It was a good cruise, and we all made it back to Newport. In my mind's eye, I was a certified commanding officer of a going-to-sea frigate. At that point in time, I'd put the age thing behind me. I'd worried about it—not worried about it, but been concerned about it. I knew I had to do everything 10 percent better to be as good, but I put it behind me once I came back from that deployment. I was sanguine about the whole thing.

Then while I was coming back, I got relieved overseas because I got orders to the Naval War College, the junior course [Intermediate Learning Curriculum for mid-career officers]. I had to be back in August, so somebody else had the privilege of bringing the ship back. But it was a great tour, great crew, and I left it and had about five fitness reports from different people, and, fortunately, I came out with a pretty good set of recommendations, and then I go matriculate at the War College.

That's a long-winded way of covering *McCloy*, but I remember *McCloy* almost day by day because of the adversity. That's what makes leadership. You have got to handle that adversity. You can't panic, you can't get excited, you have to figure out what the hell you're going to do, and do it.

SC: Admiral, let's turn now to some dynamics of that tour as CO of *McCloy*. FF-1038 was her hull designation. She was a *Bronstein*-class frigate, and you were aboard from April '72 to August '73, when you reported at the Naval War College. That ship was originally designated as a destroyer escort, or DE, when she was commissioned in 1963. Tell us about the design and roles of a DE in the 1960s.

PDM: DEs back then were supplemental. They had quite a few DEs, but the Navy had to align itself with the warfare that was ahead, not what we had done, and the warfare that was ahead with this Cold War showed that you had to have operational specialties in anti-submarine warfare, you had to have capability in air-to-air warfare, you had to have capability in strike warfare, and you had to have capability in amphibious warfare. Later on, I added a dimension called space warfare, but this is when I'm much more senior.

When I went to *McCloy*, that's what the Navy was. ASW task forces had to be able prosecute the ASW threat of the North Atlantic, which was formidable. They had their boomer boats [ballistic missile submarines] out there. They had attack submarines. So we knew that if we were going to ever engage in the North Atlantic, that you need to be able to be good at each one of those warfare areas; otherwise, you would not prevail. So the *Bronstein*, then *McCloy*, then the 1040 frigate [USS *Garcia*-class fast frigates] came after that, and we rolled out the 1052 class [USS *Knox*-class fast frigates]. They were all ASW-oriented ships, which showed that during the seventies and eighties, that we're going to have that capability that was part of the warfighting mosaic of our Navy.

SC: *McCloy* was relatively well-equipped for multiple missions with air and surface search radars, one of which you've already mentioned, sonar and a towed array sonar. Additionally, her armament included a Mk-16 missile launcher for ASROC, which is the rocket-assisted antisubmarine weapon, two Mk-33 three-inch guns [3"/50] in a forward mount, and torpedo launchers for the Mk-46 torpedo. What was the configuration when you came aboard, and did it change substantially over the years?

PDM: We did not have the towed array system [system of hydrophones towed behind the ship used for passive detection of submarines] until I came aboard. That was put on board. In fact, they took the modified helo deck that we had there and then made that where they put the towed array, but that was later on in my time as CO. The thing was, as an ASW ship, we had zero, in my view, zero anti-air capability. The 46s were fine.

ASROC, I didn't know what the Navy was thinking to put two nuclear ASROCs on board that little ship. I did not know what they were thinking. We had to go through the Navy Weapons NTPI, Nuclear Technical Proficiency Inspection. They were already there when I got aboard, so I didn't do a Navy Weapons Acceptance Inspection [NWAI], but I knew that ASROC is something that our Navy doesn't need, because I don't think we ever had viable targeting information far enough away from the ship to ever use an ASROC. [*laughs*] That's true. I don't think we did. So that was where I started making my mental notes. I made a few mental notes that if I ever got into the position that I could influence or could have the authority, that there were a couple of things that I was going to help the Navy out with. It wasn't adding capability, it was taking away capability. In my view, the Navy spent a lot of money on things we didn't need. So we had that.

We were the first ones that had—us and the *Bronstein*—had this SQS-26 sonar, very high-powered. If you were close to a submarine, it probably drove them crazy with the sound that that thing would emit into the water. But I learned a little bit about ASW. I couldn't be fooled anymore about ASW, so that was good. But it was a grand ship to be able to go to sea on, to learn to become a commanding officer. The crew was slightly less than a DDG, slightly less than we had on *Parsons*. I was able to know everybody in the crew. It was just a great experience.

SC: *McCloy* was redesignated as a fast frigate in 1975 after you'd finished your tour as CO. What dynamics caused that redesignation from DE to FF, and did it have any real substantive change for roles, missions, or capabilities?

PDM: *Bronstein* and *McCloy* were probably the only two DEs left in the force, so it was easier just to change the designation to frigate. They ran with the 1040-class. The 1040 didn't have anything that we didn't have. They had a five-inch instead of three-inch gun. They had a single-mount five-inch. But other than that, they had the ASROC, they had the 46s. The two boilers were different. They were 1,200-pound high-pressure boilers that did nothing but break down, couldn't get under way all the time, but there was no difference in the capability of any of those ships.

SC: Before you reported aboard, did you attend Prospective Commanding Officer [PCO] School?

PDM: Yeah, but it was unremarkable. I said, "What the hell am I doing here?"

SC: Tell us about that experience.

PDM: It was back up in Newport. It was at the Destroyer School, I think. It was so unremarkable, I can't tell you anything about it. I listened to rules of the road, okay, they'd tell me about writing CASREPs [casualty reports], tell me about making sure your sailors conduct themselves properly ashore. They do all those things, but it didn't move the dial, didn't move it.

SC: Was there any practical training done, such as ship handling?

PDM: I think they took us over to the ship handling thing [tactical simulation trainer], but it didn't leave an impression. I don't remember.

SC: So it was largely policies, administration, that sort of subject.

PDM: They tried to help you and gave you a little handbook to make sure that when you went to be a CO that you didn't do anything stupid. It probably did a good job of that, because you listened, you wrote the notes down. If you had a problem and you went to your notes, you wouldn't be caught doing anything stupid. So it was good. [*laughs*]

SC: You were originally from Newport and mentioned that you had not been back in many years. How had Newport itself changed since your days as a youth there?

PDM: Night and day, absolutely night and day. When I was a youngster, Fenner Avenue, going down from Jesus Savior Church, which was near One-Mile Corner to Thames Street, was just a modest two-lane road down there. There were some stores on Thames Street. Navy was by far the prominent player on Aquidneck Island, by far. But it was also while I was on *McCloy* that the rumblings came out that they were going to take some of a slice of the fleet away because they were husbanding assets in different home ports. I didn't experience it because it wasn't done while I was there, but people were getting ready for it. I knew instinctively that when you have real estate like Aquidneck Island, that even though you'd lost the Navy, it was going to be all right. First, Second, and

Third Beaches, Ten-Mile Drive, it was a beautiful place and you knew that something would come and it would build and the island would be just fine.

SC: In addition to PCO School, were there any other Navy schools that you attended in preparation for reporting aboard *McCloy*?

PDM: None.

SC: From your viewpoint as a ship CO responsible for the welfare and safety of several hundred sailors and millions of dollars of equipment, did your perspective on the value of the firefighting training change any as you were CO of *McCloy*?

PDM: Every person, every person that goes to ship in a U.S. Navy ship should go through Firefighting School. Period.

SC: Were there any schools that you attended that were more or less useful for your CO experience?

PDM: Firefighting was, I think, because earlier on I talked about a fire we had in *Papago*. I liked the damage control trainer—*Buttercup*, was that it? I haven't thought about this in a long time, but that rings a bell, *Buttercup*, in which you got in there and you learned how to put shoring up and do the basics of damage control. That's very, very useful. I think both enlisted and officers should have those kinds of basic training, as well as all the technical training they're getting to pursue their respective rate or whatever job they have as an officer.

SC: Were there any Navy schools that you would have liked to have attended or, in retrospect, might have been useful in your first CO tour?

PDM: Not other than those two.

SC: From your perspective of having held several commands over the years, how would you modify, add to, or change the school preparation for a prospective CO embarking on their first CO tour?

PDM: That's a solid question because it's been my observation that the Navy's always coming up with better ways to prepare their department heads, to prepare their XOs, COs, for assignments of that responsibility. I'm not a huge fan of longer schools. Destroyer School was six months. That could have been three months, in my view. PCO School, as I said, I have zero memory. I don't even know how long it was. If it was six weeks, it was a wasted six weeks. I think that experience that is learned on the job at sea is far, far better than any academic environment, far better. I can see the quest for trying to design, trying to facilitate classroom learning that they hope would make you a better practitioner for whatever level you're talking about. I can see the merits of that, but I never extracted from that a meaningful experience that helped me later on. I went back to that PCO School when I was going to *Luce*. [*laughs*] It hadn't changed very much since I went to *McCloy*.

SC: Well, clearly they felt you hadn't learned it the first time. "We're going to send his rear end back one more time." [*laughs*]

Let's turn now to some dynamics of your tour and more personal. You've already mentioned your first two weeks, a very interesting first two weeks as the CO, but tell us about your very first day when you walked on board *McCloy*. It's your first CO tour. What were your thoughts? What were your emotions? What were you thinking as you walked up that brow?

PDM: Probably I walked up that brow and wondered what the hell I was doing here. I had never intended on staying in the Navy. I had been acquainted with the Navy because of the boatswain that had adopted me. I remember him talking about commanding officers that he had, and he always held them in very high esteem because they had this label called "commanding officer." So, becoming a commanding officer—and you read about commanding officers in naval history—is special. You entered a special club. So I felt that I was fortunate to be able to enter that club. I felt that whatever condition that that ship was in when I walked across the brow, from that moment on was mine. I believed strongly in that, and from then until I left it, it was my total responsibility, my responsibility for the crew.

We had a small change-of-command ceremony. At that time I looked like the lieutenant ops officer. I didn't look like the "old man" that you're later affectionately called. But I knew that for some reason I had been given this opportunity before the time that it's usually given to naval officers, and I knew that I could not let down those that might follow me in being younger than most or all—that I had to do well. I had to do well. There was no other outcome but being equal to all the commanding officers that I operated with that were older than I was. I was really myopic on that point, probably too much so, because I knew I had to work harder, I knew I had to write better, I knew I had to drive the ship better, because I felt that more people were watching than normally would be watching.

So all those things swirled through me as I was taking command of that ship. And then after I went through it, I didn't say this to John Hite, I think his name was, who I relieved, but I said, "This ship's going to change." It did not pass any standard that I had with regard to shipboard cleanliness, with regard to state of repair or appearance of the crew. It didn't live up to any standard. So in my nineteen or twenty months there, I knew what was my job was.

SC: Commanding officer turnover is a vital part of the process for assuming command. Why is a solid turnover so critical, and what would you recommend to any new CO about to assume a new command in terms of the turnover?

PDM: It's a legitimate question. That's the kind of question that you get in PCO School, okay? That's the kind of question, "Oh, we have a recipe card here for you to take command, and you should make sure *a, b, c, d, e, f, g, h*, all those items are carefully recorded and taken care of." That's a different book than I read from.

I mentioned to you earlier the way that ship was the day that I took it didn't make any difference. The CASREP list should have been up to date so I knew that these were the material problems on that ship, so then the CO would have detailed to me the confidences or lack of confidence he had in the respective officers in the wardroom, chiefs' quarters, the chiefs that you could really rely on, the chief of the boat, and then who were the stars in the enlisted ranks. That was helpful, so you didn't have to learn it again. At least you could look out then to see if they were your hierarchical people. Walk to after steering, make sure the gear out there, it works. Walk down into the bilges, take up a deck plate, and then that tells you all you need to know about the chief engineer and how he keeps the ship. You just do those basic things. You don't need to go to PCO School to learn this stuff. And you take command. It's yours.

SC: Were there any particular experiences, good or bad with the turnover process?

PDM: None.

SC: In the Navy, there are many traditions that have evolved from the British Royal Navy that were handed down to the new U.S. Navy in the 1770s and have endured for over two centuries. Chief among them is the announcement of prominent visitors and the key ship's personnel, often called "bonging aboard." What's your perspective on these traditions? Are they still useful? And what's their value to the twenty-first-century Navy?

PDM: I think the maintenance of an area on the ship adjacent to the access points on the ship called the brow, and the quarterdeck, I think, that is the area that deserves the highest naval reverence that you can provide it. I'll go into this later, but as a fleet commander, both Seventh and Atlantic, I could go on a ship, I could go through the quarterdeck, and I could tell you about the rest of that ship. I could tell you about it. It's important. It's damned important.

SC: And that's not just the physical appearance, but what do the watch standers look like—

PDM: That's right.

SC:—how do they conduct themselves?

PDM: How they conduct themselves. Absolutely.

SC: We will address that more in the more senior ranks.

PDM: Absolutely key.

SC: What was your first impression of the *McCloy* as a fighting ship and the efficiency of the crew?

PDM: As a fighting ship, not so much. We had one discipline, one area of the dimensions of warfare that we've gone over. She could play in one of them. She could play very well in one of them, but in the others, not so much. But you had the experience of running and being out there with the carrier at sea. This was the Cold War. This is where ASW was probably one of the more important elements of warfare at the time, and so you were privileged to be part of it. You were able to be out there. You'd be able to see how you employ multiple assets in a combined environment. You'd send out the S-2, the buoy [sonobuoys] rings, the buoys reported back, the S-3s [Lockheed S-3 Viking, jet-powered ASW aircraft] out there, the helicopters also then get data from a SOSUS station.[52] For a brand-new lieutenant commander, this was pretty good "juju," getting this experience early on.

So it wasn't the warfighting capability as you might look at it at PCO School, because it didn't tell you all those dimensions of warfare, when, in reality, you know that you're a participant in one of those, okay, and that was good, and you learned from it. And the other aspects of it, you would go through the required exercises of each of the

---

[52] Sonobuoy are dropped from a P-3 or an ASW helicopter in specified patterns where enemy submarine activity is suspected. Sonobuoys can be either passive (acoustic noise listening devices) or active SONAR.

capabilities. You had to shoot the gun to qualify, then you have to shoot the ASROC to qualify, and you go through all that. That's fine. But as far as being out at sea with that group and watching it all come together and trying to fuse all the information, for you being a little DE or then an FF, you were getting prime-time experience.

SC: A change-of-command ceremony is one of the traditional ceremonies in the naval service. Very often it's very formal and structured, not always, but every formality and part of the ceremony has specific meanings and intentions. Tell us about your change-of-command ceremony, and what is your perspective in general on these ceremonies?

PDM: The first change of command was conducted in Lisbon, Portugal, away from home port, away from everything, so it was a very informal gathering of the crew on the helo deck. He reads orders, he says goodbye to the crew, I say, "Get to work," and the change of command's over. [*laughs*]

SC: Did you have another more formal ceremony, or was that it?

PDM: That's it.

SC: What's your perspective on those ceremonies? Useful, not useful, waste of money, waste of energy?

PDM: I have different views on things than a lot of people in that regard. For certain commands, they're important. Certain venues, they're important. But if you're in a foreign port, if you're at sea, you don't need to bring out the band and the bugles and all that stuff. You need to conduct an informal, dignified, witnessed change of command, witnessed and executed, and then the old guy takes off and new guy's got it. I'll go over the memories that I have of the perfect change of command on Seventh Fleet when we get to it.

SC: We will certainly address that. Very often, the CO is the last to arrive aboard in port and often the first to leave, and there are very specific reasons for this. Why is this the case, and what is your perspective on this procedure?

PDM: Last aboard is proper. Pull in the brow and let's get under way. So I like that. I never prescribed [*sic*] to the other one. I was probably the last to leave.

SC: Obviously that was your work ethic, as you've described over the years. Did you sense that that would have any kind of inhibiting effect on the XO, the department heads?

PDM: No, because I made sure it didn't.

SC: Very often that's the case with some skippers and XOs.

PDM: My leadership style was absolutely clear. As soon as people had whatever their responsibilities were completed, they didn't have to wait around for me to ask them questions, like so many people do.

SC: Tell us about your typical day as a CO in port.

PDM: Typical day, you arrive. I never tried to get there super early and make people think that I'm trying to check when everybody comes aboard. I always got aboard at the nominal time that the whole crew was aboard. I spent most of my time talking with not only the XO, after getting the reports in the morning, the eight o'clock reports from the XO and learning about Johnny, who got in a fistfight down at the bar, getting through all that stuff, and then material things. I tried to be the expeditor in helping any division officer or department head that needed support in getting their division back up to where it should be, because we prided ourselves on keeping everything up all the time, and I didn't mind helping them make a phone call on something, or I'd go visit the shore maintenance facility and surprise everybody that the guy wearing the CO pin over here is asking, "What the hell?"

But I was a participating crew member, as well as I was their commanding officer. A lot of people don't grasp that they're part of the crew. They have a position of responsibility called command, but they're still one of 215—or pick a number—crew members. So I was a crew member. In the ships I had command of, you'd find me. When I was Seventh Fleet (commander, U.S. 7th Fleet)—we'll get to it—you'd find me anywhere. I learned more about every command that I had from people that never normally talked to me. They had constant access to me all the time, from that network, especially on USS *Enterprise* (CVN-65).

SC: That introduces the whole concept of command personal presence, and we're going to discuss that in some detail when you're a more senior officer.

Staff meetings are a part of the regular routine on a ship, on an underway staff or shore command. Some afloat COs like to hold regular wardroom meetings or briefs, and some prefer just to meet with the XO or the department heads. What was your style on *McCloy* and what's your perspective on staff meetings in general?

PDM: The staff meetings, I seldom called them. I liked some time with the whole wardroom, not necessarily for them to meet with me, but to give others the opportunity to share what was going on in their respective departments or divisions, so that when we would go to sea, everybody had a better idea, a better appreciation, a better understanding what was going on up in SQS-26 sonar room, as well as what was going on in the after engine room. So especially with junior officers, them being able to share that they're working on this or what, or inviting them down to come see it, that's how I drove staff meetings. I didn't drive staff meetings for them to sit there and report to me, "I have two CASREPs, Captain." I already knew that. So it was to get other people involved in the ship so that everybody owned not only their space, they owned the ship, so that when they walked around someplace, if they did see something, they'd be able to say, "Hey, I had the watch and I saw this." Communications going back and forth.

SC: And that can be critical, especially if you have casualties or lose key personnel. Others have to step in and take over those responsibilities.

PDM: Absolutely.

SC: You've already mentioned some of the major operations that *McCloy* participated in during your CO tenure. Are there any others that you'd like to highlight?

PDM: No, I ran on a lot about *McCloy* because it was the first command. Your first command, it always sticks with you, the good things, the bad things. Because I had such a dynamic first fourteen days, I can still see it happening. That was, what, fifty years? No, let's see. It's forty-seven years, forty-six years.

SC: My first command was NavCommSta [Naval Communications Station] Iceland augmentation detachment, and I remember every second of it, and I remember every radioman, ET [electronics technician], and signalman in that crew.

PDM: Good COs do that; they remember it all.

SC: A major overseas deployment of six months or more happens, such as the Mediterranean, or Med, deployment, or a Western Pacific, called a WestPac deployment, and that's at least every couple of years in the life of a warship and sometimes more frequently. What were some of the activities *McCloy* conducted in getting ready for an overseas deployment?

PDM: You had a lot of textbook help on that one, too, on pre-overseas movement, POM. The supply officer had one, operation officer had one, engineer had one, you know, and those were good. I don't make light of them. Those were very good because they were tested over the years, they were changed, updated, so usually if you followed your POM checklist in the sense of material, in the sense of supply, in the sense of your electronic equipment, you're ready, because a lot of ships had deployed, a lot of ships had gone through this and they'd come back and said, "We didn't have the whatchamacallit, the whatchamaphraseit," and so they'd amend it. The Navy did a great job at that, and they spent a lot of time at it, the system did.

So you go make sure that you did all that, but you know your ship. POM doesn't know your ship. So you get together with the board and say, "Hmm. What bulkhead spares do we need?" First time I looked at one, it said have bulkhead spare. The replacement parts or whatever that we required two of, the tubes for your radar, but data shows that this ship needs more, so somehow we've got to get and then keep them in the ET's cabinet down in the engineering spaces.

For *McCloy*, it was evaporator problems. That was my biggest bane of mechanical issues, because it never made enough fresh water. You needed to make sure that you had something like tools to put in a new boiler tube and then to carefully roll the end of that tube so that it would pass the hydro test. So I didn't want one set; I wanted two sets. So you'd go through, you'd look for your weak points, and then you make sure you have redundancy to not count on the system to be able to help you stay in the material condition you want to stay in. But the Navy's gotten a lot better about that with regard to supplying spares more quickly. Back then, not so much. So you had to take care of it yourself.

But even today, if I were going to a ship today, that would be the first thing I'd do. I'd say, "What do we have problems with, guys? We're going on a six-month deployment. I don't want anything to go down for any amount of time. I want to be at 100 percent up round [ready to operate], so you go through it and tell me what we need that's extra, and there's some mechanism that we'll find it, even if we borrow it from a ship. I'll go to the ship next door, borrow it, and then they can get the one that we requested," all that kind of informal network to get things done.

SC: And you also have to make sure you have plenty of relative bearing grease [*Miller laughs*] and the Golden Rivet for the benefit of any newly reported-aboard ensigns.

PDM: Right. You need an extra mail buoy. [*laughs*]

SC: A hook for the mail buoy, absolutely essential equipment. Well, you've already pretty well described your role as a CO in getting the ship ready to deploy. Who were other key players?

PDM: Everybody was a key player. I don't like that term. There's no such thing as a non-key player. If the person was a member of the crew, he was a key player. With ship manning documents, they go through those things pretty carefully, and everybody that's on there is needed to do *x* job. So if you want that job done without having somebody else do it, he's a key player.

SC: Prior to any underway period, one of the critical evolutions is the navigation brief. As fundamental as this event is, they sometimes don't occur and, sadly, sometimes lead to trouble, such as the recent event in the Persian Gulf where two patrol boats got lost and strayed into Iranian waters. According to the investigation, they did not conduct a pre-departure navigation brief. Tell us about the typical pre-underway navigation brief that you required on *McCloy*.

PDM: That's something that was absolutely clear that before we would get under way, even from Newport, Rhode Island, that we would have a formal navigation brief, track laid out, a navigation sea and anchor detail. Why? Because I have been in and out of Newport, Rhode Island, without ever even seeing that bridge [Pell Bridge across eastern Narragansett Bay joining Aquidneck and Jamestown Islands]. So you had to know the radar points. You had to know what went on as you exited or entered that harbor. So in a foreign port, it's even more important, and the only way that you do it is a navigation brief. It's much better now with electronic charts, but you had to make sure that the changes were up to date. That's the first thing I'd ask the navigator—what was the latest change published, and if all our charts had been updated with that in it, because they would move this buoy, they would do that. It was terribly important. But the ritual of having a sea and anchor detail or pre-navigation meeting is a very, very important step in prudent seamanship.

SC: Navy warships must also prepare for possible NEO operation or the evacuation from a hostile zone of noncombatants, especially U.S. citizens. Did *McCloy* do anything special in preparation for possible NEO ops?

PDM: No.

SC: Most COs are particularly mindful of giving the crew as much time as possible off the ship before deploying, even though the preparations are typically accelerated. What is the purpose of that action and why is that a critical element of a ship's efficiency and ultimate effectiveness?

PDM: Over time, commanding officers, the Navy, they've learned that if your crew has sufficient opportunity to prepare their family for the deployment, it was equally as important as preparing the ship for deployment, because the thing that you didn't want to happen is that your crack quartermaster or your crack BT [boiler technician] get this emergency-gram from his wife that they didn't tend to something and they were having a huge problem, and it distracts him from doing his job. So you had to make sure that you did the best you could to make sure that the families were ready to deploy too.

 Becky took that upon herself to be part of the ship writ large, including the crew and those that had families, in being able to make sure there was a call list. They could first go to the wide network to help and you get all that stuff done in the pre-deployment, and if they had everything done, I didn't care. They didn't have to stay on the ship till liberty call. That's at the discretion of the department head to spend as much time getting prepared as they needed.

SC: Sometimes a new CO is leery of letting another officer get the ship under way for the first time. What was your perspective on that dynamic?

PDM: I should have highlighted it. I have, I think, reports from at least three commodores who said that I permitted junior officers to handle the ship under all circumstances. I believe strongly in that, and I think that stemmed from me gaining the confidence in ship handling from being on those ATFs. They weren't big, but you still had the same elements of tide, of wind, of relative motion impacting the ship as you did on a destroyer as you did on a DLG and whatever, and I was always confident I could handle that.

When I came to *McCloy*, I didn't even get the ship under way the first time. I said, "Who's the sea and anchor detail OOD?" I said, "Let's go." I think that surprised him. I was confident enough, particularly in the relative motion thing. I knew he was doing the right thing, and I knew that I would have to prompt him if he wasn't doing it soon enough. I wasn't one that was right on his ear, but relative motion creeps on you really quickly, and if you don't anticipate and make a change in advance of that relative motion taking full effect, you get yourself behind the problem. So it was letting them get to that position where, "I think you'd back a little harder," or do this.

I'm not blowing my own horn here, but I prided myself in teaching ship handling to junior officers. When I went to the destroyer, I became a fleet OOD in the destroyer uncommonly quickly, and I was a sea detail ship handler. I was comfortable in any ship handling situation.

SC: Tell us about your typical day at sea as CO of *McCloy*.

PDM: If it was a calm day, if we had gone down to GTMO [Naval Station Guantanamo Bay, Cuba] for refresher training [REFTRA], if it was a calm day, it was a pretty good day. [*laughs*] We could make fresh water and the sailors could be topside doing the maintenance that they needed to do, and I spent most of my time then going around talking to folks, finding out what their problem was, and the days passed, having lunch with crew. Those were unique times because you were in transit, you spent time up in the captain's chair on the bridge watching the beautiful ocean go by, and this was part of your career. You were getting paid for this. It was just beautiful.

If it was rough, it was work. The smaller the ship, the rougher the sea. That's the way it is. You can't get away from it. The less tonnage you have, the bigger rolls you take, the more bouncing you do. And on those ATFs, it was absolutely ludicrous. *McCloy*, because, as I said, the righting moment was barely, barely in specs, rough seas, you spent a lot of time holding on and eating peanut butter and jelly sandwiches.

SC: One of the toughest parts about being a CO under way is the lack of rest and the constant interruptions while you're trying to sleep. What about that aspect of command, and how did you deal with it?

PDM: If we were in a situation where I believed that I needed to be called upon lots, I would doze in a chair. I'd just be right there, and it was easier for the OOD to walk over. Then both at sea and in my sea cabins, I kept that repeater on red. Again, you either have the gift or you have to spend a lot of time acquiring it, but you knew where you would go, you knew the course and speed you were on. If the officer of the deck said, "I have this contact, x, y, z, going on course a, b, c, cross down the portside three thousand yards," or whatever, I could visually plot it. I could look at the compass and I could see it. I could see it in my mind. Fine. I wouldn't worry about it. And the same thing on the bridge, even if I was half asleep, I was able to sense relative motion, no matter what was going on at sea, even when we were in a formation steaming, which sometimes is tough. But back then, particularly in *McCloy*, the rear admiral that was in charge of the task force, liked to change the screen, the ASW screen. What he did that for, I don't know, but he liked to do that and would do it in the middle of the damn night. So you were in screen, and they told you to go to screen Juliet or whatever, and you'd have these destroyer escorts and frigates going in different parts of the ocean, that was always a challenge. I mean, you knew that you had to go over here, but that point was moving at fifteen, eighteen knots, and you knew another ship had to come from another way. So you'd figure out your maneuvering board solution, or the officer of the deck would figure out the maneuvering board solution, but very seldom it was my experience that you could ring up twenty knots and go to that without having to alter it in some ways. Great experience, but why we did it, every time we did that, I wondered, "What the hell's he doing?" Maybe he was just training us, maybe. I don't know. But what contribution it made to the overall task force readiness, it was always a mystery to this young commanding officer, a mystery.

SC: Mysteries of the sea.

PDM: It was! But they did it! You remember that!

SC: I do, indeed. This concludes our first look at your time as commanding officer of USS *McCloy*. In our next session, we'll continue with a look at your initial afloat command tour and your perspectives on effective commanding officer leadership.

This is USNI oral history interview with Admiral Paul David Miller, U.S. Navy (Ret.). This is session number five, question set number nine. The date is Sunday, December 3, 2017, and the interviewer is Professor Stan Carpenter from the U.S. Naval War College. Thank you, Admiral.

SC: This is USNI oral history interview with Admiral Paul David Miller, U.S. Navy (Ret.). This is session number five, question set number ten. The date is Sunday, December 3, 2017. These questions cover the years as commanding officer of USS *McCloy*, and the interviewer is Professor Stan Carpenter from the U.S. Naval War College.

Admiral, we're going to continue discussing your time as CO of the *McCloy* from 1972 to '73. Underway replenishment, or UNREP, is an evolution that every Navy ship goes through regularly while on deployment. What is UNREP, and what are the hazards inherent in that event, and how, as a CO, did you mitigate the potential hazards?

PDM: UNREP, as every sailor knows, is underway replenishment. You fuel your ship, you can bring stores aboard your ship, and you can exchange passengers from one to the other. It entails coming alongside the delivering ship. You're usually the receiving ship because you're smaller, particularly in the destroyer world. It's an evolution that is, I would say, easily conducted under a good sea and weather conditions, a little bit more tedious at night, and kind of rough when the weather is tossing your ship a little bit and is tossing the delivering ship a little bit, although it might be an oiler or a replenishment ship of some size. The idea is to come along relatively quickly, stop your ship where you're going to receive the lines to hook yourselves up. By "stop" I mean you're coming in at a pace where you're in an overtaking situation, and then you slow rapidly to glide into your receiving station position, which is having your fueling rig right across from their fueling rig. I looked at it as good sport. You come in hot, you're able to cut your engines, be able to glide in, then get back up to the speed that you need to be to maintain that for the next hour and a half while you're transferring whatever you're transferring. It keeps the task force or task group replenished for twenty-four-hour operations for extended periods of time, and every battle group or ship is able to conduct these evolutions. If they're routine, they should be done by the officer of the deck, whoever has the watch at the time. You set the special sea and anchor detail for fueling, for stores, or for whatever you're doing, and the evolution is conducted normally without hazard, without fanfare, and you go on back to your station or go back to your assigned position and continue your battle group operations.

I used to enjoy it. It was a challenging two hours. Nighttime, I loved nighttime replenishments. You had to get the lights proper, and somehow at night it's just like on a carrier, where you've got to get those lights right and there's not as much room for error. But it seems like you're closing faster than in the daytime, but you're not.

SC: A typical role of an FF [fast frigate] is what is called maritime interdiction operations. What's that all about and what is the ultimate objective of maritime interdiction?

PDM: We were never assigned maritime interdiction on the USS *McCloy*. I don't believe maritime interdiction became part of the vernacular until after the Cold War. It may have, but it wasn't something that was on the lips of all operating sailors. What did you want to interdict? Did you want to interdict shipping? Did you want to interdict short of a blockade, you wanted to interdict some ships that you didn't want to get into some place? In *McCloy*, we never did much of that.

Later on, as a numbered fleet commander, we became pretty proficient at it, but not on the FF. I don't even think that came up in any discussions in the waterfront in Newport. That wasn't an activity. In Vietnam, you had interdiction of whatever supplies the North may have been bringing down to the South. You'd have the different small boats, the *dhou* [small sailing vessel common in Middle Eastern waters]. Then we later had it in the Persian Gulf, but not out of Newport, Rhode Island. Everything was pretty sanguine there.

SC: Every warship typically will have a landing party designated or a boarding party. What were the dynamics of that on a fast frigate, and what sort of training or preparation did *McCloy*'s boarding party have?

PDM: We didn't spend much time on that either. Why? Because I just feared ever having to put that motor whaleboat in the water, and particularly anything but the very calmest of conditions, and then putting people out there, manned with their life vests. We did not even carry armor back then. We did carry a requisite number of rifles, long guns, and we did, of course, carry side arms, and we'd have to practice that during Operational Readiness Inspection, but we knew that that wasn't one of the things that that ship was built for, so we did it because we were prescribed to do it, but we didn't spend a lot of time rehearsing it.

SC: As a destroyer, frigate, or cruiser working with an aircraft carrier as an escort, it's a hazardous world indeed. Tell us about the dynamics of steaming in a battle group or task force with a carrier.

PDM: I think we've covered most of that. The only carrier that I deployed with on *McCloy* was the *Intrepid* and that wasn't a full air wing, as I described earlier. They were an ASW air wing. So that was a bit different, because to get those aircraft off the deck, they did not have to get thirty knots of relative wind, or thirty-five knots, depending on the weight of the attack or fighter aircraft they were launching. They could launch with less wind, and usually where we operated in the North Atlantic, they had plenty of that stuff called wind anyhow. So it wasn't that dynamic like we had in the Gulf on *Parsons*, where the carrier, you'd hear on the radio whatever the call sign was for, say, USS *Ranger*, you know, "Coming to Fox Corpen Zero-3–5 [course of 035 degrees true], speed thirty," and those carriers didn't waste one second in getting to Corpen Zero-3–5, and they could care less about whoever else was out there, and their plane guard that was astern of them. They [the plane guard] couldn't get up to thirty knots at the same rate, so it was different. I later learned that and did that. I did it when we were in the Tonkin Gulf on *Parsons*, but we did not have that dynamic in *McCloy*.

SC: What about plane guard? Give us the definition, and why is it such a critical function of a destroyer or frigate?

PDM: A plane guard was simply following astern of the carrier, usually at double standard distance or even further, one thousand yards, fifteen hundred yards, just in case the carrier had a mishap, either in launching or a recovery cycle, and somebody had to punch out of an aircraft. You were in position, your motor whaleboat was at the rail, and you had people that were ready to man the stations to be able to get lifesaving equipment into the water, get the boat into the water, to recover them as quickly as possible after a mishap. Those that worked in that position in the Gulf were exercised. We had plane guard assignments on *Intrepid* (CV/CVA/CVS-11), but I think it was because the flag was a carrier attack or fighter pilot and he liked that, but there were no ejection seats on S-2s. [*laughs*] There were no ejection seats on the helicopter. They had to ride those puppies into the water if something went wrong.

SC: All Navy vessels undergo periodic inspections that seek to assess the combat readiness and material condition. What were some of those inspections that a typical FF or DD would undergo in the early 1970s?

PDM: I respected the syllabus for going through refresher training and then having your Operational Readiness Inspection [ORI]. It gave you a sense that your crew was sufficiently trained. The inspecting party, which was generally made up of very well-trained fleet sailors—I'd call them salty and a lot of time, the engineers—you couldn't fool 'em. The signalmen had seen more on the signal bridge than your second-class [signalman] had ever seen. The quartermaster and navigation, when they came in and they put paper or whatever they put on your bridge windows and told you to get under way from GTMO imagining that was a full fog situation, you had to do what you needed to do to get out of the harbor. Those were all thoughtful and proven-over-time exercises that your crew was put through, and whether it was on *Parsons*, whether it was on *McCloy*, then later on, I prescribed [*sic*] fully. I never gave those people responsible for that a hard time. I thanked them. They always left the ship just a little bit more ready than if you didn't go through that.

SC: What inspections did *McCloy* undergo while you were the CO?

PDM: We went through all of them. We went through, of course, the ORI. We went through an NTPI. I mentioned that earlier. That was the Nuclear Technical Proficiency Inspection. We went through an INSURV, Inspection and Survey, that they do well in a year or more in advance of you going into the shipyard, in which they inspect and tear down some of your equipment to see what category of overhaul it needed, whether it needed just replacement of the bearings or it needed a whole overhaul of the motor generator set or lube oil pump or whatever. I think I went through most of the inspections in *McCloy*.

SC: As CO, what was your philosophy on inspection preparations, and how did you prepare your ship and crew for these events?

PDM: They always send you too much material to get the respective departments in the ship prepared for their coming aboard. Sharing that with the crew was easy. "This test is open book. They're giving you what they're going to do. So get an A-plus on this test, because you have all the questions in advance. If you come in with a bad report, then that's not good." So it was not hard to get prepared for them. It gave you what you needed to do, and it was just time and diligence to have your people get ready for the inspection and then for you, if you were the engineer, to meet the engineering inspectors, establish a good rapport with them, and show that you were ready, and if you showed them that you were ready, I always saw that the inspection went more smoothly and the grading was more fair, and it was just like taking any other test.

SC: Except you have the test questions ahead of time.

PDM: Right.

SC: You've mentioned already refresher training or REFTRA. That is a dreaded evolution by all surface sailors.

PDM: Yes it is.

SC: Did *McCloy* ever endure REFTRA while you were aboard?

PDM: Yes, we did.

SC: Tell us about REFTRA and what goes on there.

PDM: REFTRA, we would go down to GTMO for, I don't know, a three-week period; I forget what exactly it was. But it's just making sure that your ship was ready for a certification for fleet operations. That's why when you hear about the most recent collisions out in WestPac, you wonder, because no ship is sent to sail on a deployment without going through these steps, and they have to be trained to a certain level to be able to have those inspectors say that, "Yes, this ship is ready to do those things." And that's what REFTRA did. They went through everything, including, I remember, doing a towing and being-towed exercise. With my ATF experience, we did well in that. [*laughs*]

SC: A colleague of yours, Admiral Jim Stavridis, once remarked that, quote, "The psychology of inspections is interesting," end quote.[53] What do you think he meant by that, and how do you react to that characterization?

PDM: I don't know, but to me, he's referring to the attitude. The inspectors in any of the inspections that we've mentioned, they've seen it all, and so you have to approach it with an attitude of they're there not to find deep, dark, bad things about you, but they're there to make sure that you are reinforced with an outside look at your capability, so that when

---

[53] Admiral James G. Stavridis (1955–) graduated from the U.S. Naval Academy in 1976 and served in the U.S. Navy from 1976 to 2013. His last billet was as supreme allied commander, Europe and commander, U.S. forces in Europe from 2009 to 2013.

you complete it, you even feel better about your capability because you've had someone else give it a check. So I think that's what he's referring to.

SC: From your perspective now as a retired admiral having held significant major commands, looking back, are there any inspection regimes that are really not helpful or needed, or are there some that you think should be beefed up or made more robust?

PDM: I mentioned earlier that NTPI and NWAIs are not needed because nuclear weapons were needed neither on that ASROC ship that I had nor on the guided missile destroyer that I had. So I made the mental note to do all I can to get nuclear weapons off of surface ships, and we were successful. Period.

SC: "I can neither confirm nor deny the presence of nuclear weapons aboard this vessel."

PDM: That's it.

SC: From your perspective of a retired flag officer, what would you say to a CO in his or her first afloat command when dealing with a problematic or disappointing inspection result?

PDM: First I'd ask them, "Why did you get a disappointing inspection result?" Because you get everything beforehand except the nuclear. When we get to *Luce*, I'll save it, but that's the only surprise inspection there is. Later on when I get in *Luce*, they had a thing called the OPPE, Operational Propulsion [Plant] Examination. They had a few surprise OPPEs. I'll save that to *Luce* because it's more germane.

SC: Shipyard, that's another dreaded evolution among sailors. Did *McCloy* ever do a shipyard period while you were CO?

PDM: Towards the end of it, we did not do a full shipyard period. We went into a Boston shipyard for availability [brief repair period for minor work alongside a tender or pier or in a shipyard], but we did not do a full overhaul.

SC: What typically occurs when you go to a full availability, long-term shipyard period?

PDM: Oh, mercy. The ship's taken to parade rest, the crew's moved off. It's a nightmare for the commanding officer and the XO. For the next six months, nine months, for the carriers two years, it's just a terribly tough time on the crew, tough time on the ship, putting it back together. I worked hard to never go through that. Honestly, I worked very hard to never go through that.

SC: You've already addressed the primary mission of the frigate/destroyer community, antisubmarine warfare, ASW—

PDM: Correctly phrased, the primary mission of that brand of ship. Frigates were designated ASW units. There were others, then we had the DDGs, that were the anti-air warfare unit that had ASW capability but their primary mission was anti-air warfare. In the frigate world, it was the other way around.

SC: Tell us about the dynamics of ASW. What are some of the techniques used to detect, track, and destroy hostile submarines?

PDM: Not to be redundant, but to be really effective at antisubmarine warfare, it has to be a complex bringing together of capabilities like we had in the *Intrepid* /9CV/CVA/CVS-11) HUK [Hunter-Killer Group] group. You had surface capability; you had air capability, long range in the S-2s, shorter range in the helos. You had a fusion center to bring in the information from the SOSUS network, later on we had a fusion center that would bring in satellite information and towed array information. As we got more sophisticated with capability, we became a little bit better at understanding and appreciating and finding submarines, but it took fusion of all that information. You couldn't just do it with the S-2, P-3. The P-3 [Lockheed P-3 Orion, four-engine maritime patrol aircraft] would be able to do it better than any other single unit because they would be able to drop the sonobuoys [sonar buoys] and then they would be able to monitor them, and then they would be able to get information from the SOSUS network and be able to fuse that.[54] But any audience has to understand ASW, just like air warfare, is the fusion of information. It's very tough for a single unit to prevail by itself, but you have to fuse it all together.

SC: One of the big changes in naval warfare since World War II is the advent of the missile age. Guns are no longer the main battery of naval combatants. What are some of the dynamics of war at sea in the missile age as opposed to the gun age?

PDM: Extended range, speed of adversary—big difference—problems unfolding much quicker, so you just have to ratchet up your sensors, you have to ratchet up the fusion of information again, and then you have to make sure that the batteries that you have, in this case the missile battery, work.

SC: We'll talk in future interviews about the Navy's transition from the blue water fleet-on-fleet conventional battle that characterized a hot-war scenario between NATO and the Warsaw Pact in the Cold War era to the current littoral operations or brown water [inland rivers, coastal or littoral waters] scenario of the past three decades. How were *McCloy* and other ASW-configured warships prepared for dealing with the diesel submarine threat during the Cold War?

PDM: Diesel submarines are tough, but we weren't challenged by diesel submarines much. We were challenged by nuclear attack submarines and boomer boats [ballistic missile submarines] coming from the then–Soviet Union. They were making them quieter, they were harder to detect. Ours were harder to detect. It wasn't until we

---

[54] The P-3 Orion is a maritime patrol aircraft built by Lockheed Martin. It was first fielded in the 1960s and is a long-range maritime patrol and ASW platform capable of detecting, tracking, and attacking submarines.

transitioned to the post–Cold War that our meter on getting better prepared for diesel submarines, which is a very, very tough problem, come into being. When Iraq would buy submarines from Russia, when India had them, when Korea had them, when China had first conventional, not nuclear, ASW changed because it went from an open ocean, deep water to littoral and coastal water problem. The dynamics of sound propagation in deep water is much different than in littoral water. But during my time as both CO of *McCloy* and then *Luce*, the Cold War was still in full blossom, so we were worrying about the big bear threat from the north.

SC: In this same vein, even though we might be getting a little ahead here, what are your thoughts on how the current U.S. Navy should deal with such possible littoral threats such as diesel submarines?

PDM: Take 'em out before they get under way. Period. Then if you miss that opportunity, because a diesel submarine has no defensive function from our vantage point, defensive from an adversary's vantage point, but from ours, that diesel submarine, from the time it leaves the pier from wherever they were, is offensive in nature. And what is their mission? It isn't to just go out and patrol the littoral; it's to know where our surface ships are, to be able to operate as close as they can to them, and to be there to be able to take responses from their national command authority. So as [commander] Seventh Fleet, I always watched where the submarines, the potential adversaries, were when they were not at sea, and know where they were, in what port they were in, should something go on. That's the best place to get 'em.

SC: Although missiles have replaced guns as the main weapon system of modern warships, guns remain a key weapon system, and gunnery exercises are common. Tell us about the gunnery exercises while you were on board *McCloy*.

PDM: The only time we had gunnery exercises was during REFTRA, and let me tell you, a three-inch gun and naval gunnery may have been good at some point in time in naval history, but in the 1970s, they didn't play too much of a role. The only thing you had was some little defensive capability if you needed it, but other than that, it didn't play a role.

SC: What about the Combat Information Center, CIC, on *McCloy*? The larger the ship type, the more robust the CIC. What did you have aboard *McCloy*?

PDM: We had a small, decent CIC center, because we had an air-search radar. We had the old DRT-2 [dead reckoning tracer] plotter. We had an ECM desk, electronic countermeasures, and electronic warfare [EW] little section, so we were able to have our own little fusion center there. Was it robust? Not so much. Why? Because that ship sailed always with ASW as its primary mission. So we turned it all into fused information, on a small-scale chart or on the DRT. It tracks our movement and then we'd be able to plot all the other information and try to maintain an undersea picture as opposed to an air picture. Later on as CO of a guided missile destroyer, I maintained more of an air picture than a submarine picture.

SC: When you were CO of *McCloy*, did you spend your general quarters time in combat or on the bridge?

PDM: On the bridge.

SC: Major fleet exercises are part of the training cycle in the Navy, such as COMTUEX and JTFEX. Tell us about your experiences with major fleet exercises as CO of *McCloy*.

PDM: In my experience, I did not engage in a Northern Wedding or other large-scale combined exercise in the North Atlantic. We did do, again, ASW ops up in the North Atlantic, and if another larger-scale exercise was going on, we were the ASW commander. We weren't the carrier with ASW lead for the overarching force, but I can't recall participating in a huge combined exercise like that. I did it on the *Luce*, three of them, but we just did it mainly with the carrier *Intrepid* on ASW exercises.

SC: Admiral Stavridis has referred to missile exercises as being like, quote, "Japanese Kabuki theatre," end quote. What he meant was that they tend to be unrealistic and too scripted. How would you react to that statement?

PDM: Well, I'll respond to that when I get to *Luce*, because we didn't have any missile exercises in *McCloy*.

SC: What general observations can you make about multiship operations or even multinational operations in a combat or potential combat environment? How does this differ from single-ship or independent steaming?

PDM: Let's skip that one, too, because I was the commanding officer of StanavForLant [Standing Naval Force Atlantic] flagship, and so there we can go over all the combined ops and all the anecdotal capability of combined ops.

SC: We'll hold that question for a later interview. Let's turn now to the leadership side of being an afloat CO and the dynamics of a warship at sea and the human aspects. In a broader sense, what's the responsibility of senior officers in terms of their personal behavior, especially with juniors that they are close to and work with daily?

PDM: Two words: do right. I took that to industry. That's all. I don't have to say anything else. It's simple. There's right; there's wrong.

SC: Do right.

PDM: And particularly if you're in a leadership position. Do right. No choice.

SC: For most COs, captain's mast is the least likeable part of the job. We've discussed nonjudicial punishment, or NJP, previously in terms of being a division officer or department head and an XO, but now as a CO, the entire picture changes. What are your thoughts on captain's mast and NJP as a CO?

PDM: I think whoever authored the Uniform Code of Military Justice should be applauded, because it is unique, it is indispensable in maintaining good order and discipline in the military, indispensable. And so however way back when, when that was started, it has been groomed since to make it more effective, high marks, because it gives a commanding officer the ability to correct issues in-house, to set his standards in-house, to be able to be lenient when it's deserved and to be tough when it's required. I think it's an ingenious system, ingenious.

SC: All of us who have done sea duty have spent holidays under way such as Thanksgiving or Christmas. What is your perspective on this issue, and how did you deal with it as a ship CO?

PDM: Fortunately, I've spent some but not an inordinate amount of holiday days at sea, but when you did, people looked forward to the time off. People looked forward to the extra good food that they were going to have, extra movie sessions that they were going to see. You just make it as a comfortable a period of time that you possibly could. The Navy has changed so much. I go back to my correspondence with Becky when I was in *Parsons* in Southeast Asia, where it took three weeks to get a letter. Three weeks! Now it's different. Holidays are different because you're there. You're not there physically, but you're there because they've been able to talk to you in the morning. The kids would be able to report to Dad what came, or Mom, what came for Christmas or whatever. It's more genteel. Technology has permitted that. You know back in the sixties, seventies, eighties, not quite so much. You just had to make the best of the time that you know that the crew was experiencing, particularly those with families who were experiencing a little down time, that's all.

SC: Tell us about the homecoming following a major deployment, and as the CO, what was your attitude towards homecoming and what preparations did you make?

PDM: Not many. Homecoming took care of itself. I enjoyed watching the folks that had short-timer chains and get it down to ten days and a wakeup. [*laughs*] There were some people that carried that a little bit too far, but it was enjoyable. Homecomings took care of themselves. It needed no facilitating.

SC: Crew illness at sea is a constant problem. I remember one Thanksgiving Day coming out of Barcelona with half the ship down with the crud, not a happy scenario. What recommendations would you make to newly incoming COs as to how to deal with this dynamic, and what can one do as a CO to minimize his or her susceptibility to illness at sea?

PDM: Boy, you know what? I've never spent a lot of time thinking about that, but I guess it's probably a pretty important question, particularly in making sure that shipboard sanitation was what it should be. It mostly always stemmed from food not being cleaned properly, cooked properly, or other sanitation issues, inspecting the food before it came on board, particularly in some of the ports where food would come from. I'm just trying to run through my mind quickly if I ever knew of a ship in a fleet that I commanded that experienced that to the extent that it impacted the ship's readiness, and I can report that I have not. So things like that, they might happen, but it doesn't occur very much.

SC: What would you do as a CO to inoculate yourself against being ill at sea? Anything you can do?

PDM: That's another imponderable. You just live like you live at sea or ashore, and you take those measures that are necessary. If someone is sick and they can diagnose it and it is a particular ailment, you take the precautions to make sure that ailment doesn't spread. But that's something that I never worried about, never.

SC: You're a very athletic person. What did you do while at sea or as a CO to maintain your physical fitness?

PDM: I always made sure that every ship I was on had a weight room. If not, we made one. If it was a fan room, we made it into one. And then if you had the weight room, then if you're on a ship, a small ship like *McCloy* or the ATFs or even the DDG in rough weather, you get enough aerobic stuff just walking up and down in rough weather. But I always tried to get folks to stay in as good a shape as I was, and they did. People would follow you. We'd set up the weight room, we'd set up the bench presses, the racks of weights that we had to make sure were tied down during heavy weather. But that's what we did. We did weight rooms and other exercise apparatus before it became cool with the Navy.

SC: As a ship CO, what steps did you take to prepare the crew for port visits and liberty call in a foreign port?

PDM: You always got from a consulate or the embassy the "dos and don'ts" cultural lists, so you made sure that the crew was acquainted there. You always had the hospital corpsmen inoculate them mentally against getting themselves some disease that they didn't want or need. You'd make sure you'd go through those things, and you would reinforce the point that those judicial systems that are in other places than your ship and the USA are different, and you don't want to be involved with them.

SC: Dr. Samuel Johnson, the great British eighteenth-century philosophy and sage, said of being at sea, quote, "No man will be a sailor who has contrivance enough to get himself into a jail, for being in a ship is being in a jail with a chance of being drowned. A man in a jail has more room, better food, and commonly better company." What did he mean by that, and what does that mean to you?

PDM: It meant that he was looking back at the way the navies of the world were, not the way the navies of the world are.

This is USNI oral history interview with Admiral Paul David Miller, U.S. Navy (Ret.). This is session number five, question set number ten. The date is Sunday, December 3, 2017, and the interviewer is Professor Stan Carpenter from the U.S. Naval War College. Thank you, Admiral.

SC: This is USNI oral history interview with Admiral Paul David Miller, U.S. Navy (Ret.). This is session number five, question set number eleven. The date is Sunday, December 3, 2017. These questions cover the years as commanding officer of USS *McCloy*, and the interviewer is Professor Stan Carpenter from the U.S. Naval War College.

Many COs spend a lot of time in the captain's chair on the bridge, and you've already mentioned that a couple of times. Does this say anything, if at all, about the CO's attitude towards the watch and ship handling, or is it just a particular preference, and what was your attitude on that aspect of CO presence?

PDM: The captain's chair on a ship is part of the lore of going to sea, as is the captain getting bonged when he comes aboard. It's part of the attitude that he sets when he's on the bridge. He sits in his chair, and I tell people that that chair is not for the watch. From the first time I became a CO, I'd best not walk through that hatch and find somebody resting in that chair, and I never did. But it's the captain's place to be able to surveil what's going on, to listen to how the respective watch standers are discharging their duties, so it's a place where you can get an outstanding feel for how that section of your ship is operating, and I spent a lot of time in the captain's chair. I'd always read my messages and morning traffic there. I never read a book there. I didn't think that was part of what people should see. It wasn't leisure time. The bridge was not a place of leisure. The bridge was a place of functioning and practicing the art of seamanship. So I don't know where that came from. I never looked up who had the first captain's chair, but it is a bit of heraldry or whatever that I think is striking, and it is observed and I applauded it.

SC: I think the tradition probably comes from the quarterdeck on sailing ships, where no one entered the quarterdeck unless they had an official function. That was the captain and the officer of the deck's location.

PDM: Yes.

SC: And I think that transitioned over to the captain on the bridge.

PDM: Sounds reasonable to me.

SC: Well, we'll call it that. [*laughs*]

PDM: Sounds reasonable.

SC: What are the CO's night orders and what's their purpose?

PDM: This is one thing that PCO School would make sure that you had, that [for] example when you went on your ship, you needed to have *a, b, c, d*, all the way through *z*, things covered in your night orders. It is just those things that you expect the officer of the deck to discharge during those hours that the ship is not fully manned with all the folks in their respective work spaces. It's manned by those that are on watch. It's common sense. But the CO gets to put in the first paragraph what the parameters are that he wants the officer of the deck to follow with regard to notifying him, calling him, contacts, the air picture if you had an air picture. It just depends on the confidence of the CO.

My standing orders were probably pretty loose. Obviously, those two ships that collided, they had some officers that didn't follow them. But if they're good, you don't have to have that piece of paper there. You have that piece of paper there just because what's going to happen in the investigations. They want to know what the prescription was, but any CO of the size of a ship of a destroyer or even a larger ship, anybody that you have signed off on the qualification to be the officer of the deck, to be your representative on that ship, you should have enough confidence in and enough relationship with that he doesn't need a sheet of paper.

SC: Roaming the ship is a habit of many COs, as opposed to what has been termed, quote, "governing from an Olympic detachment," end quote. How would you describe your command style, and are there advantages and disadvantages to each style of command leadership?

PDM: Every skipper has to not only develop his own, but refine it. There is no doubt in my mind that I refined my leadership style from one command to another. It's only natural. But I'm that category of I don't appreciate the term "roaming the ship," because that connotes you just walk around and, you know, didn't have a specific purpose. I never spent time in my in port cabin at sea, but I spent a lot of time off the bridge and away from my sea cabin to just spend time in the comm [communications] shack, for instance. Back then, communications were totally different. You didn't have an iPad with all the information on it. You had those TTY teletype machines. So I'd go down there and read the scroll as it was coming over. You want to get the news. One TTY was copying the AP [Associated Press] news or whatever.

Then you'd find out what was going on with your receivers, how many of them were not functioning quite right. You'd go down to main control and you'd be able to look at all the gauges and you'd see how all the engineering equipment was functioning. Every once in a while at sea I'd go back and ask the guy in after steering how the hell he's doing. Most skippers wouldn't know where after steering was.

SC: You probably woke them up a few times. [*laughs*]

PDM: Probably, or somebody else got to them on the phone and said, "Hey, the old man's coming back," or whatever. Walk down to the paint locker. I have an affinity for paint locker. I told you that story. So I'd go down to the fo'c'sle part of the ship, open up, go down to the paint locker. I don't know how many COs have been down to the paint locker, but, you know, the guys down there are in a bad place. It's a bad place to breathe. They really appreciated somebody coming down and seeing what the hell they do. I read you three lines from a fitness report.

SC: So rather than "roaming the ship," would a better phrase be "personal presence around the ship"?

PDM: That'd be better than "roaming the ship."

SC: Most ships typically have a Navy Reserve augmentation component that brings the crew up to wartime manning levels and augments the active duty crew during exercises, special evolutions, deployments, etc. Sometimes this is a specific reserve unit attached to the ship and sometimes it's a ship-type augmentation unit. As the ship CO, how did you relate to the reserve detachment, and what expectations did you have of them, and what should a ship CO have in terms of expectations of the reserve detachment?

PDM: I did not have an affiliation with a reserve detachment till I was commander of the U.S. Seventh Fleet.

SC: Why don't we hold that question, then, for that interview?

PDM: That's right, because I didn't have any.

SC: From the first moment a new CO reports aboard, the entire ship's company looks to the new skipper for guidance and direction. How important is it to give the crew a vision statement or call it an overall strategic persona or plan?

PDM: Vision and mission statements became popular well after *McCloy*. Were they important on a military unit? Not so much, I don't think. Why? Because everyone that reports to an operational military unit has some sense of what that unit is all about. So then I viewed it as taking what a new member or whatever the crew felt when I first came aboard as a CO, of refining what they already knew. They'd been sailing that ship, they'd been flying that airplane, they'd been doing these things before you were there. You didn't have to sit down and prescribe a vision, because they might have one in place that's better than what you're thinking about. People are generally smart. I give them credit for being smart till they prove differently. So you see what the hell's going on and then you refine it. You don't write out a placard and say, "Now the USS *McCloy* vision is this." Why would one do that? That's telling that whole crew that "what you've been doing thus far isn't worthy." That's not what I did.

SC: How critical is personal appearance to a CO, especially in terms of his or her moral authority?

PDM: Personal appearance is critical. I was always on the case of people that didn't look proper in uniform, maybe to a fault, because it biased me a little bit if they didn't have the discipline to look like a member of the U.S. military, and if they were sloppy all the time, that bothered me more. I made sure in my seagoing jobs that the laundry facilities always had my attention. I would go by there in my "roaming," as you call it, to make sure that the guys could get their dungarees done, guys could make sure the chambray shirts were relatively clean. We didn't have those digital coveralls back then.

And I was a stickler for if you worked on the deck or below decks, you didn't have to have shined shoes, but you had to wear safety shoes. Too many people get off of duty because they get their feet hurt, because it's a damned dangerous environment going up and down those ladders and walking around all that equipment, particularly when it's rough. So I tried, myself, to always look like I was a commanding officer. So I put a high premium on it.

SC: What, in general, would you advise a newly appointed afloat CO in terms of where and when to take individual-initiated action and where to be more cautious and obtain higher-authority approval first?

PDM: It's a tough question. I have to know the background of what would lead to making a decision now or asking for authority, but I led my whole career as "sin bravely and then you ask for forgiveness." A lot of people can't do that.

SC: There's an authority that derives from one's actions and behaviors. What authority, attributes, actions, and behaviors do you see as essential in a shipboard CO?

PDM: That's almost a question that need not be asked of someone taking the position of commanding officer, because embodied in that position is being able to be responsible for every aspect of material and personal condition of everybody that comes onto that ship, and you can't ask—I believe strongly in that proposition that you cannot ask anybody that serves with you to do more than you do yourself, [to] look better than you look yourself, [to] write better than you can yourself if they were writing. Can't do that. So you have to show that they—I guess I would say the way that you perform has got to inspire everybody in that crew to be like you. Then you've really been successful. Some aspect of it, whether it be a seaman or whether it be the XO, but something that you did that later on in life they would copy.

SC: All humans make errors and mistakes, and some are merely minor with little impact, and some are potentially catastrophic, especially at sea, as we have seen very recently in PacFlt, sadly. What is an individual ship CO's responsibility to advise a senior officer, and let's say in this case it would be your squadron commander, probably, when he or she thinks that the senior officer has made a grave error in judgment or an incorrect decision?

PDM: Two times [sic]. You need to give that person advice when you think that what they're about to do will put them in a very bad light with their seniors, so you're being helpful, okay, just another input in to him before he triggers that. And then if they ever did something that would endanger your ship or crew, you would have to say, "WTF, Commodore?" admiral, whatever. Those two.

SC: One of the chief responsibilities of any CO is the material condition of the command. In a ship conducting periodic space inspections, called zone inspections, is a critical CO activity. What about zone inspections and how did you approach this activity?

PDM: I did have zone inspections. I did not need zone inspections, but I usually had them conducted by the chiefs' quarters, not by the officers, and the chiefs would go to a different set of workspaces than [they were] responsible for. That way I put a little bit of competitiveness into the mid-grade leadership, because they would have to report what the deck spaces looked like, as opposed to the engineering spaces, what the ops spaces looked like, because I expected the officers in the wardroom to already know everything, but the chiefs didn't. When you put them in charge of inspecting this zone, then that was different. So that's what I did.

SC: Innovation. Let's talk about that. As a CO, you were in a position to make some innovative improvements on your ship. Were there any innovations that stand out from your CO tour on *McCloy*?

PDM: Writ large, no. A small one, absolutely. I bought a Furuno radar, small harbor-type radar, for the bridge. It saved my butt a couple of times, because the surface-search radar, its fidelity wasn't sufficient to be able to get a bearing to a point and a range. The little Furuno that was the only innovation I brought to the USS *McCloy*.

SC: The great Prussian theorist of war, General Carl von Clausewitz [*Miller laughs*] described war as "the realm of chaos, ambiguity, and uncertainty." Given this dynamic, how would you recommend any incoming CO prepare for the potentially chaotic environment?

PDM: I don't think unless you experience it you couldn't prepare for it, and I never experienced that in *McCloy*. I experienced it a little bit in *Luce*, but not for real, in an exercise environment up in the North Atlantic. I experienced a little bit of it at Seventh Fleet, but nothing that was so dynamic that it reached the scale in [*sic*] which Clausewitz was talking about, legions of troops marching with each other and against each other. No.

SC: Captain's call is an opportunity to present the strategic plan or vision to the crew, address issues, answer questions. How did you conduct captain's call, and what are your thoughts on how to conduct effective captain's call as a form of strategic communications?

PDM: I do not think when I was CO of *McCloy* I had one captain's call. I had captain's call every day, not with every member of the crew, but with a hell of a lot of them every day.

SC: Is this something that might be more valuable when you have larger numbers?

PDM: Absolutely.

SC: So why don't we readdress this question, then, at the, say, fleet command level.

PDM: Yes.

SC: What is the value of crew recognition and awards for exemplary service or performance? How did you regard awards and recognition as the CO?

PDM: Awards was a currency, the only way that you could tangibly recognize exceptional performance that was a way of buoying the confidence and ensuring the recognition for that performance. It was later on—I'm getting ahead of myself, but you might remember this. There was a point in time where they gave the ship's skipper the ability to hand out the Navy Achievement Medal [NAM]. I was in the Pentagon pushing that. I think that is tremendous, where you don't have to wait for some authority to hand out a Navy Achievement Medal. Same way that at some places the guy knows that in combat if he earned a Bronze Star, he's going to get it. I think that's terribly important. It's the only currency the military has. Can't give him extra rank, can't give him money, but you can give him something he can wear that other people know that he did something good. I was for it 1000 percent, and I hated—that's a strong word. There were flag officers in our Navy that gave you a quota for the numbers of when you were deployed, numbers of Navy Achievement Medal, Navy Commendation Medals [NCM]. I did not like that at all. If someone was deserving, I supported it fully, and if nobody was deserving, I didn't. But terribly important.

SC: The Vietnam War was winding down during your time as CO of *McCloy*. Did you notice any particularly changed dynamics in the Navy or attitudes of sailors as a result of the Vietnam War dynamics?

PDM: Because we were far away from it in Newport, Rhode Island, not so much. If I had been in San Diego, which when I left the *Parsons*, a lot. But up in Newport, not a lot, because we didn't have ships deploying and coming back. In San Diego, I couldn't wear my damn uniform off the ship. That's a different atmosphere.

SC: The famous Admiral Zumwalt Z-grams were a factor of Navy life in the 1972–73 timeframe. How did these changes in Navy policy impact the *McCloy* and how you managed your role as CO?

PDM: Let me preface that with Admiral Zumwalt, who I have great reverence for and I would say affection for his leadership, was the only reason this person stayed in the Navy. So all of his Z-grams, from my vantage point, were viewed favorably and were there to assist the CO in being a modern leader. He could ratchet back from the Z-gram if his own unit prescribed for ratcheting back, but it gave him the latitude to lead in a modern way. If it wasn't for Admiral Zumwalt, I would never have been a four-star in the United States Navy.

I'd like to add anecdotally, Admiral Zumwalt followed my career, and he would send me notes along the way. When I made flag, he sent me a note. When I went to Seventh Fleet, it was a hard confirmation. He sent me a note. He knew I was one of the first that had benefited from the early promotion. Someone must have given him a list. I don't know how he knew it. He was a wonderful, wonderful not only flag officer, but person.

SC: Were there any really memorable personalities that you recall from your time as CO of *McCloy*, either positive or negative?

PDM: The two that—well, there's three. Admiral Wentworth was the Cruiser Destroyer Force Atlantic, Captain C. J. Johnson was the commodore that I told you about meeting on Christmas Day, and Captain Jex. I would not know their names if they didn't impact me in some way forty-six years later.[55] We discussed Commodore Johnson; great respect for him, great sailor. Jex, I'm going to be kind. He was my commodore. He even rode *McCloy* for a period of time. He was one of those people that made 06 because somebody said things about him in a fitness report that certainly weren't true, because he didn't deserve to make 06 in this Navy. I thought that I was going to have real issues with Captain Jex. We were on the opposite end of every spectrum. Up until Captain Jex handed me my fitness report, I had been doing quite well. There is only one fitness report in this stack, Stan, that doesn't mention accelerated promotion, one fitness report. Everything is exemplary, but that one was probably "to promote" [as opposed to "must promote" and "early promote"] and it was by Captain Jex. Why? Because he was a jealous, small person. He did not like seeing somebody as youthful as I was in a command position, didn't like it. I learned from that to never, as I got more senior, to hold it against anybody for being brighter, younger, or more in tune with what was going on. Don't hold it against it; promote it, push it. But I remember that from Jex. What I had to do about it, because I was irritated, I had two flags that I had worked for. One was the commander, the flag on *Intrepid*. (CV/CVA/CVS-11). I went to him and I said "Admiral, this is an unusual visit, and I appreciate you seeing me." I said, "We've just finished this deployment," and I had my portfolio of messages about how well the ship did. And I said, "The commodore has given me this fitness report." I said, "It's a disappointing fitness report, it's not deserved, and I would respectfully ask you to take a look at it." And I told him that I was going to take this to my type commander because it's not right. He wrote a fitness report about this many pages. Admiral Wentworth, I can show you, wrote a hand-penned fitness report to cover that. So that's why I remember those people. [*laughs*]

SC: Other than the Captain Jex fitness report, you received outstanding FITREPs for your *McCloy* tour.

---

[55] Rear Admiral Ralph S. Wentworth (1920–2010) graduated from the U.S. Naval Academy in 1944. He served in the U.S. Navy from 1938 to 1979 and was commissioned during World War II.

PDM: Amen.

SC: When you finished your tour, what was your perspective on future naval service?

PDM: I was in. I was all in.

SC: Tell us about your last day on the ship.

PDM: Unremarkable. I had completed this twenty-month CO tour. I had bad days and good days, more good days than bad days. It was a great experience, and I knew that with the paper that I had received, especially as the record was corrected by that one report—it wasn't a bad report; some people would have been thrilled with it. I was just thankful to have had the opportunity and I would use that experience to the best I could to do even do better the next time in command. That's all.

SC: Your next set of orders directed you to report to the Naval War College in Newport, Rhode Island.

PDM: [*laughs*] Oh.

SC: We'll discuss that tour at length in a future interview, but what was your attitude towards those orders at the time?

PDM: Oh, I knew I was on the first team, getting to go from CO to the War College. I knew that I was on track, and I was very pleased to have the opportunity to go to the War College.

SC: The Navy's preliminary report on the recent collisions of USS *Fitzgerald* (DDG-62) and USS *John S. McCain* (DDG-56) in PacFlt cited poor watch standing as the primary cause. What's your perspective on maintaining a proper watch and training for watch standing?

PDM: That stuff, it doesn't even deserve to be asked, because, in my humble opinion, what happened on those ships is an absolute disgrace to the maritime world, not only to the U.S. Navy. If I had been Seventh Fleet that investigation would have never gone back to Washington without an endorsement for punishment. The skipper of *Fitzgerald*, I would have assigned him a summary court-martial and the recommendation that charges would be manslaughter. That's how disgraceful they were. And if I had to draw an analogy that the youngsters around the nation would understand, if I had to describe it on TV today, I would say the bridge was texting. That tells the young people all they need to know. They weren't paying attention to what they were supposed to pay attention to.

SC: And that really leads me to my next question, which I think you just addressed. Has the evolution of electronic technology undercut basic watch standing procedures and competency, as in this case?

PDM: Electronics, they don't undercut anything. It's another tool. It's another tool. That's all it is. If the person in charge had an appreciation for relative motion, no matter where they got it from, that would have never happened. It wasn't paying attention. It was texting on the bridge. Excuse me. I didn't mean to get—

SC: That's quite all right. You have just merely synthesized what a lot of us are saying, and the very first reaction I had to the first one was, where in hell were the watch standers? Where were the lookouts? Where was CIC?

PDM: Don't ask all those questions, because they don't need to be asked.

SC: They don't?

PDM: You know what happened.

SC: Exactly. If they had been doing correct watch standing and navigational procedures, none of this would have happened.

PDM: Right. If the CO said, "No texting on my bridge," that's all he had to say. "No texting on my bridge." Because they weren't texting; they just weren't paying attention.

SC: Weren't paying attention. Here's a scenario that I would like you to comment on. Let's say that as CO, you came out on the bridge late at night and discovered that the OOD or the JOOD was standing a sloppy or careless watch. How would you react to that scenario?

PDM: It would depend on the degree of sloppiness and the tactical situation we were in. The sloppiness, you know, just because nobody was paying attention to anything, and back then, people smoked, if he was on the starboard wing of the bridge having a cigarette and there wasn't that much going on, but, still, sort of a sloppy environment, right?

But if it was a task force environment, if you go up on the bridge, the situation you described earlier, people don't have any idea of the ships moving around, where they're supposed to go to, you look at the surface-search radar, you look at his maneuvering board plot, whatever, and there's no arithmetic there that says what he's supposed to be doing, you say, "Mr. Jones, I think you've had sufficient time on the bridge. Get the—blank—off the bridge." That's what I'd do. And then whoever was the junior officer of the watch, I'd say, "Can you handle it?" And if he said, "Yes, sir," I'd say, "Do it." If he said anything but, "Yes, sir," or if he hesitated more than two seconds, I'd find somebody else. That would resound through the wardroom before the next cup of coffee was poured.

SC: Finally, tell us about family life while you were CO of *McCloy* during the early 1970s. You've already mentioned a little bit about your housing. What about your wife, your family life?

PDM: Chris, our older son, was with us. Becky Miller deserves high praise. I tell the folks in this affluent community today that I went to sea eight days after we were married. They talk about honeymoons. She gives me a dirty look. Excuse me. She gives me a look. She took over the finances of this family then and has them to this day, fifty-two years later. Same way with rearing the children. I was a workaholic, I was myopic on duty. As I got a bit more senior, I throttled back a little bit and I participated in home life. I became a commander, and the boy started to reach seven to ten years old. But in those early days, I give total credit to Becky Miller for keeping everything going as they [*sic*] needed to go, for her role as a commanding officer's wife. She pulled it off wonderfully. And we've been married for fifty-two years, so that says we got along. [*laughs*]

SC: This concludes our look at your first few months as the CO of USS *McCloy*. Are there any other areas that we did not deal with that you would like to add to the discussion to this point?

PDM: No, sir. I've rambled sufficiently. There'll be more stories to come.

SC: Thank you, Admiral. This concludes our look at your time as commanding officer of USS *McCloy*. This is USNI oral history interview with Admiral Paul David Miller, U.S. Navy (Ret.). This is session number five, question set number eleven. The date is Sunday, December 3, 2017. The interviewer is Professor Stan Carpenter from the U.S. Naval War College.

Interview with Admiral Paul David Miller, USN (Ret.)
Date: April 14, 2018

Stan Carpenter (SC): This is USNI oral history interview with Admiral Paul David Miller, U.S. Navy (Ret.). This is session number six, question set number twelve. The date is Saturday, April 14, 2018, and the interviewer is Professor Stan Carpenter.

Admiral, once you concluded your tour as CO of USS *McCloy* (FF-1038) from 1972 to 1973, you headed back to Newport to attend the U.S. Naval War College. That era is now known as the "Turner Revolution," in that the Naval War College curriculum was dramatically changed based on the Vietnam experience. The curriculum transitioned from a focus on purely operational and tactical considerations to incorporate strategic and policy areas of study. Tell us about the curriculum while you were a student at the Naval War College in those years.

Paul David Miller (PDM): Stan, I'll do that, but let me start with the following. After our last question set, I went back over some fitness reports. I saved all my fitness reports from the thirty years of service. And I was looking for something that I might share with anyone that would ever read this, what I felt was terribly important to establish beginning my mid-grade years as a naval officer, and having been given opportunity to command with less experience than most and certainly less time in service than just about all that had command. And in going through those fitness reports, I found that it laid a foundation; those documents laid a foundation for future success.

The reports written by five different reporting seniors, because I had different squadron commanders, different reporting seniors when I was deployed, they had a common thread, and the thread was performance, regardless of age, experience, that the performance of USS *McCloy* was at least equal to but just about all the time better than the other ships in the squadron, which permitted to me to get some very fine fitness reports.

And, I thought back and I said that's where the path to accelerated promotion for each of the grades really started, because I want to mention that performance is required from the day you enter the Navy, Army, whatever military service, whatever job you go to in industry, but sustained performance is even more important. You can't just perform well for two months, six months. You have to perform well for the entire cycle in which you're in command. And then if you do that, if you succeed, then you will have another opportunity to succeed, and then if you build success upon success, that will build a very, very, very successful career. So it's important that you start wherever it was, and I went back to when I was on the ATFs and the destroyer and at the Bureau of Naval Personnel. The single thread was performance, and when ranked against other officers, being the top officer. That's a terribly important ingredient.

So not a reward, but I stayed on the path by going to the Naval War College, again as a relatively young lieutenant commander, and you set the stage there with the "Turner Revolution." I personally wasn't enamored with the Turner Revolution. I did not know Admiral Turner, brilliant man, but he changed the Naval War College, as you'll recall.[56] He instituted a competitive system that I felt was not necessary for that environment. It was an academic environment, and you're supposed to have a little bit of latitude, a little bit of opportunity to know the people that you operated with in a different environment. They increased the number of participants from all the services. I think 20 percent of our class was Army, Air Force, and so that gave us an opportunity to meet other fellow career service members.

But on day one—might have been day two—he got everybody together and he gave us the lecture that, "You all are here to perform in an academic environment. I've gotten the respective authorities to say that this is equal to a master's degree." I don't know what it was equal to exactly, but that was what he tried to put out to the students to incentivize them. And he said, "You will not get a fitness report for what they used to call duty under instruction. You'll get a real fitness report and it will be broken down into three categories. You'll get an accelerated fitness report, a top 1-percenter, you'll get a top 5-percenter fitness report, or you will get a top 10 percent fitness report." And so

---

[56] Admiral Stansfield Turner (1923–2018) graduated from the U.S. Naval Academy in 1946. He served in the U.S. Navy from 1946 to 1978. His final tour was as commander in chief Allied Forces Southern Europe from 1975 to 1977. He then served as director of Central Intelligence and director of the Central Intelligence Agency from 1977 to 1981. As president of the U.S. Naval War College from 1972 to 1974, ADM Turner made substantial changes in the college's academic curriculum stressing strategy and policy and national security decision-making as well as joint military operations and operational planning. This curriculum change, largely in response to the strategic failures of the Vietnam War, has been termed "the Turner Revolution" and is more in line with a typical university graduate program.

imagine this. You have 125 guys or 150, whatever the number was, all pretty aggressive personalities. You have them there and you have the president of the college saying, "Now, you guys were all right in the operational field. Otherwise, you wouldn't be here. But we're going to see how you are academically at this level. Are you as adroit in the classroom as you were in the wardroom?"

Everybody sort of looked at each other, because then we knew that we were in a different environment. I immediately reflected, I said, "Oh, good lord." I was a pretty decent naval officer operationally. Now if I don't finish in the top 1 percent, get a fitness report at the top of this class, whoever reviews it for the next promotion's going to say, "Hey, he was a pretty good sailor at sea, but he's not quite as sharp." And then I said, "Why did he do this?" I didn't know why he did that, but he did it.

He put a real curriculum in there. You teach there now. I don't know what's there now, but he put a curriculum in there and divided it into three blocks, as I recall, and the three blocks, I think, were strategy and policy, then he had one on—let's see—naval seminar discussions, and he inserted a business block to try to get people to understand and appreciate the acquisition and business world. And so we had different professors. I don't remember any of them. I remember one professor. I don't know. I've seen his name since he was a professor on warfare tactics. That was it. Strategy, Tactics, and Business. He was a Marine.

So we go through the course, we take tests, and we write papers. And the reading list was prolific, absolutely prolific. He starts off with this thing called Thucydides and the Peloponnesian Wars, and you were supposed to have read that.[57] He sent it to you. We were supposed to have read that before you matriculated at the school. [*laughs*] I said, "Wait a minute." Anyhow, I won't go on. I knew I was in for a grind, not just attending school.

So we lived in this same house that we had when I was CO of *McCloy*, and we had one son then. Becky and I converted the closet into my study room. I spent a lot of time in that closet. I did not want to finish below the top percentage group in that school.

---

[57] Thucydides, an Athenian *strategoi* (general) in the Peloponnesian War with Sparta (431 to 404 BCE), wrote the history of the war, but more importantly, the book expresses a general analysis of the dynamics of all human conflict. A most useful translation is Robert B. Strassler, ed., *The Landmark Thucydides* (New York: Free Press, 1996).

When I look back at the fitness report, I was pleased to report that I stood in the top 23 percent of a class of 224 people, and I did achieve getting top 1 percent, and there were 60 people in the 5 percent and 70-some people in the 10 percent. So that's a pretty stark fitness report. When someone is just going through your records, he has twelve seconds to look at, "Oh, he finished at the top. That's good." But if you'd finished in the bottom group, he would have gone back and look more carefully at it, right?

And the Naval War College was a great experience. I won't belabor it. It was ten months. Met some wonderful people, especially those that were outside of the Navy, because we never had that chance before, and it was an enjoyable time because I had time to work out all the time and go over to the gym, and we had competitive basketball games. It was a memorable ten months for myself and Becky.

Then we turned to where we were going to go next, because that was an awful important departure point. Were we going to get that job that was going to proceed us on the path, with performance, to be able to keep going, or were you going to go to a staff someplace and it would be more difficult?

Fortunately—you'll segue into the next duty station—I was assigned to OpNav in Washington, D.C., on the CNO's staff, and that was an ideal place to begin Washington duty, other than at the Bureau, but in the Pentagon. And I got to know Admiral Turner a little bit there, played tennis with him. Becky and I played tennis with he and his wife. They were gracious people. But we saw things a little bit differently than he did, and I followed his career up through being [head of the] CIA (Central Intelligence Agency), and the things that I saw, the way he viewed things at the Naval War College, he sort of viewed things that way at CIA, so I'm sure that others have similar feelings. I respect him, but he tried to change things to a way that he thought naval officers should view academics, and I think he was a Rhodes Scholar, wasn't he? He was some kind of scholar.[58]

SC: In his official Naval War College portrait, he's wearing his service dress blues and a Harvard academic gown, which really created a stir in the Navy at the time.

---

[58] Turner earned a doctorate at Oxford University as a Rhodes Scholar while on active duty.

PDM: I rest my case.

SC: Well, having said all that, let's turn now to the curriculum. What courses did you find most and what courses were least challenging?

PDM: I guess the strategy part was most challenging, because the tactics part, I was pretty familiar with all of that, and the business part of it, I felt very comfortable in that world. The strategy part of it made me think. I did not read all of Thucydides and the Peloponnesian War. I did go get the crib notes on Thucydides. I did do that so I could at least talk about it. I still have some of the books in our home in Virginia. They gave you a lot of books on World War I, a lot of books on World War II. *The Long Fuse* is a World War I book about all the things that led up to the actual war.[59] And so I found it most challenging because it took the most time. You had to have read these books if you were going to write and respond reasonably effectively to the questions that would come on a test. I'm not a prolific reader, so I spent a lot of time plowing through these books. That's why that made that the toughest course. The other two, I didn't have to work as hard. I had enough background and I was able to read a little bit, answer the questions, you know.

SC: And that dynamic still exists in the "strategy and policy" and "strategy and war" courses today. You have to do the reading or you can't write the essays, although we have eliminated all the tests. It's all discussion and essay-based.

PDM: Do you have your fitness reports in three blocks too?

SC: The fitness reports have gone back to simply being, "You were here and observed."

PDM: Okay. I was lucky, wasn't I? [*laughs*]

---

[59] Laurence D. Lafore, *The Long Fuse: An Interpretation of the Origins of World War I* (London: Weidenfeld and Nicolson, 1965).

SC: Yes, you were. Well, I think you sort of preempted my next question, but maybe not. What was your most favorite and least favorite course?

PDM: The other two were—I'd put it in the same category. They were interesting, they reinforced some foundations in the respective academic areas, but they were not any trouble, so I didn't have any least favorite.

SC: What about the teaching methodology then in the 1970s? In other words, what was the manner of teaching the individual courses?

PDM: The professors would come in, and there was more lecture than discussion. There was some discussion, but most of it was them presenting the material that they had given us, the syllabus, and we followed the syllabus very, very rigorously. It was like a course at the senior level of college or graduate school, and you were left to take what the professor told you or lectured you about and try to integrate it, weave it with your readings so that you came up with some plausible approach to why that strategy was taken at that time so that in the future when you had to do that, you were able to have—I won't say a road map, but you would be able to take into account all those things that you had read about in history and what you were told about in class to make you a better officer on a staff or better leader making the decision.

SC: What we say about the strategy courses is we're trying to get students to think strategically and long after you've forgotten who shot John and how-many-cannon-on-the-hill details, that pattern of exactly what you just described, which is thinking strategically and applying a critical analysis type of thinking, that's the purpose of the program, and it's been wildly successful. Did the program require elective courses, as it does today? And if so, what elective courses did you take?

PDM: No elective courses. Three basic courses and that was it.

SC: This was a period when two great works on war, and especially strategic thinking, became the foundations of the Strategy and Policy course, Carl von Clausewitz, *On War*, and as you've already mentioned, Thucydides' Peloponnesian war history. You've already given us some of your thoughts, especially on Thucydides, but what were your thoughts on these two foundation readings at the time?

PDM: One cannot argue against foundational, to use your phrase or the school's phrase, academic work. Some students such as myself find it genuinely hard work trying to read the stuff that was written in a particular time and then trying to synthesize what they were telling you in words and then trying to bridge it to what was happening today. Some of the stuff one would say would be timeless, but taking and extracting those timeless nuggets out of there is not easy work for a student. I'm sorry. For me it wasn't. It's just not easy work. But having to have gone through that, I don't want to diminish it, but having gone through that exercise, it helps one establish a little bit of mental rigor that one didn't have, at least I didn't have it before. So it was helpful.

SC: I think you've also hinted at my next question. What are your thoughts on these two works from your perspective today?

PDM: I don't think about them today. [*laughter*]

SC: Well, I think you already answered that, the thinking and rigor and all.

PDM: That's it. That's what it did.

SC: Exactly. Tell us about your typical day at the Naval War College when you were there in the seventies.

PDM: It was just like going to a ship that was in port. You get up, they started class early, and we finished pretty early in the afternoon because they wanted to give you time to do your papers and this and that and do whatever other endeavors you wanted to do. The days were relatively easy. I didn't have any watches or collateral duties, no ship to worry about, that it was tied up properly or that the steam plant was online, offline, or whether they fixed the condensate pump. You weren't clouded with things like that, so it was a great year. [*laughs*]

SC: In the current century, the achievement of one's Joint Professional Military Education, or JPME, Phases 1 and 2, which are the intermediate and senior courses, [is] essentially required for a successful career, but not at the time you were at the college. What were the attitudes among officers in those days towards a Naval War College professional education?

PDM: The attitudes were positive. They weren't required, but students knew there that if they were selected for War College junior or senior course, they were still on track, because the military doesn't send unpromising candidates to the colleges. You knew that you had cleared a certain hurdle and were in a category that was promising. I started this section with a little bit about performance. You knew you were in that category, so that's why I put the emphasis on you're in this category, you did not know that you were going to have to perform in a competitive way, so it changed the attitude of all the students together. Some of them didn't mind. Some of them, if they finished, they didn't care. But there were half of them who really cared, and so it made it harder to get in the top percent.

SC: I once had an Army colonel say that in the Army it was harder to get orders to the Naval War College than it was to make colonel. It's highly competitive.

PDM: Exactly.

SC: What, in general, was the Navy's attitude towards officer professional education in the 1970s?

PDM: In the seventies, I think it was interesting but not compelling. You could do very, very well without going to one of those schools, but it was interesting from the vantage point if you were on that list and if you had the time to devote a year to that, it was an ideal way to take a break from the operational forces in this school to enhance your ability to view things in a different manner. I used the word "rigor" before; you did too. And that's what it helped me with. It was a good thing. It wasn't a necessary thing in my time.

SC: Today an officer cannot take up a commander-level command without having achieved the JPME Phase 1 credential. What is your perspective on that dynamic?

PDM: Hmm. [*pauses*] I'm hesitating because once the institution, in this case the Navy or all the services, put another requirement at the mid-career level that must be done, it takes away from the individual's ability to be agile in his career, because timing is such you don't always have the timing to do it when they want it done. You might want to extend for a deployment because you're on a ship and you want to finish the deployment where you can get that brand of experience instead of academic experience. So if you extend for the deployment, then you lose another year because you have to go back to fill a requirement. I'm not for hard requirements.

SC: One of the things that the Navy did realize was the problem that you just cited, and so a big push in the last twenty years has been in the old traditional correspondence course. That's gone away, the paper-based, and we went to an online web-based course and also really beefed up the nonresident program in fleet concentration areas. That was a way of getting around the problem of having to go to Newport. And we have about four or five times as many students enrolled in the nonresident program as the resident.

PDM: Well, that program, I'd be fully in favor of that latitude in permitting someone to get that designation, absolutely.

SC: In the early 1990s, the Naval War College became academically accredited to award graduate degrees, and since then, graduates in both the resident program and the non-resident Fleet Seminar Program (FSP) either receive or are eligible for the master's degree. In your opinion, was that a good move, and how does it help the services?

PDM: In my opinion, it's a "so what?"

SC: What about the international program, where officers from allied and partner nations are brought to the college and take the same or a slightly modified program alongside U.S. students? What's your perspective on that dynamic?

PDM: Super. I love it. Those guys that were there, they were the best that their country had. You learned about the way that they looked at the United States Navy, United States military. You made a couple of friends. You were able to call upon their service when you were lucky enough to have a command or have a leadership role internationally. The folks I met, I met an officer from Thailand that I was able to look up when I was the commander of Seventh Fleet. I met a U.K. commander that then when I was the Standing Naval Force flagship, I reacquainted with him.[60] So I think that bringing those folks to Newport, Rhode Island, [to] give them the opportunity to commingle with their U.S. counterparts is a very good thing. I hope they continue it. I hope it's going on today.

SC: It has and it's actually grown in importance.

PDM: Great.

---

[60] The Standing Naval Force Atlantic or STANAVFORLANT is a NATO naval force established in 1968 to act as a standing quick reaction naval force. Since 2005, it has been called Standing NATO Maritime Group One (SNMG1). The force is composed of frigate and destroyer-type warships from different NATO nations that rotate in and out of the force, which trains, exercises, and validates NATO procedures and operational concepts.

SC: And there's some statistic—I may be slightly off here—but I believe about half of all the graduates of the Naval War College international program go on to be the CNO or equivalent for their host countries.

So, the Naval War College. You're back in Newport, where you spent the first few years of your life, but the fleet had pulled out about 1972 and was in the process of moving to different home ports. How did you see those moves impacting the region and Newport in general?

PDM: I moved *McCloy* from Newport to Norfolk, Virginia. My last six weeks on *McCloy* was doing that, because the squadron had moved to Norfolk. I recall Newport; it was a very low point for the mayors and the business people and all those that looked at Newport economically. They were really down. "How are we going to make this thing work?" I think that was probably the best thing that ever happened to Newport, because Newport is a unique setting, and they've done pretty well since the operational Navy left. They still have the Navy presence there with the school's command, but it was a few years before they were able to plot some economic dots to show, hey, there is life after the Navy in Newport, Rhode Island.

SC: One of the ways they reacted very positively was they leveraged the fact that Newport is so historic and has so much there to offer; now it's a high-end tourist destination.

PDM: Absolutely.

SC: And they really played that. What social and extracurricular activities did students engage in in those years?

PDM: Social schedule was very light. I think that's one of the sort of victims of putting competitiveness into the War College, that people spend a lot of time trying to make sure that they were in the right group, and I think that at least for us, we were not very social at the War College because there was always something going on, always a requirement to get something done, and I don't know what it is now, but there weren't many organized large events. We were in a small group and you had little social things with them. My best friend up there, I remember his name today. His name was Joe Briggs, and he was a U.S. Army lieutenant colonel. He was truly a dynamic man and a good athlete. We got along really well with their family. And we had a couple of friends like that, but it was not a social year.

SC: Tell us a little bit more about your family life in Newport. Were there any activities that as a family you could partake in?

PDM: Every once in a while, we would go back to visit with my Aunt Mary and the family that I grew up with, but other than that, there was nothing remarkable. It was a year that passed quickly. We spent a lot of time with our young son there, which was great, and by the time we got our orders, we had mentally moved to Washington, D.C.

SC: Looking back from the point of view of a highly successful career, how would you judge the value of your Naval War College education?

PDM: I'm sure that somehow I leveraged some of the things that I took away from the War College, but I do not think that the War College played a material role in the outcome.

SC: Looking back from today's perspective, if you were to make recommendations to the CNO on how the Naval War College and officer professional military education should be structured and delivered, what would they be and why?

PDM: I think you made the changes. I would take away the damn competitiveness of it. Officers that are between thirty-five and forty years old, they know what the requirements are, and they should not have in their record some statistic that says they're smarter or not smarter. So I think they were changed shortly after Admiral Turner left. Maybe not. I don't know. But I'm glad they don't do that now, and I know they haven't done it for some time, because I went up there to speak, I don't know, three or four times when I was a four-star, and it wasn't going on then. The students seemed pretty relaxed and happy.

SC: Are there any other issues or areas that you would like to add regarding your Naval War College education?

PDM: I'm happy that I went there. It was an outstanding experience. I'm happier that I came out with the right paper, and I'm able to look back on it that it was a solid opportunity, but I was eager to get on to the next job and see what lay ahead.

SC: That leads nicely into my next question. What was your perspective on your future Navy career at this juncture?

PDM: I knew that having been in Washington in the Bureau of Naval Personnel, I sort of knew, and sitting on as a support person for senior selection boards, like you would have as additional duty for a JO [junior officer] detailer, where I would be working with a captain selection board for two weeks, working out records, and being somebody to help smooth the people that were sitting on the boards. I already had a good sense of the environment. We had the opportunity to observe the process, had the opportunity to listen to how selecting captains was mainly by rear admirals, how they looked at things, what was more important, what [sic] you got sort of more credit for doing this job than that job, and so I came away from that detail tour with a pretty accurate mental plot of what I had to do to succeed as quickly as I wanted to succeed. I was really fortunate to have that opportunity, because I saw it unfold. I saw people talking and sometimes observed some heated discussions why this was better than that. So I knew what I wanted to do. I knew where it was best to go.

And I don't know how it happened, just like I don't know how it happened that I got to be CO of *McCloy* at the early age. It happened, and it happened that I was assigned to OP-06. Then it was the Plans and Policies branch of the CNO staff. So I was delighted when I received orders to OpNav.

SC: Following your time at the Naval War College, you joined the CNO staff of Admiral Elmo Zumwalt in the OP-603D shop. [*Miller laughs.*] You hinted at this already, but how and why were you selected for that billet?

PDM: Again, one doesn't know how one is selected for that billet. I do know they send performing officers to OpNav. I know that they send officers that have potential to OpNav, and I can tell you where it's better to go in OpNav than other places. They have their hierarchy. In my time there, if you were a planner and programmer, you would go to OP-090, to work the budget up. If you were operationally oriented, you'd go to OP-06. If you were someone that was being sent to OpNav and were steeped in your warfare specialty, you'd go to 03, you'd go to 05, you'd go to 02. 02 was the submarines; 03 was surface; 05 was air. So it had its own hierarchy within OpNav.

They slated me to go exactly where I should go, and that was in the Plans and Policy side of OpNav, and the desk that was open when I got there was OP-603D. You're absolutely right.

SC: What were the specific areas of responsibility of OP-603D?

PDM: [*laughs*] I can't even say it. I was the command relations officer. What did that mean? Everybody in OpNav had a particular slice of staff activity to support, and in my time there, there was a *huge* revision of the UCP, the Unified Command Plan, in which they take this and divvy up the world, review that, the joint commanders for the geographical ones, the specified commanders, the support commanders, and I spent my entire time, which wasn't that long, I think it was only six months, from July of '74 to January of '75, myopic on the UCP that they were reworking on the joint staff.[61]
I spent a lot of time going down to joint staff meetings, so it gave me an appreciation for the inner workings of joint staff, and I had to brief my reporting senior[, who] was "Black

---

[61] The Unified Command Plan (UCP) establishes the missions, responsibilities, and geographic areas of responsibility (AOR) to the combatant commanders (COCOMs), who are the actual operational commanders.

Jack" Shanahan. [*laughs*] He was a great officer.[62] He was OP-60, and 60B, and his assistant was the wonderful Admiral Crowe, so I got to know Crowe really well.[63] He had to approve all of my staff papers that they had sent up, because this was an important issue to carve out, to make sure the Navy had proper representation in the Unified Command Plan, because that's where the senior officers were sent to serve. If you weren't serving in OpNav or on a staff, you were serving in one of these joint operational billets, so it was terribly important. Admiral Shanahan took a keen interest in it. Admiral Crowe was the one that grilled me and helped me and assisted me and made me go back and fight for certain things, and he later became the chairman. Admiral Bagley, then Admiral Holloway, the CNO—I had to brief them all, because there was an interest in how this thing came out.[64]

We wound that up, I think in probably December '74, and my time there was up, and I had the opportunity, I think because I had some visibility. A lot of people in OpNav never get the visibility of going up and briefing the Vice [VCNO] or the CNO or the Secretary of the Navy. I had that opportunity, and I guess I didn't stumble or stutter too much, because Admiral Worth Bagley was looking for a new flag lieutenant and I was put up for that by Admiral Shanahan.

SC: You mentioned already that in the OP-06 Plans and Policy, the UCP is a major responsibility. Were there any other major responsibility areas of the OP-06 shop?

---

[62] Vice Admiral John J. "Jack" Shanahan, Jr. (1923–2013) served in the U.S. Navy from 1941 to 1977, serving as an enlisted sailor in World War II and later a commission in 1946. His final billet was as commander, U.S. Second Fleet and NATO Striking Fleet, Atlantic.

[63] Admiral William J. Crowe, Jr. (1925–2007) graduated from the U.S. Naval Academy in 1946. He served in the U.S. Navy from 1946 to 1989. His final billet was as the eleventh Chairman of the Joint Chiefs of Staff from 1985 to 1989 and in retirement, he also served as the U.S. Ambassador to the Court of St. James (U.S. Ambassador to the United Kingdom).

[64] Admiral Worth H. Bagley (1924–2016) graduated from the U.S. Naval Academy in 1946 and served in the U.S. Navy from 1946 to 1975. His final billet was as vice chief of naval operations from 1974 to 1975.

Admiral James L. Holloway III (1922–2019) graduated from the U.S. Naval Academy in 1943 and served in the U.S. Navy from 1942 to 1978 with his final billet as the twentieth Chief of Naval Operations from 1974 to 1978.

PDM: Yeah. They dealt with everything from the daily brief, operational brief, they had a certain section that the CNO and other members, the secretariat, would come up and get a morning brief of Navy worldwide. And so they were the operational eyes and ears for the CNO and his staff. Then they had OP-60, OP-61, 63, all the operational functions of the Navy were covered, and the plans function of it all filtered through OP-06. That's why I prefaced this earlier that the two dynamic and the two influential slots for three-stars is OP-06 and then it was 090. I don't know what they call it now.

SC: Did you have any collateral duties while you were on the staff?

PDM: No, not one collateral duty.

SC: Not even wardroom mess treasurer?

PDM: Not even anything.

SC: Tell us about a typical workday on the OpNav staff.

PDM: This is where I learned that work in the Pentagon, work in OpNav was long, it was sometimes relatively intense, intense not because of the character of the work, but intense that there was an incessant timeframe. It had to be done by a certain timeframe, and you never had as much time as you thought you needed to get all this stuff done. We were not overmanned.

The office or the conditions in OpNav at that time were spartan. I can phrase it in no other way. I was surprised. When I went to OpNav, I go into this office—I still can see it—and OP-603, I think, was a captain, but then on his right—he had a small room—there were four steel desks in that room, one against four corners. Each had one of those old government steel desks. Very few pictures on the wall. It hit me that this is the premier Navy staff, and you go into this office. You spend a lot of time at that steel desk, but you spend more time out trying to go to your meetings and getting background for what you had to do. But I knew that I didn't want to stay there very long, because I knew that the best thing to do was do the best job that I could, and every time it had happened in the past that I did a good job, I got another job. So I got out of this one in six months.

SC: You were still fairly junior at this point. You've already mentioned you did a lot of briefing, but how much interaction typically did you have with the senior leadership?

PDM: I was still a lieutenant commander. For a lieutenant commander, I got a lot. By that I mean this was high on the precedence list for all the service chiefs, for the Joint Chiefs, and so with this being high on the list, they knew that they had to reform, get a new UCP out. Then the action officer for any of the services got more than their share of routine visibility with the senior officers of their service.

SC: You already said that at this point looking back, you see this as a hugely valuable tour. What about at the time? Did you see it as a positive or a negative in terms of your future career as opposed to going back out to sea after the College in Newport?

PDM: No, I knew that I had had the command, so I knew I had to go to a shore assignment after War College. I knew I would not be able to go back out to sea, so the best thing on a career pattern would be to go back to OpNav, not CinCLantFlt [commander in chief, Atlantic Fleet] staff or not CinCPacFlt [commander in chief, Pacific Fleet] staff, but go back to OpNav and get into one of those two offices that I talked about, 090 or 06, and then if I was able to do that, then I was staying on the path. I didn't know where it was taking me, but I knew that I plotted the right dot by going down there.

SC: You already had significant administrative experiences, XO in the fleet tug force and as frigate CO. Do you see this experience as a positive in terms of your duties at OpNav and your ability to carry them out?

PDM: The experience in my formative years in what I call the "junk force" in the fleet tug area and then in the DDG and in command, those experiences served me in an outstanding fashion for my sea jobs. Washington's different than being at sea, totally different, in my view. At sea, even if you're a department head, you make a decision. If you're a commanding officer, you can make lots of decisions. When you are a lieutenant commander or commander or even a captain in OpNav, you don't decide anything. You're a staff officer. The thing that you can do is influence a decision. The best officers make the decision because their ability to influence the decision maker is so keen that they know that they are making that decision, and that's how I approached it.

SC: It's been joked that captains, colonels, brigadier generals, and rear admirals make coffee and get donuts—

PDM: I don't believe it.

SC: —serving in the Pentagon.

PDM: I never saw that.

SC: [*laughs*] In other words, that old joke is just that, a joke?

PDM: I never saw that.

SC: The Pentagon is often referred to as the "five-sided nuthouse." What is your reaction to that depiction?

PDM: It's five-sided. A lot of good work goes on in the Pentagon. I'll defend the Pentagon. The problem is, is that with any large organization, there are too many people chasing too few tasks, and the work's important, but it's divided up into such thin slices that it's hard to get it all moving. I always agreed with Admiral Rickover when he said, "If you would shut the doors to one of the floors on the Pentagon and not let anybody go to that floor, it wouldn't skip a beat."⁶⁵ [*laughs*] I sort of believe that, you know. The work would just filter to some other desk somewhere and it'd all get done.

SC: You've already mentioned some personalities that you encountered on the staff, but are there any other really memorable persons from those years?

PDM: No, not on the staff at that time. Personalities will come into play as we talk more about jobs in the Pentagon, but at that time, there was nothing. I don't even remember my captain. I can't name him. I can start naming from Admiral Shanahan on, but there were none.

SC: Throughout your career, you've had atypical tours in that they were shorter than the norm, with exception of ops officer on the *Parsons*. That either indicates that you were doing a poor job and the COs want to get rid of you, or that you were doing a tremendous job and you were in demand in areas of increasing responsibility. Considering the whole of your career accomplishments, I vote for the latter. How did this dynamic appear to you at the time, and did you see it as positive or negative?

PDM: I always felt that you can take the measure of a new job pretty quickly, no matter what it is, and then once you take the full measure of that job, then you set your sights on doing something new. The only time I was a student in the U.S. Navy was the Naval War College and Destroyer School. I never wanted to be a student. I felt being a student was not a good use of my time. I didn't have much time, but it wasn't the best use of it. And then the only thing worse than being a student was having to be assigned to be a professor. Don't take it the wrong way. Because I never wanted to be on that side of the

---

⁶⁵ Admiral Hyman G. Rickover (1900–1986) graduated from the U.S. Naval Academy in 1922. After several tours in submarines, destroyers, a battleship, and shore assignments as an engineering duty officer (EDO) he was appointed as head of the Navy's new nuclear propulsion program in the late 1940s as director of naval reactors and was instrumental in the design and construction of the USS *Nautilus* (SSN-571) in the early 1950s. Known for his abrasive and gruff manner, he was retained on active duty for several years beyond the normal mandatory retirement age by act of Congress. He retired from the U.S. Navy in 1982.

desk that is teaching. I wanted to be on that side of the desk that was learning, and I would rather not be on either side of the desk. I would rather be gaining experience.

SC: You advanced rapidly in promotion during those years. To what do you credit that dynamic?

PDM: What I started this session with, as I mentioned, I look back on fitness reports, particularly in *McCloy* and even in the department head tour, was performance. That was it. And being able to gain the confidence of your superiors was the number one attribute to being a successful performer. You *had* to. And then I've worked hard to make sure I gained the confidence of every one of my reporting seniors. It's absolutely key. In OpNav, it was gaining the confidence of this crusty admiral. Admiral Shanahan was tough, but if he sees that you're right and he sees that you're right again, then all of a sudden, you can tell him what you're going to do, and he says, "I don't have time for this. Do it." That's the mode you want to get into, no matter what job you go to. And when we go to the business career, I'll show you some keen examples.

SC: In what ways did your family life change in those years in D.C. on the OpNav staff, if at all?

PDM: It did not change materially. If Becky was here right now, she'd say it would have changed materially because of the hours that the Pentagon required. OpNav wasn't too bad, but then when I migrated up to the Vice Chief's Office, it got tough, tough, but I hate to say that that was the price to participate, because it wasn't to get into the new good job. If you wanted to do what I had just laid my marker on, is gain your boss' confidence. It takes time. You have to be there when he either wants or needs you. So you have to sacrifice, and most of the sacrifice was time. And Becky will say I sacrificed a whole hell of a lot of time.

SC: Admiral, as we wrap up your time at the Naval War College and on the OpNav staff, is there anything you'd like to add to what we've already discussed?

PDM: No. OpNav staff was at that time a smooth-running organization. I don't know who triggered it, maybe it was Admiral Shanahan, maybe it was my time in front of Worth Bagley, but leaving OpNav in six months and going up to the Vice Chief's Office was a *huge* opportunity, an absolutely huge opportunity.

SC: Thank you, Admiral Miller. This concludes our look at your time as a student at the U.S. Naval War College in Newport, Rhode Island, and on the OpNav staff in OP-06. In our next session, we will discuss your time as flag lieutenant and EA, or executive assistant, for the Vice Chief of Naval Operations.

This is USNI oral history interview with Admiral Paul David Miller, U.S. Navy (Ret.). This is session number six, question set number twelve. The date is Saturday, April 14, 2018, and the interviewer is Professor Stan Carpenter. Thank you, Admiral.

SC: This is USNI oral history interview with Admiral Paul David Miller, U.S. Navy (Ret.). This is session number six, question set number thirteen. The date is Saturday, April 14, 2018, and the interviewer is Professor Stan Carpenter. These questions cover the years at the Pentagon as a flag lieutenant and administrative assistant.

Admiral, before we launch into your time at the Pentagon as a flag lieutenant and administrative assistant to the Vice Chief of Naval Operations, what do you think in particular from your fitness reports was one of the keys in terms of the Navy having a lot of confidence in you that you could be a successful flag EA?

PDM: Stan, I think there were a lot of attributes that I was able to demonstrate on the OP-60 staff, but I went back and looked at the fitness report that Admiral Shanahan gave me. It was an outstanding fitness report, but that's not the point that I want to make. What those senior officers looked for was someone that was able to do the work, do it quickly, concisely, boil it down to a recommendation that they could easily understand and appreciate, and have enough information there to reinforce that recommendation and to give the person that was going to approve it a couple of points, so if his boss asked him a question about it, he was able to have a couple of reloads, and that's the way I approached all the papers that I wrote.

Admiral Shanahan reported—and I'm reading it out of the fitness report now—"In the staffing process, Lieutenant Commander Miller was particularly adept at preparing staff responses and position papers on short notice. In every case, his work was clear, concise, and provided appropriate recommendations." That was it. They could rely on it. If a guy got a call and he was doing something in his area of the Unified Command Plan and it was getting heated towards the end of it, because each of the services were vying for respective positions in this, and once it had gone down and once it was signed, they knew it would be difficult to change, so it was terribly important to get it right. So the short-notice aspect of being able to respond to them, do it quickly, provide recommendations, and to provide reload should they ask questions about the recommendation, that's what sort of, I think, set me a little bit apart from the regular staff officer in OP-06.

And then when Admiral Bagley's office said, "I need a new flag lieutenant," who comes to mind? And I came to Admiral Shanahan's mind and went up and interviewed, and again three or four of us went up there. I was lucky and I got the assignment with Admiral Bagley.

SC: Admiral, before we launch into the specifics of your time as a flag lieutenant and administrative assistant to the VCNO, let's address some of your previous background that likely aided in that assignment. You hold an MBA from the University of Georgia. When did you complete that degree?

PDM: August of 1964.

SC: You've had a post-Navy stellar business career, which we'll address in future interviews, but for now, how did the MBA provide a foundation for your future post-Navy career?

PDM: I wasn't even thinking about it. The MBA was done because I didn't think I was going to be in the Navy. I said early on about a draft notice. If I never got that draft notice, I would never be in the Navy. It's just one of those serendipitous things that works out. So the MBA was good, but I thought I was going to go work in business. Never happened.

SC: But you have now.

PDM: But I have now, so we'll be able to go back and talk about that.

SC: We'll talk about that in our final sessions.

PDM: That's how it worked.

SC: The services now highly encourage officers to attain a graduate degree. What is your perspective on the utility of a graduate degree for the individual officer as well as for the services at large?

PDM: Education writ large is good, so I can't say that one should not take every advantage of getting the first advanced degree. I take a little bit of umbrage with the military officer that goes on to get the PhD and whatever and then comes back into a staff and now he has a PhD and he's a little bit more enlightened than all the other folks. I've gotten cross-threaded with a few of those people. But the education at the master's level, particularly if you're in the engineering world or in the acquisition world, getting a master's degree in electrical engineering if you're going to be in the nuclear power world, all that's good, but can you have an outstanding naval career without it? Yes, you can. So it's helpful, but, again, I like to use the phrase it's interesting but not compelling. It's not compelling. You don't have to have a master's degree to succeed as a military officer. It's helpful.

SC: Do you foresee a day when promotion and billet opportunities are dependent on graduate credentials other than the current JPME Phase 1 credential?

PDM: I hope not.

SC: Let's turn back and pick up your Navy career at the Pentagon, but first I want to lay a little groundwork for the Navy in the early to mid-1970s. Admiral Elmo Zumwalt, the CNO from 1970 to '74, emerged as a controversial figure at the time and in retrospect. Why was or is this?

PDM: Admiral Zumwalt was my personal naval hero. If he had not become CNO, if he had not changed the policies that he changed, I would have never stayed in the Navy. His greatest contribution was to change the selection system and give young officers a chance. I was fortunate to be a product of that decision in that first batch of young officers he gave a chance to. I look back on it as the reason that I stayed in the Navy and the reason that I was successful in the Navy.

Admiral Zumwalt was so kind. He would send me little personal notes as I advanced. The most treasured personal note from Admiral Zumwalt is one he sent me saying that I was promoted to four stars quicker than he was. It's a treasure.

Some people say he went too far with his relaxation of personal grooming standards. He let you have sideburns. He tried to get the Navy, as much as he could, to go with the social norms that were very, very interesting at the time. It was a conflict between the rigid military, but he was adroit enough to know that he had to turn the meter back a little bit at that time to attract certain young people, and he was able to do that. As you know, a lot of the senior people didn't appreciate that. They thought he'd turned it back too much, and then the people that followed him tried to tighten it back up again. Then later on, they've got it so damned tight now, people are leaving the Navy. I have two sons that will leave the Navy because of that. So he was the right figure at the right time. As controversial as he was, people like me who later became very senior officers revere him.

SC: What was Admiral Zumwalt's leadership and management style like? You've already mentioned some of those facets.

PDM: He was an officer that let individuality present itself and competency be brought forward. He didn't care if you were a commander, a lieutenant commander, or a captain. It was the competency of your work that made the difference, and someone like me just applauded that greatly and I wanted to be part of that brand of organization. It didn't turn out to be that way, but at that point in time, he gave a lot of us a hell of a lot of opportunity.

SC: You were at the Pentagon during the later years of President Richard Nixon's second term and the Watergate scandal.[66] Do you think that had any impact on how you operated or conducted your work?

PDM: No. They were across the river, and we had work to do on our side of the river, and that was interesting news and that's all it was for me.

SC: Going further, how did the Watergate affair impact the Navy and DOD in general, if at all?

PDM: The level that I was at, it did not impact it at all. Whether it impacted down in the Office of the Secretary of Defense, I wasn't familiar with at the time.

SC: You were in D.C. in the final years of the U.S. involvement in Vietnam. How did that dynamic impact your work in the Navy command structure in general?

PDM: They were difficult years. When I went down to Washington, it was difficult for me to appreciate, to understand why I wasn't wearing a uniform to work every day,

---

[66] President Richard M. Nixon (1913–1994) was the thirty-seventh president of the United States, from 1969 to 1974. The Watergate Scandal was created when Republican operatives bugged the headquarters of the Democrat National Committee at the Watergate office complex and were captured. The ensuing cover-up and threat of impeachment forced Nixon to resign in August 1974.

because it was still the spillover to the military [of the Vietnam War]. There was a lot of acrimony between the civil side and the military side. The uniformed officers were being sort of blamed for Vietnam. Most of us, we didn't do anything but carry out the orders that were given to us, but still, it was a difficult time. I experienced it when I was in the bureau and then even when I came back in '74, and then it gradually, gradually got better, but it was a tumultuous time in Washington, D.C., during the Nixon years and during the Carter years. It's tough.

SC: In terms of the final part of the Vietnam War, did you take part in any of the planning of any operations or was yours strictly a planning and policy role?

PDM: No, we were not part of sort of the tactical planning. Most of that was handled out at CinCPac. I later learned, being the EA to CinCPac, how that Unified Command Plan that I helped put together worked. [*laughs*]

SC: We have previously mentioned the famous Zumwalt Z-grams and the impact at the individual shipboard level. Review for us, please, what these were and what was their intent.

PDM: Admiral Zumwalt's intent was to get this rigid naval institution not to relax, but to turn the dial back a bit to be able to absorb the changes that were going on in our culture and our society. I mean, when you look back at that time, between drugs, race relations, dress, grooming, it was a very rocky period, and the Chief of Naval Operations had to get an organization that was based upon discipline to be able to not lose that, but be able to attract into [*sic*] and then to work with young people that were different than those that came in the military in the early sixties and the fifties. It was one of those—I guess if you're using a metaphor for geology—one of those tectonic shifts, and that was happening in the seventies culturally. And he did his damnedest to adapt as he could to the changing situation. I gave him high marks. I tried to pattern some of my leadership styles after him. There was no one individual that I had higher respect for in the uniformed Navy.

SC: You've already mentioned several ways in which the nature of the Navy changed in the early seventies and the immediate post-Vietnam period from when you were commissioned in the 1960s. Are there any other observations that you would make on those changes?

PDM: We witnessed during the Vietnam era what happens to a force that has worked hard for protracted periods and not given sufficient resources to be able to stay current in maintenance and training. You see what happens in the ability to keep a ready force. Sadly, we've experienced that with this thing called sequestration in the last decade. We've worked our ships really hard, we've worked our people really hard, and we've been in a war now protracted even longer than Vietnam, and you can't do it. It'll bite you sooner or later. We suffered it throughout the seventies, and it wasn't until the shift, as you well know and as the record shows, the shift in administrations and bringing in [President Ronald] Reagan. So all those things were happening. It was a tough time in the seventies for the military, tough.

SC: You went from OP-06 to be the flag lieutenant to the Vice Chief of Naval Operations, Admiral Worth Bagley.

PDM: Yep.

SC: First, describe the duties and positions of a flag lieutenant.

PDM: The duties are just as you would think they would be. I had a myriad of protocol and social responsibilities. It wasn't my favorite job. It's probably one of my least favorite jobs, because I didn't like doing that stuff, but you learned how to observe, and it was helpful for future assignments. I came into daily contact with very senior military people, senior government officials. I had to exercise a pretty keen sense of diplomacy, which probably wasn't a strong suit at the time, but I learned how, because it was really required.

One of the most difficult things was when a very senior person came in to visit the Vice Chief and the office was running behind time, and you had to sort of entertain. You couldn't just let someone sit there idly. And so those periods of time were very, very helpful in learning to get comfortable with whoever it was and meeting whatever person it would be from industry, or be from the military.

But I was only the flag lieutenant for three months. I saw that the person that was the real worker on the paperwork side of the office, he was leaving to go to command, and I said, "Hmm. I wonder if I can just go from Side A of the office to Side B of the office." So one day I just simply said, "Admiral, Pete's leaving, and instead of going through the process of finding somebody, why don't you just let me slip over? I'm familiar with the office. You're familiar with me. And then I'll just go to that side and then you'll be leaving." We knew that he was leaving the overall office in that summer. "You'll be leaving in the summer, and there'll be a good transition for the new Vice Chief to have somebody on that side of the office that was experienced when he brought in his team."

And he said, "Sure," and so I went over to that side of the office and I dropped all the protocol responsibilities. I was happy.

SC: In those three months that you were the flag lieutenant, did you have any perspective or opinion on how this would impact your career progression and possible future assignments and promotions?

PDM: No, but I did come away with the perspective of always making your flag lieutenant, which is a necessary job, but always making him feel that he was more than a flag lieutenant, that he was an integral part of your staff. So whenever later on I got to have a flag lieutenant, I used that as the design for his not only helping me with what he had to help me with from the protocol and the personal side, but he felt that he was a real staff member, not just what in that day we called them "Hey boys." "Hey, boy, I need this. Hey, boy, I need that." To make sure that they didn't feel that that's what it was.

SC: So, more than just a social director.

PDM: Absolutely.

SC: Or a cruise director.

PDM: Absolutely.

SC: So what, in general, is the VCNO position all about and what are the typical responsibilities?

PDM: The VCNO is a tough job. I didn't know how tough it was until I got in to probably my second vice chief, which was Hal Shear, and I'll get into that, because I know you're going to give me more questions on that office.[67] Hal Shear was 180 degrees different than Admiral Bagley, 180 degrees.

SC: Well, let's look into that. Serving in D.C., one sees many different leadership styles. Which leadership style did you observe as being the most effective and how about the least effective?

PDM: Oh, wow. The most effective was putting the attributes of Admirals Bagley, Shear, and Long into one pot and stirring it around, and you had the best damn leader that could ever be.[68] [*laughs*] I spent four years [at the Pentagon]. I went to Admiral Bagley's office in February of '75. I left the War College, six months in OP-06. February of '75. Then I had Admiral Shear's whole tour. Six months with Admiral Bagley, Admiral Shear for two full years, and then Admiral Long for three-quarters of his tour or at least half his tour. So that was a long period of time seeing three different leadership styles.

---

[67] Admiral Harold E. "Hal" Shear (1918–99) graduated from the U.S. Naval Academy in 1942, shortly after the Japanese attack on Pearl Harbor (December 7, 1941) and served in the U.S. Navy until 1980 as the vice chief of naval operations from 1975 to 1977 and then as commander in chief, Allied Forces Southern Europe from 1977 to 1980.

[68] Admiral Robert L. J. Long (1920–2002) graduated from the U.S. Naval Academy in 1943 and served in the U.S. Navy until 1983. His last billets were vice chief of naval operations from 1977 to 1979 and commander, U.S. Pacific Command until 1983.

The dynamics of the Vice Chief's Office were terribly interesting. I went through one EA with Bagley, two EAs with Hal Shear, and another EA with Admiral Long, and these were all post-major command captains that knew they were on the road to rear admiral and very difficult to work with. Each one of them was very difficult to work with.

On the administrative side with Admiral Bagley, I took that as a learning period. I had three months before the new vice chief would come in. The Vice Chief's Office handles an enormous amount of paper to keep the naval staff on track, to keep the Navy on track, and to filter to the CNO for decisions only those that had what they called completed staff work and then the CNO decision panel to make the big decision, whether it be to build a new class of ship or whether it be to look at the operational evaluations of the Navy force. I was shocked at the amount of paperwork that came in to run an organization like the Navy from the staff level, from personnel to submarine, each of the platform sponsors, to the budget. The budget took up 30 percent of the time by itself in trying to do tradeoffs and listening to the tradeoffs of why you put this much budget into this slot and this much into that. It was a very, very tough desk. And the CNO had the Joint Chiefs of Staff responsibilities, he had lots of traveling responsibilities, and so the buck stopped for, I would say, 80 percent of the decisions at the vice chief's desk. Terribly important job in the Navy.

SC: Before we get into the leadership style of the individual, the three vice chiefs that you served under, describe for us first what your typical day was like as the flag lieutenant.

PDM: Flag lieutenant, I'd just get there before the boss and leave after the boss and help him get through the day. I was the "Hey boy" sometimes. I'd have to go over and talk to Mrs. Bagley when they were having some kind of social function. It was work that I did not like, but that I did, and I did it the best that I could, and I must have done it all right, because they moved me to the other side of the office. That's all.

SC: Well, let's talk about that. Describe your typical day as the VCNO administrative assistant.

PDM: That's where I was initiated in long days, because I would get there before everybody, before the EA, of course before the vice chief. I took that job with every package that came through there, and every package had—the Navy has what they called the chop list. It had been around to all these offices and there were initials from everybody that had to have seen that paper come in to the vice chief before it would go off. The Vice chief would either make a decision or pass it on. Papers were anywhere from a letter that was a point paper, two pages to a stack of two and three inches of paperwork, voluminous. But early on, I tried to review those packages as if I was Vice Chief. It took time. I just did not take that all these three-stars had signed off on that paper to just give it to the vice chief and say that "all the work was done already, and you just have to sign it." I would write a concise, clear précis of what this thing was about, with a recommendation, and sometimes I would recommend against some of the things that three-stars had chopped. I put down why, and then I'd give him a draft that he could write on the paper to send it back. It took me a long time to do this.

I got cross-threaded with each of the executive assistants that worked at that desk because I saw the paper first and I'd put this on there, put it on the left side. They didn't know what to do with it. They didn't know whether to agree with the paper as submitted by the staff or to let this paper go in with what I had said. It's a difficult situation. I was fortunate in that the position was gapped [not filled] for a bit because one had made flag with Admiral Bagley and the other one hadn't arrived yet. So with Hal Shear, he was getting my notes for, I don't know, a couple, three weeks. And the new guy that came in there, I'd do it the same way, but I was finding out that he'd taken out my paper because he thought he should be the one doing that. Fine, until Admiral Shear got a couple of these and he said, "Where's Paul's note?" A sticky wicket, sticky wicket.

So with Hal Shear, tough, tough man. He was an original diesel submariner and then finally offered transition to nukes. He was from the old Navy school, I mean the *old* Navy school. He wanted everything done properly. I can still see him at that desk. He didn't even like reading my notes, and he would never read two inches of paper. He had direct lines. He used the phone all the time, much more than paper. He'd call up the chief of naval material, he'd call up the admiral of 06 or whatever, "I've got this paper here. Tell me what am I supposed to do with it." And that was his management style. He wasn't deep into reviewing staff work. He was deep into, if he had confidence in somebody that told him to do something, you know, he'd rather do it that way.

But back then, it's important to note that a lot of the phone conversations were monitored. I monitored most of the conversations with three vice chiefs for three years. I learned a lot. And if he was talking about something significant, he would say, "Clear line," and then you're supposed to get off the phone. With Admiral Shear, I'll never forget the day he was talking about—it was a pretty important—the topic's not important, but he said, "Clear line, clear line." So I hung up.

Afterwards, he says, "What did he say?" He buzzed me and he said, "What did he say?"

I says, "Admiral, I don't know. You told me to clear the line."

He really got angry. "When I say, 'Clear the line,' it's for the idiots on the other end of 'Clear the line.' It's not for you to clear the line. I want you to listen so I don't miss anything." It was amazing. I never left the line, and some of the things that I heard I can't report in this presentation. It was absolutely amazing, and what an education it was on how to handle different situations, how to handle different issues, because you were hearing two very senior people or you were hearing [the] CNO and him talk. It was amazing, the education, from the education vantage point. So that when I got more senior, I would have heard all these discussions before and how they go back and forth and how decisions are made. Terribly important, wonderful, wonderful experience. And I got along with Admiral Shear really, really well. He was tough. He didn't suffer fools. We would go into meetings, he would be pinpoint with regard to how to quiz and how to challenge the recommendations. In his last six months, he was getting tired. Sometimes I'd watch him and you'd think that he wasn't paying attention, but he would surprise you. He was looking like he might take a little snooze, but he wasn't. He was an amazing individual. He went off to be—we had CinCUSNavEur [commander in chief, U.S. Naval Forces Europe] at the time. He went off to be the head of European CinCUSNavEur after being Vice Chief.

He tried to get me to go nuke and said, "The only thing wrong with you is you're not a trained nuclear power officer." He tried to get me, before I went to command, to go that way.

I says, "Admiral, it's not for me. I probably couldn't even pass the school." I mean, I wasn't steeped in the math and everything else. I says, "I appreciate it, but I'm going to have to stay as just a regular old sailor."

He says, "You'll do fine." He gave me three fantastic fitness reports, handwritten notes all over them. He's passed now, but he was just a tremendous officer.

So he left and Admiral Long came. I'm on my third vice chief now. Admiral Long was totally different than Admiral Shear, different type of decision maker, much broader in outlook, much broader. And he came up from OP-02. He was keen for the new submarine programs that we were bringing forward, and, if you can be, he was good friends with Admiral Rickover. He watched over the nuclear power community carefully funding-wise. But he was a genuine administrator of the Navy staff for the CNO.

The staff worked really well under Admiral Long, and we continued. He had an EA, but Admiral Long and I got—we became closer than I was with Admiral Shear, regardless of who was the EA there. The last EA, I said, "I have a great relationship here. I'll do everything that I possibly can to help make you the right paper and recommendations for flag, but I've got a relationship with him and I'll do my job." Just tough. I'm stuttering because it was a very tough almost three and a half years because I had someone in between me and the vice chiefs, so it was hard, tedious, but it all worked.

That period of time, I was selected early to commander. I hadn't even been to my commander command yet, and the experience that I had tucked away about large organizations, about strategic thinking, about listening to all these briefs about what the maritime force of the future would have to be, when I finally left there, I had a kit of experience that was absolutely second to none of any brand-new commander in our Navy.

SC: You've described the leadership style of Admirals Shear and Long. What about back to Admiral Bagley? How would you characterize his leadership and management?

PDM: Admiral Bagley was probably, in my short time with him, probably more traditional. He liked to have the finished staff product more so than—I know more so than Shear and even more so than Admiral Long. His brother was chief of naval personnel at the time, which was interesting. This was his last six months that I was with him, so I knew that he wasn't going to go on to another four-star job. This was a wonderful person. He did not get another four-star job. So his style was more traditional. He was very smart. But, the time that I served with him, particularly the last three months, when one is leaving, you know, it's different. The days are a little bit different. He's got to get other things done as opposed to just grinding through. He ground through it, but then he retired from being Vice Chief. He was a four-star. So it was a six-month period.

But as far as the ability to really articulate, that's what I took away from him. I would listen to him in large CNO Executive Board sessions, and he was a studied, articulate decision maker, and he was able to provide rationale as to why he went one way or went the other way.

The three men were very different. Each of the three men were immensely competent. Their personalities, of course, were different, but the Navy was served well and the CNOs, the two CNOs were served well by having those three people as vice chief between 1974 and 1978 or whenever Admiral Long left.

SC: Were there any positive or negative traits, characteristics, or behaviors that you observed between the three officers that you adopted or avoided as you advanced in seniority and greater positions of responsibility?

PDM: [*laughs*] No, I can't tell you about one that I adopted from Admiral Shear. It's precious. But I adopted a little bit from Admiral Bagley, more from Admiral Shear, but a lot from Admiral Long because Admiral Long let me go to sea when he became CinCPac. I got a message one day and it said, "You will be in receipt of orders to be my EA at CinCPac." So then I was with him for another eighteen months or two years, so I really adopted—I mean I was really influenced because I saw him operate operationally within the Navy staff and then operationally with the Pacific Command.

SC: In terms of an officer's future promotion and advancement, what would you advise a young post-command-at-sea officer to do if offered a billet such as you had at the Pentagon?

PDM: Take it.

SC: Were there any other memorable personalities, positive or negative, from your time at the Pentagon or on the VCNO's staff?

PDM: I don't remember names, but the answer is yes. The most difficult personality on a large staff like that are probably the 06s or the captains that have a keen desire to become a flag officer. I saw many try too hard and many that would never cross the finish line work in a fashion that they thought they should. That's where the difficult personalities were. The younger personalities, they were just trying to get their job done and getting out to go to command or go to major command. They were all fine. The admirals, they were all fine because they had made it, you know. They were promoted to two stars out of the box, even though they weren't for pay grade, so that'll be a sort for SecNav. But they were promoted, so they were all pretty comfortable. They were wearing two stars already, so they knew that the Navy only had thirty-three three-stars, so they knew that the chances to go to three stars were limited. Most of those people were pretty comfortable in having made two stars, and if they made three stars, that was great, but it wasn't what they were trying to do. But there were a lot of captains in a big staff like that trying really hard to become rear admiral or brigadier general. Those were the ones that were difficult.

SC: We're going to talk, as we get down the road, about the whole process for captains being selected for admiral and some of the dynamics there.

Once you completed your administrative assistant tour, you requested assignment to the PMD, which is the executive management course at Harvard. What is that program and who is the intended audience?

PDM: Admiral Long—I had to say it's time for me to go, because it was comfortable. I've been in that situation where I've had somebody that I was comfortable with. I said, "Admiral, it's a long time."

So he said, "Where do you want to go?"

I can't remember who triggered me to this program, but the Navy, as you'll recall, left Harvard when they took the NROTC unit away during Vietnam and hadn't sent anybody back to Harvard. It was a visitor—I can't recall who said that "you have an MBA. You ought to go to the Harvard Business School Executive Management Program."

I looked it up and there were two executive management programs. They had what they called PMD, the Program of Management Development, which was a fourteen-week program. It was a good program, fourteen weeks long, and it was for mid-level executives in industry. And then they had one advanced management, which was for CEOs and the like, or near-CEOs. So I knew I fit the age and the criteria for the PMD, and so I had somebody in the office get all the data. I remember the school was terribly expensive, at least from my outlook. I filled out some paper, and so I asked Admiral Long to fund this from OpNav and then to okay the Navy being reintroduced to Harvard University. I was the first officer to go back sponsored by the Navy since we left the campus a decade earlier. They did. They paid the freight and approved the assignment. I was accepted up there.

But why did I do this? I did this because I did not want to go to a new construction ship, which was a *Spruance*-class destroyer which everybody else wanted. I did not want to do that because I'd spent too much time getting a new ship operational, going through all the things, and by the time I'd finished my CO tour, all I would have done was get a new ship into the Navy. So I looked at the slate, and there was this thing called the *Luce* (DDG-38), and it had just come out of the yard, so I wanted to give the new skipper three months or so, four months or so, to get all its problems fixed, and then I would have an operational ship totally around for the time that I would be CO, and that's where I would make it or not.[69] So I needed to spend some time. That's where the Harvard PMD program came into play. The Navy did not have a program to send me to. I had a program to send me. It happened to work out. But then after I left, the Navy sent other people up there. It became a program.

SC: The program is comprised of about thirty mid-level business leaders.

PDM: Yep.

SC: Why would the services sent an officer to this program, and what would be the expected benefit to the service?

PDM: Because they could. Because the vice [vice chief of naval operations] paid for it, and I didn't know exactly what the benefit would be. It was just that. I was a naval officer amongst, I think, twenty-eight or something, U.S. and international mid-level businesspeople. It was a wonderful experience.

SC: Were there any other services represented?

PDM: No.

SC: You were the only one.

PDM: I was the only military person there. They didn't know if I had two heads or not.

SC: [*laughs*] Well, describe for us the typical day as a student in the PMD program.

---

[69] USS *Luce* (DLG-7/DDG-38) was a *Farragut*-class (DLG-6/DDG-37) guided missile destroyer commissioned in 1961 and decommissioned in 1991. *Farragut*-class destroyers were commissioned in the early 1960s initially as guided missile destroyer leaders or DLGs, but beginning in 1975, were re-designated as DDGs or guided missile destroyers. *Luce* had a complement of 21 officers and 356 enlisted crewman. She was rated to thirty-three knots speed and carried a 5"/54 gun, ASROC launcher, Mk-32 ASW torpedoes, and a missile launch system. Later in her career, she was back fitted with Harpoon anti-ship cruise missiles.

PDM: We operated as an adjunct to HBS [Harvard Business School]. We had selective cases that the business school had done. It was the full case study methodology. Was it rigorous? No. Was it intense in that I was surprised particularly from the foreign students of how driven they were to succeed in that program and the amount of time that the foreign students spent in addition to the time that was required to do this collaborative work, because all the cases, most of them were collaborative, in which the whole class was put into three- and four-person elements to come up with the case, come up with a solution, and then present it as you would if you presented to your board to get something done. So it was good from that vantage point.

That's where at least the MBA [University of Georgia, 1964] came into a little bit of practice, particularly in these case studies. I used it, I learned from it, and I left it. Was it necessary? I look back. Did it change PDM [Paul David Miller] to become a better leader? I don't think so. Did it add a narrative that I had not seen on the Navy staff looking at these mid-grade industry people and how they approached their work? Did it add something to do that and put that into my kit of leadership? Yeah. So you don't graduate. I mean, you get a certificate or whatever, that you paid a lot of money for, that the Navy paid a lot of money for, and then I was anxious to go on to command.

SC: From your perspective today, would you recommend that a mid-career officer seek to be appointed to such a management development program?

PDM: Absolutely.

SC: Were there any memorable personalities from your time at Harvard?

PDM: A couple of professors were different, different, but the students, to a person, were polished. You could tell that these people, when they'd go back to their respective firms, were going to do very well. I made a couple of acquaintances there. One was Japanese—very, very sharp Japanese guy. I think he worked for one of the large machinery companies in Japan. There was a person from India that worked in their engineering software world. They were outstanding people. You knew they were going to be successes. We had reunions for about ten years, but now it's been forty years since I went. It's history. But I can see some of the people that were there.

It was good. If somebody has a chance to do it, whether it be from the Navy or other services, they should go. I sent some of the people when I was a CEO to University of Chicago and a couple of other schools to give them an opportunity to experience who they were facing. This is their competition in industry. These are the people they're going to lead, businesses that are going to be your competitors in your respective field, and it was very helpful to them.

SC: As we wrap up this session, is there anything that you would like to add to the discussion of your time at the University of Georgia, at Harvard, or at the Pentagon on the VCNO staff?

PDM: No. Each of them were a unique opportunity to gain experience, to perform to the best measures that I could, and I knew each of the tours of duty were being measured in different ways, and to be able to get through those tours and then be able to go to the HBS thing and then go to a ship of choice, I knew that a path had been given me to continue to be a successful naval officer. And as I said at the beginning of this session, performance, once you get on that train of success, it continues until you derail yourself. I knew that I was on the train, and now I had to be the best ship's captain that I could possibly be—compete with the other captains the best I could, so that I would become, just as I was in *McCloy*, the number one CO in the Squadron and solidify an opportunity to get promoted early to captain. Was it the best way to approach command? I don't know, but it was a successful way to approach command. Each one of those opportunities was unique. Subliminally, I would think I haven't been derailed yet. A couple times in *Luce* I thought it was coming. You'll hear about them. However, with a great crew, we gained a top notch Fleet reputation for *Luce*.

SC: Thank you, Admiral Miller. In our next session, we will discuss your tour as CO of the *Luce*.

This is USNI oral history interview with Admiral Paul David Miller, U.S. Navy (Ret.). This is session number six, question set number thirteen. The date is Saturday, April 14, 2018, and the interviewer is Professor Stan Carpenter.

SC: This is USNI oral history interview with Admiral Paul David Miller, U.S. Navy (Ret.). This is session number six, question set number fourteen. The date is Saturday, April 14, 2018, and the interviewer is Professor Stan Carpenter. These questions cover the years as CO of USS *Luce* (DDG-38) and as CinCPac executive assistant.

Admiral, after your Pentagon tour and period at Harvard in the PMD program, it was time for you to return to sea duty. You specifically requested a billet as CO of a DL. That's a ship designation no longer used in the current U.S. Navy, so let's start with some definition. What was a DL and also a DLG?

PDM: DL was what they called the destroyer leader, and then a DLG was a guided missile destroyer leader. The capability of a DLG was 5"/54 [gun], ASROC Tartar missile systems, a 1,200-pound engineering plant, and it's probably, what, 1,000 tons more than a regular destroyer, just a little bit bigger. But then they renumbered it [*Luce*] to DDG-38. They dropped all the DL designations.

SC: You mentioned ASROC and Tartar. Tell us a little bit about those weapon systems and the capabilities.

PDM: The ASROC system is the rocket-thrown torpedo, comes out of a box launcher, armored box launcher on the bow, in front of the pilothouse. We weren't a designated ASW ship, but we had the ASROC and Mk-46 [torpedo] capabilities for antisubmarine warfare. We were designated anti-air warfare ship and we had the Tartar missile system. It made it perfect for integration into carrier group operations. It was a very capable ship, very tough to maintain with the 1,200-pound engineering steam plant, very seaworthy. I spent the entire time as commanding officer in some form of operation at sea. It had just come out of the yard, as I have mentioned. The ship wasn't known as the best ship in the fleet, and I think I can sum it up in the first sentence of the first fitness report that I received from my squadron commander. It says, "Commander Paul Miller is my number one commanding officer. The reason for this is that he assumed command of a ship that needed a strong, positive leader. The ship morale had deteriorated, which, in turn, had infected to considerable extent her overall reliability. He took positive steps in the following areas: accessibility to the commanding officer was vastly improved, habitability was improved, less rigidity in command, and, above all, a greater willingness to make known his desires, combined to turn around a mediocre ship. *Luce* is an outstanding ship."

Now, I read that sentence verbatim because earlier, Stan, you asked about Admiral Zumwalt, and I think in that one sentence I followed what I had seen in Admiral Zumwalt as the Chief of Naval Operations. "Needed a strong, positive leader." Admiral Zumwalt was that in my mind. "Accessibility to the commanding officer was vastly improved." That was taken from Admiral Zumwalt and then each of the four-stars that I worked for. They gave me accessibility, and by accessibility, I was able to communicate, learn what the particular mission they wanted to accomplish, was able to do it and do it more quickly and correctly. "Less rigidity in command." I think I talked about Admiral Zumwalt in looking at the way that he changed the cultural things. He was less rigid in making sure that everybody had to be out of the military centerfold with regard to haircut, uniform, shoes, etc. All that stuff was important, but you can achieve it by being less rigid in the way you approach it.

So I cite that sentence to say that I learned along the way as to trying to take the attributes from the leaders that I worked for and put them into practice when I had the opportunity to lead a warship. So I took the tour at *Luce* and it was probably the best twenty months I had in the Navy.

SC: In the 1970s, the DLs and DLGs such as those of the *Belknap* (DLG-26/CG-26) or the DLG-26 class and the *Farragut*-class (DLG-37/DDG-37) such as the *Luce* were re-designated as cruisers, CGs, or guided missile destroyers, DDGs.

PDM: Right.

SC: Why was this change made?

PDM: You know, I don't know. They were able to categorize ships more easily and particularly put them all into one class, because I think they were going through an organizational change with regard to how they were going to assign ships, and they took the DLGs and made them regular DDGs, and they grouped them into a squadron with other DDGs, and so the COs were reported upon in the same vein, regardless of your capabilities. One had a little longer-range mission than another one, but they grouped them all. And the way they had it organized during my time, I was in Mayport [Naval Station, Mayport, Florida, near Jacksonville] and every cruiser-destroyer ship in Mayport worked for one commodore, and that commodore was in charge of maintenance and training of those ships. And then when you went on an exercise or went on a deployment, then you worked for what they called an operational DesRon [destroyer squadron] commander. He was responsible only for tactics and completing of the mission at hand. They changed the designation of the ships, I think, to coordinate with the way they wanted to operate the ships.

SC: What was the typical departmental organization of a DDG?

PDM: Much as we were organized in USS *Parsons* (DDG-33). There was the weapons officer. I think now they have a combat systems officer. You had a supply officer, operations officer, and engineering officer, and operations officer. Those were the department heads, and each of the department heads had numerous division officers that covered the ship stem [bow] to stern. It was everyone's task to keep the ship running efficiently and keep everything in proper working order so that when you went to sea, you were able to complete every evolution assigned.

SC: You had already done a ship CO tour on the *McCloy* as a lieutenant commander. That was a frigate, and now you move to a larger ship as CO of a destroyer. Let's look at a command tour at sea for a young commander. What characteristics does the Navy then and now look for in sending an officer on their first commander-level command at sea?

PDM: Whether it be command at sea of something designated for a captain, a commander, a lieutenant commander, or a lieutenant, command at sea is command at sea. It starts with safe operations every time you took the ship to sea, making sure you go from Point A to Point B, not hitting any buoys, not hitting any ships, but sailing it properly. That goes whether it be on an ATF [fleet tug], frigate, DDG [guided missile destroyer], fleet oiler, or a CVN [nuclear aircraft carrier]. As ships get larger the only thing you add is complexity. You add complexity in the weapons systems, and then you add range. You're able to extend your war fighting capability with the larger ships with more complex weapon systems. That goes for propulsion systems; no matter what you had, the responsibilities are the same. Regardless of designation—diesels or whether they be 600 or 1,200-pound [pounds of pressure per square inch] boilers, even nuclear power or now gas turbines—you need to make sure that that ship is ready to "answer all bells." Operations are pretty similar, except for the larger the ship with more capability, you're going to have to deal with more complexity. Simultaneity comes into play. When you're with a battle group, you might have to be worrying about your AAW [anti-air warfare] picture, and all of a sudden, you have an ASW [antisubmarine warfare] contact that you have to prosecute. So there is more complexity but the basic attributes that you need to command are the same. Knowledge, leadership, and confidence are key.

SC: What type of billets should one have accomplished successfully in order to be competitive for selection as an at-sea CO?

PDM: You're asking the wrong person, because I went to be CO of a frigate and many said that I did not have the experience and I was too young. Many. But somehow I had a pretty successful tour as the CO of *McCloy*. I had a very successful tour. For me, what I learned along the way, both at sea and ashore, made me the more successful CO in *Luce*. The ability to deal with the complexity that I just talked about is, for the majority of naval officers, particularly surface warfare officers or in the aviation community, squadron commanders, the pattern that they've established. A department head, an XO, and then go to CO tour is probably the pattern that fits 92 percent of the people, but the system isn't adroit enough to accommodate the other 8 percent of the people. They squash those 8 percent of the people with the 92 and don't treat them any differently. If I had a chance to do it, lead it differently, I would make sure that the 8 percent of the people had a path also, because I ardently believe that whether it be the military or business, there's a certain cadre of people that are able to perform better, more adroitly, more correctly, more quickly than the majority of people, and those people should be given a different path.

SC: What in your record and credentials do you think caused the Navy to send you back out for a second warship command at sea?

PDM: Well, the Navy was rigid in that they'd had command for lieutenant commanders, commands for commanders, and commands for captains. The ship that I had as a commander in capability was no different, except for the range of the missile, than what they had as a captain. You take the ship that you served on, the *Josephus Daniels* (CG-27). They had the Terrier missile system, but other than an extended range from twenty-five to forty miles, they had no other capability, but yet it needed to have this thing called a captain to be the commanding officer. So they had to create the necessary matrix to get people the experience, to experience them for the next rank, and then they had those ships, because *Josephus Daniels* had 410, I don't know, and *Luce* only had 302 people, so they had a few more people because they had a little bit more capability, but they had to care for nuclear weapons.

Back then, we had nuclear weapons on those damn ships. I can say today that one of the things that I said to myself, if I was ever in a position to get nuclear weapons off of surface ships that would be one of the things that I would work hard to do. They do not have nuclear weapons on surface ships today.

SC: You've said that you specifically requested command of a DL. Why was that?

PDM: Because it was the premier ship for commander command. It was larger. The missile capability puts you in a different operating environment. That's why I really tried to steer not going to a *Spruance*-class destroyer, because they were new, they had the new engineering plant, but they didn't have the multiwarfare capability, and I wanted to be a practitioner in each of the areas of warfare that a ship of the line, the best ships of the line had.[70]

SC: If you were to advise a mid-career officer facing their first command at sea of a ship the size of a destroyer or, in those days, a DL or DLG or DDG, what would that advice be?

PDM: It's really hard to give advice to aspirants to command, because I believe you have to build your own style for command. Command is an awesome responsibility. People don't appreciate the authority of a commanding officer and the responsibilities of a commanding officer at sea. Unless you've been in the milieu to serve onboard a ship like that, you don't appreciate it. And then when you have that capability and then when you deploy it to sea and operations that are complex, it's tough. There's so much going on in a battle group when, say, you're in an exercise in the North Atlantic, then remember this was the Cold War going on and you were exercising against the then–Soviet Navy in three dimensions of warfare. You were under surface, surface, and air warfare. We hadn't brought in space warfare at that time.

But even in those three dimensions of warfare, when you had planes flying and you had everything going on in your naval tactical data system [NTDS] and your status boards, and it was full of adversaries and friendlies, and then, as I mentioned, you had a submarine contact, which you did in those big Northern Wedding and other style operations, the pace of activity was frantic. And then if you superimpose upon that some kind of casualty to the engineering plant, and your mind is going, "How am I going to piece all this stuff together?" It puts a hell of a lot of stress on not only the commanding officer, but everybody that's on that ship. And then you throw in something that you can't control, some really bad weather, and then your ship is rolling twenty-three, thirty

---

[70] The *Spruance*-class DDs (DD-963 to DDG-997) were commissioned beginning in the mid-1970s and were designed primarily for ASW. They did not carry a missile system except for the last several that were missile-equipped for AAW defense and designated as DDG. They were gas-turbine powered with variable-pitch propellers, which gave better maneuverability and the ability to come up to speed faster.

degrees, and you're trying to keep everything online, you sort of ask yourself, "What in the world is going on here?"

It is tough work. You don't learn how to do that. You just do it. Because until you get into that position, you don't know. You do not know how you're going to react. You hope that you react properly, but the biggest thing that I saw as a commanding officer is people were watching how you react. People gain confidence in their commanding officer as they watch their commanding officer under stress and how he would handle that stress, and then if they were a junior officer who aspired to stay in the Navy, you would have made an impression on that junior officer and you would hope that he—or now she—would have learned how to handle the situations and become a better CO because of it.

SC: For a warship the size of a DDG, the captain cannot have the span of control that he or she might have on a much, much smaller vessel. Given that dynamic, how did the relationship between the CO and the XO and the department heads change as opposed to the smaller frigate? Or did the relationship change at all?

PDM: I would argue that the premise of the span of control is different. I would argue that the span of control is the same. The only thing that is different is the extension of each of those spans, the span in engineering, in weapons, supply, and operations. It just reached a little bit further, but the span of control and your knowledge, to me, had to expand from when I was CO of a frigate to when I was CO of a big DDG. The span of control, I had the same span of control on that big ship that I had on that smaller ship. It was just extended. I had four department heads on each ship. I had four department heads. But I had a little bit further reach on the DDG. I had to know the condition of all the missiles that were aboard. I didn't have that before. But I wouldn't give up having that span just because I was on a larger ship. The span of control went from the bow to the stern, no matter what ship it was, and the reach was further. I think I'm trying to say this correctly. But you had the same span of control. It didn't change.

SC: The frigate that you were on was basically an antisubmarine warfare vessel—

PDM: Correct.

SC: —whereas the DDG, because it had the missile systems—

PDM: Was anti-air warfare.

SC: —was anti-air warfare. What other missions or warfare areas was the DDG capable of, in addition to the anti-air warfare?

PDM: We were capable in antisubmarine warfare, but we didn't have a long-range sonar. We did have the submarine weapons that could be used, but we did not have the sonar so we were limited. The only other limitation it had, we did not have a certified helo deck on the DDG. That was a limiting factor for its particularly ASW capability. So whenever we were at sea, we were put in the AAW role, the air warfare commander role, and the ship was very seldom used outside of that.

SC: You were assigned to USS *Luce* (DDG-38). Tell us about the *Luce* itself.

PDM: *Luce* was a great ship. It was an older ship, though, particularly the engineering plant. The Navy was going to gas turbines, and it still had these 1,200-pound boilers. I was surprised by that. I had experience on 600-pound boilers. I thought I knew a little bit about engineering and steam plants, but anybody that's ever served on a 1,200-pound steam plant respects 1,200-pound steam. It's a dangerous atmosphere and you have to run things meticulously. The only thing that made life a little bit easier on *Luce* than I had it on *McCloy* was we had two evaporators on *Luce*, one on *McCloy*, so I did not worry quite as much about boiler feed water on the *Luce* as I did on the *McCloy*.

It was twin-screw, a dream to handle. I loved ship handling. I think it's a lost art in the U.S. Navy today, because everything, every time I see a ship, it's got a tug alongside it. You know, back then, it was a stamp of pride that you bring that ship into the pier and you park that puppy. But the Navy sort of lost that along the way. Being in the destroyer force like that, you were proud of it. You taught people how to drive ships.

On *Luce*—I think I'm being perfectly honest with myself—I docked the ship once or twice, but I do not think I was ever at the conn for underway replenishment. I always used that as a training evolution. I made people want to do this, be proud of doing it. Sometimes I would stand there and watch and I'd have to hold my breath, and I'd just look and I'd try to anticipate is he going to make the correction that he needs to make, and maybe once or twice I nudged and helped, but I had great pride in fitness reports reflected in having youngsters from ensign through lieutenant commander take the conn, do the evolution day, night, smooth, rough seas, and everybody felt, once they did that, they really felt part of the ship. It wasn't just your sea and anchor detail or your special OOD that did every one of them. Whoever was on watch took it. The OOD or JOOD, they took it.

And I could sense, by the time I left *Luce*, all the officers felt that they had real ownership in this ship. They could drive it, they could put it into harm's way and at nighttime they were unrepping [underway replenishment] from an oiler or whatever, in rough seas. It was a tough evolution, but most of them had done it. They were proud of it. My job as a CO was to build the proudest ship that I could to turn over to the next commanding officer, and have those junior officers reflect on their time and under my supervision that it was as enjoyable a ride that they could have and they learned something all the time, because they were the ones making it run, not the captain.

SC: What deployments did *Luce* make while you were the CO?

PDM: We made one deployment, was only a ten-week, three-month, to the North Atlantic on a combination of combined exercises with the NATO [North Atlantic Treaty Organization] Alliance on Northern Wedding and another exercise even further north than the GI-UK Gap, and the numbers of ships out there, it was amazing.[71] We had, I don't know, three carrier battle groups; we had a British carrier battle group, two of ours, and then we went all the way into the fjords into Norway and transited from Stavanger in

---

[71] GI-UK or GIUK Gap is the sea space between Great Britain, Iceland, and Greenland through which the Soviet forces would have to pass to get to the North Atlantic.

the fjords up to Narvik to try to get that far north without being picked up by surveillance of the then–Soviet Navy. That was one exercise, one deployment.

I did not make a Med deployment, because when we came back from that, we had to workup to become the flagship for the Standing Naval Force Atlantic, StanNavForLant, and it was the U.S. turn to take the commodore role. So we embarked a commodore for the full deployment for StanNavForLant, which is a six-month deployment.

But in that Northern Wedding exercise, we'd already gone up the fjords. Then we went into the Baltic and we made a port visit to Helsinki [Finland], and the commodore was embarked. For some reason—I cannot recall the exact detail—we had to be in Portsmouth, England, at a certain time, and they had put into the schedule a respectable sixteen knot SOA [speed of advance] or whatever to get there. We got under way from Helsinki and, without exaggeration, you couldn't see the damn coast. We had a pilot help us get out of the harbor, which is a tough harbor, lots of little islands, and the pilot boat comes up, he drops us, and can't see anything.

What's this captain going to do? I can go three knots, blow the horn every sixty seconds or whatever the periodicity is, drive myself and the crew crazy, or we could go fast. So I sped up, set a watch in combat with not only the surface scopes but the NTDS system, trained all the useful radars that we had, including the gun directors that could take bearings on them, all feed back into where I was observing. Then we put a line through the Baltic, and I figured, going fast, I'd only have to worry about a couple of quadrants, because everything back here I'm going to leave in the dust, particularly if they're going slow in the fog. The commodore, I know, wanted to say, "What the . . . ? What are you doing?" He just left the bridge. It was forty-eight hours over that, to get out of the Baltic, the Skattagat, then down the channel.

My summation is—and this was Captain Hannagan—he talked about my training the ship. [*reading*] "The result, predictably, was that the ship constantly improved as the crew developed skills and maturity. Commander Miller pushes himself hard and has tremendous stamina, which paid off. When the ship was required to make a high-speed transit from Helsinki to England in the densest fog imaginable, his ability to make the right decisions quickly, under adverse conditions and much pressure, was tested time and time again. He proved to my complete satisfaction that he can take the heat and come through with flying colors."

I attribute that forty-eight hours to me performing as CO as making the difference, in the eight ships that were deployed, of me getting the top fitness report. I give that and write that it is things like that that separate commanding officers, separate staff officers. You have to know when to take the prudent risk and have the confidence in yourself and in the people that you have trained and rely on, to perform, to have the mission completed without any problem. I could tell that story, but unless I quote it, somebody else, they'll say it's a sea story. That is not a sea story. That commodore experienced it all the way, and he was absolutely surprised.

SC: You had command of *Luce* in the immediate post-Vietnam period. We've already addressed certain aspects of that period, but what do you think were the most significant changes in Navy culture from before the Vietnam War period when you first entered the service and the mid-1960s to the late 1970s?

PDM: The period you're talking about is a complete sine wave. When we were in the first part of Vietnam, everything was going—even the prosecution of the war was going. People could just [see] it for themselves. But ships would go over from small boats, from swift boats to riverine forces [small combatant craft for inland water operations such as the swift boat], to carriers. Everybody was proud, honorable, do their job, do their duty then come back. Some of us went back again.

Then you get up to that period in the early seventies where you get frayed edges. We knew that things were turning south, and we came out of there in a less than glorious way, right? And then you were into the early seventies, where you had the cultural and the social things that we talked about. Admiral Zumwalt comes to be the new CNO. He has to deal with all that stuff. He deals with it. Some people say he loosened the valve a little bit too much. And then crank back a little, closed a little bit in the mid-seventies. We're talking about now the late seventies. The Navy, material-wise, isn't in the best condition, but we could put ships to sea and we operated in the North Atlantic, Mediterranean, and Pacific. But then, the ship that I had the pleasure to command, it was an operating ship. It took a lot of work to make it that way, but there were a lot of commanding officers that felt the same way about their ships. So we were on an upward trend, but the ascent was slow. It wasn't until after Reagan came in that we got to be able to get back up to the Navy that we needed, that everybody respected, that every ship in the force was as ready as it should be and was manned as it should be.[72]

SC: Tell us about wardroom life on *Luce*. Was there a different dynamic with the larger ship as opposed to the smaller wardrooms on the *McCloy* and the fleet tugs?

PDM: No. Dynamic was the same. People were different, the numbers were different, but I was of the school, properly or improperly, that believed in an informal wardroom. Life at sea is tough enough without having to have people come down to dinner at a prescribed time and in a prescribed uniform. We did everything family style from the mess decks, and the officers that I had, they appreciated that. They had the latitude that they needed to do their job, and that's the environment that I fostered.

SC: When a husband or wife is a sailor, the spouse and children join the Navy as well. Tell us about your family life in the late 1970s while you skippered the *Luce*.

PDM: I was not home very much. We had two sons at that time. Becky was a wonderful CO's wife, because at that time, the tradition was to have a close wardroom for the spouses when ships were away, and she filled that function perfectly. Mayport was a small community and it was probably easier to do that in Mayport than it was to do it in a large port like Norfolk where people lived in a greater geographic area. News traveled rapidly in Mayport because of its size. So I think that the spouses of the overall shipboard family unit writ large were well cared for, from not only the *Luce*'s vantage point, but the whole destroyer squadron that we had down there, because we were helped by size.

---

[72] Ronald W. Reagan (1911–2004) was president of the United States from 1981 to 1989. A goal of the Reagan administration was to rebuild the US Navy back up to six hundred hulls.

SC: You've already described a great deal of your leadership style as CO of the *Luce*. Any more to add?

PDM: No. I describe it, but it wasn't a description of a false narrative. I lived it. That ship was part of me. I knew everything that went on in that ship. I would walk around that ship at least once a day, maybe twice a day. I would visit each of the engine rooms and each of the boiler rooms. I would visit the laundry. I'd talk to the guy that was down there doing the laundry. I'd go into the comm shack [radio central]. I'd go to the burn bags [classified waste stored in brown paper bags labeled as CLASSIFIED designated for destruction by burning] and sit down on the burn bags and talk to the radiomen on watch. But people could see that. People could see that I cared.

I don't know if you remember a thing called the OPPE, the Operational Propulsion Performance Examination [periodic examination of the ship's propulsion system and operating procedures]. Those were legendary in the surface force during that period of time, and if you blew, if you failed an OPPE, it was bad news. This 1,200-pound plant, we had to take an OPPE before we went on this Standing Naval Force assignment. There were engineers that were absolutely—I'll use the word "surprised"— when they saw me after working hours, in the evening, in number two fire room, in the bilges with the youngsters, cleaning a bilge pocket that I wasn't happy with. I was in there in coveralls, and we had rags and we were cleaning that thing, because those inspectors were not going to find anything in our bilges that they could talk about. Word like that spread, you know, all over the place. They knew that I believed in that ship, that I believed in them, and we were going to do this, because for a 1,200-pound ship to go out there and complete an OPPE, make full power, and come back in, that was a rare occurrence. We did it. That's just an example. As a captain, I'm the captain but I'm also a crew member of the ship, and I can't separate the two. I take the responsibility, okay? But I also work just as hard as anybody on that ship to make it the best ship that we possibly can.

SC: Did you establish any specific goals for the *Luce* when you reported aboard?

PDM: Yeah, be the best damn ship in the squadron and in the whole force.

SC: And the second part of that question, how well did the ship achieve these goals?

PDM: I think I just read it to you.

SC: Absolutely. If you could go back to the late 1970s as CO of *Luce*, what, if anything, would you do differently?

PDM: The only thing I would do is that I would lobby for a different deployment schedule. We were active all the time, but for the crew's sake, I would have lobbied for a battle group deployment to the Mediterranean so that we would have been able to exercise the ship's capability with other destroyers in that environment. That would be the only thing.

SC: And there's also the great port visits in the Med, and that's something that every sailor that's done it talks about to the end of their days.

PDM: That's exactly right.

SC: You were CO for nineteen months. Traditionally, a CO tour has bounced back and forth between eighteen months and three years over the past century. What was the standard in those days for a CO tour length?

PDM: The standard was two years, twenty-two to twenty-six months, but I was taken off that ship early because Admiral Long, he was going to leave the Vice Chief's Office and become commander in chief of the Pacific, unified command, and he wanted me to come out there, so he sent me a message and said, "You're coming to Hawaii." So Becky and I, when I got relieved, we went to Hawaii. Change of command was in Edinburgh, Scotland. It was in Rosyth [Royal Navy naval station near Edinburgh, Scotland].

SC: After nineteen months, you received a "Personal For" message with this new billet assignment. Before we delve into that new billet, and for those not familiar with the Navy message system, what is a "Personal For" message and why is it different from a regular naval message?

PDM: There are different tasks. I'm trying to phrase this properly. There's different nomenclatures for naval messages. There's the regular general routine message that everybody can see. If you want it delivered to a particular person, you put "Personal For Commanding Officer," and then it goes up higher in classification if it's something that you don't want to be seen by very many people. And the "Personal For" got the ship's attention because it was coming from the Vice Chief of Naval Operations, "Personal For" CO *Luce*, and of course they read it. [*laughs*] So word spread pretty quickly that the captain was going to get relieved. And it just evolved, but I did not try to stop it or argue it. I looked at it as a compliment that Admiral Long wanted me to go work for him again. And Becky and the kids and I went to Hawaii.

SC: Navy radiomen are the chief source of any information you want to know.

PDM: [*laughs*] There you go.

SC: You received orders to become the EA at Pearl Harbor for the commander in chief Pacific, or CinCPac. That would be Admiral Long. That is a hallowed position held by officers such as Fleet Admiral Chester Nimitz et al.[73] What is the scope of duties of CinCPac? And tell us a little bit about that command.

PDM: Before I do that, before I leave *Luce*, I just thought of something that I have to put on the record. It has to do with nuclear weapons again. There are two inspection

---

[73] Fleet Admiral Chester W. Nimitz (1885–1966) graduated from the U.S. Naval Academy in 1905 and served in the Navy 1905–66. In World War II, he served as commander in chief Pacific Fleet and Pacific Ocean Areas, and later as Chief of Naval Operations. Fleet admirals remain on active duty until death rather than their actual retirement from active duty date.

programs that when you carry nuclear weapons that you have to go through to maintain your certification. You have the NWAI, Nuclear Weapons Acceptance Inspection. That permits you to load the weapons on board. I'm saying this because I'm so happy nuclear weapons aren't on surface ships. It's a personnel program, it's an inventory program, but you do that inspection. We had two ASROCs and we had some nuclear Terriers too. Then you had this thing called the NTPI, Nuclear Technical Proficiency Inspection. These are the guys from Los Alamos [New Mexico] that can come to any ship or any facility and go on board, with short notice, and test the proficiency of your handling of nuclear weapons. They came aboard and they found a discrepancy, and they called the commodore and they wanted to offload the nuclear weapons from *Luce*. Needless to say, I was a little bit disappointed. So this colonel was in charge—and my memory's not failing—I asked him to leave the ship. "As far as I'm concerned, your inspection's over." He was a little bit surprised. I knew I was fighting, I was playing with fire, but whatever the discrepancy was—and I wish I could name it—but in my view, it did not reach the bar for declaring that we were incapable of guarding and handling those weapons. It just wasn't. And I was going to go to the mat. Asked him to leave, and he responded, "Let's go talk to my boss."

I worked it out with Commodore Goldie. I said, "You send your people over and you determine whether this discrepancy merits decertification." And messages go out to everybody when a ship is decertified.

My point of bringing this up, if anybody ever reads this, if you believe in something strongly, if you really believe it and you know that you're right, you have to stand up and take on the system. You have to. In this case, my judgment was correct. It may not have been correct. If I had somebody, might have been somebody different, I would have blown my whole career at that point right there. That's important for people to know that they have to do it, but they have to do it when they feel that they're right, and you have to stand up for it, and if you are right, the majority of time it'll happen just like me. And that was one of the other things that made me number one commanding officer out of twenty commanding officers, because most people would have let him decertify the ship and put their tail between their legs and say, "We'll fix it. Now we'll fix it." But it's too late. Once they send a message out to the world that this ship is decertified, you're decertified. It's tough to recover. And you have a crew from another ship come aboard your ship to take the weapons.

After you've worked hard to build the esprit on a ship, commanding officers have to be able to have the self-confidence to do that when they know they're right.

SC: What is CinCPac and what is its responsibility?

PDM: Commander in chief Pacific is one of five area commanders. I knew this well when I was going there, because I had been the officer for the UCP [Unified Command Plan] and I knew all the things that were in the commander in chief Pacific's portfolio. He resides on Camp Smith in Hawaii, it's a big headquarters, and his command stretches from the North Pacific all the way through the Pacific to the Indian Ocean, to Australia, into the Indian Ocean to Africa, and at that time he had operational command of the Persian Gulf. That is one massive sea and land area, and he's got the typical combined staff of officers from all the services to run operations in that domain. So that's what I was entering into.

SC: You were still a commander at this point. Wasn't it a bit unusual for such a relatively junior officer to be the EA to a major commander such as CinCPac?

PDM: You're absolutely right. I went out there in the same awkward position that I had in the Vice Chief's Office. There was an Army colonel that was in zone for BG [brigadier general]. I went through the same thing I went through in the Vice Chief's Office. I had a great relationship with the CinC. I knew exactly how to support him. The Army colonel was myopic on doing everything right, because he wanted to make BG. So it was a difficult situation, but this colonel, his name is Pat Patrick, he's a Georgia boy, he had the common sense to see almost immediately that he did not want to get into a tussle about who is subordinate to whom with regard to Admiral Long. He was able to read the landscape.[74]

So until he made BG—he had a great combat record—we felt that this was all going to happen and we sort of bifurcated the duties. I let him take—this is four months, I think, we went this way—I let him take all the trips. He took all the trips with Admiral Long, which was great, because it gave me opportunity to—I knew I was going to move into that desk in four months, whatever—to work with the staff, to get everything the way that I would want it run once Patrick was gone. And it worked out perfectly. We exchange Christmas cards. He couldn't be more delighted when I made four stars. He sent me a letter that was just precious. But it's always difficult when that happens. So he goes on to be a BG and he retires as a three-star general. I learned something from him, though. He retired as a three-star general when I was the Commander of Seventh Fleet. When I went to commander of Seventh Fleet, I visited him. I said, "Why did you retire? Why are you retiring?"

He was on his way to four buttons [stars]. His son had a drug problem. His son blamed him. "Because you're always working. You didn't care." Pat Patrick turned in his letter of resignation an hour after that conversation with his son. He shared this with me. He said, "Don't make the mistake."

I say that and share that because you have to know people's personal circumstances and learn from them. It's so important. He's a great man.

But Admiral Long and I, for two years, not quite two years were together. The Pacific Command was a wonderful, wonderful assignment. I learned a lot. The highlight, for the record, is that Admiral Long had OPCON of the operation, the rescue operation in Iran.[75] We went for months, three, four months, having special access program [information] about the training that was going on, about the plan to insert the helicopters to rescue the hostages. We had the latest in communications equipment.

---

[74] Lieutenant General Burton D. "Pat" Patrick (1935–) graduated from North Georgia College, was commissioned through the Army ROTC program and served in the U.S. Army from 1957 to 1988. His last tour was as the commander of the combined U.S. and Republic of Korea forces in South Korea.
[75] OPERATION EAGLE CLAW was the joint operation intended to rescue the fifty-two U.S. hostages from the U.S. Embassy in Tehran, Iran, which failed on April 24, 1980 due to equipment failure followed by a collision between a helicopter and a C-130, killing several servicemen.

We were in flag plot, and I will not forget that night we heard, "Launch the insertion," and then the news of what happened. I took away from that, watching Admiral Long, of how a commander handles adversity. You could see on his face he was just widely disappointed, but he was stoic. He immediately went into the damage control mode as to what needed to be done, from public affairs through the operations out there a long way away. This is in the Indian Ocean. It was an experience and it was a lesson. I was able to put that lesson into use a couple of times in my career. But that was the biggest thing that happened in his time as CinCPac.

The other important thing was the relations with Marcos in the Philippines.[76] I learned a lot of that. I learned much of that from the political-military association that they had together. And you never know. I learned that you never know when a leader of a country that's important strategically or geographically, how relations can turn on a dime if you don't nurture all aspects of a relationship with any country that you think is going to be needed to be an ally or, if not an ally, someone that would be supportive if you needed to lay down a contingency operation or need access to airfields.

So the unified commander's job is he has to work all these countries that he has under his domain. It's a big job and it's an important job, because you have to keep that landscape ready to respond to lots of stuff, lots of it. And so I was able to learn a lot about that when I went out to be Seventh Fleet, to be able to try to keep those arrangements that I had with the respective governments where we had ships and where we had other capability, to have it work out pretty well. But it was experience. That's all I did at CinCPac.

SC: Tell us about your typical day as the CinCPac EA.

PDM: Admiral Long was not a workaholic. I'd probably get in there at 6:00 o'clock. He wouldn't come to work till about quarter to eight. At eight o'clock, we'd have a great big briefing, and sometimes it lasted too long, but the CinCPac area, the span of control of CinCPac is huge, and there is always, always something going on. [*laughs*] I mean, you

---

[76] Ferdinand E. Marcos (1917–1989) was president and head of state of the Philippines from 1966 to 1986 and was forced to flee to Hawaii due to public pressure following a fraudulent reelection victory in 1986.

cover, I don't know, eight time zones or whatever. But there's always something going on over there.

After that, then it would be the protocol duties of a unified commander. They are huge. There's always someone visiting, and then there's always someone visiting from Washington because they're on their way to wherever in the Western Pacific and they always come in from secretary of state, secretary of defense. They want the in-briefings [phonetic]. It was always full of stuff.

Then we'd just do the regular business of the command, and he would see the respective "J" officers, the J-1, the personnel, the operations, intelligence. Intelligence probably took up most of the time. But then as a unified commander, you have something called a POLAD, a political adviser, and we had an ex-ambassador who was a really good guy and he knew the Pacific well. He had been ambassador to Indonesia. And we spent a lot of time country by country, especially in trip preparation so that he would be cognizant of what was going on and what he needed to do. And then in writing briefs, cables, as they call them in the State Department, after Long would see an influential leader in the Pacific. Sending it back was always a task.

So it was a busy time, but because of the time difference, it wasn't overwhelming. We were fortunate, because Washington's day would end and we would still have time, so that was very fortunate. I enjoyed it. He spent three years out there. I only spent the first two, not quite two, with him, and then he retired and he subsequently has passed, but he was an outstanding officer.

SC: What was life like for a senior officer on a major staff in Pearl Harbor in the late 1970s, early eighties?

PDM: I wasn't a senior officer when I went out there. Luckily, I made captain early, so I became a senior officer.

Housing in Hawaii is tough, and Makalapa is where most of the captains live. It's right by CinCPacFlt Headquarters. I came out there as a commander. Admiral Long said, "Get him a house in Makalapa." So you know how things like that cause issues. But we lived in Makalapa the whole time and it was very nice, and I was glad when I put on four stripes, because then I belonged. [*laughs*]

SC: Did assignment to a senior staff in Pearl Harbor change your family life in any significant way?

PDM: Yes, it was significant because everybody really enjoyed it, and we had some time. I didn't travel in the first four, five months because I had Colonel Patrick. He did all the traveling, so I had a little bit of time there, and then when I did travel with him, I only went to the key, key jobs. I let the flag lieutenant do his protocol duties, and he was very happy with that because I kept things up. He didn't have to read anything. He read one message, one page a day. He knew if it wasn't on that page, that when somebody gave him a message board, he read it, because he wanted to. He didn't have to. So that's how I did my work.

SC: You were early selected for captain, or 06. What does it mean to be below-the-zone selected?

PDM: It goes back to Admiral Zumwalt. The Navy keeps careful arithmetic on how many people it can promote in each grade, and they have criteria with regard to year groups when people were commissioned that can be selected. They had a policy, I guess for some time, where every once in a while they would pick up an outstanding officer that was just outside that zone, particularly if he had special attributes that they needed for a job.

But Admiral Zumwalt, as I said before, he wanted to change that. He wanted to change the "no wine before its time" mindset. He said, "There's some people out there that can contribute quicker than others. That's just the way human nature is." And he expanded the window to 15 percent of the numbers of people selected for lieutenant commander to one or two years early. That upset the system. By the time I reached captain, there was a different Secretary of the Navy, different CNO. They had the window—they still got the two years in it, but they had narrowed the percentage markedly. It was a handful; it wasn't percentages. So when you're selected below the zone, it's that you're below the cutoff point with regard to time in grade and years in service to be selected, and so if it was four years in grade as a commander or five years in grade as a commander, that was the bottom of the zone, then the precepts of that selection board would let them go below that and pick a few people, and I was fortunate enough to be in the under-the-below-zone pick.

SC: There's a significant break point between promotion to commander and promotion to captain in the Navy. Why is that, and what are the practical implications for a career officer?

PDM: The significance is arithmetic. If you have one hundred officers commissioned, you'll have 96 percent of them make lieutenant (junior grade), you'll have 90 percent of them make lieutenant, and then you have 90 percent go to lieutenant commander and you'll have, I think, 75 percent of that 90, so that brings it down to 68, 70, or whatever, right? And then of that 70 that's left to make commander, it'll come down to about 55 percent, and so you have 55 percent of 70. And then when it comes to captain, you'll have less than half of that percentage. So out of the one hundred, you'll probably have twenty, twenty-two make captain. That's the significance of it—that you're in the top quartile of everybody that came in the Navy with you as an officer that made it a career at that point in time. The arithmetic is pretty astonishing. Then when you make flag, it's rugged.

SC: We'll talk about flag selection in a while. We've already hit on this issue tangentially prior to this interview, but at this level, the stakes for the Navy in terms of the captain selection and promotion are much higher. Please review the process or procedures for selection to captain. How does that system work?

PDM: For the selection board to captain, having sat as a helper on captain selection boards when I was in the Bureau of Naval Personnel, I knew mentally what exactly was going on in that room when a captain selection board was ongoing, particularly when I was in front of it. Each of the gentlemen on the selection board, you get a stack of records for them to go through, and then they're able to brief those records to the assembled group, and the assembled group votes. It's as simple as that.

The vote, though, is the "yes" or "no," but the "yes" vote comes with confidence. Complete "yes" is one hundred, but you could hit eighty, sixty, forty, twenty, or zero. So if someone wanted to say, "I want to vote for the guy, but I really don't care," he just sends in the lower confidence number and then the overall number goes—the integrated number goes up on the board and that says numbers when they cut it off somewhere, these people above it, these people below it.

I think the process, as demanding as it is, is fair. Why do I say that? Because whether people like it or not, whether an officer likes it or not, when he gets a stack of paper written by other people, when he gets that written on him, by the time he's going up for captain, if he were honest and he read all those reports, he would know already himself whether he was going to be selected for captain or not. The same way for admiral. Maybe not. There's some misses in admiral because the nuances are different. But he would know whether he would be in the basket for admiral. That's the system. It's relatively fair. And the process itself, from ones that I've chaired and the ones that I've helped on, I've never seen any skullduggery in any of it, never seen trying to bias it. It's a pretty fair system.

SC: There's an old adage in the Navy that to be promoted to captain in the active duty Navy, an officer must have had a successful command afloat, a CO tour as a surface warfare officer or submariner, or, if an aviator, a squadron command. In the Navy Reserve, one must have had several successful reserve unit commands. What is your take on that statement?

PDM: Historically, it was correct until they designated major shore commands as equivalencies, and once they did that, they made it very difficult for selection boards to equate commander of Naval Station Norfolk with CO of *Josephus Daniels*. It then called on the selection boards to make some judgment factors here, and then it sort of said, "You guys, we're asking you now to vote on potential. Which one of these gents, if you only pick one or two and they're different, who sort of has the potential to do what the Navy needs done next?"

That was a big deal. I was surprised that the Navy did that—that they took the spotlight off of command at sea. No matter how important the shore assignment—and I don't mean to say it's not important, because I'm not. It's terribly important for the support and shore establishments to be recognized, and the maintenance, all that, but to try to draw an equivalency with the CO of a naval station with the CO of the USS *Carl Vinson* (CVN-70), it's tough. It's really tough.

SC: We're going to wrap up here with a question that you've already answered in a lot of ways, but I want to sort of pull things together here.

PDM: Good luck.

SC: [*laughs*] What in your career and accomplishments do you think helped your selection to captain, particularly two years below the zone?

PDM: What helped me get two years below the zone for lieutenant commander? What helped me get two years below the zone for commander? The same thing: performance. Go through the stack of fitness reports and had multiple people—I mean multiple; I'm talking tens to twenties—and all of a sudden, you see a thread in these fitness reports. [*reading*] "Recommended for promotion to captain and assignment for billets to flag rank as soon as possible." As a commander. The fitness reports say it. I detailed, when we talked about *McCloy*, how the only fitness report that I have that's not accelerated promotion was by a commodore that I had during a deployment on *McCloy* because, number one, he didn't know how to write fitness reports, and, number two, he was an inept commodore and he should have never made captain himself.

Any naval officer will find that in a career that he's working for someone like that. The selection boards are astute, crafty, and precise enough to say, "This is an outlier. These are the ones that count." And so it was performance.

SC: As we wrap up your tour as the CO of USS *Luce*, EA to CinCPac, and promotion to captain, are there any other areas that you would like to explore?

PDM: No, you just ran through some pretty interesting seven years of service in the last five hours. [*laughter*] My memory was—I mean, this process with your questions really facilitates pulling those things up that happened, and after the first couple, I had to go back out and dig these fitness reports out, because they detail exactly where you were, what you did, like the thing I read to you about the fog so that helped me to get ready to try to be a little bit more concise in answering your questions today, and I will be really concise when we go on to the next ones.

Right now you're up to finishing CinCPac. I finished there in 1980 or '81, '80, so we still have thirteen years to go.

SC: We will get through them all.

PDM: But the next thirteen years go faster.

SC: That's what I found in these interviews, is once you do get to this very senior officer rank, you don't have as many tours. They tend to be longer, and we can bore in with each session.

PDM: That's right.

SC: And one thing about the fitness reports, as an historian, I look on these as primary-source historical records, the fitness reports. They encapsulate your entire career from start to finish.

PDM: Right.

SC: So that's why they are critical.

PDM: Yeah, and something like you're writing there, taking a couple of these things and putting them in there says it all. They do it better than I can do it, because they're summing up a finite period of time, and memories are fresh. I'm glad I pulled those things out. I had to dig for these things. [*laughter*]

SC: That's one thing I always have told people, don't ever throw away a piece of paper the Navy gives you. In our next session, we'll cover your time as executive assistant to the Secretary of the Navy.

This is USNI oral history interview with Admiral Paul David Miller, U.S. Navy (Ret.). This is session number six, question set number fourteen. The date is Saturday, April 14, 2018, and the interviewer is Professor Stan Carpenter.

Thank you, Admiral Miller.

PDM: Thank you.

[End of April 14, 2018, interview]

Interview with Admiral Paul David Miller, USN (Ret.)
Date: April 15, 2018

Stan Carpenter (SC): This is USNI oral history interview with Admiral Paul David Miller, U.S. Navy (Ret.). This is session number seven, question set number fifteen. The date is Sunday, April 15, 2018, and the interviewer is Professor Stan Carpenter. These questions cover the years as SecNav EA.

Admiral, after your tour as CinCPac EA, you went back to the Pentagon as EA to the new Secretary of the Navy, John Lehman, from 1981 to '85. Having been with Admiral Long for almost two years at CinCPac, how were you selected as the SecNav EA?

Paul David Miller (PDM): Carefully. SecNav Lehman reported to Admiral Long that I came to his attention and he needed the best captain the Navy had, to assist in his ambitious task of orchestrating the Navy recovery program and fleet expansion to the six-hundred-ship Navy. With that said, Admiral Long got a call one day, and the secretary told Admiral Long that I'd come to his attention and that he wanted to interview me for the position when he came out to visit both Admiral Long and also CinCPacFlt [commander in chief, U.S. Pacific Fleet] commander.

A few weeks proceeded. He made that trip. He came out and an interview session was set up. But during that period, I tried to do some sort of homework on John Lehman. I knew he had been nominated and then confirmed as the Secretary of the Navy, but I did not know thoroughly his background, other than what had been put out in public affairs sheets announcing him as SecNav. I found that he was a remarkable young man. He had a PhD from Penn, he was a graduate of Cambridge [Cambridge University, England], he finished college at Saint Joseph's. He came from a very well-known family in Philadelphia. In fact, I learned that he was a cousin of Princess Grace of Monaco. He was from a background of the Navy. His father had served in World War II; he had command of a small ship in World War II. I found that he was a real historian, and I found that at Cambridge he was in a debating society that won him accolades. But most importantly, I found out that John Lehman was Secretary of the Navy and he was six months younger than I was. And, honestly, I thought I was doing fairly well, having recently been selected two years early for captain.

So I knew that when I was preparing for this interview, that I'd better get things right if I wanted that job [*laughs*], because he knew what he wanted to do and he knew where he wanted to take the Navy with regard to the six-hundred-ship Navy. So it was important that he find someone that the chemistry was correct and that could assist, where he could, in promoting the goals that John Lehman, under President Reagan, had set for the Navy of the future. But this wasn't going to be really easy, because Admiral Long was on his last tour, he was revered in the Navy, he was the Navy's most senior admiral, and he didn't want to go through another personnel shift in his last year in the Navy, and he felt, quite honestly, that there were a lot of qualified captains in the Navy and Secretary Lehman could pick any one of them that he wanted to.

So the secretary came out, set up an interview. I went down and interviewed with him, and it was sort of a wide-ranging interview, what I felt about the condition of the Navy, what were the main elements that he believed he should focus on as the new secretary, you know, those types of questions. But then he asked me a very peculiar question. I still reflect on that. I've reflected on this often. He asked me point-blank, "The Navy is resisting my appointing Admiral Ace Lyons as CinCPacFlt."[77] And he went on with some rationale, and I listened very carefully. And he said, "Should I appoint Admiral Lyons as CinCPacFlt?"

My mind was spinning at that time, because I knew this was a very, very important question. I said, "Mr. Secretary, you are the Secretary of the Navy. Part of that task is to populate the Navy with the finest leaders that you believe will serve the Navy and the nation in such an important position, and you should, as Secretary of the Navy, appoint Admiral Lyons, a four-star, and name him as the next CinCPacFlt commander. Full stop." I think that answer may not have been exactly phrased properly, but it was the right answer, because shortly after the interview, Admiral Long got a telephone call and [Lehman] said that "I'm going to send Paul orders to come back to be my EA."

---

[77] Admiral James A. "Ace" Lyons Jr. (1927–2018) graduated from the U.S. Naval Academy in 1952 and served in the U.S. Navy until 1987. His final billet was as commander in chief, U.S. Pacific Fleet from 1985 to 1987.

To my amazement, Admiral Long said no. [*laughs*]

And John said, "Okay. In deference to Admiral Long, I'll take another look."

And not a week later, he came back and said, "He's going to get orders to come back."

I was listening. With Long, I listened to conversations. I listened and I could not believe what I was going to hear next. Admiral Long said, "John, do you know that's like stealing somebody's maid?" [*laughs*]

I looked at the phone and, of course, had to chuckle. But it was done, the ribbon was tied around it. I received message orders the next day and made all preparations to go back to Washington. Admiral Long, he was very good, and the best way to summarize his feelings, he just took his pen and he wrote a few lines on my final fitness report. He said [*reading*], "Captain Miller is being assigned as executive assistant to the SecNav. It is with deep regret that I see him go. He is, in my judgment, clearly one of the outstanding naval officers I have personally observed during my time in the Navy. He has the strength of character, integrity, judgment, intelligence, and balance to go to the very top of our Navy. I strongly recommend that he be selected for flag rank at the earliest opportunity. He has much to give our Navy." I couldn't have asked for a better set of words from someone that I genuinely had great affection for as a naval officer and as a man.

So with that and a few farewells, Becky and I and the boys go back to Washington. Luckily, we had kept a house in McLean [Virginia] and went back to that same house, got the boys in school. Chris was going to St. John's. Both of them went to St. John's, which was a small Catholic school not far away. But we settled very, very quickly there, and I reported to SecNav Office to begin work.

What did work consist of in the SecNav's Office? It was a very interesting assumption of duties. He had in place an EA that had been with the previous SecNav. He had not put together a staff yet, but I knew that we had to do everything the way that a SecNav Office needed to be set up for someone who wasn't just going to administer the Navy, but for someone who was going to change the Navy. After reading what he had put out, knowing that the political framework was set with SecDef Weinberger, then President Reagan, I knew that it was clearly an administration goal to enhance this nation's maritime capability.[78] So the previous office setup for just administering the Navy was insufficient.

So I had to, upon arrival, sort of evaluate the efficiency of all aspects of the secretariat. I briefed SecNav on the weaknesses and had to implement some tough actions that substantially streamlined the organization. Secretary Lehman, to support him properly, needed a streamlined, not a bureaucratic organization. So we restructured and we fine-tuned the workings of the immediate staff, but, importantly, very importantly, established a close working relationship with the CNO's Office to ensure this thing called SecNav-CNO cooperation. We had so much to do. He was so intent and he had such a clear vision of where the Navy needed to go. We needed a practical long-range agenda for the accomplishment of this Navy recovery program. It wasn't going to be easy, but it had to be relatively structured and it had to be long-ranged because, in my view, Secretary Lehman was going to set the pieces of the Navy—by pieces I mean set the force structure of the Navy to affect the Navy for thirty years to come. It just wasn't over the horizon. This was an extended-range plan, if fully implemented, would still be affecting the Navy as you and I are talking in 2018, and this was in the eighties, and I think you would agree that there are ships sailing out there right now that were part of that six-hundred-ship Navy that John Lehman built in 1981 through '87. So that was terribly important.

All the while, because John Lehman wasn't just a figure for the Navy, he was a figure for the Defense Department and he was a figure outside the confines of the Pentagon, because he had close relationships with a vast network, some of which I had to learn because I had not toiled in some of those vineyards before. So I had to maintain effective contacts with OSD and surely with Congress, surely. We had close relationship with Congress, even the White House. The job was to make sure everybody knew and everybody was sort of supporting on the same—pulling the same way about a fast-moving policy and fast-moving issues, and we had to influence the outcome of each. That was why I was brought back to help in those assignments.

---

[78] Caspar W. "Cap" Weinberger (1917–2006) graduated from Harvard in 1938 with a B.A. and with a J.D. in 1941 with a keen interest in politics, which shaped his future career. He served as an Army officer in the Second World War and then started a law career. He served in the Ronald Reagan Administration as secretary of defense from 1981 to 1987.

SC: You'd served previously as a junior officer detailer who determined an officer's next assignment based on the needs of the Navy and the career dynamics of the individual officer. You already told us a little bit about how you were selected for the EA billet, but, in general, what about the billet selection process for a senior officer billet such as EA to a major commander or for a very high-ranking civilian official? What does that typical selection process look like?

PDM: Many times the individual that has taken a position that requires a strong, I like to call them military assistants, if they are civilian, or executive assistant, or however you want to phrase it, if they were in uniform. I would say in the vast majority of the cases, the individual has a short list of their own, particularly the military side, not so much the civilian side.

So on the military side, the detailers would get a look at Admiral "X" wants to look at Captain "Y" to be his number one guy. They'd pull the dossier, they'd pull the record on those to prepare a book, but then they would always have someone that wasn't known but truly deserved to be in one of those positions, and then they would add one or two extra people. That book would be delivered, and the principal, as we'll call them, would go through there, check all of them out. For the military side, it was much easier because they knew they could call up, "That's two reporting seniors." It was pretty easy to test the water. And then if the principal did not know him—and now it would be she—did not know them, there was always the interview thing to check the chemistry.

Chemistry is the most important of all the ingredients. You can make up for some of the other things, but you can't make up the chemistry. John Lehman and I had great chemistry. Admiral Long and I, Admiral Shear and I, Admiral Bagley and I, the chemistry was absolutely important.

That makes me add something for any individual that might ever be in that position to be selected for one of those positions. What's the number one ingredient than chemistry? Humility. It has to be. You come into any interview with a proper dose of humility and then take it from there. But at least if you do that, you have a chance to see if the other things that go along with the personality, chemistry check work out, but if one doesn't come in there with that as the most important ingredient, he has a very steep hill to climb. So that's how the process goes.

SC: Why do you think you were selected as the SecNav EA?

PDM: I wondered about that often. I think I was selected because by that time, having served for three four-stars, having a sound operational reputation within the surface Navy, that I would appear on any list that Secretary Lehman was given. Later on, I found out that that's exactly what happened. Somebody—and I know who it was—said, "John, you ought to look at this captain that's out with Admiral Long right now." It takes a bit of that. It takes a little bit of serendipity that somebody you know knows the principal and gets you in the hut. After you get in that list and someone says you're going to be interviewed for a particular job, then it's 100 percent on you, because you've already passed the performance tests. He's not going to go back and say, "Oh, this guy didn't do well at this," whatever. No. It's going to be the chemistry check and then it's upon you to pass the chemistry test.

SC: Once you were selected, you spent four years at the Pentagon as the SecNav EA. That's an unusually long shore tour. Why was that?

PDM: The short answer, Secretary Lehman wouldn't let me go. Okay? That's the answer. But I had worries. Actually, I think it was four and a half years. That's a long time. And I had received, back in December 1980, notice of having been screened [approved and acceptable for appointment] for major command. [*reading*] "I am very pleased to inform you that you've screened for major command in fiscal year '81." Cruiser-destroyer list. I'm on the right list. So I thought that I was going to leave CinCPac, go direct to major command early. I mean, I had been screened but I had to go early, and I'd be—boom! [*snaps fingers*] I'd be right there, ready for, if I'd done well in that command, my third one, I'd have been in pretty good shape for vying for flag at an early age. Time out. This thing sat on the shelf. This thing sat on the shelf year after year, so, you're right, I did get a little concerned about that.

But John Lehman is an individual who is loyal to the people that work for him, just as he demands loyalty from the people that work for him. John Lehman wrote just prior to—no, John Lehman didn't write. Before the flag board, '83 flag board was going to meet, somehow Admiral Lando Zech, who was then the chief of naval personnel, he wrote a memorandum for the record.[79] [*reading*] "Subject: Assignment of Captain Paul David Miller, USN." It's a short memo. It says [*reading*], "This memorandum is to appraise detailing and selection board personnel that although career and professional development considerations would have logically called for the assignment of Captain Miller to major command afloat, his tour of duty as executive assistant to the Secretary to the Navy has been extended to July 1984. This extension is made at the direction of the Secretary of the Navy in order to provide necessary continuity while numerous issues critical to the Navy's future are under consideration. Captain Miller's superb performance in his present assignment further justifies this action. It should be clearly recognized that the needs of the service rather than Captain Miller's professional development have dictated this extension of duty." Cover. Because my first flag look was in '83. So this was at the top of the pile.

SC: For those not familiar with the term, what does the Navy mean by major command?

PDM: Major command is those ships designated as being the primary warfighting units of the Navy. They're aircraft carriers, they're cruisers, they're capital amphibious ships, they're commodore assignments, which places a captain in charge of seven or eight destroyers or seven or eight amphibious ships. It's a prized assignment to know that you have served well in a subordinate command and that you are being given an opportunity to command not only the finest but most important maritime capability that the United States has. The same goes for naval aviation, same goes for the submarine force. The major command in submarine force are squadrons and some of them are the capital Trident [ballistic missile submarines] ships in the nuclear world that hold so much responsibility when they go to sea and stand the watch as part of the nuclear triad.

---

[79] Vice Admiral Lando W. Zech Jr. (1923–2011) graduated from the U.S. Naval Academy in 1944 and served in the U.S. Navy until 1983. His final billet was as the chief of naval personnel.

So it's a place, if you've made a naval career, it's aspirational. The Navy, I forget the year they made the decision, but they came to the decision that it was as important to have shore commanders reflect being part of the major command community because of the importance that they played in supporting the afloat forces or the air forces or the submarines. And so during the eighties, there were some major commands that were so designated and they qualified for participation for selection to flag rank by going to those commands. So it's absolutely key. Major command is known by any professional that has made the Navy a career.

SC: And in those days, it would have included the battleships as well.

PDM: Not until we brought them back. In '83, we hadn't brought them back yet. That was part of the thing we were doing. But that would have.

SC: You've already told us a little bit about Secretary Lehman, but can you expand on that in terms of how he operated and how he conducted his affairs as SecNav?

PDM: John Lehman had a remarkable appetite for information. One didn't have to spend time going over anything told to him twice, but he didn't suffer folks that briefed him that were unable to tie a knot around their presentation. He was looking for what someone was recommending, why they were recommending it, and if he agreed with it, what needed to be done to implement it swiftly. He was very efficient.

Later, he believed strongly in delegation. We had infrequent staff meetings, because they were usually timely, but when we did, we had them in his office. There were a limited number of participants, and he was able to take care of lots of the smaller issues in a session like that, because once he had been informed, like, say, of an R&D issue by the ASN(RDA) [Assistant Secretary of the Navy for Research, Development & Acquisition], told about it, he would delegate it. He wouldn't get wrapped up into him having to take the action to implement it.

He was keen on moving forward with the big issues, the six-hundred-ship Navy, the contracting of multiple carriers at one time, those acquisition measures that had to be implemented to get our shipbuilding program moving quicker. There are too many illustrations for this forum to detail them all, but one remembers clearly the *Arleigh Burke* destroyer decision, limiting the cost of the initial ship, what tradeoffs had to be made for capability to make sure that cost wasn't breached.[80] Lots of time, lots of analysis.

When we went through the first one, it was clear that we needed to beef up our own Office of Program Appraisal, they called it, OPA. It was a mini-appraisal shop that the CNO had in OP-090. So we looked for an officer to take that position to help with critical analysis, to make sure that what we had been given by the system passed the common-sense test. Two different things.

The individual that Secretary Lehman picked was Admiral Frank Kelso, who was a submarine officer who was exactly the right personality for that assignment.[81] He was very well respected by the Navy in the submarine community. So he came to that for a couple of years to help in that particular measure, making sure that the secretary had benefit of a second look at analysis, program analysis, and making the good decision, the right decision. He also had a very, very strong ASN for shipbuilding [Assistant Secretary of the Navy, Shipbuilding & Logistics], and between OPA and a gentleman called George Sawyer, he was the ASN shipbuilding, we had lots of talent. So when the system put something forward, the secretariat was able to either validate it or offer the Secretary another avenue to get there cheaper, faster, or whatever we needed to do to get this 600-ship Navy moving along.

SC: What were some of the practical implications of the six-hundred-ship Navy as a policy goal?

---

[80] The *Arleigh Burke*-class destroyer was named for Admiral Arleigh Burke, Chief of Naval Operations from 1955 to 1961. USS *Arleigh Burke* (DDG-51) was commissioned in 1991. They are equipped with the Aegis system based on the AN/SPY-1 radar system and are armed with missiles, gun, and torpedoes. The class of DDGs are a current main surface combatant in the U.S. Navy as the Ticonderoga-class cruisers are decommissioned.
[81] Admiral Frank B. Kelso II (1933–2013) graduated from the U.S. Naval Academy in 1956. He served in the U.S. Navy until 1994. His final billet was as the twenty-fourth Chief of Naval Operations from 1990 to 1994.

PDM: The practical aspect of it was building ships in the most cost-effective manner possible so that we would have the ships for decades to come, because one knows that Washington doesn't always work with a budget going up, so you have to take advantage of those times, because we see what happens when budgets are going the other way. We've talked about the seventies, the retrenchment after Vietnam, and so the ships were tired. Our new-built program was barely to keep yards in business.

So when the philosophy and the administration changed, you have a certain amount of time to get as much as you can accomplish to get accomplished. It wasn't trying to throw money at things that we didn't need, it wasn't trying to be wasteful in any fashion, but it was trying to build the Navy that would serve this nation for the next three decades, and that's what the six-hundred-ship Navy did. We did it for the destroyer force, we did it for the carrier force, the submarine force, but the secretary probably looked at another arm of the Navy with equal or even more importance, and that was naval air. We know that he was a reserve officer as an A-6 BN [bombardier/navigator], and he was a very important and a very [sic] admirer of naval aviation capability. We had the F-14s, we were going into the F/A-18, we were reworking some of the Tomcats, looking for better weapon systems.[82] There were so many things that were going on simultaneously in each of the warfare directorates, 05 for air, 03 for surface, and 02 for subs. My mental plot every day was getting jostled by what we were doing here, here, and here, because other than OPA, we didn't have them. There wasn't a big staff. Before that paper got in to the secretary, there was not many stops that it took.

He used meetings, CEB [CNO Executive Board], executive board decisions, but he was a secretary that would go into one of those meetings, and if it lasted four hours, it didn't make any difference. Very few appointed officials have, number one, the patience and, number two, the knowledge to grill down [sic] and ask questions that needed to be asked about programs that you were trying to fast-track to get into production and out to the fleet. So that's how things were done.

---

[82] The F-14 Tomcat was an interceptor, air-superiority fighter in service from 1974 to 2006. The A-6 Intruder was an attack aircraft is service from 1963 to 1997. The F/A-18 Hornet is a multirole fighter in service since 1983.

SC: Secretary Lehman, as you pointed out, was a Naval Reserve officer and specifically an A6 Intruder bomber-navigator. How did that factor impact relations with very senior officers at the Pentagon?

PDM: It didn't have any impact. John went on active duty for two weeks a year, predominantly down in Oceana [Naval Air Station, Oceania, Virginia] and flew down there. He had a lot of close friends and contacts in that community. I guess OP-05 may have been a little bit concerned with his spending two weeks down there, of what he'd come back with, but sometimes he came back with little things, the black shoe-brown shoe controversy, you know. "Why do we all have to wear black shoes, Mr. Secretary? Huh?" And soon after one of those times down there, put out a little something that naval aviation could wear brown shoes with the appropriate uniform. He'd come back with one of those every once in a while, but that added to the aura that this gentleman, John Lehman, had built as Secretary of the Navy. He was one of them, also all the while being the Secretary of the Navy and an integral part of OSD [Office of the Secretary of Defense], and be able to move the Navy forward. So it was unique.

SC: As EA, how much interface did you have with other Navy senior commanders' EAs?

PDM: Not only with senior commanders, but with the deputy secretary of defense, the secretary of defense. Colin Powell was "Cap" Weinberger's military assistant.[83] Because John was a personality that operated outside the limits of the naval secretariat. If you'd pick up the *Washington Post* some morning, I would submit that John Lehman had as much ink, if not more ink, than the secretary of defense. That might not be correct, but I think if someone went back and checked, it'd be pretty damn close, because he was out on point, selling the six-hundred-ship Navy, working with Congress for the six-hundred-ship Navy, working with the airplane programs, taking EB [General Dynamics Electric

---

[83] General Colin L. Powell (1937–2021) graduated from the City College of New York and George Washington University. He served in the U.S. Army from 1958 to 1993. His final billet was as chairman of the Joint Chiefs of Staff from 1989 to 1993. As a civilian, he served as the secretary of state from 2001 to 2005.

Boat] to court for the submarine construction debacle. There were so many things going on, that a lot of them deserved press outside the Navy.

SC: How about interface with other service EAs, and how about interface with Congress?

PDM: Did not interface with the other services all that much. With Congress, heavily interfaced with them. We had to keep a balance. We had so many programs that were so important to some congressional districts. We were expanding the Navy. We were looking at homeporting issues, where should they take place, and every time you made a step, it impacted a district, or it might impact in the wrong way another district. So the Congress liaison was terribly important.

We made sure that we had the right flag in charge of OLA [Navy Office of Legislative Affairs], and on the administrative side of the office, we kept clear file [sic] of correspondence to congressional delegates, so that when I had to go back and refresh my mind quickly on what went on with Congressman "X," [snaps fingers] I would pull it up like that. We didn't have the capability we have now on the computer, but I could pull it up quickly and get the little file, refresh myself on it, and then brief the secretary, and whether he had to see him, talk to him, whatever, I always made sure that he was exactly up-to-date with what we were doing.

SC: What about any other federal agencies outside DOD? Any interface with them?

PDM: Not a lot, I guess. I guess maybe the Department of Energy, because now might be a good moment to talk about a significant event of that time, which was the firing of Admiral Rickover. It's an event I won't forget. It's an event that's detailed in John Lehman's book *Command of the Seas*, which sort of goes over lots of this stuff, but in much more detail about his time behind the desk.[84] But Admiral Rickover, he had reached that point where it was his time. Lots of people thought so, except for Admiral Rickover.

---

[84] John F. Lehman, *Command of the Seas* (Annapolis, MD: Naval Institute Press, 2001).

I called him one day and asked him to come by and visit with the Secretary of the Navy. I probably shouldn't detail what he said, but who's going to read this? Admiral Rickover said—I'm getting this about right; it might not be perfect—"Tell that pissant that I'm not coming over there because I know he wants to fire me." [*laughs*]

So I looked at the phone and said, "What am I going to do with this?" So I let that rest.

We finally were able to get a meeting of the two. It was very short. But as the record shows in the book and other places, Admiral Rickover said the president was the only person that could fire him. So that was set up. John, President Reagan, and Admiral Rickover met, and it took that much to properly and thankfully have Admiral Rickover move aside for a younger but a qualified person to take over Navy nuclear power. It wasn't an easy thing, because this wasn't going to be a two-year assignment. Admiral Rickover had been covered by congressional paper, so we had to put together, you know, the framework for that terribly important job as a director, terribly important, and he had a dual line with Energy Department. That's why I brought that up.

And Admiral Ken McKee, an outstanding submariner with a thoroughly qualifying nuclear background, was chosen as the first officer to follow Admiral Rickover as director of naval reactors, and the time in service was eight years, so it gave him the longevity that the system couldn't impact him very much, because he was going to be there if someone demanded a change in something, he would change it back so they couldn't challenge it. It all worked.[85] And to this day, Naval Reactors is an exalted slot, and the same safety, the same operating not only parameters, but the focus to ensure that there would never be a nuclear incident with a naval reactor, all those processes are still in place. Admiral Rickover did a great service to this country, great service.

SC: Were there any particularly memorable projects that you worked on while SecNav EA?

---

[85] Vice Admiral Kinnaird R. "Ken" McKee (1929–2013) graduated from the U.S. Naval Academy in 1951 and served in the U.S. Navy until 1988. His last billet was as director of naval reactors.

PDM: I've mentioned a lot of them. The first one was probably the most interesting. And I got asked this question a lot: How did the six-hundred-ship Navy come about? Why six hundred ships? Why not 572? That was a question. It's a legitimate question. And it came about by looking at the system. The system never generated the right rationale. They generated some stuff, but they didn't generate the right rationale.

Remember this was Cold War, Soviet aggressions at sea, Soviets sort of showing that they could control the North Atlantic. Their submarine force was getting pretty damn good. They had found their secret to quieting, and all the reports that one would read about would show that, hey, every submarine that goes out there now doesn't have that clear distinct signature, the reduction gear spike or whatever it was.

And so putting the six-hundred-ship Navy together was sort of relatively reasonable—not easy, but it was reasonable. It started with the centerpiece of the Navy fighting force, and that is the battle group. So you have all this domain. So you go down. In a full-fledged conflict, how many of these set pieces do you need? And it turned out to be, with a couple in the yard at any one time, we needed fifteen aircraft carriers. And then associated battle groups. How many amphibious ready groups did we need? We sent those around. How many surface support ships were required? How many nuclear submarines in both nuclear-response capability, triad [ballistic missile capability—nuclear submarines, manned bombers, and ground-launched missiles] capability, and attack boats do you need? How many small mine warfare force do you need? You'd go through all that against a scenario that some would say would be ambitious, because some would say you wouldn't be doing it at the same time, but if you're building a maritime force to have command of the seas, this is a force that you would need to make sure that you did. And honestly, when you total them up, it probably totaled up to 587 or pick a number. But six hundred had a magic ring to it, and so the six-hundred-ship Navy was it.

SC: Tell us about your typical day as the SecNav EA.

PDM: Busy, always busy. SecNav, to his great credit, was not a workaholic. He could do an inordinate amount of work in a relatively short time. He did not get into the office till eight or sometimes after, and then I'd have things laid out and what he needed to do, why he needed to do it, and we used his days fully.

He had a wide net of contacts throughout Washington, D.C., so oftentimes our day would be interrupted with someone that would come see him. I would always schedule these long meetings when absolutely necessary, when we couldn't work out the issues any other way, and then Admiral Kelso and I would talk to him about a particular decision that needed to be taken and then would spend whatever time necessary to do that.

There were so many illustrations of visiting the fleet and seeing that we needed to view things differently. I could go over scores of them, but an illustration for the record might be us visiting—I forget the name of the carrier, and the *New Jersey* (BB-62) off of Lebanon after the sad bombing of the Marine barracks, the killing of 250-plus Marines. And the Navy had ordered a strike shortly thereafter, and the strike itself didn't go over well. It's when we had Lieutenant [Robert] Goodman captured. I think another plane was shot down. It wasn't naval aviation or the United States Navy's finest day. So the secretary wanted to visit it. We set up a visit. We visited, talked to the air wing, talked to the CAG [commander, Air Group] captain, skippers whose pilots flew the missions. The secretary learned that it was very similar to the Alpha strikes flown in Vietnam. Was this the place? Was this the time? Was this the environment to fly an aluminum cloud into some fairly decent anti-air capability? The record would show it wasn't, because we didn't do that well. The secretary took all that information, but it clearly came back that something was askew with training and tactics. It wasn't quite right.

On the plane home, I could clearly mentally see me sitting across from the secretary and talking through what we just saw and what might be a training element that would give our squadron commanders and naval aviators a different look at how to train and plan strikes. So out of that discussion, the secretary decided that we were going to put together this thing called Strike U, Strike University, in Fallon, Nevada. That was the place because that's where they had the facilities. But to get the right naval aviator to command it and to buy into this had to be a major command. [*laughs*] And we've talked about major command. He probably had to spend a good amount of time there initially to get the thing set up. The Air Force has a similar place at Nellis, I think. I'm not sure, but I think they do.

So it was created. Squadrons, before deployment, would go through there. It became the thing to do to get your squadron through there. If you go visit out there, it's a wonderful place to fly, to do adversary work, to do all the stuff that you need to do to make sure that your squadron is expertly trained to look at the situation and not go back to the Vietnam carrier playbook and send an Alpha strike at everything you've got to strike. But that's just an illustration. It didn't take a lot of staff work to do that. He visited it, a couple of conversations, a couple of decisions. It was hard implementing. You do a lot of work to take that from talk to write up the right decision memorandum, put it into the system, then to make sure the system followed the decision memorandum, didn't slow the decision memorandum, all those things. That's what took up my days. [*laughs*] Little things like that.

SC: One of the big roles of Navy reserve aviation since that time has been playing the role of the aggressor squadrons.

PDM: Yeah.

SC: So we've discussed three major initiatives here: six-hundred-ship Navy, the aviator training, Strike University. Were there—

PDM: The list would fill your sheet.

SC: Pick one. Pick one more.

PDM: Contracting multiple carriers. Not done before. It was sort of a two-for-one. Even talked about three-for-one, not one for the price of one, but the one buy. Carriers are so complex, long lead time. You know, when you make a reactor pump one at a time, it's pretty damn expensive, but if you assured that you had two of them, a little bit less expensive, and then if you sort of had a promise of a third one down the way in the shipbuilding plan that hadn't been totally approved but was sitting there waiting, shipyard might go ahead and order more of the long-lead items at a better price. Spent a lot of time on the shipbuilding program, the carriers, DDGs, as I just mentioned, the amphibious ships. So the summation would be the acquisition patterns that were required to have a shipbuilding program at a pace you needed to reach your six-hundred-ship Navy. All these things take a lot of time, effort, energy.

SC: In a lot of ways, that harkens back to the World War II model, where we were turning out the *Essex*-class carriers.

PDM: Yes, illustratively you're exactly correct, but what we were trying to turn out in 1985—or pick a year—were so complex, that the engineering that was required, the safety overlay that was required for the nuclear weapons makes it an exponent of a thousand times harder than that illustration, but the illustration is true. We took America's industrial capability, put it to work to try to get the job done. That illustration's true.

A fifth thing that I feel was a secretary contribution was personnel assignments, getting the right flag officers out there in the fleet that believed in and that supported the brand of Navy that the secretary was trying to build. Oftentimes, the Secretary of the Navy would sign off on flag assignments as given to him by the CNO. They had to be approved by the Secretary of the Navy.

I'm not talking out of school. Too much water has passed beneath the keel since then. But there was some—is competition the right word?—between the SecNav's Office and the CNO's Office about who should go to certain jobs, and so there was lots of discussion between the secretary and Admiral Hayward first, then Admiral Watkins about the flag assignment, not only policies, but the brand of officer that was going out there to be the important fleet commanders and then the CinCs, terribly important.[86] I tried my

---

[86] Admiral Thomas B. Hayward (1924–) graduated from the U.S. Naval Academy in 1947 and served in the U.S. Navy until 1982. He was the twenty-first Chief of Naval Operations, from 1978 to 1982; Admiral James D. Watkins (1927–2012) graduated from the U.S. Naval Academy in 1949 and served in the U.S. Navy until 1986. He was the twenty-second Chief of Naval Operations from 1982 to 1986. Following his Navy service, he was the secretary of energy in the George H. W. Bush sdministration from 1989 to 1993.

best to work that with the EAs, the CNO's EA. I had a wonderful counterpart with the CNO's EA in Admiral Jeremiah, wonderful man. We could resolve most of them. He left after making flag and went out to do his CruDes job [cruiser-destroyer].[87]

A name you'll recognize would come in there, named Mike Boorda.[88] That probably wasn't the best for relations between the two offices. Relations got a bit strained between myself and him, but it all got worked through. He was—I shouldn't say it. Sadly, he's passed. We all know what happened. I had made flag a year before him in my first look. He thought maybe that he should be ahead, maybe. It did not help relations.

But flag assignments were terribly important. Sometimes it took the CNO and secretary to have pretty tough discussions about matters. But the secretary was absolutely rigid in his brand of warfighter that he wanted out there in the fleet, and he traveled so much, he knew these people. He knew everyone in naval aviation. They could not put somebody up in naval aviation that wasn't the very, very best that naval aviation had, because he knew them all in spades. I knew most of the surface people and Admiral Kelso knew most of the submariners, so flag officer detailing was very, very exciting.

One other item for the record that I think is important. I will say that every officer that retires as a one-star in the United States Navy since about 1985 or '84 should send me a thank you note that they are not called commodore (retired).

SC: Those were the first-term years of the Ronald Reagan administration. Were there any noticeable or significant changes in the surface climate from the President Jimmy Carter years of the late 1970s?[89]

---

[87] Admiral David E. Jeremiah (1934–2013) graduated from the University of Oregon and George Washington University. He served in the U.S. Navy from 1956 to 1994. His final billet was as the vice chairman of the Joint Chiefs of Staff and briefly as the acting chairman of the Joint Chiefs of Staff.

[88] Admiral Jeremy M. Boorda (1939–1996) originally enlisted in the U.S. Navy and was later commissioned from Officer Candidate School in 1962. He served as the twenty-fifth Chief of Naval Operations until his suicide in 1996.

[89] The Goldwater-Nichols Act of 1986 was co-sponsored by Senator Barry Goldwater of Arizona and Congressman William Nichols of Alabama. The thrust of the legislation was to promote jointness between the services, but it also granted more authority to the chairman of the Joint Chiefs of Staff and made the line of operational command authority from the president and secretary of defense directly to the combatant commanders bypassing the service chiefs.

PDM: Night and day. Renaissance, new birth, choose it. It was totally different. Once President Reagan got in there, put his full backing behind restoring America's armed forces, totally different. People stepped a little bit livelier. I probably wore a uniform every day to work, every day. It was just night and day, totally different.

SC: Jointness was bubbling about in the DOD in the early 1980s and eventually resulted in the Goldwater-Nichols Act of 1986. What is meant by jointness and why had it become so powerful a concept by the early 1980s?

PDM: That is a tough question that I took on as a flag officer, became embroiled in, and later I'll tell you how I broke my pick in it. But it came about in the time period, to answer your question, in the mid-eighties there with Goldwater-Nichols. It came out after all those studies that were done on our sad failure in the '80 rescue in the desert. Were we using all of the capability that the nation had? And so there were complaints from unified commanders with regard to the talent that they were receiving. Even, honestly, Admiral Long had that complaint, and I can see it at CinCPac. Each of the services were sending good people, but their best people were kept for the air staff, the Navy staff, and Marine Corps staff, the Army staff, or for the component commands. You know, it was better to be assigned to CinCPacFlt in operations than CinCPac in operations. And so it all came together about that period of time that they needed a mechanism to raise the bar with regard to serving in a joint billet, and then that way giving both joint staff and the operational CinCs the ability to have the talent from the services that they need to view every operation from the joint prism as opposed to the service prism. That's how all that came about, and that's Goldwater-Nichols, where big components of it, they were all briefed on it and they sign on to it, and that's where all the fallout from you needed to have joint duty, etc., etc., etc., came from.

SC: The joint orientation of the services that emerged from the 1980s made major changes in the roles and duties of the Joint Chiefs of Staff, especially the chairman. What's your perspective on those changes?

PDM: They were important, but that leads to the discussion that I'll save and I'll come back to it, of who the unified commanders worked for. They worked for the secretary of defense, not for the chairman of the Joint Chiefs, and we'll expand on that greatly in probably the last segment when I was CinCLant.

SC: The modern component commander concept is very important. What are component commanders, or COCOMs, and what's their role in the modern service dynamic?

PDM: That's easy. Each of the geographic operational CinCs, when they have to pull together forces for some type of operation, they have to call upon a joint force. For ease of operations, each of the CinCs has a naval component, an Army component, and air component reporting to them. Illustratively, CinCLantFlt, CinCPacFlt, they work for the CNO for the training and administration of the force, but for operations, it's conducted under the unified commander, so he is a component of the unified commander for the execution of the operational mission, two hats for all components.

SC: As the SecNav EA, how engaged were you in the efforts to promote service jointness in the early 1980s?

PDM: Honestly, it wasn't on my scope. That thing came into being, it was handled by the chief of naval personnel and the CNO. The secretary had comments on it, a little bit to do with it, but we did not get involved in it.

SC: What were, in general, the stumbling blocks to service jointness in the early 1980s?

PDM: Service commitment to assigning people to joint billets. Before there was a requirement to assign to them, there was always a demand pull on top-quality people. It happens in industry, it happens in the military, it happens in OSD. There are only so many people that are in the top 10 percent, only so many people that are in the top 20 percent. Everybody wants them. How many times did someone call up and say, "Send me someone that's in your bottom group to be—?" How many times did they do that? Huh?

Not many. So that's the important aspect of this. That's where it all came to why that happened, why everybody had to have a qualification. Then everybody meant the top 10 percent, too, now, so you couldn't avoid sending the top 10 or top 15 percent to the joint command, where you certainly could avoid it all the time that I was in the Navy up until that happened. I had never even thought about a joint command. As a pretty successful naval officer, it had never crossed my mind. So, you know, that's why that action was taken.

SC: The last Maritime Strategy major plan of the late Cold War period came out in the mid-1980s. How much connectedness to that development process did you have?

PDM: I think that with the premise of the six-hundred-ship Navy, with the implementation of the battle group structure that was put into place that was one large set piece of any national strategy, where we would have those battle groups in peacetime and how we would be able to surge in wartime. It was all predicated upon the capability that was built into that six-hundred-ship Navy.

SC: If you were to advise a young officer who aspired to billets such as EA to a major commander or even SecNav or SecDef, what would you say?

PDM: One doesn't aspire to that billet; one is detailed or selected for that billet based on the attribute that I have woven throughout every answer that I've given you.

SC: Performance.

PDM: Performance. If the performance is there, it will be recognized, and if it is recognized, you then go to the better jobs or the demanding jobs, of which those that you mentioned are a part of. It's as simple and elementary as that. There's no *kabuki* [a highly scripted and formal Japanese dance form]. You just start from day one and put every job that you go to, as I've been through here with you. If anybody's starting on an ATF and work[s] his way out of the "junk force" of the Atlantic Fleet through one thing, performance, and wind[s] up where we wound up on this with early selection to flag during this period, it's evidence that it is. It can't be anything else.

SC: If you went back to your time as SecNav EA and could have a do-over, is there anything you would do differently?

PDM: Not a thing.

SC: As EA, you, no doubt, encountered difficult personalities.

PDM: No, I take that back.

SC: Okay.

PDM: There is one thing that I would do over, but it's between me and the secretary. It's a very important thing, very important. But if I failed the secretary in any one thing, it was this. It was probably a very important decision, the only time that I didn't stand strong enough. That's enough said. One time I didn't stand strong enough. The secretary made a decision that probably wasn't the best. But changing one thing in four and a half to five years ain't bad. One thing. The secretary knows exactly what that is, as do I.

SC: We will leave that where it lies.

PDM: Leave it where it is.

SC: As EA, you, no doubt, encountered difficult personalities. How did you deal with such a person?

PDM: Oh, that is a very good question. I had been fortunate to work in high offices for many years with the three vice chiefs, with Admiral Long at CincPac, so I had experience with difficult personalities, and it made it a little bit easier when that occurred. I always gave a difficult personality the opportunity to benefit from my experience and to benefit from the relationship that I had with my bosses, and if they knew better and they didn't want the benefit of any recommendation, I let the difficult personality proceed into the situation that I could have written out how it was going to end, and I will say that 98 percent of them ended the way that I forecasted.

And then the difficult personality went away and then he never received any help, but most of the time, I never saw them again. Most of the time, the really difficult personalities I never saw again, because whatever they wanted to get done, the answer was a flat no, or the answer was to go back and have it redone, and most of the time the same personality didn't present the issue the second time. I made sure of that. And there were ways to do that. So that's what I did. I didn't have time for the secretary to get agitated because someone was difficult to deal with. It wasted too much energy. It wasted too much time. So that was my pattern. I offered every time, quietly and with he and I. I believe strongly in four eyes. I believe strongly in four eyes. Nobody else in a conversation I ever had with people like that.

And I believe strongly, and to this day, everything that I'm telling you is from total recall. I never kept a memorandum. I never kept a log. I never kept a little yellow pad or a little spiral notebook, never, because if something went south, they would all have to be submitted, and I never wanted to put any of my bosses into that situation. And things do go wrong. So whether it was a difficult person or a difficult situation, I always tried to remedy it with four-eye meetings and I always entered any discussion the way I entered any interview, I did it with humility. I was a person who has experience, and if you wanted to benefit from it, I'd be glad to share. It was from not that "you have to do it this way." That was important.

SC: You've always been very athletic. What athletic pursuits did you undertake in those years to stay sharp physically and mentally?

PDM: In the Pentagon, both in the Vice Chief's Office and in SecNav's Office, it's probably a combination of seven years, eight years. Seven? Yeah. Maybe more. I had played a lot of tennis, but then I became a squash player. I went down to the POAC religiously, every day. I told my boss that every day I went down to POAC [Pentagon Officer's Athletic Club], found an hour, hour and fifteen minutes to go down to the POAC. I had a list of squash people to find out who I could play with, and I learned squash in the Pentagon. When I was in the Vice Chief's Office, they played with the hard ball. I'd come home sometimes and Becky would ask me, "What is that on your back?" And I played it and it's a demanding game, but it keeps you in shape. Forty-five minutes of squash plus fifteen minutes in the weight room, a little steam and a shower, and get back up and that was it.

SC: What was life like in D.C. in the early 1980s for a senior officer assigned to the Pentagon?

PDM: I don't know. I didn't have one. [*laughter*] I'm not being facetious. I'm being serious. I went to work early, came home late. We went to a few functions. The secretary was kind. We had a very good relationship with him and Barbara. But we didn't do that much. We didn't have enough time. Weekends were quieter. I didn't work many Saturdays with the secretary. We had to every once in a while, but not many. With the CNO, it was different. With the vice chief, it was different. But the secretary never went in on Saturdays unless he had to. But we had two boys that were engaged in football, basketball, whatever the season was. We had the house to keep up. But we were not that active socially.

SC: In 1985, near the end of your EA tour, you were early-selected to flag rank at the twenty-one-year point, and that's a topic that we will take up in our next session and also start with your first billet as a flag officer. As we wrap up this session, as you were the SecNav EA, is there any issue or topic that you'd like to add to or discuss?

PDM: There's much that I left out, but I would summarize it, four, four and a half—I'm going to find out exactly how much time I spent with the secretary, but it was about four-plus years. It was a period of learning, a period of performing, and, proudly, a period of contributing to the Navy that was built during that time, to the improvements that were made in training that Navy, and I benefited from all that for the ten years or so, or eight years, nine years that I served on active duty after I left that office. I couldn't have been prouder of my link with the secretary, my friendship with the secretary, and the time that I contributed to the success that he had as secretary that had the most impact on the warfighting capability of this nation of anyone who had served as Secretary of the Navy, and I say that unreservedly. The record will show that ships that were produced, and the airplanes that came off the assembly line were attributed to that secretary.

SC: Thank you, Admiral Miller. In our next session, we will cover your promotion to flag rank, your time as a battle group commander and as a cruiser-destroyer, or CruDes, commander.

This is USNI oral history interview with Admiral Paul David Miller, U.S. Navy (Ret.). This is session number seven, question set number fifteen. The date is Sunday, April 15, 2018, and the interviewer is Professor Stan Carpenter.

[End of April 15, 2018, interview]

Interview with Admiral Paul David Miller, USN (Ret.)
Date: July 28, 2018

Stan Carpenter (SC): This is USNI oral history interview with Admiral Paul David Miller, U.S. Navy (Ret.). This is session number eight, question set number sixteen. The date is Saturday, July 28, 2018. The interviewer is Professor Stan Carpenter. These questions cover the years as a battle group commander.

Admiral, in 1985, near the end of your EA tour, you were early selected to flag rank at the twenty-one-year point. That is usually the point where commanders are promoted to captain. How unusual was your promotion to flag at that very junior point in your career?

Admiral Paul David Miller (PDM): There are many that thought it was unusual, but when I looked at my progression through the rank of lieutenant commander, commander, captain, I was with a year group that had probably five more years, six more years of service than I had at the time of selection to then commodore. So it wasn't unusual in that I had gained two year-group years at a time for selection to lieutenant commander, commander, and captain, so it put me with a group of people who were what they would consider to be on time, if they were going to be selected to flag. So it was only unusual to those that looked at age only, but if they looked at the experiences that I was fortunate enough to have, coupled with early selections, then that would put me in that group, and then I just happened to be selected among a new group of cohorts which was probably year group '60, '61, as opposed to '64, '65.

It was early selection by two years for each of the more junior ranks, lieutenant commander, commander, captain. By doing that, you gain just a little bit of notoriety. Then you add it to the high-level jobs that I was fortunate enough to have, with three vice chiefs of naval operations, with the commander in chief of the Pacific Command, and being in the Office of the Secretary of the Navy, plus the performance at sea, and it all linked to put in front of the selection board screen a career that deserved a keen look at flag. I had done what most had done for selection in the past, and so being put in the group, that selection board just felt that I should be among the twenty-five that were selected that year. So I didn't look at it being junior; I looked at it being with that group, having gotten there by a different way.

SC: If you were to advise an officer just starting a Navy career and who aspired to flag rank, what would you advise him or her in terms of how they should shape their career?

PDM: Do not aspire to flag rank. Take each job and do everything you can to be successful in that job, because if you do not enjoy a great deal of success in each iterative job, you will never reach flag rank. I like the analogy that you hear about professional golfers play one shot at a time. And so play one tour at a time and then if you are able to string together a number of tours, just like a professional golfer, he strings together a number of successful holes, like eighteen of them, and you string twelve assignments together considered for flag, you'll be in good shape. But you don't aspire to it. If you're fortunate enough to be selected to it, that's a big day. But there are so many qualified people, and the Selection Board can only choose but a few, so there should be no disappointments, although I know there are in some that I've met, but it's such a grind and everything has to come together.

So don't be disappointed in yourself if you do have that aspiration when you reach captain. That's when you can have an aspiration, because you look back and you said, "I've done everything that I needed to do," but it might or might not happen.

SC: What billets or career experiences or education or training would you recommend that commanders and captains seek out in their career?

PDM: Clearly, operational. You must be at the top of the ladder in any operational command that you have. I think the record shows that jobs that are intense, particularly in the Navy staff in Washington now and joint duty, are considered greater qualifiers for flag rank than would be someone on the fleet staff in Hawaii or Norfolk. So working for people that are leading the Navy, the military, the Defense Department, working for them directly is no impediment, because you're being exposed to the flag-level environment, flag-level decision processes. That's what you want to link together, those kinds of tours to put yourself in a position to be considered for flag.

SC: Let's look at flag selection. What is the actual selection process? How does that work, and is it different from the process for captain and commander promotion selection?

PDM: Not different, more intense. You go through the same designation of being what they call in zone for selection for flag rank. You have a primary year group that most of the selectees should come from that year group. You have a few selectees that have had previous looks but might be caught up a year or two after their primary year and, conversely, a year or two earlier than might otherwise have happened.

 The precepts of a flag selection board are generally straightforward: select the best. But you have a dynamic in flag selection that's just a little bit sharper, a little bit crisper than it was for captain or commander, and that's warfare specialty. They try to maintain a balance in the warfare specialties, and so you'll have an equal number of aviators, submariners, surface warfare officers on a flag selection board, and they will usually have a clear appreciation for their community. And when records are briefed at the flag selection room, you not only have the briefer briefing the record, you also have probably a community input, because the flags that are in that community know every candidate personally, it's all put together, mixed around, and twenty-five people come out as flag selectees.

 But I contend that if you had thirteen different flag officers in that room, that list of twenty-five may have ten names that are different. There might be fifteen names that will be selected by probably any group, but there are probably 40 percent that might be selected because of the different backgrounds and the different views of the admirals on the board.

SC: While you were the SecNav EA, did you have any particular mentors, and how did they prepare you for your future flag duties?

PDM: I had no mentors except maybe Admiral R. L. J. Long. He's the vice chief that I worked for. Then he took me to CinCPac. So he gave me two looks. Within the vice chief, it was my third vice chief, and they were all different. And then at CinCPac, he gave me a look at the Pacific Command when traveling with him. He gave me the opportunity to view operational issues from a much different platform than most captains review them from, and so you take the operational command stuff, you take the Washington command high-level offices, and then working directly for the CinC of a unified commander, you're being mentored in a different way. You're seeing the problems that those desks face and you're seeing different leaders, how they address and solve those problems, so you're being mentored by having the opportunity to sit at those desks. Then if one catches your eye, like I caught Admiral Long's eye, then you have an opportunity to really sit with him, travel with him, talk with him, and able to participate in decision-making. My point that I want to get across is what that does for an individual is that when you face those decisions, they're not new to you. You remember them because most problems that military people face have been faced by somebody before. There are a few nuances. So if you're learned how to address them as an apprentice, so to speak, then you're able to go right to the end process of decision making. You don't have to learn; you're able to do it.

SC: We have discussed a D.C. or Pentagon tour in terms of promotability to captain and commander, but now we're in an entirely different realm: flag promotion. How critical are D.C. tours for flag promotability, and what tours are especially helpful in terms of making oneself competitive?

PDM: You'll get a lot of different answers to this question, Stan. I think that the tours within the Pentagon, those associated with your warfare specialty are fundamental. You're known as a keen staff officer, decision-maker among your community. I mentioned that community will have representatives on the flag board, so in that business, of course working for the top-level jobs, the vice chief, the CNO, the Secretary of the Navy, the secretary of defense, the chairman [of the Joint Chiefs of Staff], all those jobs support your selection for flag because of the answer to my last question: you get to see how large decisions are taken.

Then you have to be able to take that experience when you're outside the Pentagon, when you're outside of Washington and you happen to have a job as a chief of staff somewhere, some important slot like the Seventh Fleet [Western Pacific and Indian Ocean] or the Sixth Fleet [Mediterranean], you are better prepared; it's terribly important. The common factor in all of those is you're working closely with the top leader in some position of our military. The closer that you work to that desk, the better opportunity you have to learn and the better opportunity for that particular boss, whether he be a three-star, four-star, or civilian secretary, to understand you and be able to write about your capabilities and your potential better than anyone else.

SC: Let's speculate here. If you had to pick from your previous Navy experiences the most critical aspects of your career that made you a good candidate for flag selection, what would they be and why?

PDM: Oh, mercy. Number one would be finishing at the very top of any list in operational command at sea. Without that, you won't qualify. Then having the opportunity to work your way up and work for the individuals that I've just described, the then leaders of our Navy, of our military, our joint commands, our Defense Department, working at the very top of the ladder, working for those individuals sets you up better than any other pattern that I can name. If you take the flag list any year, you'll see that operational success is by far the most important ingredient, and then you look down the list of who those individuals currently work for or have worked for recently, and I'll suggest that they will fill in those desks that I talked about along the way.

SC: At that time, the Navy was going through the process of making the one-star a more definitive rank. Previously, a one-star was a rear admiral (lower half), but when promoted, you pinned on two stars. When you were promoted, the title was actually commodore. Why and how did that title create a lot of chaos in the Navy at the time?

PDM: I could give a very long-winded answer on this one, because I do believe that every rear admiral (lower half) that retires owes me a "Thank you." Why do I say that? A revered congressman by the name of Ike Skelton is the one who permitted the "commodore" title to reenter our naval ranking system.[90] There was some bill going through, and there was a lot of—not a lot, but there was enough chatter from the other services as to why in the Navy you got to be promoted direct to two stars. Well, you weren't promoted direct to two stars; you wore two stars, but they were still pay grades of 07 and 08. But, still, you wore it, and there was just a bit of, for want of another word, professional jealousy, because when you were going into a meeting, when you were at a dining table, a freshly-minted Navy rear admiral with two stars would get seated above an Army brigadier that may have been more senior than the Navy guy.

So Ike Skelton is the one that let it go. The Navy didn't fight it. Navy didn't fight it. So it happened. So it came out that we changed the one-star list to commodore. I was with John Lehman at the time. I didn't think about it too much till I was selected as a commodore. It just didn't feel right. What does that mean, selected as a commodore? The Navy has—I bet it has 100, 150 honorific commodores, you know. An individual has command of a destroyer squadron, he's a commodore. Aircraft wing, commodore. Submarine squadron, commodore. Amphibious squadron, commodore. So the name was used within the Navy, but it was honorific. It was not a pay title. You weren't assigned as a commodore, okay?

So I thought about it, and then when I was selected, it just left a bad taste in my mouth. I didn't have any—I'll phrase it differently. I thought that I had a very good chance of going beyond commodore, so it wouldn't trouble me too much because I think I was positioned well to make two stars at least. But I felt that there will be a lot of gentleman that worked awful hard to make rear admiral, and then they would be stuck with the title "commodore." And as you know, half of our rear admiral ratings, half of them will have to retire as a one-star because only half get promoted to two stars, and the others slip and proceed with a one-star rank. They would have slipped and proceeded

---

[90] Congressman Isaac N. "Ike" Skelton (1931–2013) graduated from the University of Missouri with a law degree in 1956 and represented Missouri from 1977 to 2011. As a powerful member of the House Armed Services Committee and Chairman from 2007 to 2011, he was a promoter of service education.

back into community life as a commodore. So his title would have been "commodore." Some of them would go back to seaport towns and be introduced as "Commodore," and one might wonder if he was a commodore of the Yacht Club or maybe this thing called a commodore in the Navy. They wouldn't be able to link it with great naval personalities such as Commodore Perry.[91]

I asked Secretary Lehman about changing it, and he said, "If you want it changed, change it." So that's the kind of relationship we had. I thought about it and thought about it. I decided in my spare time to work on that issue. To wind up this question, I started a series of chats with Ike Skelton, and finally I wore him down. There was a bill going through the process, and he said, "Okay, what do you want me to do?" Inside the Navy, it was never a formal structure, but we had to settle on what were we going to call it, and there were all kinds of names or modifiers to [one-star] admiral. "Commodore admiral" even was one of them. That was probably the one that received the most notoriety. "Brevet admiral." You know, there was all kinds. But what finally settled on—well, the way it was before, rear admiral (lower half) was an 07, rear admiral (upper half) was an 08, and so they had the title "rear admiral" either way because no one's going to check the parenthetical upper half/lower half. So that was it.

I took it over to Ike Skelton, he put it in the bill, it was passed, and so all those gentlemen that are now retired that happened to retire as a one-star or lower half, are called admirals, not commodore. I bet you didn't know that.

SC: I did not know that. I remember going through the "commodore admiral" thing and wondering what in the world is going on here. For those not familiar, the title "commodore" basically can be any actual rank, as long as you command a squadron or a flotilla or some type of multi-ship group.

As we wrap up your time at the Pentagon as SecNav EA and promotion to flag, are there any other areas that you would like to explore?

---

[91] Commodore Matthew C. Perry (1794–1858) was an American naval officer who commanded the 1853–54 expedition to Japan to open trade, which eventually set the foundation for the Westernization of Japan in the later nineteenth century.

PDM: The opportunity to be able to work at the, for want of another expression, at the top of the food chain, permits one to gain the experience, to gain the confidence, to gain the awareness of how and what to do when one gets in those positions, future positions. For anyone that would ever be fortunate enough—and I didn't say "aspire"—be fortunate enough to find themselves with an opportunity to work in those very top jobs, I would say do not shy away from them because of the long hours, because of the travel, because of all those things that one might not want to do. The payoff is huge, not only in potential in the Navy, but the payoff is huge for the rest of your professional life.

SC: As you departed the Pentagon again for a return to sea duty in a major leadership position, what was your perspective on your future Navy career?

PDM: I was going to go to sea. I was fortunate enough to be going to a CruDes group that was embarked in a carrier. I knew that as a one-button [one-star rear admiral, lower half], I had to have a full deployment, an operational deployment, as a battle group commander. That's what we called them then, not strike groups. And I was going to take this one step at a time because if you didn't succeed there, then you wouldn't have to worry about anything else. So I go back to that analogy about one shot at a time. Having the good fortune of going to an operational CV [aircraft carrier] was absolutely key to having the opportunity to gain that experience.

SC: Typically, command of what we call today a carrier strike group, then, as you say, it was battle group, is a first or second flag tour and a real opportunity to show one's ability to command multiple warfare arms, from fixed and rotary wing air, to cruiser-destroyer-type ships, to the subsurface when a submarine's attached in direct support. Other than obvious differences in size and numbers of ships between a squadron and a strike group, what are the command dynamics' difference between being a surface squadron commander and a battle group commander?

PDM: Night and day. The surface squadron commander deals with one segment of a battle group's activity, worries about those surface warfare issues, particularly antisubmarine warfare, and operates in support of the battle group commander. The battle group commander has to deal with each of the phases of maritime warfare and has to understand, appreciate the air wing's contribution, because operations and capabilities of that battle group center on the CV and its embarked air wing. So the battle group commander's job is far-reaching. It is in degree of complexity, I would say, three times as complex as the commodore's job is, and the opportunity to misstep as a battle group commander is far greater than it is in any command that is part of that battle group.

People have little appreciation for when a battle or a strike group is at sea and they get involved in operations from the sea. The dynamics of putting the immense capability of that battle group into action are absolutely challenging to anyone who has had the best of experiences up to that point. Not being a naval aviator I had a little bit of makeup to do in on-the-job training from the day I relieved as that battle group commander.

SC: For those not familiar with the concept of a battle group as, as it's called today, carrier strike group, could you describe the structure and roles of the various components?

PDM: A battle group, the composition, nominally ten ships, nine, eight. The centerpiece, when you set the table, is, of course, the carrier and its air wing. The composition of the air wing is key, with its fighter attack aircraft. The numbers of combatants and their capabilities are important.

I was in a nuclear carrier and we had two nuclear cruisers, the *Texas* (CGN-39) and the *Arkansas* (CGN-41), as part of that battle group, and then we had five other destroyers, 963s and 1052s at the time, and then we had the oiler, or the AOE, to provide logistic support.[92] At times, we had a submarine attached, but not all the time. So when you go over that inventory of capability, you see that your staff and then you have to be

---

[92] *Spruance*-class destroyers were named for Admiral Raymond Spruance (1886–1969). The USS *Spruance* (DD-963) was commissioned in 1975 and decommissioned in 2005. The destroyers were not missile-armed, which created an anti-air warfare defense concern. The *Knox*-class frigates were commissioned between 1969 and 1974 and were ASW platforms with limited AAW capability. The AOE is the fast combat support ship and is the Navy's largest combat logistics ship for underway replenishment of fleet units.

able to integrate that capability to make sure that each phase of it is trained, each element of it is materially ready, each subset is particularly groomed, like the long-range strike capability, the surface warfare capabilities, the ASW capabilities, because you just don't know what was going to be called into action when.

For me personally, it's important to record that I was fortunate to have as a chief of staff one of the top naval aviators. He was the second Top Gun skipper, and he contacted me early on, and he said, "Admiral, you're coming to be the battle group commander without any aviation experience. This hasn't been done much. So you're going to have to gain the confidence and respect of their air wing, regardless of what you have on your shoulder." That phone call really helped. He said, "If you can, come here with all your qualifications to fly, and then we'll take it from there."

So I went to Pensacola. You have to go through all the physiology routines to get your card, to say that you've passed your survival, you've passed your ejection seat capability to be able to fly from an aircraft carrier. That was absolutely key, because when I went to the battle group, I joined it right after it had completed its WestPac transit. It hadn't started any operations yet, but it had completed the transit. That's where I had the little modest change of command.

Soon after getting under way and the first couple of days of flight ops, I started flying with the air wing. Initial flights were with the COs of each of the embarked squadrons, 202 Aardvarks, 214 Black Lions. I remember them all distinctly. I had my flight suit with Velcro on it, and whatever squadron I was going to fly with, I would put that patch on before we hit the flight deck. I flew in the helicopters, flew in the A-6s [Intruders].[93] The A-6s were the Warlords. And I'm sitting here talking to you today, Stan, and I can remember each of those squadrons like yesterday. So by flying with them and then the air wing commander, who was Denny Gladman, he wasn't offended about supporting this blackshoe in getting a real naval aviation background, so he put me on the flight plan, so I'd look to see who I was flying with. I got a lot of flying done during that cruise. Then I'm able to record that I never visited a carrier, to my recollection, in other than a jet, from being the battle group commander through being the CinC in Norfolk.

---

[93] Grumman A-6 Intruder medium-range all-weather attack aircraft in Navy service from the early 1960s to the early 1990s.

The battle group is an intense twenty-four-hour-a-day operation, and you have to pay attention to all segments of it, because you are on the board worldwide as a forward capability of this country. You're in the Pentagon, you're in the CinCs, you're in Europe, you're in Japan, you're in Hawaii. So this is your time to be able to make sure that you're ready to answer all bells, and that's what we're talking about when you put all the battle group capability together.

SC: In general, what is the overall mission of a battle group?

PDM: Readiness. We've gone over all its capabilities, and then the overall mission is to be able to respond when needed, and making sure—I can't emphasize too strongly—making sure that the advertised capabilities are there, are ready, and can be counted upon without notice.

SC: You already started hitting on this particular question, but let me ask it again another way. An argument might be made that because of the background in carrier aviation, an aviator always ought to be the battle group commander. What's your thinking on that issue?

PDM: To be kind, rubbish. We do not groom a leader to have only a stovepipe range of capability, so when you have the centerpiece of our forward deployed and strike capability, to say that you need to preserve the top job in that capability for a particular brand of individual or particular warfare specialist, I think is wrong. I think you need to send your best leaders, to send your leaders with the most potential to those jobs, so that when one gets beyond that particular capability, one has that experience in his kit, so that he can be better informed in making command decisions, which will affect not only the carrier but the whole damn fleet. So I think it's terribly important to let the individuals that have the talent, that have the experience, not necessarily in aviation, but writ large, experience writ large to go do those jobs.

I was a strong proponent of sending submariners to be battle group commanders, because we've seen a lot of submariners reach CNO, and fleet commanders. If you do it properly—and am I saying I did it properly? I'm saying that I did it gingerly. I did not go in there just saying, "I'm the battle group commander." I went in there with the attitude that I wanted to learn everything that was to know about that carrier and that air wing's capability in the first month I was there.

I worked on each of the gangs that run that carrier from the aviation point of view. They wondered, "What the hell's he doing?" I can show you a caricature. I wore the jerseys as my uniform. They started to print one with one star on it, but I wanted to go down and work with the yellow shirts, the blue shirts, the grapes [purple shirts], which were the fuelers, and I would go spend a day with the chief, take me around, and I participated with those guys to learn what they do, how it works there.[94]

Then with the aviators, I'd go to the ready rooms different times of day and night to listen to the ready room brief as to what mission they were going to go on. Then I had the privilege of being able to fly with the guys and attend the ready room sessions. A month into that, I knew a lot about carrier operations. I immersed myself in it, in addition to being the battle group commander. So that stood me in really good stead, as we proceeded into this deployment, of being able to crank into any decision I had to take in the battle group, but, more importantly, with what I was writing back to my seniors with regard to our capability and our readiness.

SC: Tell us a bit about the billet selection process for a major command tour such as a battle group commander.

PDM: It isn't the process per se. By that time, you're down to a few individuals within each group that have been put into this group that should receive the opportunity to command a strike or battle group, so then it depends upon availability, it depends upon the CNO, the chief of naval personnel, the secretary. How you get slated is just a process, but you have to have the prerequisites.

---

[94] Roles on a carrier deck are designated by specific shirt colors for ease of recognition. White is quality control, safety, and medical; red is ordinance, crash, and salvage; purple is aviation fuel; yellow is officer aircraft handling; brown is plane captains, green is catapult, arresting gear, and maintenance; blue is aircraft handling and elevator.

To be sure, in the early days, I wasn't the first one that was in a battle group, but I think I was the first one to fully deploy a carrier battle group. We had, I think, two or three they called strike groups centered on battleships, not many, but there was a surface warfare group, DesGru [destroyer] commander in charge of that. But then after myself, a few more, then I think warfare specialty didn't make much difference, but they stopped the battle group commander from flying with the air wing.

SC: What's the turnover of command like for a new battle group commander? What type of information is most critical for the outgoing commander to pass on to the relief?

PDM: Brief me on the operations schedule, brief me on the staff and the commanding officers of the respective ships in the battle group, and say, "Thank you" to them, and he proceeds and you take charge. That's it.

SC: What was your day like under way as the battle group commander? You've already described your first month or so, but once you were in the routine, what was a typical day like under way?

PDM: Each day that I had the privilege of being with that battle group, which wound up being—well, I joined it probably thirty days into the deployment. I still had a seven-month deployment with it. [*laughs*] So each day had to do with getting your staff together, figuring out—it was always trying to stay one step ahead of the schedule, trying to make sure to stay one step ahead of what we were going to prosecute that day, and oftentimes the days, particularly in the northern Arabian Sea, were not that challenging operationally because we were there but we had to be ready. There were many days that you weren't getting ready to do anything imminent. That's tough, to have ten ships, to be able to keep them well-trained, to keep them sort of not only trained, but in the readiness mode for periods of time, for weeks. It's tough. You've been there at sea. You can only groom your EW [electronic warfare] equipment so much. You can only reload a missile so many times to make sure it all works. So the challenging thing for me on a routine basis in the northern Arabian Sea was to make sure that each of those ships felt that they were part of a national response capability.

I would rotationally visit all the ships. I would brief the crew. I would spend time walking through there, making sure they knew why they were there, what the battle group's capability was, and trying to set them up to go to some liberty ports, but there are not very many in the northern Arabian Sea.

Those days were long, but we were so very fortunate because the alarm bell rang, and our alarm bell was the National Command Authority wanted another carrier in the Mediterranean. Otherwise, we would have spent the whole time there in the northern Arabian Sea, carrier on watch, and we would have just come back to Alameda [California] without a lot of, you know, stuff to talk about. And there were many carriers, as you know, that spent six months, seven months in the northern Arabian Sea before the activity started. That bore a lot of holes in that ocean, did a lot of training flights in those skies, but never got an alarm bell rang.

SC: One of the most critical tasks of a battle group staff is the daily staff briefing. What's your philosophy on how these staff meetings should be conducted? What did you require from your staff officers? And just in general, what sort of qualities did you look for in a successful staff officer?

PDM: I was not a commander who dwelled on long staff meetings. I wanted to hear what the problems were and what I could do to help facilitate remedying those problems. I wanted to know where each of the ships in the battle group were, what their activity was, what their problems were, and that's about all. My staff meetings were probably ten minutes.

What I looked for in a staff officer was someone who did not require any supervision, oversight—you choose the word—an individual who told me when I needed to know something when I needed to know it, not necessarily at a staff meeting, who worked hand-in-glove with the chief of staff, bringing me into it when they thought it appropriate and necessary. I gave that staff a great deal of autonomy to not only write and send messages on my behalf, so that it wouldn't slow any process down, but also represent me in any dealings with the battle group or outside staff, and tell me, after the fact, what they had done. I was perfectly happy with that. I never required them to come to me for "May I?" until they mucked it up. Then you used that as an event that—I think the phrase of art now is "a learning experience." You used that as a learning experience.

But that's how I led all my staffs. I was not one to interfere with their jobs. They had their jobs, and if everything went smoothly, I never heard about what the hell they did, because I didn't need to. So it's leadership. I've been looking for a word for a long time for it, but it's just leadership by leaving or letting people do their job, giving them everything they need to succeed, and let them alone to do it, and then support them when they need support. And that's how I ran it. It was ideal.

SC: The total opposite of the micromanager.

PDM: I had a couple of those along the way, and they drove me absolutely crazy. I told myself if I was ever in a reverse position, that I was going to be so far away from being a micromanager, some would say I was lax, because, as I mentioned, I spent a day away from not even seeing the damn staff. I'd go down to quarters with the blue-shirts and that's where I'd spend my day on a carrier. Even the COs of the carriers wondered what the hell I was doing. But at times, I bet I knew as much about his ship as he did.

SC: You made an extensive deployment, an eight-month deployment. You arrived thirty days into it, so you had a seven-month deployment. In general, tell us about that deployment and any real-world operations during the deployment.

PDM: I'll go over this as quickly as I can. The alarm bell rang, northern Arabian Sea. Admiral Kelso wanted three carriers in the Mediterranean for operations against Libya in 1986. They were going to get the third carrier because a carrier from the East Coast was coming in to relieve another carrier. This carrier had been at sea for a long time. They had some operational issues or whatever, so they decided to take the unorthodox action to reach into the Pacific Command and bring a carrier into the Mediterranean. We would have to go through the Suez Canal.

Up to that point, no nuclear-powered aircraft carrier had ever gone through the Suez Canal, so that was the first thing we did, was go to, quote, "general quarters" to try to get all that planning done to get to get a ten-ship battle group through the Suez Canal and up into the Mediterranean, and then to be able to find out what were the commander Sixth Fleet's rules, regulations, procedures, and then get ourselves ready to chop to the Sixth Fleet, then because of Libya, to make sure the air wing was totally refreshed and ready to go. So as you can imagine, it was a busy battle group from the time that we were in the northern Arabian Sea.

We go into the Red Sea, we set up a scheme to go through, but we couldn't. They wouldn't let us through. It took President Reagan's intervention to get this carrier through the canal, and I remember they halted all the operations in the canal. They positioned us to go through at nighttime. We went through the canal at nighttime without incident; everything went smoothly. An aircraft carrier is a big ship, and there were a couple of places in that canal where I'd be on the bridge and I'd look this way, guess what I'd see. Land. I look this way. More land. [*laughs*] So it was very interesting going through that thing. The captain did a great job.

A funny anecdote that I'd like recorded. We had to pay a toll to get through the canal. My recollection was clear. We had to pay $250,000 in cash to get the battle group through the canal. A good thing a carrier goes to sea with a lot of cash. But this was supposed to be for a roundtrip ticket. So we go through. We report to Admiral Kelso. We were assigned a position north of the Gulf of Sidra. The actual evening of the strike in Libya had taken place just before we got there because they had the three carriers before they detached as we were coming in to fill in. So they gave us a position in the Central Mediterranean north of Libya, with lots of assignments and requirements to fly certain patrols, and then I spread out the battle group to do what battle groups do in such situations in ASW and Alpha Whiskey [AW—anti-air warfare] stations, airborne warning stations, to make sure that we had total control of the air picture because we took that over.[95]

---

[95] OPERATION EL DORADO CANYON (April 15–16, 1986) was a strike against Libya in retaliation for the support of terrorist operations against U.S. servicemen in Europe by Libya and as a preemptive strike against the Gaddafi regime's ability to provide for state-sponsored terrorist attacks.

It was serendipitously that this young flag officer was able to be in the carrier and gain the opportunity to participate in a huge real-world event of that time, and exercise all the capabilities of the battle group, spend lots of time at sea. We got four days in port during that whole time, and then go back out to sea and wondered when they were going to let us go. I think that was in April that that event took place. We were there in May, got there. They still didn't figure out when we should be able to go back to the Pacific Fleet because there was a requirement, a vacancy there. We thought we'd come up two or three weeks, and boom!

We had a problem. We didn't have a problem, but the Navy had a problem. Egypt would not let the nuclear-powered ships go back through the canal. Even with input from our highest offices, they wouldn't let us go back through. And it boils down to we were one of the carriers that participated in striking that Muslim nation. And they would let the conventional ships go through, so we detached the destroyers and the support ship to go back through the canal, but *Enterprise*, *Arkansas*, and *Texas* stayed as a task element until they decided to let us go home.

I tried, I tried *hard* to get Admiral Lyons to permit us to sail across the Atlantic and go around the Cape of South America and up to California, and that's how the deployment would end. He would not let me do it. Back-channel messages, I finally got the message, "You've asked enough." I had read books about how sailing ships went around the Cape. I laid it out how we could do this. The problem was it was wintertime and we had eighty-three planes that we could not put them all in the hangar. We had them on topside. I think the staff and he, they were concerned that a carrier would go through there, we'd have damage. So he did not let us go through there. I would have let us go through in a heartbeat minute or any carrier go through. If you studied enough, you'd know you could go into the lee of the east side of South America, and as soon as the weather changes, but I was confident that even in between fronts, with nuclear knots, you would get through there and get to the other side and you wouldn't have anything happen, but I couldn't convince my superiors.

What we did, we went around Africa. That is a long sea journey. Went around Africa and the southern Indian Ocean. If you want to take a cruise and be in nowhere, try the southern Indian Ocean from the Cape of Africa to Australia. That is a long way, long way. So that's what we did.

SC: The flagship was the USS *Enterprise*.[96] What about the relationship that you had with the commanding officer of the *Enterprise*?

PDM: The relationship at the beginning, of course, he's worried about the new boot flag officer coming aboard the *Enterprise* without aviation experience. That soon passed. There was a curiosity about my leadership style. They had not had a flag officer putting on flight deck jerseys before. They hadn't had a flag officer roaming the ship from stem to stern, going down in the galleys, just saying "Hi" to folks, being up and eating midrats [midnight rations for the ongoing and off going watches] with flight crews before they'd take off for a—because we maintained a twenty-four-hour CAP [combat air patrol] in the Libya station.

So the relationship was good. They were an outstanding carrier. I reported on the CO and the ship accordingly. It was a great experience for the embarked staff and myself, but it was even a greater experience for the ship, in which they wound up making a full eight-month deployment and going around the world and then participating in an actual real-world event, exercising the Navy strike capability. So it all worked harmoniously, and he later was promoted to flag rank and retired as a Navy three-star. So I would say that he received a good report for his time in command. [*laughs*]

SC: Being a flag officer very often puts you in the role as an international diplomat, and that might be a question for later in this interview series, but did you have any diplomatic functions at that point?

PDM: We'll save that for later. My function was totally an at-sea commander.

---

[96] The USS *Enterprise* (CVN-65), the first nuclear-powered carrier, was commissioned in 1961 and decommissioned in 2017.

SC: As I write this question, I'm looking out over Narragansett Bay at a very large container ship making its way up Narragansett Bay. This observation leads me to a question about the role of the modern Navy in the international setting. As you advanced to more senior commands, your world perspective became much more globally focused, so many questions from here on will address that dynamic. But let's start with that container ship. In the twenty-first century, what do you see as the Navy's essential mission set in terms of trade and international commerce?

PDM: The Navy's central strategic contribution and, thereby, mission has not changed: command of the seas, to permit that container ship to go anywhere in the world on an ocean or series of oceans that are free, that the skipper of that ship didn't have to worry about a peril from on, under, or over that ocean. And so I see the Navy that's being built today having the same role that our maritime force had since we took it over from the British when they lost the prescription for being able to maintain a navy that controlled the seas, and which permitted them to have a world-reserved currency ensured by their maritime capability and trade. When we took that over [1945], we've been able to maintain it, and now the leadership has got to restore the capability that was built through the Lehman years that I went into depth on earlier, because we gained command of the seas. We still have it, but we're being challenged for it, and I pray that this nation doesn't become a Great Britain and cede command of the seas to China or another nation.

SC: As we wrap up your tour as the USS *Enterprise* battle group commander, is there anything that you would like to add?

PDM: It was a wonderful experience that, while I was only in the ship for seven months, I was able to learn, participate, and appreciate the capabilities involved in that carrier and its air wing and its battle group capability that permitted me to then become a better numbered fleet commander, fleet commander, and unified CinC. Without that seven months, I do not believe that I would have had the necessary requisite on-hand knowledge to succeed as I think I succeeded in the positions that I just described. It was essential, but more importantly, it was fun. What surface warfare officer has the opportunity to be in the backseat of an F-14 with the skipper of the Black Lions? It demonstrated to me the capabilities of that aircraft. How many surface warfare officers have taken a 9G turn? How many have gone straight up and stalled that puppy and turned it over? That's the kind of experiences that I was able to have and do low levels in an A-6 off of Indonesia. It was just a tremendous set of capabilities that I will have fond memory of forever.

SC: Thank you, Admiral Miller. In our next session, we will cover your time as a cruiser-destroyer, or CruDes, commander at ComCruDesGru 3 and your assignment to a fleet command in the Pacific.

This is USNI oral history interview with Admiral Paul David Miller, U.S. Navy (Ret.). This is session number eight, question set number sixteen. The date is Saturday, July 28, 2018, and the interviewer is Professor Stan Carpenter.

SC: This is USNI oral history interview with Admiral Paul David Miller, U.S. Navy (Ret.). This is session number eight, question set number seventeen. The date is Saturday, July 28, 2018, and the interviewer is Professor Stan Carpenter. These questions cover the years as CruDesGru 3 and as commander of Seventh Fleet.

Admiral, when you detached from the *Enterprise* carrier battle group, you were assigned command of Cruiser Destroyer Group 3 in San Diego. Before we launch into the particulars of that tour, tell us about the general nature and composition of a CruDesGru in the late 1980s.

PDM: The cruiser-destroyer group command is that you have both operational and administrative command over a number of ships. It varies. I think Cruiser Destroyer Group 3 has something like thirty-five. It was not a great number, but if you weren't chosen to go on a deployment as a battle group or then the few strike groups that they have in battleships, you would spend your cruiser destroyer group time and most of the emphasis would be placed on training and material readiness of the squadrons that composed your destroyer group and making sure that they were ready for deployment.

We shouldn't spend too much time on this, because I got back from my deployment June, end of May, and then it was a scant four months or so before I was relieved and went on to Seventh Fleet. Too much of my time as the group commander was spent trying to get clearance for my next job.

One thing that we left behind in the last session was as we were coming around Africa to Perth, Australia, I received a personal message that said you were to try to get back to Washington while the ship was in port because you had been nominated for Seventh Fleet, and you had interviews with the secretary of defense and the chairman of the Joint Chiefs to have that nomination cleared. I said, "Oh."

We arrived in Perth. I jumped on commercial air from Perth to Sydney to Los Angeles to Washington for a couple of days in Washington. Based on the strength of the battle group and, I know, reports from Admiral Kelso and conversations probably between Kelso and John Lehman, the decision was made to nominate me for Seventh Fleet, because I'm absolutely positive that I wasn't in the queue on the CNO side of the ledger to move to Seventh Fleet that soon. But the nomination went forward. I had three hurdles to clear: my discussions with "Cap" Weinberger, my discussions with Admiral Crowe, and then any discussions I needed to have with the Senate staff in trying to get that clearance, all done before I could proceed.

I flew back to Washington and then had my meeting with SecDef. That meeting is as crystal-clear as I'm sitting across the table from you, Stan. I had known "Cap" Weinberger because, of course, he was the secretary of defense when I was SecNav's EA, so paths crossed. Colin Powell had been his military assistant. And sometimes John was not in trouble but had reasons to have extra time with the secretary of defense. So I knew. I mean, it wasn't like walking in and not knowing the secretary of defense, which was very, very helpful. I walked in the for interview, and he says, "You know you've been nominated." He said, "But, Admiral, I must share with you that I've had some pushback about your going to Seventh Fleet at this time, particularly because of your age."

I don't know where it came from, but I paused and I said, "Mr. Secretary, I'm getting older as fast as I can."

Weinberger chuckled. He said, "Admiral, don't push it. It comes soon enough." He said, "It was great seeing you again." Took out his hand and said, "Congratulations." I left the office, told very few people about that because they wouldn't believe it. But I went down to Admiral Crowe. He started off with the same thing, "Got some pushback." He says, "How was your interview with the Secretary of Defense?"

I says, "It was pretty brief." I told him about the age question. I recall that Crowe had the same pushback, age, experience. I told him the secretary chuckled at my answer. And he said, "Congratulations." And Admiral Crowe had a few pleasantries and said, "Congratulations."

So I flew from Perth, Australia, probably for a total time of less than ten minutes of interviews. So that was done. SecDef signed off on it. It goes to the [Capitol] Hill. I get on a plane to go to Washington to San Francisco to Manila, over to Cubi [Naval Air Station Cubi Point] and back to the ship, because they had gotten under way during this period of time and they were sailing up through the Lombok Straits to pick up their detachment left at Cubi, and so I rejoined the ship for the remaining sail to Alameda.

But then the word was clear that even when I got back to San Diego, that I was the cruiser destroyer group commander having been nominated for Seventh Fleet. In San Diego, there was a few news clips, but then we heard that I had a hold put on my nomination from Senator Nunn and Senator Dixon.[97] Huh! So in addition to my CruDesGru job, my main job was trying to get the Senate to decide that I was worthy of being cleared for Seventh Fleet. This process was just that: a process. The well had been poisoned, and clearly those detractors that didn't agree with this assignment had influenced Senator Nunn, in particular, and then Senator Dixon because it would be stronger if they had two holds on it. There were some that probably thought that this drill was over, with such a name as Senator Nunn against it.

So the process started. I had to talk to some senators. The staff was led by a gent whose letter I just read a moment ago, Arnold Punaro. At that time, he was a Marine

---

[97] Senator Samuel A. Nunn (1938–) graduated from Emory University law school in 1962 and represented Georgia in the U.S. Senate from 1972 to 1997. Nunn served in the U.S. Coast Guard (active and reserve) from 1959 to 1968. He was chairman of the Senate Committee on Armed Services. Senator Alan J. Dixon (1937–2014) served as a senator from Illinois from 1981 to 1993.

Reserve colonel, and he asked for *lots* of information, lots. He asked the bureau for my fitness reports. He asked for me to pull together a block diagram that had other early-promoted officers to three stars. He wanted time at sea, how long it took them to make commander, captain. He wanted the numbers of months in command. He wanted all this in a block form. I had to get some help in pulling that together. The flag detailer helped me pull some of that together. The Congressional Liaison Office helped me pull some of this together. But I remember clearly on the list was, of course, Admiral Zumwalt, Admiral Bobby Inman, Admiral Stansfield Turner, Admiral Staser Holcolm, and maybe one more, that had made three stars early.[98]

So we did that. I'm glad I did that, because some surprising things came out of that, about time in command. Hmm! Because I had had the benefit of nearly two years in *McCloy* and then *Luce*. My time in command was not the least. Aha! So they couldn't say that was it, time at sea, because I spent my first five years totally at sea without a break of anything, and then the *McCloy* and then *Luce* and then *Enterprise*. Time at sea was in the bucket. So, hmm! Can't do that. Then time in, I think, the Pentagon, whatever.
It came out that this had been done before. It wasn't new. It had very seldom been done, okay, but it was done. There were officers in the sixties and seventies and now me in the eighties that had been promoted to three stars at a relatively young age. So that took some of the string out of the critics trying to get the senators to use that way to stop my progression.

It boiled down to them having my fitness reports over there, and then going through them and seeing that this had been reinforced by such officers as Hal Shear, Admiral Worth Bagley, Admiral Long on numerous occasions, and those were officers that had been confirmed and had been testifying in front of the Senate, so they were known by Senator Nunn and Senator Dixon. So they let me linger. Is that a good word? They let me cook—[*laughs*] is that a good word—for a couple of months until they finally decided to put the nomination up to committee for vote. And that's when Senator

---

[98] Vice Admiral M. Staser Holcomb (1932–) graduated from the U.S. Naval Academy in 1953. He served in the Navy from 1953 to 1985 and commanded U.S. Seventh Fleet. Admiral Robert R. "Bobby" Inman (1931–) graduated from the University of Texas in 1950 and served in the U.S. Navy from 1951 to 1982. His last billet was as deputy director of central intelligence and he was the first naval intelligence officer to achieve four-star rank.

Dixon and Senator Nunn, particularly Senator Nunn in his remarks, said that they had thoroughly looked at the qualifications and the performance of this officer, and they were withdrawing their hold and would vote affirmatively for the committee to pass this on. That was an interesting period for an individual to go through to sort of try to get himself promoted [*laughs*] to three stars. It's a tough system, and you hear about it all the time, a senator putting a hold on a nominee, and sometimes when that happens, it just stays there and that person never passes "go." Fortunately, with a lot of help, I was able to get through. It was uncomfortable, with the lengthy sessions that I had with the staff director and with him pulling all the information together, particularly the fitness reports. I was pleased that this time the system worked, even though it was troubling, but it worked and I got to go to Seventh Fleet.

I remember that was my time as CruDesGru 3. It wasn't on the waterfront, sadly. The chief of staff did that, because I was preoccupied with trying to get all this stuff done.

SC: Your critics said at the time that you had the benefit of Secretary Lehman's support. How did you react to that charge then and today?

PDM: Guilty as charged then. Today I look back, and I guess this is probably as good a time as any to put it on the record, my record at Seventh Fleet. I have fitness reports from two outstanding, tough fleet commanders. One is what this book is about [*taps finger several times on book*]. Admiral "Ace" Lyons was my first fleet commander, and the second was Admiral David Jeremiah, two totally different personalities. I'll put the fitness reports that I have by them against anybody.

The Lehman thing was absolutely true. Do I think that I would have become a fleet commander if it wasn't there? The answer would have been yes. I had a Chief of Naval Operations tell me that there was little doubt that I would have been a fleet commander, but the timing may not have been as quick, particularly after the reports from Kelso, that it was all there. Timing. Was John [Lehman] the facilitator? Yes. That's why I said guilty.

But then there was a body of people that thought that when Secretary Lehman left the position, that somehow I would go away, but they didn't take into account that maybe the performance that's in those records deserved another tour, deserved another time to show that the record was put there by hard work, and so the opportunity to go to another key three-star job was there, and it was performance there, including at Seventh Fleet, two very demanding three-star jobs, that I was able to get four stars. And then John certainly teed it up with sending me to Seventh Fleet, but then after that, I was just another fleet commander in another operational DCNO [Deputy Chief of Naval Operations] that was in the basket for four stars. So I didn't have any particular mentor at that time. So what you have there is true. I'm proud of it, and it worked. [*laughs*]

SC: The noted naval historian and analyst Norman Polmar said of you at the time, quote, "He's one of the most qualified flag officers we have," end quote. What exactly did he mean and why did he state that?

PDM: Somebody asked him that, I'm sure, when we were going through with this. I did not know Mr. Polmar well, but he obviously knew of some of the things that I had done, and he was someone very familiar with the Navy, as you know. So having people like that in your corner is helpful.

SC: You've already mentioned that operational command at sea is perhaps the most critical aspect. Would you say that that was one of the big reasons for your selection to fleet command, your operational command at sea experience?

PDM: No. The operational command at sea experience was the prerequisite to be considered between command of ships and command of the *Enterprise* battle group. Prerequisite. But then I would say that potential was equal, that you get selected based upon the performance, but you do not get selected as it being a reward. You get selected for Seventh Fleet, for CinCLantFlt, for greater responsibilities because you have the potential to do well in those assignments of greater responsibility, but you don't get to participate unless you have the requisite performance in the command structure.

SC: Seventh Fleet is based in Yokosuka, Japan, and covers the Western Pacific and Indian Ocean. What was it like for you moving to and operating out of Japan?

PDM: It was the best experience that I had and my family had in our Navy career, full stop. Japan, from the family side, "What? We're going to where? Japan?" Of course there was a degree of absolute wonderment by Chris and Colby, our sons. Becky, she was such a supporter all the way, as I've mentioned before. She was looking forward to this enthusiastically too.

We go off to Yokosuka, Japan, and we move into a different house on top of the hill right there in Yokosuka. That was the Japanese navy's [Japan Maritime Self-Defense Force] main base then. We were thrilled to be there and I was absolutely awestruck at being able to command in the U.S. Seventh Fleet. Think about it. It goes back to World War II, and this was still a time before iPads and iPhones, and Seventh Fleet was someone out there on the point of the spear in the Pacific. At that time, our operational theater was from the Kamchatka Peninsula to the Persian Gulf, all that geography, and you had nominally seventy ships a day under your command at Seventh Fleet. Who could not be absolutely enthusiastic and thrilled about moving to Yokosuka?

SC: Seventh Fleet in the Western Pacific and Sixth Fleet in the Mediterranean are considered the U.S. Navy, quote, "fighting fleets," end quote. What exactly does that mean?

PDM: I just covered the geography we had, and then the Mediterranean and its relationship with the European Command, that's where all the action was going to take place in the period that I was in command. For them to deserve that reputation as the fighting fleets, that's where all the action was taking place post–World War II. Seventh Fleet was the predominant fleet commander during the Vietnam issue, and the Mediterranean, all the action that took place post–World War II, there was no big combat operation conducted, but all the hot spots, Lebanon, Libya, Balkans, that was all Sixth Fleet. So that's how they deserved that bumper sticker, because that's where the action took place.

SC: Describe the typical operations and missions of a numbered fleet, especially in such a volatile area as the Pacific, Western Pacific.

PDM: When a ship CHOP'ed, change of operational command, to a forward-deployed fleet commander, Sixth or Seventh Fleet, you were supposed to be receiving what I would call an all-up round. It had been through its type training, its predeployment training, its COMTUEX as sort of a multi-unit training, and so they were to come out to the fleet commander, Sixth or Seventh Fleet commander, as ready.[99] They had been organized into battle groups and strike groups now, but then we had other things like amphibious groups in the fleet, you had individual ships, the support ships. So, like I say, nominally we would have seventy ships from the Persian Gulf up through northern Japan at the time there. Then your task as the fleet commander was to employ those ships where you thought that their contribution would be best to address the issues of the time that you had command.

You had a lot of help, because the Middle East, the Persian Gulf thing was just beginning to boil over. We'll probably get into this in a minute. There were operations down there that deserved a lot of attention. The Korean Peninsula always deserved attention. The relations with the Japanese Maritime Self-Defense Force always deserved attention. So you had a full menu to select from of where you were going to place your emphasis, and you had a great flagship, but that theater was too large and it moved too fast for you to be tied to that flagship. So you had great contact with the staff on that flagship, but you had to move around that domain to understand, to appreciate, to be able to effect outcomes. You couldn't do it all from the command flagship, USS *Blue Ridge*.[100]

SC: Were there any real-world operations that Seventh Fleet engaged in in your two years as the commander?

---

[99] COMTUEX is the Composite Unit Training Exercise to prepare a strike or battle group for deployment and is conducted predeployment.

[100] USS *Blue Ridge* (LCC-19) is the 7th Fleet command ship commissioned in 1970 and stationed in Yokosuka, Japan. She was purpose-built as a command, control, communications, computers, and intelligence (C4I) platform.

PDM: Lots. None of them made the front page of the papers, but there was lots going on. Korea was festering. I did two Team Spirit operations in which we put together real brigade-level amphibious landings in conjunction with the Korean and U.S. Army. I would go over, and that's the only time that I would move the flagship and stay on it for two solid weeks and participating, but I myself would be physically embarked with the other commanders in the command center.

I learned that the Korean Peninsula—it comes home every day now that we talk about it—if there was ever a war started, my mental plot says there has been no war in history that has been more rehearsed, that the two sides know more about each other than the North to the South and the South to the North, and they regarded each of those annual exercises supported by other exercises as critical. You may have had a reserve assignment to one of them, because they get lots of people from the reserve to support those two big exercises a year on the Korean Peninsula. So Korea occupied at least—and at certain times of year—my full attention, in addition to what was going on in the fleet.

On the other side of the spectrum, the Arabian Gulf [Persian Gulf] was heating up. You may recall we had ship escort responsibilities, and the name for them was Earnest Will.[101] While they had the commander, Middle East, two-button, in charge of the Gulf, it was during my time at Seventh Fleet where I clearly knew that was not sufficient, and we moved and established the first Joint Task Force Middle East, JTFME. I took CTF-70, Admiral Denny Brooks, and made him the first Joint Task Force Middle East commander.[102] That was the igniter to show that the U.S. was going to pay more attention and our involvement in the Arabian Gulf was going to become greater.

I had Diego Garcia activity there. I haven't decided whether I'm going to detail it or not, because very few people know about it. We brought an amphibious ready group [ARG] from the Mediterranean this time to support operations in the Arabian Gulf, as

---

[101] OPERATION EARNEST WILL initiated in July, 1987, was the convoying and escort of Kuwaiti oil tankers by the U.S. Navy that had been reflagged as U.S. registry until the end of the Iran-Iraq War in 1988. Iran had been conducting attacks on the Kuwaiti tankers to intimidate the Kuwaitis, who favored the Iraqis.

[102] Rear Admiral Dennis M. "Denny" Brooks (1934–2018) graduated from the U. S. Naval Academy in 1957 and served in the U.S. Navy until 1992. His final billet was as director, Naval Space Command and military director of the National Reconnaissance Office (NRO).

opposed to us supporting operations in the Mediterranean. We had opened up the fluidity of forces flowing one fleet to another.

So I can spend too much time on operations that I conducted at Seventh Fleet. It was a full, full twenty-four months. But a sidebar that I want to go on record was the relationships with the Japan Maritime Self-Defense Force.

SC: As the fleet commander, how much operational independence did you have?

PDM: Total. I was shocked that there was—I don't remember ever receiving an order to do something. I don't know if I phrased that correctly. But in my time at Seventh Fleet, I tried to be on top of every single operation, and I was always asking for support to do this or do that, but I do not remember being told to do something, other than that amphibious group that I talked about earlier that was in Diego Garcia.

I had watched ships move from Korea to here. I had watched ships that I knew we needed to do something about, so I would ask, since it was a national thing, I would go up to my Pacific Fleet commander and ask for an okay that we were going to take down this civilian ship because we had to look at it. But I didn't need Washington to tell me to look at that ship. I had been following that ship of interest for a long time. So I just put together a plan and told them, "I'm taking it down." They could tell me no, but I don't remember—I honestly don't remember them ever giving me an order to do something.

SC: As a fleet commander, what was your relationship to the CoCom, or area combatant commander, which was commander, Pacific Command, and under him, commander in chief, U.S. Pacific Fleet?

PDM: [*laughs*] I did not have a direct line to CinCPac, who was the unified commander. All my ships appeared on his board every day too. He came out to do his political stuff. I would dutifully brief him on the latest stuff, but other than that, it wasn't an operational-type thing.

Admiral Lyons, he was into operations. If you weren't a step ahead of him, you were way behind him. There was no equal ground. Recall, Stan, that the Cold War was still going on. We were still doing very sensitive submarine operations in the Sea of O-, Sea of Okhotsk. We were still intercepting any Soviet aircraft that flew into my AOR [area of responsibility]. So we had that dynamic. It was the Cold War, still, mentality, but it was being diverted a little by what was going on in the Indian Ocean, in the Arabian Gulf.

Admiral Lyons had a damn board, and he was ahead of me in time, and it was more than once that I'd get a telephone call pretty damn early in the morning, and there is one that I'd like to be on record with. One time the red phone rings in my bedroom in Yokosuka and Admiral Lyons, bless his heart, he said, "Can't you see what's going on?" That was the first sentence out of his mouth.

I said, "No, sir. You just woke me up." [*laughter*]

He's in the flag—I can picture him. He's in his flag plot and he has a perfect picture of what's going on. [*laughs*] He said, "Get down to the flagship!"

I said, "Roger."

So he was an operational guy, and this had to do with a sensitive Soviet issue. He was tough. You had to stay awake and be ahead of him on anything operational, particularly with the Soviets, because [*taps finger several times on book*] what's detailed in this book he did at Second Fleet, he didn't drop a trick when he became the Pacific Fleet [commander]. He just didn't have direct control of the assets, so he had to manage it from his flag plot, but he was no less as intense as he was as a Second Fleet commander in wanting every Soviet entity covered from your assets.

SC: And I might mention that the book that you just referred to is *Oceans Ventured: Winning the Cold War at Sea* by John Lehman.[103]

PDM: Correct. And the largest personality in this book is Admiral "Ace" Lyons, who was the Second Fleet commander, who strung together a lot of exercises, annual exercises that challenged the Soviets in the North Atlantic.

---

[103] John F. Lehman, *Oceans Ventured: Winning the Cold War at Sea* (New York: W. W. Norton and, 2018).

SC: At about the time that you took command, Congress had just passed and DOD was implementing the Goldwater-Nichols legislation that mandated increased jointness in the U.S. military. What is your perspective on jointness between the services?

PDM: I'll do this question great homage when I'm into my last set of questions when I'm the U.S. Atlantic commander, but quickly, I began earlier than Seventh Fleet to see the efficacy of joint operations, probably in the battle group. I believed in them, I supported them. Goldwater-Nichols I looked at with a bit of mixed reviews because I know that was centered on staff work, not operational work, to make sure a person had so much time on a joint staff. But I thoroughly believed in it operationally, and we will get into it, and I broke my pick on it. By that I meant I really got some people upset later on with my push towards jointness, but I believed in it so strongly that I used it as a template with the Japanese. And whatever question you have on that, I'll save it for that.

SC: As a fleet commander, you're constantly engaged with foreign allied and friendly political and military officials. What were your roles in terms of diplomacy and foreign relations, now that you were a fleet commander?

PDM: I personally took that part of my job, except for a few cases, and put it on the back burner. The office, the command, the Pacific Fleet commander, and the unified commander were out visiting the Pacific a number of times, and I'd let the PolMil [political/military] aspect of it remain with them, and I did not try to interfere. If they needed support in something, I'd be happy. I was there. If they needed some groundwork done on an issue and it was too far, we were local and we had a command structure throughout that domain, I was there. But I did not try to run over and see every ambassador or to get myself involved in things political. I was totally operational and in support of political military stuff.

SC: How much interaction did Seventh Fleet have with the Chinese People's Liberation Army Navy, or PLAN, in the late 1980s?

PDM: Very little, but it was a blossoming relationship, and I worked to get a port visit to China. I wanted to do that on board a Seventh Fleet ship, but I didn't quite make it. Hank Mauz, my successor, did make it, so he was able to finish up all the groundwork laid and to try to advance the nascent relationship with China that I knew was going to be important because I had made a two-week trip to China with John Lehman in 1984, and I had visited their shipyards at Dalian.[104] I was the first flag officer to visit a Chinese nuclear submarine. I had spent time with their East Fleet commander. So I knew that this was coming, this force was coming. So when I got to be Seventh Fleet, I tried to say, "We need to be engaged," but that political ball rolls slowly, so it didn't happen on my watch, but I was enthusiastic about it.

SC: What was your perception of the Japan Maritime Self-Defense Force, or Fleet, and its capabilities at the time?

PDM: This is going to take a minute. I went to the Seventh Fleet, as you know, at a relatively young age, and all of my counterparts were appreciably older. The two Japan Maritime Self-Defense Force commanders were a decade older or more, Admiral Koga and Admiral Higashiyama. I became friends of both those individuals, but I would try to watch their operational pattern because they were in Yokosuka, and I would invite them to view what I was doing with the Seventh Fleet not only in the North Pacific but throughout the theater, because the Japanese had, and do have, tremendous capability.

But I tried to get the JSDF and the Japan Self-Defense Force, the army, I tried to link them together in the most elementary ways when I first got there, and I saw four distinct stovepipes that had little to do with each other operationally, so I said, "I'm going to really make it an effort to try to bring those capabilities together in exercises, to show that if they work their capability with each of the capabilities of the other forces, that the sum is really better." How did I start that? I invited each of them to visit an aircraft carrier at sea with me, to brief them on how that battle group as it was either transiting to

---

[104] Admiral Henry H. "Hank" Mauz, Jr. (1936–) graduated from the U.S. Naval Academy in 1959 and served in the U.S. Navy until 1994. His final billet was as commander in chief, U.S. Atlantic Fleet from 1992 to 1994.

the Gulf or doing operations on the Korean Peninsula would show them how they would view the capabilities of the other services.

Admiral Higashiyama, who was the naval person who later became their chairman of the Joint Chiefs, was happy to fly to an aircraft carrier with me because he was the first Japanese pilot trained in P-3s at Pensacola. He spoke English very well. So he was happy to do that. We did it together. The air force commander was not enthusiastic, but he was air force; he wanted to fly an F-14. The army guy wouldn't touch it. Repeated invitations. "Get out of my way." The chairman of the Joint Chiefs wouldn't touch it. But Higashiyama relieved him.[105]

So during my whole two years, we worked on small exercises and working with setting up Japanese air working with naval air, because there was a barrier, and so we made great progress. I went up to an army brigade that stands watch over the Urals from the north sector of northern Hokkaido, the northern island in Japan. They wondered what in the *world* was this Seventh Fleet commander doing getting a brief from the commander of the brigade on the northern forward point of Hokkaido looking north at Russia. But that little visit influenced the army to talk to the navy.

When I came back, there was a sergeant that gave me a memento. I think I showed it to you. This memento is a hand-carved bear with its mouth wide open and its teeth showing, and that sergeant said, "Admiral, this is what we do every day. We look down the throat of the bear," speaking of the Soviets across the way. But I was able to use that. I brought that back and showed, "Here you have a sergeant in Hokkaido thinking that that's his contribution. What is your contribution, Admiral Higashiyama, to have your naval forces support that sergeant?" Hmm. We got into some key discussions.

And then the intel [intelligence] that you have, shared not with just stovepipes, but with the whole force, we worked very hard over that two-year period to bring jointness, because I was a card-carrying joint officer. Even though I wasn't one by code, I was one mentally.

The Japanese did something at the end of my tour. I got relieved of Seventh Fleet in Singapore, but they asked me to fly back to Tokyo. Up on that wall is a citation—I'm

---

[105] Also known as the chairman of the Joint Staff Council or the chief of staff, Joint Staff of the Japan Self-Defense Force.

pointing at a wall—all in Japanese, and they gave me the Order of the Rising Sun, highest degree. They've given other Orders of the Rising Sun, whatever other degrees there were. Many foreign countries have different degrees. But that one is chopped by the emperor, and Higashiyama and their secretary of defense, upon awarding of it, emphasized my work with not only the Seventh Fleet but with the Japanese Self-Defense Forces, in trying to find those areas where cooperation and operational activity brought them closer together. I was very proud of that.

SC: This was the late Cold War period before the collapse of the old Soviet Union. How much, if any, interaction did Seventh Fleet have with the Soviet Pacific Fleet?

PDM: More subsurface that surface, more air than surface, but I think I'm correct, either I or Admiral Lyons or Jeremiah knew about any Soviet combat capability—I'm not speaking of merchant ships of Russia—combat capability that roamed the Seventh Fleet without having a friend close by.

SC: Clearly, the maritime security picture in East Asia and the Western Pacific has changed dramatically since the late 1980s when you commanded Seventh Fleet. What is your perspective on this dynamic from thirty years later?

PDM: The geography is as important as it ever was and is growing in importance every day, with the rise and with the enthusiasm of the Chinese to play a greater role in having a navy that will challenge this country for command of the seas. They have proven out-of-area operations. It came home strongly one year ago this month when I happened to be in the Baltic and I was going to visit St. Petersburg, and two Chinese combatants were operating with the Russian Navy in the Baltic. How far away from that is the East Fleet in Shanghai or the shipyard in Dalian? They're there. They're present. It has changed. Full stop.

SC: Are there any other dynamics of either fleet command or Seventh Fleet during your tour that you would like to add?

PDM: No. I've used too many words in describing all of this. The wrap is, those forward commands, whether they be fleet or when they get put into a joint element, are the forward footprints of the military capability of our country, and the readiness that commanders are responsible for is sacred, and you never know when it's going to be used. Most recently, the highlight of it would be the Tomahawks fired into Syria on zero notice just months ago. The depths of it would be two U.S. Navy ships colliding with merchant ships. One would wonder, are they ready, as demonstrated by the Tomahawks? Or are they not so ready, as demonstrated by those two warships? But it's the fleet and joint task force commanders' task to make sure that they are ready, as witnessed by those TLAMs [Tomahawk Land Attack Missile] that were fired.

SC: Thank you, Admiral Miller. In our next session, we will cover your time as deputy chief of naval operations for naval warfare, as commander in chief, U.S. Atlantic Fleet, or CinCLantFlt, as supreme allied commander, Atlantic, or SacLant, and as commander in chief, U.S. Atlantic Command.

PDM: You got it.

SC: This is USNI oral history interview with Admiral Paul David Miller, U.S. Navy (Ret.). This is session number eight, question set number seventeen. The date is Saturday, July 28, 2018, and the interviewer is Professor Stan Carpenter.

SC: This is USNI oral history interview with Admiral Paul David Miller, U.S. Navy (Ret.). This is session number eight, question set number eighteen. The date is Saturday, July 28, 2018, and the interviewer is Professor Stan Carpenter. This session covers your time as deputy chief of naval operations for naval warfare, as commander in chief, U.S. Atlantic Fleet, as supreme allied commander, Atlantic, and commander in chief, U.S. Atlantic Command.

Admiral, when you detached from Seventh Fleet, you returned to the Pentagon in another three-star billet, as the deputy chief of naval operations for naval warfare. Before we launch into the particulars of that tour, tell us a bit about the general nature and composition of the OpNav organization as it existed in the late 1980s.

PDM: First, leaving the United States Seventh Fleet, where there was a huge degree of autonomy, where daily activity was fast-paced, where you could measure your successes, where you could engage on a timetable that you prescribed, where you had little interference from higher authority, to leave that one day and report *x* number of days later to the Navy staff in the Pentagon was a huge change. You take the attributes that I just mentioned and then you step into an environment where you had very little autonomy, the pace of activity was slow, the tasks didn't seem all that important because you couldn't measure your successes on a reasonable timeline. You were contributing to an overall picture that moves on a budget cycle, and at the end of it, the only way you measure your success is how many of your programs actually made it through the different budget wickets and wound up being included in the DOD budget that went to the Hill.

I think it would be a summary to say that I didn't particularly enjoy that environment. I accepted my tasks and did them, I think, fairly well, but it was two years that I felt like I was sort of in Navy purgatory, not being punished for anything that I did, but I needed a place to continue to contribute, to see if I was going to, on this merry-go-round, grab the ring that was going to take me to four stars.

When I went there, there was a set of activities going on that was grooved with the budget cycle, but nothing that I can recall that left a memory that I could talk about right now, so it was just being a dutiful staff member and moving the paper along as quickly as I could. That was OP-07.

SC: There's often a lot of confusion, especially in the media and in popular entertainment, about the precise role and responsibilities of the CNO and the OpNav organization. Can you clarify for us what exactly is the difference between an operational warfighting organization in the DOD and the administrative functions of OpNav?

PDM: DOD doesn't have any direct warfighting organizations so I think I'll start with what most people do not realize. The warfighting elements of our armed forces, that is, the combatant commanders, work directly for the secretary of defense. They don't work through their respective service chiefs, but they have a direct operational line to the secretary of defense. The Chief of Naval Operations, along with the chiefs of staff of the Army, Air Force, Marine Corps, they have the duty to train and equip forces, and after they get through a certain level of training, then their operational command is passed to the unified commanders. That's how that is supposed to work. Most of the time it works that way. Sometimes, not so much.

The CNO has that role in which he provides and trains forces. He spends much more of his time in working all the budget issues to provide the capability for future fleets to employ. If there's any place that doesn't show the immediate troops, it's when you're in a job that has a shipbuilding or an airplane building program. You're signing on to decades; you're not signing on to "We'll approve this ship today." It might not reach the fleet for five years, and most of the people that approved it the first time around won't even be there.

That OpNav place, it's hard to get everything through there, because in my experience, there are a whole hell of a lot of people that can say no, and not so many that can say yes. It was my experience that they would take this thing called coordination. On the surface of things, you would think that something was being coordinated; that means people that should know, know, would be a good thing, but that network, in its attempt to coordinate or let everybody know, puts a lot of restraints on moving actions through the CNO staff quickly. It becomes labor intensive because every coordination level requires some kind of meeting to make sure they understand what's going on and to move it forward.

It was two years that I tolerated, but didn't enjoy. Did I think it was necessary? I wonder, because the desk that I had, I wasn't there to try to prescribe the numbers of ships of the future, the airplane of the future or the submarine of the future, but I was right alongside what they called the platform sponsors, which were those, and they needed someone to pull together the warfighting capability that those hulls, air frames had, so that you'd be able to work them better in a coordinated environment at sea. So we worried about the aircraft and what bombs they would drop, what kind of antisubmarine warfare capability we would have, what kind of amphibious lift we required. So all those things that didn't belong immediately to the platform belonged to this office called Naval Warfare.

So when you understood and appreciated what was included, which was a whole hell of a lot of capability that those platforms used, and you needed to put those in the right flow to get their budgets together in coordination with the actual platform, then you had a total force moving forward. That's how it was designed. It worked that way 62 percent of the time. It never worked that way totally, except maybe in a very significant amphibious study to figure out what did the country and the Navy really need in amphibious lift and forcible entry capability.

I was never a fan of amphibious warfare. In fact, I wondered sort of why did we still have that capability. I became rather a student of it when we were doing all of this, and the percentage of littoral area that you could easily conduct an amphibious operation with surface craft is very, very small, given the coastlines that the world has. But anyhow, the Marines live and die by that capability. They want to make sure they have a forcible entry capability.

So General Gray was the commandant of the Marine Corps, and the Chief of Naval Operations was Admiral Watkins.[106] There were few that in my time there believed that I could get a total force amphibious study, laying it all out, ships, lift, forcible entry, laying the whole recipe for amphibious warfare into a binder and say Amphibious Force whatever, experience, of the Future, and have it signed by General Gray and Admiral Watkins. I spent eighteen months trying to bring that about, and when Admiral Watkins signed it, he even mentioned that "I didn't think this could be done." [*laughs*]

But that's what [OP-] 07 is; that's what they do. The Navy got rid of OP-07 for a while because they weren't seeing any results from it, but then for years, I'd say in the early eighties and maybe in the late seventies, when they got rid of it, they were missing

---

[106] General Alfred M. Gray, Jr. (1928–) graduated from the State University of New York and served in the U.S. Marine Corps from 1950 to 1991. He was the twenty-ninth commandant of the U.S. Marine Corps, from 1987 to 1991.

something. There was too much getting dropped because the platform sponsors were only really excited about platforms. But there's a whole hell of a lot of capability that you need to make sure that you analyze and do some tradeoffs of what kind of ASW weapons are better, a whole lot of analytical capability, and so they needed a shop to do that. So that's how I spent two years.

SC: What was your actual code as the naval warfare deputy CNO?

PDM: OP-07. [OP-] 02 was the platform submarines; [OP-] 03, surface ships. [OP-] 04 was somewhat like myself, it was logistics, but no one paid attention to logistics. It wasn't warfighting. So logistics was logistics; [OP-] 05 was naval aviation; [OP-] 07 was naval warfare requirements, naval warfare; and [OP-] 08 was the budget.

SC: Shortly after you took up the billet, a new CNO arrived, Admiral Frank Kelso. What was it like working with Admiral Kelso, and what can you tell us about his leadership style?

PDM: Admiral Kelso was the gentle prince. He was a submariner. He was very, very smart, analytically driven. I knew him from working for him as a battle group commander in the Mediterranean. I had known him years before in the Pentagon. There was no doubt that he would be a potential CNO candidate, but that becomes, as you know, quite political, so you never know who's going to get that seat. But he was the right person at the right time. I knew that he had a good chance, because the submarine community had a pretty good hold on the Navy at that time, and with Admiral Watkins moving, a submariner, the chances of bringing in another submariner were pretty good. But he had the intellect, he had the leadership demeanor, and, most importantly, he had the respect of the senior military leadership. So it was not a surprise, but it was an applauded event when they named him CNO.

SC: What sort of staff did you have working for you as a deputy CNO?

PDM: I had a miniaturized CNO staff. What do I mean by that? I've gone over what the CNO has, and all the platform sponsors, budget, whatever. Well, I had a flag deputy, but I had O-6s [Navy and Coast Guard captains, colonels in all other branches of the armed forces] that were linked to the platforms. Another O-6 was linked to the budget, another O-6 that was linked to the Marine Corps. So we were able to work warfighting capability that goes on these platforms with the same setup that they had with the organization writ large, and that's where all the cross-connecting took place that we put the budget together for that portion of it that needed to have the warfighting capability on the platforms.

SC: Tell us about your typical day at the Pentagon as a deputy CNO.

PDM: Boring. I had to just slow down, because after Seventh Fleet, you come into that office and things don't move the same way. You had meetings and you have decisions, CNO Executive Board decisions, at which I had a seat at the table, but you don't have things that needed to be done right now. So your day consisted of lots of meetings, and a lot of meetings internally with your respective—I would call them group commanders, because they were really wrestling with things that wouldn't fit in that single sock because we knew we had budget guidelines. So more time was spent with them than with things going on.

But we did have one element that got my attention, and I spent more time on it probably than I should have. I can't detail all of it, but we have a couple of houses outside the Pentagon that work on elite capability, and it's in the black. By black I mean they're special-access programs. Since almost all of those programs involved some type of warfare capability, we played a good role in all of that, along with the guy that ran the budget for it. So I got pretty schooled on future capabilities or special capabilities that the Navy could employ.

SC: Did you ever have to testify before a congressional committee? And if so, tell us about that experience.

PDM: The answer's yes, but there was nothing that was out of the ordinary. The vast majority of them were perfunctory. They had a budget to get experts over, and very seldom was it by myself. They just had to go through asking questions on hot buttons that they had on some capability, so you'd go over it, but it did not take up that much time, nor did I make any special contribution in doing it.

SC: You've already mentioned this amphibious warfare study and the special programs. Were there any other particular issues that stand out in your mind that you dealt with at that time?

PDM: No. [*laughs*] No.

SC: Short answer follows.

PDM: Yes.

SC: How much of your time and attention was paid to actual budget issues?

PDM: Well, the budget was handled by what they called OP-090. It was put together by other shops under the CNO, when they started with a blank sheet of paper and a justification and the costing data. That's where it really started. I spent more time on that side of the budget than on the side of the budget that put a number into the POM [Program Objective Memorandum] that required x capability. So it was activity that was important, more important as it was being put together, being added on that blank sheet of paper, than it was when the conclusion was made there and it was simply plugged into the larger budget, because then it was just a number that was being plugged in for x, y, and z. But if you didn't get it right down here, in the initial start of what you were trying to justify to buy and to put in the budget, then it was harder. So that's what I spent more time on.

SC: At the end of your tour at the Pentagon, the U.S. and coalition allies were engaged in Operations Desert Shield and Desert Storm. Did your office play any role in that conflict?

PDM: The answer is yes, but the only role that we played was that I briefed CNO, Admiral Kelso, and went with him when he briefed and I briefed the secretary of defense, the chairman, and the unified commander, General [Norman] Schwarzkopf.[107] It's a very special capability that was used in the initial stages of that conflict.

SC: The Pentagon is often referred to as the, quote, "five-sided nuthouse," end quote. [Miller laughs.] In addition to the hearty laugh, what is your reaction to that characterization?

PDM: Oh, mercy. The Pentagon has many labels. That's as good as any. I liked Admiral Rickover's approach to the Pentagon, who often said that if they were to ring off one floor of that building, one whole floor, not let anybody go to that one floor, you wouldn't miss a thing. I can understand that and appreciate that, and I believe fully what Admiral Rickover said. [*laughs*]

SC: As we wrap up your final Pentagon tour as deputy CNO, is there anything that you'd like to add or expand on?

PDM: I was quite pleased that I was given the opportunity to come back to a significant role in the Pentagon, because I knew with that I was still in the running for four stars. I had heard that they had me penciled in for a second three-star job—because you can't ask a fleet commander that had been successful to leave; that wouldn't be good form. I was going to go to be the deputy space commander. I had heard that. What in the world would that be? But it would do what some in the system wanted to do, was to get rid of me and to show that it was just John Lehman that helped me along, to get me up, okay?

---

[107] General Herbert N. Schwarzkopf Jr. (1934–2012) graduated from the U.S. Military Academy in 1956 and served in the U.S. Army to 1991. His last tour was as commander, United States Central Command (CENTCOM) from 1987 to 1991. He was the overall commander for OPERATIONS DESERT SHIELD (1990–91) and DESERT STORM (1991).

But serendipitously, the individual that was slated to go to OP-07 was the Sixth Fleet commander, but he had gotten himself into a heap of trouble and he was asked to retire because of his trouble, so they didn't have anybody that had the qualification. They could have put a new three-star in there and he would have been lost. They didn't have the background, the experience to go into a job like that. So I got assigned to OP-07. No one ever mentioned the Space Command to me. Was it true? I think so, because I knew there was a part of the system that knew that if I'd get another star, I wouldn't be easily controlled by the Navy. So that was fair.

But with this opening, I got a call that I was going to be OP-07. And when I first came back, I met with Admiral [Carlyle] Trost and I had dealt with him when I was in the CNO's Office.[108] He was very fair. We had a little history from my SecNav days, but when I came there, we reviewed some stuff. But the key thing he did that I still remember, he didn't have to do it, but I knew that I was okay with him, he doled out, himself, three-star quarters because it was such a perk. And the person that drew the thing up was going to put me in the Navy Yard someplace. Admiral Trost said, "No, we're going to put him at the Naval Observatory. He's got two young boys still in school, and the Navy Yard's no place for that." Did he have to do that? No. He didn't have to do that. That was a very fine gesture on his part to sign us to go to the Naval Observatory as opposed to the Navy Yard.

We talked about the amphibious force. He said, "We have to do this." And he's the one who told me right then, he says, "You're never going to get me to sign." He didn't use those words, but Al Gray and I signed the same document. We had a tough assignment. So it was Trost. So it all worked. It all worked.

SC: In February 1991, you were promoted to admiral and pinned on the fourth star. You'd now reached the pinnacle of a military career in terms of rank. Looking back on how your career started as a junior officer assigned to a fleet tug, what was your perspective now as to that promotion?

---

[108] Admiral Carlisle A. H. Trost (1930–) graduated from the U.S. Naval Academy in 1953 and served in the Navy from 1953 to 1990. His final billet was as the twenty-third Chief of Naval Operations from 1986 to 1990.

PDM: Wonderment. How does one start on a fleet tug and make it to four stars? What were we talking about earlier, what advice would you give someone about wanting to be a four-star? Never want it, right? Never, ever, ever want it. Just do what you did. I did what I did along the way. We've gone over it all. I've shown you fitness reports. I've read them. It was performance that brought me to that level. When I told people I started on a fleet tug, I was almost ashamed of that. But I wasn't ashamed of receiving orders as a fleet commander as a four-star, because in my view, everything that the Navy asked me to do, I did well and put one job after another in succession, that when they looked at the people, when Admiral Trost left, when they looked at those that were eligible for four stars, I was the one given—there were three four-stars selected during that time. There were more candidates than that, but there were three, and I happened to be one of them. The other two were at least five or six or seven years older than I was. So the youth aspect hadn't quite caught up with me, but it was close. [*laughs*]

SC: You were assigned as commander in chief, U.S. Atlantic Fleet from July '92 to October '94. What was the scope of your new responsibilities?

PDM: Different than Seventh Fleet. This was a fleet that was an extension. CinCPacFlt and CinCLantFlt are extensions of the CNO, to train and equip forces to be assigned to the operational commanders under the Unified Command Plan, the UCP, the CoComs, the combatant commanders, to be used by them for warfighting. Many people don't understand that. So when I go down to Norfolk, I put together the staff to make sure that we carried out every maintenance, training, readiness, people assignment task that we needed to make sure that that fleet was at its best state of readiness ever. That was my goal.

SC: What, in general, was the composition of the Atlantic Fleet in the early 1990s?

PDM: We were just about at the pinnacle of our numbers, just about. We were going to get that six-hundred-ship Navy. It didn't quite get there, but we had lots of ships there.

We had more ships than we had money. We had more ships than we had people. So it was a balance, but we were turning the screws on those ships so hard.

I had not taken over yet, but I remember watching it on television because I was in limbo. I was in the pre-command phase where you were getting acquainted with the fleet staff. I remember watching on television the air campaign of Desert Storm. I remember watching that. I remember after the change of command, of getting the list of every ship that we had there, every airplane that we had there, squadron, and then what our logistics requirements were, and I became very, very myopic on that part of my job the first *x* number of months there, because that was the big thing, then the training of what was going to flow when we relieved them. That was the fleet job. It wasn't like Seventh Fleet. I didn't fly around everywhere and see people. I didn't have an AOR. My AOR was the command center and the piers at the respective home ports on the Atlantic coast. That's not a very big AOR. It's not a very sexy AOR. It's just ships, planes, people that needed to have someone represent them, to make sure that they had all the support required to maintain that they were ready, to maintain that they had the proper ammunition loads, that the equipment was calibrated, all those things, and that's what a fleet commander does, unless you're a numbered fleet commander. Then you have the operational side. It was good.

SC: What were the command relationships and command structure up and down the chain at the time? What was the command structure that you had to deal with?

PDM: The CinCLantFlt structure is that I had two bosses. I was the component commander for CinCLant, who was the combatant commander, and then I had a dotted line to the CNO because I was his representative on the training and maintenance and support line. So those were my two bosses. And then from that, we had a relatively large staff to support all the things that we did. Operationally, we were linked with the Second Fleet. If the combatant commander wanted to get to the Second Fleet for operations in the Atlantic, that would come through me.

But Second Fleet also had a NATO hat called ComStrikeForAtlantic, commander Strike Force Atlantic, and he could have his forces employed by NATO, in a NATO hat.

And the Second Fleet commander had a NATO command hat, so when he would deploy on exercises, he would report to the NATO chain more so than to the U.S. chain. Then we had folks that did the maintenance, we had the shipyard commanders, we had the huge Navy supply center, we had all those support mechanisms under us. The submarines, they were a little bit different. They operated under ComSubLant. Operationally, he was under CinCLantFlt, and then on certain operations would go to the CoCom, but a lot of them not.

The Marines, I had commander, Fleet Marine Force Atlantic. That was the link to Camp Lejeune and the link for our amphibious forces to embark and to sail with Marines. So you had a lot of cross-turns there. The lines were clean once you understood them, but when you talk about them, they look a little spaghetti-like, but that was because you had the combatant commander, the notional U.S. commander, and then underneath all of that, you had two separate forces, an amphibious force and you had the Navy, and trying to lace it all together to put a battle group to deploy and to put an ARG [amphibious ready group] to deploy. That was our task, and we never missed one. We didn't miss one.

SC: To take up your new command meant moving back down to Norfolk, Virginia. What was family life like in Norfolk compared to the Washington, D.C., area?

PDM: We liked Washington, D.C., because of living at the Naval Observatory. Our family had great experiences there because we moved there when George Herbert Walker Bush had just been elected president and he lived at the Naval Observatory as the vice president.[109] He wins the election. The president was gracious to us when we moved into it. I had met him and Mrs. Bush when they visited *Enterprise* in the Arabian Sea when I was in *Enterprise*.

Then he was relieved as vice president, or when he moved over to the White House, Vice President Quayle moved into that house. The Quayles have a couple of sons just like we do. The younger son got along very, very well with the middle son of the

---

[109] President George H. W. Bush (1924–2018) graduated from Yale University in 1948 after service in the U.S. Navy as an aviator in World War II. He served as the forty-first president of the United States, from 1989 to 1993. Daniel Quayle (1947–) served as the vice president.

Quayles. So even though we were in Washington, D.C., it was routine family life there. Our older son, just as we were leaving the Observatory to move to Norfolk, he goes off to college, so he didn't experience it in Norfolk.

A unique thing happened there too. Admiral Edney had been the unified commander.[110] I was going to relieve Admiral Edney as CinCLant. When I moved down to Norfolk as the fleet commander, he did not want to move out of the house that he was in, which was Missouri House. So I moved into Virginia House, the big house, because he knew that he was going to leave in the not-too-distant future. So it was amazing living in that house for four years, two years as fleet and then as CinCLant/SacLant. Everything about as normal as it could be with, all of a sudden, first time we ever had three mess specialists and a house that was 14,000 square feet. Other than that, it was pretty damn routine.

Trying to find Colby a school was the hardest thing. I had gone to high school in Norfolk, Virginia, so options were to go to Norfolk Academy, go to a public school, go to the Catholic school. I felt that Colby should go to the school that most of the fleet sailors went to, so he went to Murray High School, which was a rich experience in itself, because it was probably 50 percent or more black, rich experience. It served him well, but it taught him a lot of life lessons. Chris was off to college and he was doing just fine. So here we did quite a bit of traveling, not as the fleet commander, but once I had moved to get the CinCLant and SacLant hats, I became a full-fledged member of the alliance and had to go over there monthly for meetings. So life was different once we made that transition.

I'll tie a ribbon around it and then go. To tie a ribbon around the fleet, as long as you knew that the responsibilities flowed from CNO to training and maintenance, then watching it, I became an advocate of why do we have two fleet commanders in charge of the same thing in two different fleets? Because I'd do some checking and I'd look at what the regulations were with regard to refresher training in the Atlantic Fleet and the Pacific Fleet, and, you know, they were different. I'd question. We had one fleet. Why are they

---

[110] Admiral Leon A. "Bud" Edney (1935–) graduated from the U. S. Naval Academy in 1957 and served in the U.S. Navy to 1992. His final billet was as supreme allied commander, Atlantic from 1990 to 1992. He had previously served as the vVice chief of naval operations from 1988 to 1990.

different? Well, over time, they just had separated and you had different everything. So I became an advocate of get rid of a fleet and have one fleet commander. But that took about eight years after I left, but they finally did it. Fleet Forces Command runs all the ships, airplanes, the training, readiness, support that get assigned forward or to the combat commanders. It made a lot of sense to me then, and I think it's working. I'm not sure. I hear different things. Because it kept the CinCPacFlt name. They're still in Hawaii. But I still think it's better to have one guy in charge of all the ships, as opposed to two.

Go ahead. I'll be ready to go to CinCLant anytime you want.

SC: How would you describe your leadership style?

PDM: My leadership style has never changed, never changed. I stated at the beginning, I work hard initially to find the people that work for me that can do their job without supervision. I don't interfere. I've said that throughout, whether it be CO of *McCloy* or the battle group or whatever, and I concentrate on the couple of officers that are what I would say NQR, not quite right, and then bolster them and spend my time there. I always—and I've given anecdotal evidence throughout this oral history—that I care about and that I would work with our sailors. That may have been taught to me by the boatswain that I mentioned early on, about going to the ships that he was on and working with the sailors. I've given illustrations, the CO of *Luce* being in the bilges on *Luce*, wearing flight deck jerseys on *Enterprise*. I never changed.

My leadership style was simply boiled down to find the leaders, let them lead, assist, help, or otherwise decide whether they have the capability to assume the job and complete it as they should, and if they can't, cut them off at the beginning and don't let them have a half a career by just passing them along. And then working on down the chain, have great relationships with intermediate management. For the Navy, that's the chiefs' quarters, or at the Marine Corps, the sergeants' mess. No matter where you go, know them, have them know you. And then down at the sailor level, know them, spend time with them, spend days with them. I can't remember the numbers of days that I spent working as a sailor and I was a commander, a captain, a flag officer, because I think they appreciated it and, more importantly, I knew what they were thinking and I knew where I could best utilize my position to support them.

SC: In 1992, you were named as the supreme allied commander Atlantic, or SacLant. It's a NATO command. What are the roles and responsibilities of SacLant?

PDM: I can tell you what they were on paper. In real life, it's different. On paper, this was when the [Berlin] Wall had already come down, so it was beginning to fracture. NATO was beginning to be questioned, the readiness of NATO, the exercises that they were conducting, the money that they were spending. So the paper role was still to be able to secure the North Atlantic if needed, and to support the continent as required. Did a lot of that activity take place in my two years there? Nah. A lot of meetings took place.

This is where I sort of broke with convention. I want to be careful with this part, because this is where I got myself into—not into trouble, but I was probably getting more detractors than attractors. On the U.S. side, I will start there. I mentioned a couple of times early on that I believed strongly in joint warfare. So I was at a desk, finally, where I could put something down and no one would be able to say, "You can't forward that." So initially I came up with a proposition that the U.S. needed a joint forces command to train and equip all our forces and then assign them to the unified commanders with the capability that they required to fulfill a task. Intellectually, it's pretty good, but I didn't appreciate the china that I had to break to even talk about it because of the stovepipe nature of our services.

The staff, I brought in an Army three-star to be the deputy. They said, "What do you want an Army three-star for?" Because I wanted an Army three-star. I wanted to show I wanted to make that staff really joint. Had a Marine, Air Force. I had a mini joint staff right as soon as I got into that job. And I told the staff what I wanted to do. I said, "I want to put forward a proposal to change the U.S. Atlantic Command to the Joint Forces Command." Ambitious, yes.

We all decided to put together a briefing that I could take to Washington and a plan to do it. I have it all somewhere. It was good. I made a fifteen-minute video, the staff did, and I was in that. It's somewhere. And in it I used a Rubik's Cube as my prop. The

Rubik's Cube—it's in Florida—one side of it had Navy capability, one side of it had Army capability, Marine capability, Air Force capability, the support aspects of it, intelligence, moving of logistics, the civilian side of it, different agencies. And the scheme was that if there was a capability required, it was like turning on the Rubik's Cube and—boom!—you'd come up with a set of—this is it! This is what he needs! And it should all have been trained, and—boom!—we have it. And you would be able to do it like an Army, Navy, Air Force, Marines, and then the agency capability, and you'd move them. I used to give this in talks about you'd move them just like the fingers on your hand, that fast, that easy. We do things too slow, too cumbersome.

It lit initially. In Washington, I had some problems. Of course they didn't want any of this. So with regard to the command structure, Colin, General Powell, he was the chairman, he would agree to support it, he knew intellectually this was good, but he wouldn't go as far as to give me command of the West Coast, not Hawaii, but the West Coast, where we have all our capability so I could integrate them into the overall concept. I told him, "You ask me why do we need to do this. It makes a hell of a lot of sense, you know that, budget-wise, training-wise, more efficiencies. But here's why we need it. You have just seen unfold the Desert Shield operation. Okay. Successful."

But in doing what I'm talking about doing, and with that in the backdrop, I wanted to give anecdotally how are we doing it for real versus how we train for it. So I started off with the air order of battle because I had read that there was some consternation between Navy and the Air Force and coming out with a daily op plan. So I got the colonel in charge of the Air Force ops over there and the captain that was air wing commander in the Navy, invited them all the way to Norfolk to talk with the staff about what training they went through and then operations they carried out.

After that meeting, I was absolutely positive that I was on the right path and that we would miss a huge opportunity if we didn't do this. The first time these two combat commanders had met each other was in my office in Norfolk, Virginia, after hundreds of sorties by airplanes from the Army and Air Force never being trained together, trying to sort it out on the go.

I told that to Colin. I said, "That's prima facie evidence that we're doing things the wrong way. The real world's telling us we're doing things the wrong way." Still couldn't get the West Coast. He let us and SecDef Perry—I spent so much time with him too. We became not the Atlantic Command, but the USA Command. Okay? That was a first step. It wasn't enough, but it was a step. So we changed the heraldry, so we were making progress. In the interim, we were working it out, we were putting things together. I started writing about the new national strategy and what forces would be used for. I wasn't averse, as many of them were, for the U.S. to participate in what they called peacekeeping operations at the time. I didn't like "nation building," but I looked at some peacekeeping operations as nothing more than good training activities. You have to pull everything together to pull off one of those. The ROE you had to have, but you didn't engage. So I wrote about that.

On my NATO hat, I wrote about and briefed "Retaining Alliance Relevancy: NATO and the Combined Joint Task Force Concept." Because that's what I was doing. Everything that I would send to a combatant commander that we would have trained at USACom would be a combined joint task force. I was saying, "NATO, get off your ass and start."

You talk about something that fell flat. I briefed this to this Military Committee and the ambassadors of NATO one day, and the field marshal that was in charge of the Military Committee, a British field marshal, he said to me, as I was walking out the door, "Do you know how far you have set back relations of the Navy and SacLant with NATO?" [*laughs*]

I chuckled. I said, "No, sir. I think this is a *good* idea."

He went crazy. They saw that somebody was trying to move NATO from their patterns of complacency, so therefore, in 2018, when I see [President Donald] Trump doing what he did with NATO, I applauded.[111] If you look through this book, there ain't much difference. I didn't have the horsepower to get their attention, to knock their heads together, but I was certainly advocating to restructure SacLant, and I was advocating how they should be organized for the new security environment, their coalition potential. And none of them had any capability. It's a ruse! But what they did have to put together to

---

[111] Donald J. Trump (1946–) was elected as the forty-fifth president of the United States in 2016. Previously, he was a real estate businessman in New York City.

have one NATO Combined Joint Task Force that could move when they had to made sense to me. Didn't make sense to anybody over there.

So that was the first stumbling block I had. I hit a stone wall over there, and I was beginning to hit a stone wall back here. After writing four of these things, I knew I was in trouble because they wouldn't clear this in the Department of Defense. Came back. You know how they do things, red lines. You probably know the people. The Institute for Foreign Policy Analysis at Fletcher [Fletcher School of Law and Diplomacy at Tufts University, Medford, Massachusetts], I had them print it. They did. They printed them as Paul David Miller, not as Admiral. Do you think that angered—not angered. Do you think that got some people's attention? But, still, I was on the right track. I still believe today I'm on the right track.

We continued to try to advance things. The chairmanship came up. I've got some press clippings about that, too, none of them very—I had a lot of complimentary things, but I think the worse thing they said about me, which I'm proud of, they called me an iconoclast. But I am! I am.

I anticipated that Shalikashvili would become the chairman.[112] He did. He was a good man. He was SacEur when I was SacLant. But then I got the opportunity to demonstrate what I was talking about.

SC: There's a NATO operational force known as Standing Naval Force Atlantic, or StanNavForLant, and since 2005, that's been called the NATO Maritime Group 1. What's that force and how did it come about, and what's its mission?

PDM: I think you recall that in our *Luce* review I was the flagship for the Standing Naval Force Atlantic, and its mission then was to sail a force comprised of four or five combatants from NATO nations in the Atlantic, to support general operations of the alliance. Truthfully, it was to show the flag, NATO flag, because we would participate in some exercises and then we would go to ports and represent NATO. But when I was the

---

[112] General John M. D. Shalikashvili (1936–2011) graduated from Bradley University in 1958 and was commissioned from Army Officer Candidate School (OCS) at Fort Sill, OK, in 1959. He served as the chairman of the Joint Chiefs of Staff from 1993 to 1997.

CO of a ship, we had a role in those exercises that I talked about that were conducted in the North Atlantic. They were real exercises against the Soviets. This is when I had command back in '78, '79. Move forward to when I was SacLant, what were they doing? They were going from port to port, representing NATO, and not doing too much on the exercise front.

SC: A major real-world operation during your tenure was the Haiti interdiction operation. What was that all about and why did the U.S. get involved in the Haitian situation?

PDM: This is what I wanted to get to when I said I had a chance to sort of show what I was talking about actually worked. About the beginning of 1994, we started to collect migrants from Haiti, a few and then many, and then we had migrants from Cuba, because there were press reports that we were collecting them. Where were we collecting them? Guantanamo Bay, Cuba. This goes on for weeks. The numbers on the island grow. We set up camps that you wouldn't believe. We set up facilities to feed them, clothe them, but when we got up to 30,000, we said, "Time out. We've got to do something. This ain't gonna work."

Getting Washington to move was really tough. I tried to get people down there to look at this. There's lots of literature on it. I've got crap all over. We named the operation Uphold Democracy. I've got videos, everything you'd ever want to know on it. There's been a book written about it called *The Immaculate Invasion* [by Bob Shacochis].[113]

Finally, through lots of backroom briefings telling the real story to State, telling the real story to Defense, we finally got an audience to lay down a plan to send them back. There were many in the administration that did not want to send them back. The last line of anytime I briefed it, I said, "There are nine million Haitians on that island, on that side of Hispaniola, and every one of those nine million want to become your neighbor. When do you want me to bring one there?"

If we had not taken them back, I believe strongly that there would have been a continued mass exodus and we'd have had to do something. The Cubans knew that. They were coming almost as fast. But we had two different paths. The Cubans, once they got

---

[113] Bob Shacochis, *The Immaculate Invasion: A War Story with No War in It* (New York: Viking, 1999).

outside of Cuba and they reached the United States, they could come into the country. They had that special exemption, right? Guantanamo Bay is not the United States, but you could easily slide into a decision that they made it to Gitmo, we've been caring for and feeding them. It's easier to send them back to Cuba, which was a "hostile," quote, territory, right, than to bring them in. That's what happened to the Cubans.

But the Haitians didn't have a "Get out of Gitmo" pass like that, so the only way to take them back was to take them back, but at the same time, they were having real problems in Haiti. They were having problems with the leadership that had ousted President Aristide [who had been democratically elected in 1991]. The country was falling apart. So we put together a plan called OPERATION UPHOLD DEMOCRACY, and we briefed it, and it made sense.[114] But here we used my Rubik's Cube. We put together what capabilities we needed. I wanted to make it totally joint, so it shows the 18th Airborne commander as the joint task force commander, to be on the flagship of the Second Fleet, who is going to be the deputy joint task force commander, gave them the planning responsibilities, and over a couple of months, we put together this plan called OPERATION UPHOLD DEMOCRACY.

But it became really clear during the planning for this operation that military commanders did not think joint, didn't do it. He's 18th Airborne. He wants to jump some people into Haiti. I didn't think that was necessary, but it's a great training exercise, you know, to do that. But we were going to take the country—boom!—then get rid of the regime, bring in people, so we needed more than what we were going to jump in.

I'm not exaggerating. I go down to Fort Bragg, get a brief. I see the jump and I understand that. Then I see these huge numbers of troops being transported by helo from Hurlburt [Field] over to Haiti. I'm saying, "What?" The first thing, I said, "General, I want the NC rates [nonoperational] for the last year of all the helos that you would use in that operation, because I don't think we have sufficient numbers of helos to carry those troops without having an accident." Hmm. Said, "While you're getting those numbers,

---

[114] OPERATION UPHOLD DEMOCRACY was conducted by multinational forces to restore the democratically-elected government in Haiti through economic sanction, military operations in country, and a maritime interdiction in summer 1994 to spring 1995.

give me another number. How many acres of land do you need to run that operation safely and timely?"

Okay. Fast-forward. I never really got the NC numbers. I knew it. I mean, you know, operating those damn things, I knew what they were. But I did get the number of acres. He said, "We need four acres," or five acres, something like that, to spot [land and take off] the helos.

So, I said, "Okay, need an aircraft carrier. I'm going to send out a message to the fleet commander to take the Navy air wing off a carrier. You'll have OpCon of that carrier to put Army helicopters onboard." The aircraft carrier has a big deck. It's land. We move it two miles. They have no offshore capability, so you move it two miles off the coast of Haiti. Those guys jump in, fly two miles. If you want to go one mile, I don't care. But you're not going to lose anybody. You're going to be fast. And then we were going to use a modicum of Special Forces because they are trained. So I gave them another. I gave them the *America* (CV-66) for five days or something like that, not very much, but we took the air wing off that too.

The Chief of Naval Operations went crazy, nuts. What am I doing? I'm showing that the taxpayers of this nation pay for an aircraft carrier, and I'm saying that the aircraft carrier can be used for more than one thing, and that's flying sorties out of it with jets. They did not like it, but we did it. In the garage, I have a picture of the carrier with Army helos onboard.

That operation was done. One morning we were going to have to go in hard, but hard was still soft because there was nothing to go hard against. But once they saw all this, that President Clinton was serious, so they back off.[115] So they changed it from the hard entry to just flying in, no jump, just flying into the airport, dropping some troops there and other places.

But I had the ROE [rules of engagement] because there were some bandits in Haiti that said they were going to resist. I says, "They'll resist for about eight microseconds." So the ROE was clear. If you took a shot or you thought you took a shot,

---

[115] William J. Clinton (1946–) was the forty-second president of the United States from 1993 to 2001. He had been previously the governor of Arkansas.

deadly force was authorized right then and there. We put the Marines in up at Cap Haitien. Someone fired at them. They killed six Haitians, and boom! I mean, that spread through Haiti like wildfire, that they were serious. So absolutely nothing happened. We had every contingency covered. We had engineers to get their electric power back up. It wasn't nation building, but it certainly was nation helping, because the place was an absolute disgrace. The operation worked perfectly. We take all of them back peacefully. That operation goes into the dustbin of history, and the only reason that it received no notoriety is because why? Nothing went wrong. All those moving parts, and not one thing went wrong.

SC: You were credited with being able to, as the *Washington Post* characterized the plan, quote, "quickly change the sequence of forces," end quote. Would you say that what you did in Haiti was an example of what you call, quote, "adaptive joint force packaging," end quote?

PDM: Yes. Ultimate adaptive joint force package. But all those things were against the catechism of services. They lose some control, right? When I really knew I failed, I knew I failed. The moment I got relieved, I knew I had failed. Not a good feeling. But when they slammed it [*slaps hands together*] home was in Florida probably about eight years after I created USACom, I received an invitation in the mail for the disestablishment of the Joint Forces Command.

I still think this country will go to that. It'll go to it because at some point in time, they'll wonder about the money, they'll wonder how much technology can overcome some of this hardware. It'll come to it. But anything, if you have a long enough history, good ideas surface, good ideas get batted back down until the temperature's right for the seed that you plant to grow. It wasn't right for this case.

What that did do was leave me an exit strategy. I'd done a pretty successful operation. Chief of Staff of the Army liked it. I mentioned there's not too many officers that have the Distinguished [Service] Medals from all services. So it was a good note to leave on, but inside, I knew that I'd failed, and I don't like failure. But it wasn't right.

The timing wasn't right. So that's how I ended. Started off with a tug and then failing, trying to change the command structure of the country, but it was a good ride in between.

SC: As we wrap up your time as the Atlantic commander, is there anything that you'd like to add or elaborate on?

PDM: Anybody that has the privilege to serve our nation in a top military position is one of the luckiest professionals that this nation has in its stable of citizens. The opportunity to be with all those young people for such a long period of time just gives me magic memories, just as we've discussed today. It's permitted me to recall things that happened that I haven't thought about for a long time, but were just an absolute thrill to be able to do and to participate.

I would add that service doesn't come without lots of sacrifices. Those that sacrifice in a combatant situation sacrifice the most, to be sure, but those that serve in being able to maintain the readiness and capability that the nation needs twenty-four hours a day, year after year after year after year also make lots of sacrifices. And I learned that those families that endure—and I chose that word carefully—the hardships of that service deserve equal applause with the members that participated in our military. I believe that strongly, and it was a privilege to be part of it all.

SC: Thank you, Admiral Miller. In our next and final interview, we will address your retirement from the Navy in October 1994 and your subsequent business and professional career.

PDM: Roger.

SC: This is USNI oral history interview with Admiral Paul David Miller, United States Navy (Ret.). This is session number eight, question set number eighteen. The date is Saturday, July 28, 2018, and the interviewer is Professor Stan Carpenter.

SC: This is USNI oral history interview with Admiral Paul David Miller, U.S. Navy (Ret.). This is session number eight, question set number nineteen. The date is Saturday, July 28, 2018, and the interviewer is Professor Stan Carpenter. These questions cover the Navy retirement, post-Navy business career, and your perspective on the twenty-first-century national security environment.

Admiral, you retired from the U.S. Navy in October 1994, after your years as CinCLantFlt, SacLant. What were the dynamics that led you to retire from the Navy after thirty years of service?

PDM: After two years as USACom, SacLant, I had run out of air speed and altitude, so to speak, and it was time, to use an old British naval expression, it was time to slip and proceed. All the indicators were there. I had served in most of the positions that I was eligible for. I was not picked as the chairman, which was fine. Within the Navy, I had passed up an opportunity to compete for the CNO nine months earlier than retirement because I believed so strongly in the joint application of military forces, that I liked what I was doing right there, and serendipitously, it came out that the Haiti operation showed the uniqueness of capability and how you can turn around your forces to do different things rather quickly. So it was a successful time to leave, and I was maybe even just a little smugly saying, "I'm leaving the Navy, having been able to obtain a full career and the rank of four stars, and I won't have my thirtieth anniversary till two months later." So I actually left the Navy with twenty-nine years and ten months of service.

It was a wonderful ride, and it was time to slip and proceed, as I said, to go on to another career, because I was fortunate enough to leave the Navy with a lot of runway left. So that's what I did, and I thanked everyone for the opportunity to serve. When I left the *Enterprise* again, because the ceremony was conducted on *Enterprise* on a Friday afternoon, on Monday morning I reported to my first civilian, quote, "assignment" in Charlottesville, Virginia.

SC: Tell us about your retirement ceremony.

PDM: The retirement ceremony was regal. I neither deserved nor did I ever believe this sailor would draw the attention that it did for me leaving the service. NATO was there with the head of the Military Committee, with many of the ambassadors, chairman, CNO, most importantly the secretary of defense, who I learned to have great reverence for and became friends with. So the ceremony was spectacular. I've never looked at the filming of it because I just want to hold those memories myself. For a family that had gone from seaman with my adopted dad, to four stars, and then having sons that were following, there was no better way to end it with kind words and a few accolades, and closing it out and moving forward.

SC: How did your wife, Becky, and the family feel about your Navy retirement?

PDM: Becky was probably relieved that it was finally over. I have not said much throughout these hours of her contributions, but there are no expressions that I could voice that state clearly the role that she played in whatever success that I achieved. First five years were very, very difficult because she was by herself. I spent lots of time at sea. When we had our first child, I was in my first Washington assignment, and then she had the task of having the lion's share of the job in raising those two great youngsters, because I was captive of work and then captive of going to sea again. And then as I got greater rank, more responsibilities, more time, more efforts, as is often the case with people on that treadmill, things that happen at home get cut short a little bit, never intentionally, but that's the way that, sadly, that happens. But she made up for all my shortfalls, and her support for the military, the military family, our family leaves her with lots of medals that she never got, but she deserved every one that I received.

SC: As you took your final salutes in uniform, what did you think your future would entail, and what were your post-Navy career objectives?

PDM: I did not look at leaving the Navy as a retirement. I looked at it that I had had a magnificent job for thirty years, I was leaving it, and I, fortunately, was going to another job on Monday morning. I had no idea where that was going to lead. The only thing that I knew, that I was going to try to make that next phase as successful as I had made my military phase, and it would do two things this time around: it would continue to hold the proud family together, but it would also probably monetarily secure a future for my family. So with those as my missions, I stepped off the ship, the brow, saluted, and jumped in the car and did not look back.

SC: Looking back on your Navy career, are there things that you might have done differently, different decisions or roads taken or not taken?

PDM: Too many. I was happy, I was thrilled with my Navy career up until my last job. I knew what I wanted to do, but I knew that the timing was suspect, and I knew that the breadth of what I was trying to change might be just a little too much for a bureaucratic system to handle. At least I knew that that was liable to be an outcome, so I wasn't terribly surprised that it came out that way.

SC: If you were to advise a high school student just graduating and contemplating service or even a career in the military, what would you advise them?

PDM: I'm going through that with a granddaughter right now. I'm trying to not advise her, but she's been recruited by the U.S. Naval Academy. She's a top-notch swimmer. I would be very proud if she went there, because I believe any youngster that is lucky enough to serve as an enlisted person or an officer in our military gains a degree of experience more quickly than otherwise possible in anything that they would ever do, and the job that they do right out of the gate is of such importance that they will look back forever as whatever time they spent serving, it'll be a cherished amount of time in their life. I would support any youngster that asked me about it. I would support it unequivocally that they should do it.

SC: From your perspective now as a highly successful naval officer, what do you regard as the most important career objectives that a young ensign just starting out should strive to achieve in the twenty-first-century Navy?

PDM: The objective is to do your job that you were given to the best of your ability, learn all that you possibly can about the next step, and don't worry about anything after that. Period.

SC: Well put.

PDM: If you do that, it'll take care of itself.

SC: Since your retirement and while you were still on active duty, you've published several articles on defense and security matters, such as "Both Swords and Ploughshares" and "Harmonising the Alliance with the Dynamics of Change" in the Royal United Services Institute journal and, more recently, "America, Don't Give Up on Afghanistan." Tell us about your central arguments or main points in these publications.

PDM: I think a lot about our national security future. Right now I'm myopic on a topic that I mentioned earlier in this set of interviews, and that's command of the seas. I am afraid that if we slow down in the current rebuilding of our Navy, we court trouble. It was built during the Reagan time. I mentioned that often. There was a plan there clearly, and we had a clear adversary. Things aren't so clear now. We're getting some funding, but I don't see the roadmap to x numbers of ships. I don't like counting ships, but I like counting capabilities to make sure that we aren't replaced on the high seas by a maritime force of another country.

I do not think there is any doubt—any doubt—that China wants to replace the United States Navy as that force that controls the sea lanes. We saw what happened—and I mentioned it to you before—about Great Britain. They lost it. There were probably many discussions before that. They didn't think they could ever lose it. They lost it. All of a sudden, the dollar replaced the pound. I hope this nation doesn't ever think we can't lose it, and the *yuan* [Chinese currency] replace the dollar. Times rolls on. Strategically, that would mean so much to this country in an adverse way. We're at the cusp. We can stay ahead, but it's going to take determination, it's going to take leadership, and I'm hopeful that we have it, because if we lose it, one has to look back and see what's happened to other countries that have had command of the seas and other countries that have had the reputable world's currency, and where those countries are today. That's not a line that I want the USA to fall into.

SC: You've served as CEO or in a senior executive position of companies such as Sperry Marine, Alliant Techsystems, and Litton Industries. Tell us about those experiences.

PDM: My initial business tour was with Sperry Marine, a small company, hundred-million-dollar company in sales. It had been purchased by a private equity company led by John Lehman. He knew I was leaving the Navy, and he said, "You want a chance to run the company?"

"Yes." So I went there the Monday after I retired. I learned about private equity financing quickly.

He said, "Oh, by the way, you have $78 million worth of debt. You have revenue of about ninety-some million to cover that debt. The mission is grow the company, because we want to sell it in three years."

"Okay." And we were in the field of marine instruments. The good thing we had was a recognizable name. Sperry was a vintage old name. So I won't go into what we did or how we did it, but I fulfilled the mission.

Litton Industries came in even before three years, and we had grown the company, we had instituted into the Navy a fog gyro and digital, and we were clearly ahead in the navigation instrument world, so Litton purchased it. But a funny thing happened: I was sold with the company. So I had to stay with Litton after the closing of the deal, so I had a one-year contract with Litton.

There was an opening to possibly go to Litton after I finished that one year, but in the interim, a headhunter came and asked if I wanted to put my name in the hat to be CEO of this modest aerospace and defense company called Alliant Techsystems in Minneapolis. I looked at it, and what I found it to be is after the [Berlin] Wall came down, there were quite a few defense companies that said, "All bad things have come to an end. Why do we need to have this segment anymore?" So they spun off everything related to defense to shareholders of Honeywell in about 1994, '93, something like that.

They gave a share of this new thing for two shares of Honeywell. Anyhow, it was a public company on the New York Stock Exchange.

That intrigued me to go from running a small private equity company to having a New York Stock Exchange company, so I had to meet with the person who was going to make the decision. There I got my first surprise. I wasn't going into the structure of the company; I was meeting with this young hedge fund manager from Gotham Capital who was one of the first corporate raiders. He saw that there was value in this company, so he had bought up sufficient shares to take control of it, and he noticed, he and his little staff, that we've got to start with bringing in a new CEO. So he called the headhunter. That's how I get an opportunity. They had about five or six people in the pot, as any headhunting company would.

I get set up with a meeting to have dinner with him, and then I was probably fifty-five, fifty-six. He was probably forty-two. I thought that very interesting. He had written books about investing. His name is Joel Greenblatt, very bright guy, very bright guy.[116] And he asked me a bunch of questions, and fortunately, because of my apprenticeship in which I had to learn everything from cash management to legal liabilities in this smaller company, I was able to answer business questions not like a retired admiral, but like a business dude.

He told me at the end of the thing that I should go up to take a look around, and Minneapolis would be this. I remember clearly I looked at him and I said, "Joel, if I take this job, it's going to be like taking another set of Navy orders. I'm going to go up there, I'm going to take the company and it is going to be what it is, and then it'll be my command and I'll take it from there, except there's going to be one thing that's going to change."

He said, "Yes?"

I said, "You're going to have to relinquish the chairmanship and give it to me, because I want to be responsible for the whole company. I need both positions to do that. And if that's satisfactory to you, then I'll be happy to do it."

---

[116] Joel Greenblatt (1957–) graduated from the Wharton School of Business at the University of Pennsylvania and is a hedge fund manager, investor, and author of several books on successful financial management and investing.

I looked at him, and he didn't exactly know what to say. Then he said, "Well, maybe we can start with what kind of contract would you want. Have your lawyers look." I said, "Joe, I think you missed part of my conversation. I'm going to take this like I took command of a Navy ship. There was no contract; there were just orders. So just tell me that you want me to do it, and I'll go do it. I'll leave all the remuneration up to you. I'm not sophisticated enough to know all the nuances, and I don't want to get involved with some lawyer and give you something and you give me something back. I don't want to get into that. Just write down what I'm worth to do this, and I'll go do it." [*laughs*]

He says, "This is different." But he did it.

I went up there within two weeks of when I had told Litton I was leaving, and what I found, I wasn't happy with. I did not have the premier ship in the squadron. Had a lot of debt. I had maybe four or five hundred million dollars in sales. It was a very small cap company. Had a lot of distributed assets. I went up there. Becky and I moved to Wayzata, Minnesota, established a house, and I just went to work. I had to clean up the leadership. The leadership drove me crazy. My leadership pattern of looking around for people that I knew could do the job and leave them alone, out of everybody up there in the top management, I had one. The others had to go. It was hard finding the right replacements, but I went back to offering somebody that worked for me at SacLant, an Army guy, I offered a job to him, I put in play people that I could trust, started to rework what we wanted to do, what lanes we could expand.

I bought a small company. It didn't move the needle. But then the opportunity came up to buy—you'll know the name—Thiokol, which was space boosters. It's too long to get into why that was available, but it was available. It was an auction. I knew that people would say we can't afford it, but I knew we had to have it. We put together a plan. I was bidding it against Aerojet and a company that you would say why did they own Thiokol. It was Alcoa. Alcoa owned it because they had bought a company called Cordant, which was the largest aluminum fastener company, and they're in Utah and they happened to own Thiokol because Thiokol's in Utah.

NASA didn't want Alcoa to own Thiokol because they knew nothing about rockets. One of the segments we had from the old Hercules company was rockets in

Utah, so we figured out how we could put these two together, the synergies and all of that, and we put in a bid that I knew was paying too much, but we had to have it. We won it. What do I do next? How do I pay for it? The cash streams, they had non-compete contracts, so we were good there. NASA would pay. But I had to refinance what I already had on the books, so I had to go borrow $1.1 billion from the street. The bankers said, "You're going to do what?" One-point-one. Adding Thiokol into the business that I had, it took my leverage to 5.2. That's really extreme. Nominally, a good company's at 2. A leveraged company's at 3.5, maybe 4. A superbly, highly, highly, highly leveraged company's at 5.

I went to the street. We had to sell bonds. They put together this audience in New York, all the youngsters, twenty-six, you know, they were like all the lieutenants. I gave them a brief about what we were going to do, and I just stood up, said, "Half of you have fallen asleep here. You really don't care about this stuff." That got their attention. "You've got the numbers. You all will run them, you all will decide whether yes or no." I said, "You know that I spent thirty years in the military, retired as a four-star officer. Now I'm making another run, this time in business. I'll tell you the following. If you all support this, I'll take it as I'm taking on my personal mortgage and I'll start paying back 10 percent of this mortgage every year, whatever the subscription is." I was oversubscribed by 25 percent. I drove the rate down. You'll love this rate. They wanted 9 percent because I was a junk bond. I got it down to 8 because they were oversubscribed. But that kicked it off.

Then I went into ammunition. That was the lane: rockets, ammunition, fuses. We built a great company. So we built it. One anecdote that's important, I bought Federal Cartridge, which is an ammunition company. Three months after I buy that, we look at the Army ammunition plant where President Truman grew up. He put it there. We did some research on that. It had a sole-source contract to Winchester since 1946, never competed. I said, "Since we've just bought this ammunition company, let's put in an unsolicited bid for that."

The Army said, "You can't do that."

I said, "Compete it." This was with a two-button [major general] at Rock Island. "Compete it." We had never competed it. Sounds like a good time to me. He wouldn't do it.

I went to the Naval Material Command, but it was soon enough after my leaving that he knew I was real. Had a meeting with him. He said, "They don't want to compete it."

This is what I said, and I've put it on the record before. "General, if I don't see a letter soliciting competition very soon in the *New York Times* or the *Washington Post*, one, we'll carry a front-page story of how the U.S. Army has spent millions or maybe hundreds of millions on a cost-plus contract with one company since 1946. Is that good for Army procurement?"

They competed it. We competed it with Winchester, us, and some other company. We agonized over that competition. I spent more time analyzing how much it cost to manufacture a bullet. I wanted to add one more penny to the price-per-bullet on a fixed-price contract. The guy that I trusted—I told you earlier I had one guy—he said, "No, you won't win it." [*laughs*]

I said, "Come on. I'll still win it with one penny." But he was hard. He had been a pro in this stuff. I said, "Okay, use your numbers."

We did win it. It was a competitive contract. We won it for three years, and then they competed again.

Three months later, maybe four, the terrorist attack—I mean the terrorist act, the subsequent activity in Iraq and Afghanistan. Do you know how many bullets the Army needed? It was just good fortune again. It wasn't good fortune that we're going to war, sadly, no, but it was good fortune that we had made business transactions and we were going to give a better deal to the government than Winchester would have ever given them. So that launched us. We bought other companies after that.

And then I left when I got prostate cancer, and I stayed on boards after that, and it all worked out.

SC: How well do you think your Navy career helped in your post-Navy business world?

PDM: Oh, it helped immensely. It helped with—you know, you have a reputation and you have a degree of confidence. I'd have never been able to go in and sort of lobby or, you know, cajole for competing [for] a contract. It helped immensely.

SC: And that's why retired senior naval officers or military officers are so valuable to the business world.

PDM: And not enough of them retire soon enough to have the runway I had to reach the senior levels.

SC: Right.

PDM: It's not that they can't do it; it's that they don't have enough time left.

SC: Did you ever consider a post-Navy career other than the business world?

PDM: No.

SC: Let's turn to something different. You've already mentioned you're very proud, and justifiably so, of the Order of the Rising Sun from Japan. Are there any other particular honors or awards that you are especially proud of?

PDM: Nine Distinguished Service Medals. I have five from the Navy and one from each of the other services. We talked about it during the Vietnam stuff. I never received a combat award. I was never in the position. But on the other side, I think I rang the bell. There's not too many with nine, is there? I don't think.

SC: Don't think so. If you were to recommend one overarching national security imperative to President Trump and the current administration, what would it be?

PDM: Build your Navy.

SC: If you were to recommend one overarching national security imperative to the Department of Defense, what would it be?

PDM: Change the overall format for career service in the United States military. I believe strongly that the military is a young person's game. I believe strongly that Secretary Rumsfeld moved to keep officers on active duty till they're age sixty-four was a move in the wrong direction.[117] I think the Israeli model is absolutely directionally correct. It might not be exactly that, but it's something between where we are now and where they are. We'd have a lot of people serve and a few people at the next level, and you don't need to have as many folks as we do right now in uniform, because I think you can do it with not only fewer people, you can give more responsibility to younger people, thereby narrowing out the pyramid to the top.

SC: If you were to recommend one overarching national security imperative to Congress, what would it be?

PDM: Fund the military capability of the nation to maintain the position that it currently enjoys, and on a couple of fronts might lose it if it is not supported by Congress with the strength and vigor it deserves.

SC: As we wrap up your post-Navy business career, is there anything you would like to add?

PDM: No. I've been blessed in both careers, and the military, it was astonishing, in business almost equally so, but the rewards were different. To put both of them together, one has to just look back and say thank you, Lord.

---

[117] Donald H. Rumsfeld (1932–) served as secretary of defense in the Gerald Ford administration (1975–1977) and again in the George W. Bush administration (2001–2006). A U.S. Navy aviator (three years active duty), he graduated from Princeton University in 1954 and served as CEO for several corporations in addition to his political career.

Launched in 1969, the U.S. Naval Institute's award-winning oral history program is among the oldest in the country. Used in combination with documentary sources, oral histories offer a richer understanding of naval history through candid recollections and explanations rarely entered into contemporary records. In addition, they help depict the atmosphere of a particular event or era in a manner not available in official documents.

The nonprofit Naval Institute accomplishes its history projects through contributed funds and gratefully accepts tax-deductible gifts of all sizes for this purpose. This support allows the Institute to preserve the life experiences of today's service men and women so they may enlighten and inspire future generations.

For information about opportunities to underwrite Naval Institute oral history projects, please contact the Naval Institute Foundation at 291 Wood Road, Annapolis, Maryland 21402; by phone at (410) 295-1054; or by e-mail at foundation@usni.org.

Index

Numbers
1MC (1 main circuit), 119–20, 120–37, 138
5"/38 Dual Purpose gun, 30, 30–8

A-4 Skyhawk aircraft, 157, 157–51
A-6 Intruder aircraft, 304, 304–93, 314
AAW (anti-air warfare), 251
adaptive joint force packaging, 350
admiral title, 300–301
advice
   for commanding officers, 164–65, 182, 197
   on crew illness at sea, 189
   for department heads, 82–84, 87, 90, 98, 101, 140
   on education and training, 227, 243, 296–97
   for executive officers, 51–53, 60–62
   for first-time command-at-sea officers, 249–50
   for high school students, 7–8, 13–14, 354
   for junior officers, 36, 38, 50–51, 101–2
   on leadership skills, 53–54
   on national security, 361–62
   for new ensigns, 22–23, 354–55
   for officers aspiring to department head role, 71
   for officers aspiring to flag rank, 296–97
   for post-command-at-sea officers, 239
   for senior officers, 274–75
   on taking a stand, 259–60
   on working with difficult personalities, 60–61, 87, 291–92
AFFF (Aqueous Film Forming Foam), 130, 130–45
Afghanistan War, 360
African Americans in Navy, 44
aircraft. *See also* helicopters
   A-4 Skyhawk, 157, 157–51
   A-6 Intruder, 304, 304–93, 314
   in carrier strike groups, 303–4
   cold cat (catapult launch), 111, 111–30
   F-14 Tomcat, 279, 279–82, 314
   on *Intrepid*, 157
   P-3 Orion, 184, –
   P.D.M.'s experience with, 304, 313–14
   plane guard for, 179
   S-2 Tracker ASW, 157–58, 157–51, 179
   Vietnam War, rescues during, 114–15
Air Force, U.S., 343–45
air search radars, 127, 127–42, 155
Alcoa, 358–59
alcohol use and abuse, 53, 101–2
Alliant Techsystems, Inc. (ATK), x, 356–60

Alves, Charlie, 42, 56
America (CV-66), 348
"America, Don't Give Up on Afghanistan" (Miller), 355
amphibious warfare, 332, 340
AN/SPS-29 air search radar, 127, 127–42, 155
AN/SQS-26 bow-mounted, low frequency SONAR, 155–56
Anteon International Corporation, x
anti-air warfare (AAW), 251
antisubmarine rocket (ASROC) system, 94–96, 94–25, 159–60, 244–45
antisubmarine warfare (ASW)
    battle groups for, 303–4
    destroyers and, 125–26
    Light Airborne Multi-Purpose Systems for, 115–16, 116–35
    Luce capabilities for, 251
    North Atlantic patrols during Cold War, 157–59
    techniques used in, 183–84
    weapons for, 159–60, 244–45
AOE (fast combat support ship), 303, 303–92
Apollo 12 Atlantic recovery force, 72
Aqueous Film Forming Foam (AFFF), 130, 130–45
Arabian Gulf. *See* Persian Gulf
Arabian Sea, P.D.M. as battle commander in, 307–8
Arkansas (CGN-41), 303
Arleigh Burke-class destroyers, 278, 278–80
Army, U.S., 343–45, 359–60
ASROC (antisubmarine rocket) system, 94–96, 94–25, 159–60, 244–45
ASW. *See* antisubmarine warfare
Atlantic Fleet, 338–39. *See also* CinCLantFlt, P.D.M. serving as
Atlantic Marine, Inc., x
awards and recognition of crew members, 198
awards for P.D.M.
    Distinguished Service Medals, 361
    list, xi
    Order of the Rising Sun from Japan, 327–28

B-27 Superfortress bomber (*Enola Gay*), 48–15
Bagley, Worth H., 219, 219–64, 233–35, 317
basket leave, 85
battle group commanders, 302–3, 305–7. *See also Enterprise* (CVN-65), P.D.M serving as battle group commander
battle groups, 110–13, 303–6, 306–94
Berra, Yogi, 9
billet assignment process, 69, 69–19, 143–47
Bissell, Alan, 56, 59
bitch boxes, 120–21
Blue Ridge (LCC-19), 321, 321–100
boarding parties, 178
boatswain's mate of the watch, 119–20
Boorda, Jeremy M., 287, 287–88
"Both Swords and Ploughshares: Literary Roles in the 1990s" (Miller), x, 355

Briggs, Joe, 216
British Royal Navy
    Polaris ballistic missile system tests with, 72
    traditions adopted by U.S. Navy, 165
Bronstein-class frigates, 158–60
Brooklyn Navy Shipyard, 3
Brooks, Dennis M. "Denny," 322, 322–102
Burke, Arleigh, 278–80
Bush, George H. W., 340, 340–109
Buttercup damage control wet trainer, 26–27, 162

Camp Smith, Hawaii, 260
captain's call, 197–98
captain's chair, 191–92
captain's mast, 187–88
career development, Navy
    admiral, promotion to, ix, 337–38
    awards, xi, 327–28, 361
    battle group commander, 297–314
    captain, promotion to, 264–67
    commander in chief, U.S. Atlantic Fleet, 337–43
    commanding officer of *Luce*, 240–60
    commanding officer of *McCloy*, 154–204
    Cruiser Destroyer Group 3, command of, 314–18
    at Destroyer School, 59, 68–70, 73–79, 160–61
    division officer of *Papago*, 19–36
    enlisting in Navy, 14–17
    executive assistant for CinCPacFlt, 258–69
    executive officer of *Seneca*, 37–67
    flag rank, promotion to, 295–99
    influences on decision to join Navy, 1–6, 16–17
    lieutenant commander, promotion to, 148–49, 153–54
    lieutenant junior grade, promotion to, 37
    at Naval War College, 205–18. *See also* education
    as Navy detailer, 143–49, 151–53
    operations officer of *Parsons*, 80–143
    overview, ix–x
    at Pentagon
        as command relations officer in OpNav, 218–25
        as deputy chief of naval operations, naval warfare, 329–37
        as executive assistant to Secretary of the Navy, 270–301
        as flag lieutenant and executive assistant to VCNO, 226–39
    Reserve to USN augmentation, 143, 150
    retirement from Navy, ix, 352–53
    screened for major command, 275–77
    Seventh Fleet, commander of, 315–29
    short tours, promotions and, 223–24
    supreme allied commander Atlantic, 343–51
    temporary additional duty on *Hawkins*, 68, 71–72
career development, post-Navy. *See also* publications by P.D.M.

with Alliant Techsystems, 356–60
   with Litton Industries, 356
   MBA from University of Georgia, 226–27
   Navy career influence on, 360–61
   overview, x
   with Sperry Marine, 356
carriers
   aircraft, rescues of, 114–15
   in battle groups, 110–11
   maintaining station in sector screen, 123–24
carrier strike groups (CSGs), 302–5. *See also Enterprise* (CVN-65), P.D.M serving as battle group commander
Carter, Jimmy, 287–88
CDOs (command duty officers), 28–29, 29-7, 135
celestial navigation, 33, 42–43, 119
chairman of the Joint Chiefs of Staff (CJCS), 315–16
change-of-command ceremonies, 167
charged fire hoses, 103
chief engineers (CHENGs), 117, 165
childhood
   education, 2, 6, 10
   home, 1–2
   personal heroes, 8–9
   reflections on, 15
   sports participation, 2–3
   working in Navy ships, 3–4
Chinese People's Liberation Army Navy (PLAN), 325–26, 328, 355
Chopper submarine, 72
CICs (Combat Information Centers), 125–27, 186
CinCLantFlt (commander in chief, U.S. Atlantic Fleet), P.D.M. serving as
   advocating for creation of Fleet Forces Command, 341–42
   assignment to, 338
   command structure, 339–40
   composition of fleet, 338–39
   family life, 340–41
   leadership style during, 342–43
   roles and responsibilities, 338
CinCPacFlt (commander in chief, U.S. Pacific Fleet), 257–60, 271, 324. *See also* executive assistant for CinCPacFlt, P.D.M. serving as
classified communications, 94
Clausewitz, Carl von, 197, 211
Clinton, William J. "Bill," 349, 349-115
closest point of approach (CPA), 76, 76-20
CNOs (Chiefs of Naval Operations), 230, 289, 330–32, 338–39, 349. *See also* OpNav, P.D.M. serving as command relations officer
Coast Guard icebreaker ship, P.D.M. on, 31
cold cat (catapult launch), 111, 111-30
cold iron, 104–5
Cold War
   ASW patrols during, 157–59
   Luce deployed to North Atlantic during, 252–53, 252-71

Maritime Strategy major plans, 290
  P.D.M.'s Seventh Fleet command during, 323–24, 328
  Soviet Pacific Fleet, 328
  Soviet submarine technology and, 283
  submarine detection during, 184–85
College of William & Mary, Virginia, ix, 11–12
Combat Information Centers (CICs), 125–27, 186
ComDesGru 3 (Cruiser Destroyer Group 3), P.D.M.'s command of, 314–18
command duty officers (CDOs), 28–29, 29–7, 135
commanding officers (COs)
  advice for assuming new command, 164–65
  advice for inspection results, 182
  captain's chair and, 191–92
  CEOs compared, 66
  chaotic environments, preparing for, 197
  essential actions and behaviors of, 195–96
  executive officers, relationships with, 48–49, 54–55, 250
  illness of crew at sea, challenges of, 189
  leadership skills of, 141–42, 173–74
  of *Luce*. *See* Luce
  of *McCloy*. *See* McCloy
  as mentors, 49–50
  night orders, 192
  personal appearance and, 195
  senior officers, relationships with, 196
  sleeping on ships, 175
  zone inspections and, 196–97
Command of the Seas (Lehman), 281, 281–84
command personal presence, 169
commodore title, 299–301
communications aboard ships
  1MC (1 main circuit), 119–20, 120–37, 138
  bitch boxes, 120–21
  classified, 94
  Combat Information Centers, 125–27
  EMCON (emissions control), 122, 122–40
  engine order telegraphs, 120
  FleetTac radio circuit, 124
  radio silence and, 122, 122–40
  signal flags, 122
  sound-powered phones, 121
  TTY teletype machines, 193
communications officers, 80
component commanders (COCOMs), 289
Composite Unit Training Exercise (COMTUEX), 321, 321–99
ComStrikeForAtlantic (Commander Strike Force Atlantic), 339–40
conditions of damage control readiness, 137
Congress. *See also specific legislation*
  commodore title, changes to, 299–301
  national security advice for, 362
  P.D.M. as EA to SecNav and, 273, 281

P.D.M. testifying before committees of, 334–35
CPA (closest point of approach), 76, 76–20
Crestar Bank, x
Crestar Financial Corporation, x
Crowe, William J., Jr., 219, 219–63, 315–16
CRTs (cathode ray tubes), 127
CSGs (carrier strike groups), 302–5. *See also Enterprise* (CVN-65), P.D.M serving as battle group commander
Cuba, Guantanamo Bay
   Haitians migrating to Cuba, 347–48
   Papago deployment to, 20–21, 27
   Seneca deployment to, 47, 54
cultural values, 9. *See also* wardroom culture

damage control and fire brigades
   Aqueous Film Forming Foam for, 130, 130–45
   conditions of readiness and, 137
   Damage Control Central, 128–29
   damage control lockers, 128–29
   Halon system and hoses for, 129
   Oxygen Breathing Apparatus for, 32, 129, 129–44
   Papago experiences with, 32
   Parsons experiences with, 94–95, 95–26
   training on, 26–27, 128–29, 162
Damage Control Central (DCC), 128–29
dead man's stick, 117
Dead Reckoning Tracers (DRTs), 44, 44–12, 126, 186
Decca Navigator System, 46, 46–14, 125
"the declination of Aries," 43
delegation of authority, 66–67
department heads
   advice for, 82–84, 87, 90, 98, 101
   aspirants to, 71
   discipline issues of sailors and, 85–86, 100–101
   division officers, relationships with, 80–81
   efficiency evaluations and, 52
   ideal, 98
   junior officers
      fitness reports, 83–84
      relationships with, 82
   leadership skills of, 87
   moral authority and, 88
   personal issues of sailors and, 84–85
   responsibilities of, 78
   senior leadership, relationships with, 81, 86–87
   time management and, 140
Department Head School, Surface Warfare Officers School (SWOS), Newport, 23, 23–4. *See also* Destroyer School, Newport
deputy chief of naval operations, naval warfare, P.D.M. serving as, 329–37
   assignment to, 329–30

budget issues, 335
congressional committee testimonies, 334–35
roles and responsibilities, 331–33
staff of, 333–34
typical day, 334
DesRon 15 (Destroyer Squadron 15), 99
DesRon 28 (Destroyer Squadron 28), 156–57
destroyer escorts (DEs), 158–59
destroyer leaders (DLs), 244
destroyers
aircraft, rescues of, 114–15
in battle groups, 110–13
bridge watch and functions of watch standers, 117–22
Combat Information Centers on, 125–27
helicopters on, 115–16, 115–34
weapons systems of, 112
Destroyer School, Newport
coursework at, 69–70, 73–76
faculty of, 74–75
foundational knowledge for, 78
maintaining station in sector screen, practicing, 123
P.D.M. attending, 23, 59, 68–70, 73–79, 160–61
Prospective Commanding Officer School, 161, 163
renamed, 23–4
typical day, 73
detailing and billet assignment process, 69, 69–19, 143–47
discipline issues, 85–86, 100–101, 187–88
Distinguished Service Medals, 361
division officers, 52, 70, 80–81, 83, 89, 136. *See also Papago*, P.D.M. serving as division officer of
Dixon, Alan J., 316–18, 316–97
Donaldson Company, Inc., x
dream sheets, 69, 69–19, 143–44
Drone Anti-Submarine Helicopter (Gyrodyne QH-50 DASH), 115, 115–34
DRTs (Dead Reckoning Tracers), 44, 44–12, 126, 186
Duxbury Bay (AVP-38), 2

Edney, Leon A. "Bud," 341, 341–110
education
advice on, 227, 243, 296–97
childhood, 2, 6, 10
Destroyer School, 23, 59, 68–70, 73–79, 160–61
Florida State University, BS in economics from, ix, 11–14, 17
Harvard Business School Executive Management Program, ix, 239–43
junior college in Jacksonville, Florida, 6, 11
Naval War College, 205–18
curriculum, 209–11
effect on career, 217–18
extracurricular and social activities, 215–16
fitness report from, 208
officers' attitudes toward, 212–13

        teaching methodology, 210
        Turner Revolution and, 205–7, 206–56
        typical day, 211–12
    Naval War College Intermediate Learning Curriculum, 158
    Navy Firefighting School, 26–27, 162
    Officer Candidate School, 15, 15–1, 18–19, 24–25
    Prospective Commanding Officer School, 160–63, 192
    University of Georgia, MBA from, ix, 226–27, 242
    William & Mary, transfer from, ix, 11–12
efficiency evaluations, 52–53
electronics maintenance officers, 80
electronics technicians, 126, 126–41
electronic warfare technicians, 126, 126–41
EMCON (emissions control), 122, 122–40
engineering officer of the watch (EOOW), 27–28
engine order telegraphs (EOTs), 120
Enola Gay (B-27 Superfortress bomber), 48–15
Enterprise (CVN-65)
    commissioning of, 312–96
    P.D.M serving as battle group commander
        aircraft experience for, 304
        billet selection process for, 306–7
        daily staff briefings, 308–9
        flagship relations, 312
        leadership skills for, 305–6, 309
        lessons from, 313–14
        in Mediterranean Sea during Operation El Dorado Canyon against Libya, 309–12, 310–95
        preparation for, 297–302
        promotion to, 295–97
        roles and responsibilities, 302–9, 306–94
        typical day, 307–8
    P.D.M.'s retirement ceremony on, 352
evaporators for freshwater, 155–56, 171
executive assistant for CinCPacFlt, P.D.M. serving as, 258–69
    assignment to, 238, 258
    early selection for captain and, 264–67
    family life, 263–64
    fitness reports from, 272
    Operation Eagle Claw, 261–62, 261–75
    orders for, 258
    roles and responsibilities, 261, 264
    typical day, 262–63
executive assistant to SecNav, P.D.M. serving as, 270–301
    commodore title, Navy changes to, 299–301
    expansion of Navy and, 278–79, 283
    family and social life, 293
    interview for, 270–71
    lessons from, 291–92, 302
    Maritime Strategy major plans and, 290
    mentors during, 297–98
    personnel assignments, 286–87

    physical fitness during, 292–93
    relationships with senior commanders, 280–81
    roles and responsibilities, 272–73, 281–82
    screened for major command during, 275–77
    selection for, 270–72, 274–75
    service jointness and, 287–90
    shipbuilding program, 285–86
    typical day, 283–85
executive assistant to VCNO, P.D.M. serving as. *See* flag lieutenant and executive assistant to VCNO, P.D.M. serving as
executive officers (XOs). *See also Seneca* (ATF-91), P.D.M. serving as executive officer of
    commanding officers, relationships with, 48–49, 54–55, 250
    delegation of authority and, 66–67
    difficult superiors, relationships with, 60–61
    fitness reports of junior officers, 52–53
    junior officers, relationships with, 50–51
    leadership skills of, 53–54, 60–62, 64–65
    as mentors, 49–50
    roles and responsibilities of, 65–66
    senior leadership, relationships with, 49
    wardroom culture and, 51–52

F-14 Tomcat aircraft, 279, 279–82, 314
"fam fire off the fantail," 103
family
    granddaughter, Naval Academy recruitment of, 354
    Japan, moving to, 320
    Naval Observatory, living in, 340–41
    son: Chris
        birth, 147–48
        childhood, 203–4, 272
        college, 341
    son: Colby, 272, 340–41
    step-father: influence on career choice, 1–4, 163
    wife: Becky Miller (Norcross)
        child rearing and financial management of home, 203–4
        education, 12, 17
        life in Norfolk, 36–37
        marriage to P.D.M., 20
        meeting Princess Grace in Monaco, 47–48
        as Navy wife, 29, 58, 105–6, 173, 255
        retirement of P.D.M. and, 353
        San Diego, move to, 79–80
        support for P.D.M.'s career, 17–18, 353
        Washington, D.C., family life in, 147–48, 151, 224
Federal Cartridge, 359–60
feed water, 155–56, 171
fire brigades. *See* damage control and fire brigades
Firefighting School, 26–27, 162
fitness reports

department heads writing for junior officers, 83–84
executive officers writing for junior officers, 52–53
of P.D.M.
    as commanding officer for *Luce* (DLG-7/DDG-38), 244–45, 253–54
    as commanding officer for *McCloy* (DE-1078/FF-1078), 157, 158, 200, 205–6, 224
    as command relations officer for OpNav, 225–26
    as division officer for *Papago*, 34
    as executive assistant for CinCPacFlt, 272
    as executive officer for *Seneca* (ATF-91), 60
    as flag lieutenant and executive assistant to VCNO, 237
    from Naval War College, 206–9
    as operations officer for *Parsons* (DDG-33), 89, 91, 97
    for promotion to captain, 267
    for promotion to lieutenant commander, 148–49
    for promotion to Seventh Fleet command, 317–18
    for temporary additional duty on *Hawkins* (DD-873), 72
as primary-source historical records, 268
Fitzgerald (DDG-62), 134–35, 135n46, 201–3
flag lieutenant and executive assistant to VCNO, P.D.M. serving as, 226–39
    challenges in, 239
    fitness reports, 237
    qualification for, 226–27
    roles and responsibilities, 231–38
    selection as, 225–26
    traits and behaviors learned, 238
    typical day, 234–35
flag rank
    advice for officers aspiring to, 296–97
    P.D.M. promoted to, 295–99
    selection process for, 297
Flanagan, William J. "Bud," 97, 97–28
fleet exercises, *Seneca* and, 47
Fleet Forces Command, 342
Fleet Marine Force Atlantic, 340
Fleet Rehabilitation and Modernization (FRAM) program, 30, 30–8, 72
Fleet Seminar Program (FSP), 214
FleetTac (Fleet Tactical) radio circuit, 124
Fletcher Scholl of Law and Diplomacy, Tufts University, 346
Florida State University (FSU), ix, 11–14, 17
Forrestal (CVA/CV-59), 26, 26–6
FRAM (Fleet Rehabilitation and Modernization) program, 30, 30–8, 72
fueling detail, 130
Furuno radar, 197

Garcia-class fast frigates, 159
Gearing-class destroyers, 72
geedunk stand, 132
General Quarters (GQ), 32–33, 32–9
GI-UK Gap, 252–53, 252–71
Gladman, Denny, 304

goal setting and meeting goals, 2, 60, 256–57, 272–73, 278–79, 338
Goldie, (Commodore), 259
Goldwater, Barry, 287, 287–89
Goldwater-Nichols Act (1986), 287–88, 287–89, 325
Goodman, Robert, 284
Grace (Princess of Monaco), 47–48
Gray, Alfred M., Jr., 332, 332–106, 337
Greenblatt, Joel, 357, 357–116
Greenwich Bay (AVP-41), 2
Guantanamo Bay, Cuba
    Haitians migrating to Cuba, 347–48
    Papago deployment to, 20–21, 27
    Seneca deployment to, 47, 54
guided missile destroyer leaders (DLGs), 244
guided missile destroyers (DDGs), 245–46, 251
Gulf War, 336, 339, 344
gun decking, 63–64, 63–17
gun lines, 110–13
gunnery exercises, 185–86
guns vs. missiles on ships, 184
Gyrodyne QH-50 DASH (Drone Anti-Submarine Helicopter), 115, 115–34

Haiti interdiction operation, 347–50
Halon fire suppression, 128, 128–43
Hannagan, (Captain), 253–54
harassment and interdiction (H&I) fire, 109, 111, 113–14
"Harmonising the Alliance with the Dynamics of Change" (Miller), x, 355
Harvard Business School Executive Management Program, ix, 239–43
Hawkins (DD-873)
    FRAM program and, 72
    P.D.M.'s temporary additional duty on, 68, 71–72
Hayward, Thomas B., 286, 286–86
helicopters
    delivering sailors to ships, 116–17
    helo in-flight refueling for, 115–16, 157–58
    Light Airborne Multi-Purpose Systems, 115–16, 116–35
    vertical replenishment by, 137
helmsmen, 120
helo in-flight refueling (HIFR), 115–16, 157–58
Higashiyama (Admiral), 326–28
highlining, 116
Hite, John, 164
Holcomb, M. Staser, 317, 317–98
holding quarters, 139
holidays under way, 188
Holloway, James L., III, 219, 219–64
homecoming following deployment, 188–89
Honeywell, 356–57
Hunter-Killer Group (HUK) deployments, 157, 183
Huntington Ingalls Industries, Inc., x

The Immaculate Invasion: A War Story with No War in It (Shacochis), 347, 347–113
Imperial Japanese Navy, 129
Inman, Robert R. "Bobby," 317, 317–98
innovation, 197. *See also* technology improvements
Inspection and Survey (INSURV), 180
Institute for Foreign Policy Analysis, 346
International Code of Signals (HO 102), 122, 122–39
international commerce and trade, 313
Intrepid (CV/CVA/CVS-11), 157, 178–79, 183
Iran, Operation Eagle Claw in, 261–62, 261–75
Iran-Iraq War, 322–101
Iraq War, 360
Italian navy, 41

Jacksonville, Florida, P.D.M. living in, 5–6, 11
Jacksonville University, Florida, 6, 11
Japan
   atomic bombing of, 48–15
   Imperial Japanese Navy, 129
   Order of the Rising Sun awarded to P.D.M., 327–28
   P.D.M. and family move to, 320
   Seventh Fleet, P.D.M. as commander of, 315–29
Japanese Maritime Self-Defense Force, 321, 326–27
Japan Self-Defense Force (JSDF), 326–28
Jeremiah, David E., 287, 287–87, 318
J.F. Lehman & Company, x
John F. Kennedy (CV-67), 115
John S. McCain (DDG-56), 134–35, 135–46, 201–3
Johnson, C. J., 156–57, 199–200
Johnson, Samuel, 190
Joint Chiefs of Staff (JCS), 221, 288–89
Joint Professional Military Education (JPME), 212–13
Joint Task Force Middle East (JTFME), 322
junior officers
   advice for, 36, 38, 50–51, 101–2
   department heads, relationships with, 82
   duty department head duties, 104
   fitness reports on, 52–53, 83–84
   navigation, learning, 173–74
   officer of the deck duties, 102–4
   shore patrol officer duties, 101
junior officers of the deck (JOODs), 119

Kelly, Jim, 97
Kelso, Frank B., II, 278, 278n80, 309, 315, 333
Knox-class fast frigates, 159, 303–92
Koga (Admiral), 326
Korean Peninsula, fleet exercises on, 322

Lafore, Laurence D., 209–59
LAMPS helicopters, 115–16, 116–35
landing parties, 178
Landing Ship Medium (Rocket) LSM(R)s, 114, 114–33
leadership skills
  adversity and, 158
  advice on, 53–54
  of Bagley, 237–38
  of battle group commanders, 305–6, 309
  of commanding officers, 141–42, 173–74
  delegation of authority and, 66–67
  of department heads, 87
  differences in, 233
  of executive officers, 53–54, 60–62, 64–65
  of Kelso, 333
  lack of, 84
  leadership styles and, 64–65, 89–90, 168, 192–93
  of Lehman, 277–78
  of Long, 233–34, 237
  moral authority and, 53–54, 61, 88, 101
  of officers of the deck, 134
  of P.D.M.
    childhood influences on, 3
    CinCLantFlt and, 342–43
    Luce command and, 256
    McCloy command and, 168, 192–93
    Papago and, 38
    Parsons and, 89–90
    Seneca and, 43–44, 63, 64–65
  personal problems of sailors and, 53–54, 84–85
  rapport with sailors, 53–54
  of Shear, 235–36
  subtlety in, 64–65
  wardroom culture and, 51–52
  of Zumwalt, 229, 245
lee helmsmen, 120
Lehman, John
  background of, 270–71
  Command of the Seas, 281, 281–84
  commodore title, Navy changes to, 300–301
  expansion of Navy and, 278–79
  on firing of Admiral Rickover, 281–82
  improvements to office and Navy, 272–73
  leadership style, 277–78
  Oceans Ventured: Winning the Cold War at Sea, 324, 324–103
  personnel assignments by, 286–87
  relations with senior officers, 280
  selection of P.D.M. as commander of Seventh Fleet and, 315, 318–19
  selection of P.D.M. as executive assistant, 271–72

Sperry Marine, purchase of, 356
  Strike University, creation of, 284–85
liberty ports
  favorites of P.D.M., 47–48, 55–56, 99–101
  junior officers, issues with, 100–102
  preparing crew for, 190
  rope yarn liberty, 131–32
  shore patrol officers for, 101
Libya, Operation El Dorado Canyon in, 309–11, 310–95
Light Airborne Multi-Purpose Systems (LAMPSs), 115–16, 116–35
limited duty officers (LDOs), 24, 24–5
Litton Industries, Inc., x, 356
littoral areas
  amphibious warfare capabilities and, 332
  submarine threats to, 184–85
Long, Robert L. J.
  commander in chief of Pacific, 257–58, 261–63
  fitness reports for P.D.M., 272, 317
  leadership style of, 233–34, 237
  as mentor to P.D.M., 298
  Operation Eagle Claw, 261–62, 261–75
  overview of service, 233–68
The Long Fuse (Lafore), 209, 209–59
lookouts, 118. *See also* watch standing
LORAN (Long Range Navigation), 21, 21–3, 42, 119
Luce (DLG-7/DDG-38), P.D.M. serving as commanding officer of, 240–60
  complexity of ship, 247
  deployments of, 252–53, 257
  family life, 255
  fitness reports from, 244–45, 253–54
  leadership skills, 256
  missions and warfare areas of, 251
  navigating, 251–52, 253
  nuclear weapons inspections, 258–60
  overview of ship, 241–69, 251
  request for command of, 240–41, 248–49
  span of control, 250
  wardroom culture, 255
  weapons system of, 244–45
Lyons, James A. "Ace," Jr., 271, 271–77, 311, 318, 323–24

maneuvering (MO) board, 76–78, 123, 175
Marcos, Ferdinand E., 262, 262–76
Marines, U.S., 332, 340, 343–45
Maris, Roger, 9
maritime interdiction operations, 177
Mauz, Henry H. "Hank," 326, 326–104
maximum condition of readiness, 32–33
Mayport, Florida, 246, 255
McCloy (DE-1078/FF-1078), P.D.M. serving as commanding officer of, 154–204

assignment to, 154
ASW work in North Atlantic, 156–59
change-of-command ceremony, 164, 167
Combat Information Center, 186
communications aboard, 193
education for, 160–61
first day on, 163–64
fitness reports from, 157, 158, 200, 205–6, 224
freshwater issues, 155–56, 171
impression of warfighting capability, 166–67
innovations and improvements on, 197
inspections of, 179–82
last day on, 201
leadership style, 168, 192–93
navigating, 155, 172–74
pre-overseas movement, 170–71
refresher training of, 181
shipyard period for, 182–83
staff meetings and wardroom culture, 169
storm and loss of mast, 155
submarine detection on, 184–85
typical day at sea, 174–76
typical day in port, 168–69
underway replenishment of, 176–77
weapons system on, 159–60, 185–86
McKee, Kinnaird R. "Ken," 282, 282–85
Mediterranean Sea
   P.D.M. as battle commander in, 308–10
   Seneca deployment to, 41–42, 47
mentors
   for new junior officers, 27–28, 82
   of P.D.M., 297–98
   XOs and COs as, 49–50
Military Sealift Command (MSC), 33, 33–10
missile exercises, 186–87
missiles vs. guns on ships, 184
mission and vision statements, 60, 194
Mk-16 missile launchers, 159
Mk-29 air search radar, 127
Mk-33 three-inch guns (3"/50), 159
Mk-46 torpedoes, 159, 244
moral authority, 53–54, 61, 88, 101
Morris, Robert, 151
motor whaleboats, 178–79
Mr. Roberts (film), 30
MSC (Military Sealift Command), 33, 33–10

NATO (North Atlantic Treaty Organization), 214, 214–60, 253, 339–40, 345–47. *See also* SacLant, P.D.M. serving as
NATO Maritime Group 1, 346–47. *See also* StanNavForLant

Naval Academy, 16
naval gunfire liaison officers (NGLOs), 109–10
naval gunfire support (NGFS), 108–14, 125–26
Naval Material Command, 360
Naval Observatory (Washington, D.C.), 340
Naval Special Warfare Command, 114, 114–32
Naval War College, Newport
   graduate degree program of, 214
   Intermediate Learning Curriculum, 158
   international program of, 214–15
   P.D.M. attending, ix, 158, 201, 205–18. *See also* education
   Turner Revolution and, 205–7, 206–56
navigation
   celestial, 33, 42–43, 119
   instrument companies for, 356
   learning, 173–74
   LORAN (Long Range Navigation), 21, 21–3, 42, 119
   on *Papago*, 21, 24, 29, 33, 36
   on *Parsons*, 119, 126, 136
   pre-departure navigation briefs, 172
   satellite navigation (SatNav), 119, 130–31
   on *Seneca*, 42–43, 54
   Suez Canal, navigating battle group through, 309–11
Navy, U.S.
   African Americans in, 44
   battle groups, 303–5
   British Royal Navy traditions adopted by, 165
   change-of-command ceremonies, 167
   command of the seas, continuation of, 355–56
   commodore title, changes to, 299–301
   detailing and billet assignment process, 69, 69–19, 143–47
   flag selection process, 297
   Fleet Forces Command, 342
   Fleet Rehabilitation and Modernization program, 30, 30–8, 72
   Military Sealift Command, 33, 33–10
   Officer Candidate School, 15, 15–1, 18–19, 24
   P.D.M. advocating for joint forces command, 343–46, 350–51
   Reagan administration expansion of, 255, 255–72, 270–71, 273, 278–79, 283, 285–88
   recategorization of ships, 245–46
   selection process for captains, 264–67
   service jointness and, 287–90, 325
   surface squadron vs. battle group commander roles, 302–3
   surface warfare officers, creation of designation, 107
   trade and international commerce, role in, 313
   Vietnam War, effect of, 231, 254
Navy Achievement Medal (NAM), 198
Navy Bureau of Personnel, P.D.M's detailing assignment at, ix, 143–49, 151–53
Navy Enlisted Scientific Education Program (NESEP), 81, 81–23
Navy Firefighting School, 26–27, 162
Navy Reserve augmentations, 194
Navy Tactical Data System (NTDS), 127

Navy Weapons Acceptance Inspections (NWAIs), 159, 182
Navy Weapons Nuclear Technical Proficiency Inspection (NTPI), 159, 180, 182
NEO operations, 172–73
New Jersey (BB-62), 109, 111, 284
Newport, Rhode Island. *See also* Naval War College, Newport
    Naval fleet leaving, economic impact of, 215
    P.D.M. attending Destroyer School in, 23, 59, 68–70, 73–79, 160–61
    P.D.M. moving back to, 161–62
    P.D.M.'s childhood in, ix, 1
    Surface Warfare Officers School, 23, 23–4, 76, 76–20. *See also* Destroyer School
NGFS (naval gunfire support), 108–14, 125–26
NGLOs (naval gunfire liaison officers), 109–10
Nichols, William, 287, 287–89
Nimitz, Chester W., 258, 258–73
Nixon, Richard M., 229, 229–66
nonjudicial punishment (NJP), 187–88
Norfolk, Virginia
    family life in, 36–37
    moving to Virginia House, 341
    P.D.M.'s childhood home in, 1–2
North Atlantic
    ASW patrols during Cold War, 156–59, 186, 346–47
    fleet exercises in, 186
    Luce deployments to, 122, 252–53, 252–71
    SacLant position and, 343, 347
    SOSUS system installation in, 46, 125
Northern Wedding exercises, 186, 249, 253
NTDS (Navy Tactical Data System), 127
NTPI (Navy Weapons Nuclear Technical Proficiency Inspection), 159, 180, 182
nuclear weapons
    on *Luce*, 258–60
    on *McCloy*, 159–60
    Nuclear Technical Proficiency Inspection (NTPI), 159, 180, 182, 259–60
    Nuclear Weapons Acceptance Inspection (NWAI), 159, 182, 259
    on surface ships, 248
Nunn, Samuel A., 316–18, 316–97
NWAIs (Nuclear Weapons Acceptance Inspections), 159, 182, 259

OBA (Oxygen Breathing Apparatus), 32, 129, 129–44
Oceans Ventured: Winning the Cold War at Sea (Lehman), 324, 324–103
Office of Program Appraisal (OPA), 278
Officer Candidate School (OCS), 15, 15–1, 18–19, 24–25
officer of the deck (OOD)
    characteristics and personality traits of, 134–35
    defined, 113–31
    duties and responsibilities of, 102–3, 119–20, 126, 133
    P.D.M. as, 113, 117, 134–35
    qualification regime for, 133–34
    security issues and, 103–4
    underway replenishment and, 138–39, 177

Officers' Club, Subic Bay, 100
Olongapo City, Philippines, 99
On War (Clausewitz), 211
Operational Propulsion Performance Examination (OPPE), 256
Operational Readiness Inspections (ORIs), 179–80
Operation Desert Shield/Desert Storm (1990–1991), 336, 339, 344
Operation Eagle Claw (1980), 261–62, 261–75
Operation Earnest Will (1987), 322, 322–101
Operation El Dorado Canyon (1986), 309–11, 310–95
operations officers. *See also Parsons* (DDG-33), P.D.M. serving as operations officer of
    general duties of, 70, 93–94, 96
    naval gunfire support missions and, 113
    preparation of, 75
operations specialists (OSs), 126, 126–41
Operation Uphold Democracy (1994–1995), 347–50
OpNav, P.D.M. serving as command relations officer in OP-603D, 218–25
    assignment to, 208
    career development and, 221
    difference from being at sea, 221–22
    family life, 224
    fitness reports from, 225–26
    roles and responsibilities for, 218–20
    selection for, 218
    typical day, 220–21
OpNav organization, 218, 330–33
OPPE (Operational Propulsion Performance Examination), 256
Order of the Rising Sun from Japan, 327–28
ORIs (Operational Readiness Inspections), 179–80
Oxygen Breathing Apparatus (OBA), 32, 129, 129–44

P-3 Orion aircraft, 184, 184–54
Pacific Fleet. *See* CinCPacFlt
Papago, P.D.M. serving as division officer of
    assignment to, 19–20
    family life, 29
    fire aboard, 128
    first day on, 27–28
    fitness reports from, 34
    General Quarters, 32–33, 32–9
    lessons learned from, 33–34, 38
    navigation of, 21, 24, 29, 33, 36
    roles and responsibilities, ix, 21, 28–32, 34–35
    ship overview and duties, 19–2
    Thor cable layer, assistance for, 46, 125
    wardroom culture, 24, 51
    worst and best days on, 35–36
Parsons, William S. "Deak," 48–15, 68
Parsons (DDG-33), P.D.M. serving as operations officer of, 80–143
    arriving onboard at Kaohsiung, 80, 92–93
    assignment to, 48, 68

best and worst days on, 90–91
  bridge watch and functions of watch standers, 117–19
  Combat Information Center on, 125–27
  communications aboard, 119–22
  division officers, relationships with, 80–81
  family life, 105–6
  favorite ports, 99–101
  fitness reports from, 89, 91, 97
  general quarters station, 94–95
  junior officers, relationships with, 82
  leadership styles during, 89–90
  lessons from, 91–93, 141–42
  naval gunfire support missions, 107–14
  navigation of, 119, 126, 136
  personnel inspections and, 140
  radar types on, 127
  roles and responsibilities, 93–94, 134, 137, 139
  senior leadership on, 81, 88–89
  ship overview and duties, 48–15, 94–96
  SWO pin received during, 107
  Vietnam, tour of duty in, 97–98
  wardroom culture, 83
  weapon systems on, 94–96, 94–25, 109, 112–13
Patrick, Burton D. "Pat," 260–61, 261–74
PCO (Prospective Commanding Officer) School, 160–63
peacekeeping operations, 345
Pentagon, P.D.M. working at
  as command relations officer in OpNav, 218–25
  as deputy chief of naval operations, naval warfare, 329–37
  as executive assistant to Secretary of the Navy, 270–301
  as flag lieutenant and executive assistant to VCNO, 226–39
  flag promotion and, 298–99
  national security advice for, 362
Perry, Matthew C., 301, 301–91
Persian Gulf
  Gulf War, 336, 339, 344
  Operation Earnest Will, 322–23, 322–101
  ships on rotation in (1950s), 1–2
personal appearance, 195
"Personal For" messages, 258
personnel inspections, 140
Personnel Qualification Standards (PSQ) system, 107–8, 107–29
physical fitness, 189–90
PLAN (Chinese People's Liberation Army Navy), 325–26, 328, 355
plane guard, 179
Planned Maintenance System (PMS) records, 63–64, 63–18, 108
PMD (Program of Management Development), Harvard University, 239–43
Polaris ballistic missile system, 72
Polmar, Norman, 319
Powell, Colin L., 280, 280n83, 344–45
pre-departure navigation briefs, 172

pre-overseas movement (POM), 170–71
Prevail (AM-107), 1–2
professionalism, 53–54, 84–85
Program of Management Development (PMD), Harvard University, 239–43
Prospective Commanding Officer (PCO) School, 160–63, 192
PSQ (Personnel Qualification Standards) system, 107–8, 107–29
Pub. 102 (*International Code of Signals*), 122, 122–39
publications by P.D.M.
    "America, Don't Give Up on Afghanistan," 355
    "Both Swords and Ploughshares: Literary Roles in the 1990s," x, 355
    "Harmonising the Alliance with the Dynamics of Change," x, 355
    "Retaining Alliance Relevancy: NATO and the Combined Joint Task Force Concept," 345
Punaro, Arnold, 316–17

quartermasters of the watch, 119

race relations, 44
radar
    air search radars, 127, 127–42, 155
    Furuno radar, 197
    surface search, 127
radarman (RD) rating, 126, 126–41
Radford (DD-446), 59
radio silence, 122, 122n40
Rainier (Prince of Monaco), 48
readiness
    battle group mission and, 305–8
    CinCLantFlt and, 338
    conditions of damage control readiness, 137
    executive officers and, 65
    General Quarters (GQ), 32–33, 32–9
    importance of, 329
    maximum condition of readiness, 32–33
    NATO and, 343
    Operational Readiness Inspections, 179–80
Reagan, Ronald
    firing of Admiral Rickover and, 281–82
    Navy improvements and, 255, 255–72, 270–71, 273, 283, 285–88
    Suez Canal and, 310
Redgrave (Captain), 69, 73
refresher training (REFTRA), 181, 185–86
refueling
    helo in-flight, 115–16, 157–58
    at port, 137
    at sea, 130, 137–39
regular overhaul, 141
relative motion, 76–78, 123
Renown (Great Britain), 72
"Retaining Alliance Relevancy: NATO and the Combined Joint Task Force Concept" (Miller), 345
retirement from Navy, ix, 352–53. *See also* career development, post-Navy

Rickover, Hyman G., 222–23, 223–65, 281–82, 336
RIM-2 Terrier missile weapons system, 95, 95–27
RIM-24 Tarter missile weapons system, 94–95, 94–25
Rizzuto, Phil, 9
roaming the ship, 192–93, 195, 312
Robinson, H. J., 37
rope yarn liberty, 131–32
Royal Navy
    Polaris ballistic missile system tests with, 72
    traditions adopted by U.S. Navy, 165
Royal United Services Institute (RUSI), x, 355
Rumsfeld, Donald H., 362, 362–117

S-2 Tracker ASW aircraft, 157–58, 157–51, 179
Sackett, Albert M, 146–47, 146n47, 153–54
SacLant (supreme allied commander Atlantic), P.D.M. serving as
    advocating for joint forces command, 343–46, 350–51
    assignment to, 343–44
    Haiti interdiction operation and, 347–50
    roles and responsibilities, 343–44
    Standing Naval Force Atlantic and, 346–47
safety of ship and sailors. *See also* damage control and fire brigades; *specific inspections*
    aircraft rescues during Vietnam War, 114–15
    charged fire hoses, 103
    command duty officer role and, 135
    conditions of damage control readiness, 137
    crew sickness at sea, 189
    fam fire off the fantail, 103
    gun decking and, 63–64, 63–17
    helicopter delivery of sailors to ships and, 116–17
    officer of the deck duties and, 102–4
    personal or professional conflicts, 54–55
    plane guard for, 179
    Planned Maintenance System records and, 63–64, 63–18
    safety shoes, 195
    security teams, 103–4
    watch section, 104
satellite navigation (SatNav), 119, 130–31
Sawyer, George, 278
Schwarzkopf, Herbert N., Jr., 336, 336–107
sea and anchor detail, 136
sea daddies. *See* mentors
SEAL (Sea, Air, and Land) Teams, 114, 114–32
Sea of Okhotsk, 324
Second Fleet, 339–40
Secretary of Defense (SecDef), 280, 315–16, 331
Secretary of the Navy (SecNav), 270–71, 276, 280–82, 286. *See also* executive assistant to SecNav,
    P.D.M. serving as
sector screens, 123–24
security teams, 103–4

Seneca (ATF-91), P.D.M. serving as executive officer of, 37–67
   assignment to, ix, 37–41
   benefits to career, 57–59
   best and worst days on, 56
   defensive armament, 44–45
   family life and, 57–58
   favorite ports, 55
   fitness reports from, 60
   fleet exercises, 47
   in Guantanamo Bay, 47, 54
   leadership style, 43–44, 63, 64–65
   in Mediterranean Sea, 41–42, 47
   navigation of, 42–43, 54
   propulsion plant on, 45
   roles and responsibilities, 41–42, 45–46
   ship overview and duties, 37–11, 41–42, 47
senior leadership
   commanding officers, relationships with, 196
   department heads, relationships with, 81, 86–87
   XOs, relationships with, 49
Seventh Fleet, P.D.M. as commander of (Com7thFlt)
   diplomacy and foreign relations, 325–28
   family life, 320
   operations and missions, 321–23
   readiness, importance of, 329
   selection for, 315–20
   superiors, relationships with, 323–24
Shacochis, Bob, 347, 347–113
Shalikashvili, John M. D., 346, 346–112
Shanahan, John J. "Jack," Jr., 219, 219–62, 224, 226
Shear, Harold E. "Hal," 233–37, 233–67, 317
ship store, 132
shipyard periods, 182–83
sidearm use and qualifications, 102–3
Siemens Product Lifecycle Management Software, Inc., x
signal flags, 122
signalmen, 122, 122–39
Sixth Fleet, 320–21
Skelton, Isaac N. "Ike," 300–301, 300–90
sonar
   AN/SQS-26 bow-mounted, low frequency, 155–56
   sonobuoys, 166, 166–52, 184
   SQS-26, 160
sound-powered phones, 121
Sound Surveillance System (SOSUS), 46, 46–13, 124–25, 157, 184
South China Sea, 94
South Korea, Team Spirit operations with, 322
Soviet Union. *See* Cold War
Spahn, Warren, 8–9
Spanish navy, 41
Special Ops forces, 114, 114–32

Sperry Marine, Inc., x, 356
Spruance (DD-963), 303–92
Spruance, Raymond, 303–92
Spruance-class destroyers, 240, 248–49, 249–70, 303–92
SQS-26 sonar, 160
staff meetings, 169
StanNavForLant (Standing Naval Force Atlantic), 214, 214–60, 253, 346–47
Stavanger, Norway, 101
Stavridis, James G., 181, 181–53, 187
Strait of Gibraltar, navigation to, 42–43
strategic communications, 15–16, 40, 91–92
Strike University, Nevada, 284–85
Subic Bay, Philippines, 99–101, 141
submarine detection, 184–85. *See also* antisubmarine warfare
Suez Canal, navigating through, 309–11
SunTrust Bank, x
surface search radars, 127
surface squadron commanders, 302–3
surface warfare officers (SWOs), 76–20, 107, 247, 313–14
Surface Warfare Officers School (SWOS), Newport, 23, 23–4, 76, 76–20. *See also* Destroyer School, Newport

tactical action officers (TAOs), 78–79, 78–21, 96–97
tactical training, 25, 92
Team Spirit operations, 322
technology improvements
   sector screens, replacement of, 123
   ship accidents and, 202
   Spruance-class destroyers, 240, 248–49, 249–70
Teledyne Technologies, x
Texas (CGN-39), 303
Thiokol, 358–59
Thor (ARC-4), 46, 125
Thucydides, 207, 207–57, 209, 211
Tonkin Gulf, 90, 94, 96
towed array systems, 159
trade and international commerce, 313
Trial by Fire (training film), 26
Trost, Carlisle A. H., 337, 337–108
Trump, Donald J., 345, 345–111, 361
Tufts University, Massachusetts, 346
Turner, Stansfield, 206–8, 206–56, 208–58, 317
Turner Revolution, 205–7, 206–56

UGS Corporation, x
underway replenishment (UNREP), 137–39, 176–77, 252, 303–92
Unified Command Plan (UCP), 218–19, 218–61, 226, 338
Uniform Code of Military Justice, 188
University of Georgia, ix, 14, 226–27, 242
unmanned aerial vehicles, 115, 115–34

Valletta, Malta, 55
vertical replenishment, 137
vice chiefs of naval operations (VCNOs), 233–34. *See also* flag lieutenant and executive assistant to VCNO, P.D.M. serving as
Vietnam War
   draft letter for P.D.M., 14–15
   effect on Navy, 231, 254
   naval gunfire support missions, 107–14
   Naval War College curriculum changes based on, 205
   Parson support in Southeast Asia during, 90, 94, 96–97
   P.D.M.'s visit for detailing research, 146–47, 149, 152–53
   public attitudes toward, 24–25, 58, 145, 198–99, 229–30
vision and mission statements, 60, 194
Voge (FF-1047), 155–56

wardroom culture
   leadership advice for, 51–52
   on *Luce*, 255
   on *McCloy*, 169
   on *Papago*, 24, 51
   on *Parsons*, 83
   staff meetings and, 169
watch quarter and station bill, 131
watch standing
   discipline for sloppiness, 203
   duties and responsibilities of, 117–19
   electronic technology and, 202
   ship collisions and, 135–46, 201–3
   training for, 76, 201–3
Watergate Scandal, 229, 229–66
Watkins, James D., 286, 286–86, 332
Weinberger, Caspar W. "Cap," 272–73, 273–78, 280, 315–16
Wentworth, Ralph S., 199–200, 200–55
Weschler, Thomas R., 154, 154–50

Yokosuka, Japan, 320

Zech, Lando W., Jr, 276, 276–79
zone inspections, 196–97
Zumwalt (DDG-1000), 118, 118–36
Zumwalt, Elmo
   career overview, 153–48
   changes made to Navy, 228, 230, 264–65
   early promotion of, 317
   influence on P.D.M., 245
   leadership style, 229, 245
   personal notes to P.D.M., 199, 228
   promoting young sailors, 148, 153

Z-grams of, 140–41, 153n48, 199, 230
Zumwalt class destroyers named for, 118–36

www.ingramcontent.com/pod-product-compliance
Lightning Source LLC
Chambersburg PA
CBHW080622170426
43209CB00007B/1494